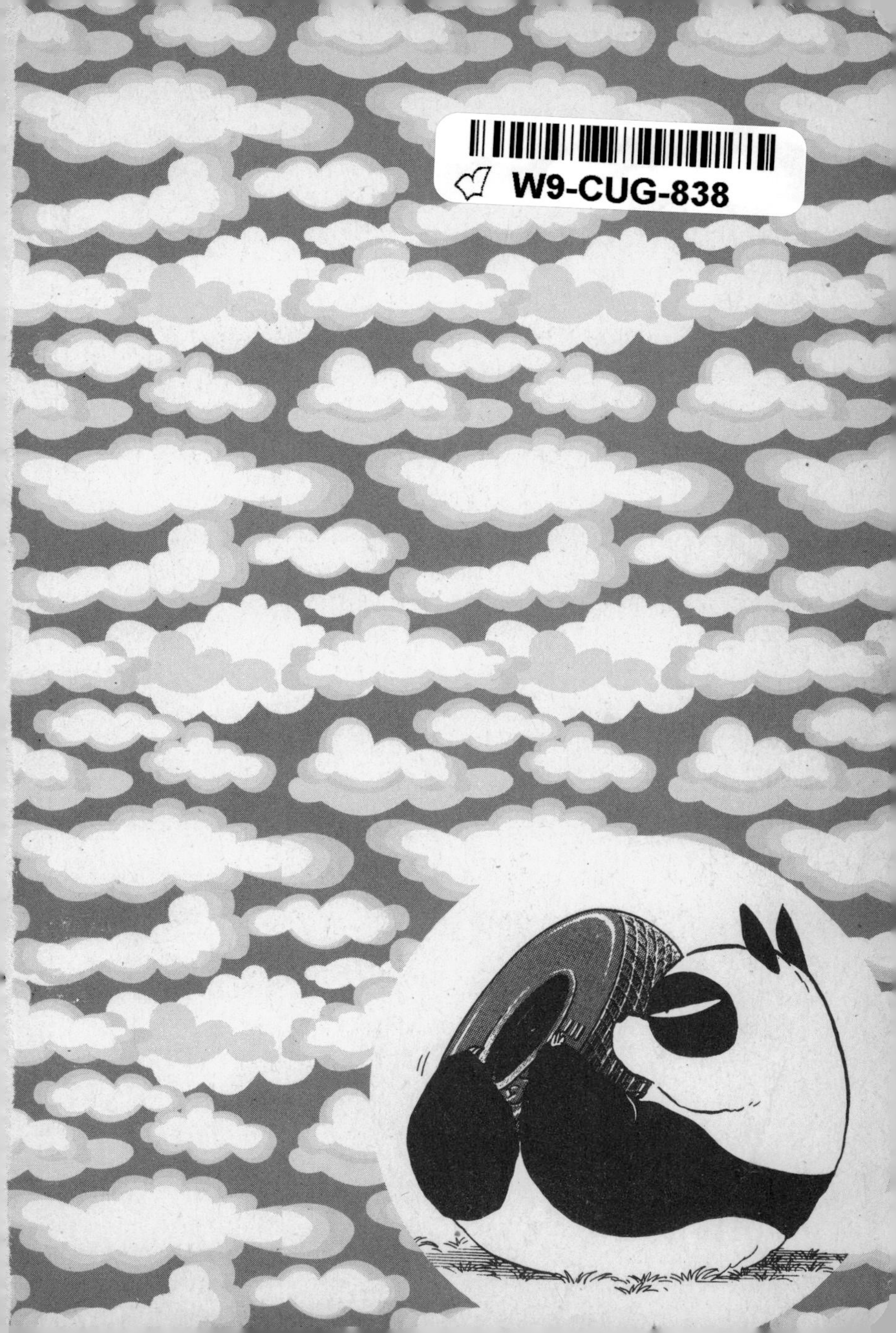

VOL. 20
Action Edition

Story and Art by
RUMIKO TAKAHASHI

English Adaptation/Gerard Jones and Toshifumi Yoshida
Touch-Up Art & Lettering/Wayne Truman
Cover and Interior Design/Yuki Ameda
Editor (1st Edition)/Julie Davis
Editor (Action Edition)/Avery Gotoh
Supervising Editor (Action Edition)/Michelle Pangilinan

Managing Editor/Annette Roman
Director of Production/Noboru Watanabe
Vice President of Publishing/Alvin Lu
Sr. Director of Acquisitions/Rika Inouye
Vice President of Sales and Marketing/Liza Coppola
Publisher/Hyoe Narita

Printed in Canada.

Published by VIZ, LLC
P.O. Box 77010
San Francisco, CA 94107

1st Edition Published 2001

Action Edition
10 9 8 7 6 5 4 3 2 1
First Printing, July 2005

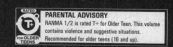

Ranma ½

VOL. 20 — Action Edition

STORY & ART BY
RUMIKO TAKAHASHI

STORY THUS FAR

The Tendos are an average, run-of-the-mill Japanese family—on the surface, that is. Soun Tendo is the owner and proprietor of the Tendo Dojo, where "Anything Goes Martial Arts" is practiced. Like the name says, anything goes, and usually does.

When Soun's old friend Genma Saotome comes to visit, Soun's three lovely young daughters—Akane, Nabiki and Kasumi—are told that it's time for one of them to become the fiancée of Genma's teenage son, as per an agreement made between the two fathers years ago. Youngest daughter Akane—who says she hates boys—is quickly nominated for bridal duty by her sisters.

Unfortunately, Ranma and his father have suffered a strange accident. While training in China, both plunged into one of many "cursed" springs at the legendary martial arts training ground of Jusenkyo. These springs transform the unlucky dunkee into whoever—or whatever—drowned there hundreds of years ago.

From then on, a splash of cold water turns Ranma's father into a giant panda, and Ranma becomes a beautiful, busty young woman. Hot water reverses the effect...but only until next time. As it turns out, Ranma and Genma aren't the only ones who have taken the Jusenkyo plunge—and it isn't long before they meet several other members of the Jusenkyo "cursed."

Although their parents are still determined to see Ranma and Akane marry and assume ownership of the training hall, Ranma seems to have a strange talent for accumulating surplus fiancées...and Akane has a few stubbornly determined suitors of her own. Will the two ever work out their differences and get rid of all these "extra" people, or will they just call the whole thing off? What's a half-boy, half-girl (not to mention all-girl, *angry* girl) to do...?

CAST OF CHARACTERS

THE SAOTOMES

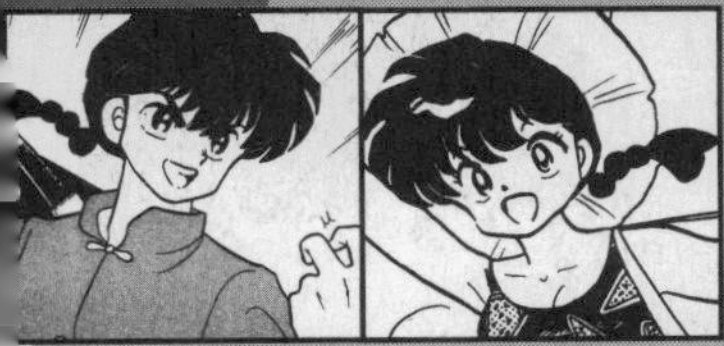

RANMA SAOTOME
Martial artist with far too many fiancées, and an ego that won't let him take defeat. Changes into a girl when splashed with cold water.

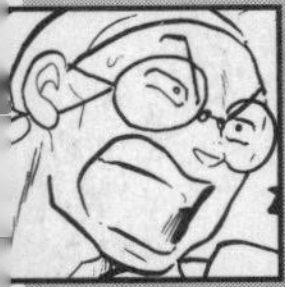

GENMA SAOTOME
Genma's father. Changes into a roly-poly, sign-talkin' panda when wet.

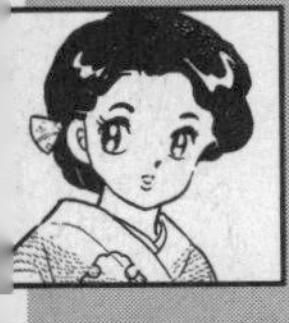

NODOKA SAOTOME
Genma's oh-so-traditional wife and Ranma's oh-so-deadly mom, Nodoka has taken an oath to eliminate *both* her dearly beloveds should her boy grow up to be less than manly. Um....

THE TENDOS

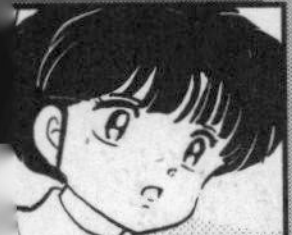

AKANE TENDO
Martial artist, tomboy, and Ranma's reluctant fiancée. Still totally in the dark about the "Ryoga/P-chan" thing.

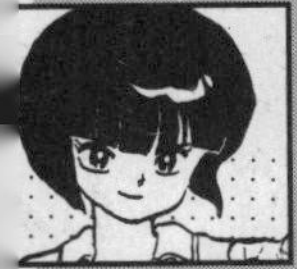

NABIKI TENDO
Middle Tendo daughter. Nothing comes close to her love of money.

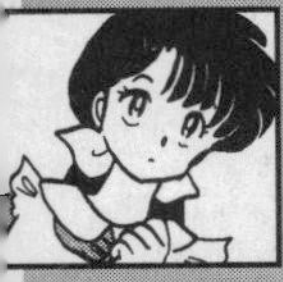

KASUMI TENDO
Eldest Tendo daughter who's the sweet-natured, stay-at-home type.

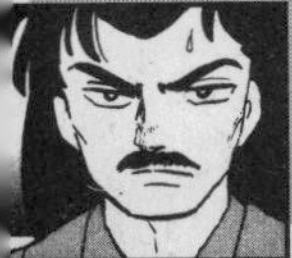

SOUN TENDO
Tendo family patriarch and former Happosai disciple. Easily excitable.

THE MASTER

HAPPOSAI and COLOGNE
One's a pint-sized pervert and the other's the pint-sized proprietor of the Cat Cafe. Your guess as to who's who.

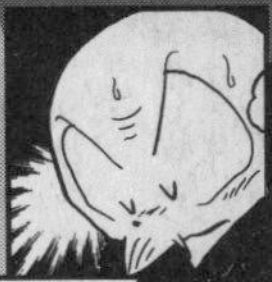

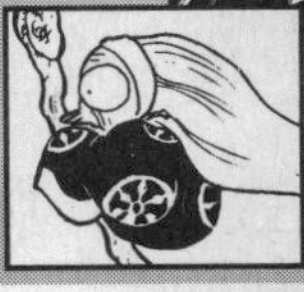

THE SUITORS

SHAMPOO
Chinese-Amazon great-granddaughter to Cologne. Has come all the way from China to either kill Ranma...or marry him.

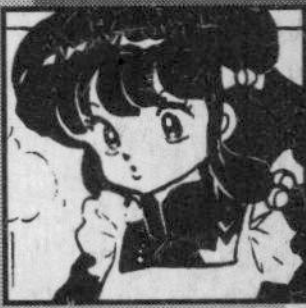

MOUSSE
Myopic master of hidden weapons. Continually thwarted (however inadvertently) in his pursuit of Shampoo by Ranma.

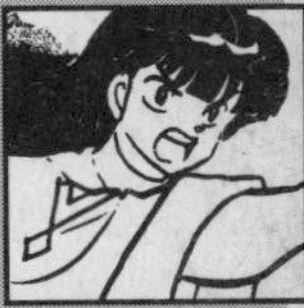

UKYO KUONJI
Spatula-wielding, childhood-betrothed, would-be sweetheart of Ranma's.

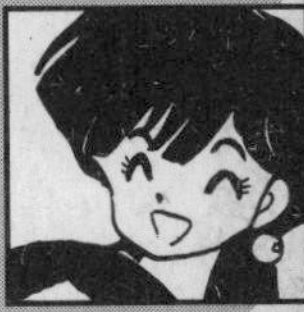

AND IN THIS CORNER...

MARIKO KONJO
Cheerleading champion of Seishun ("Seisyun") High who, heaven knows why, falls in love with Kuno and enters a "cheer-off" against Ranma to prove it.

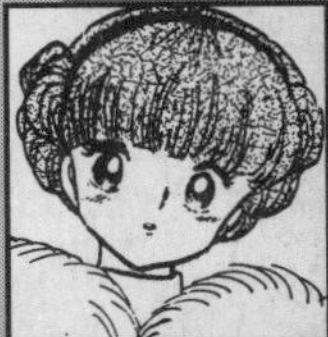

CONTENTS

Part 1

LOVE ALWAYS WINS

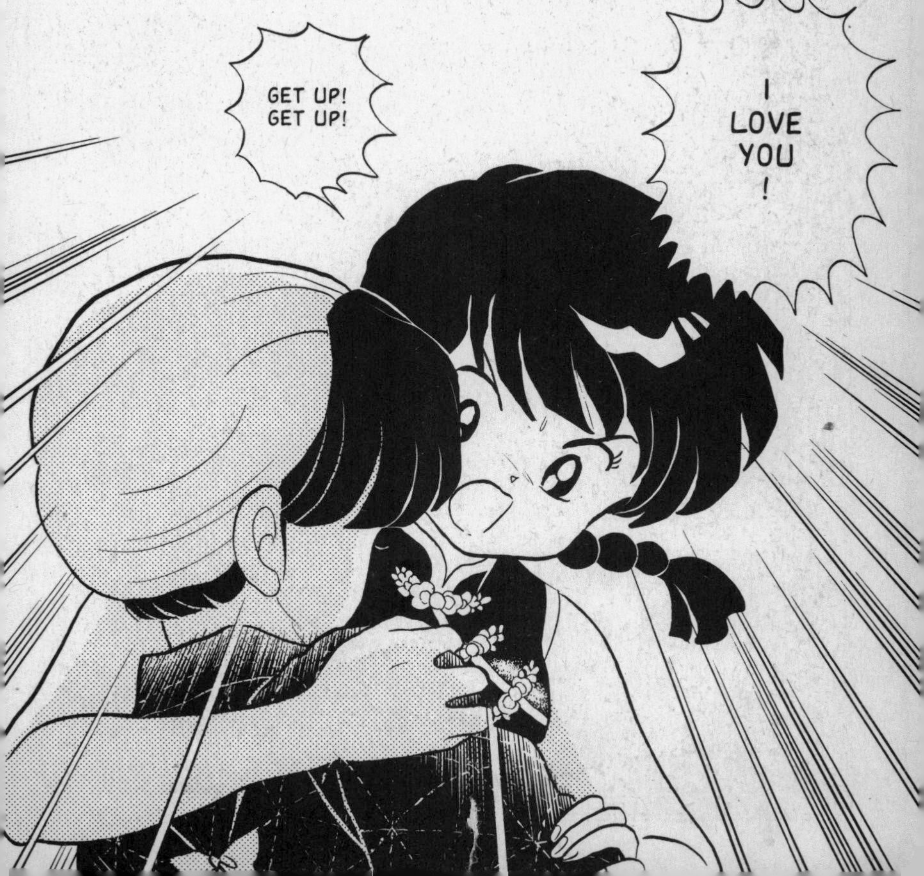
GET UP! GET UP!
I LOVE YOU!

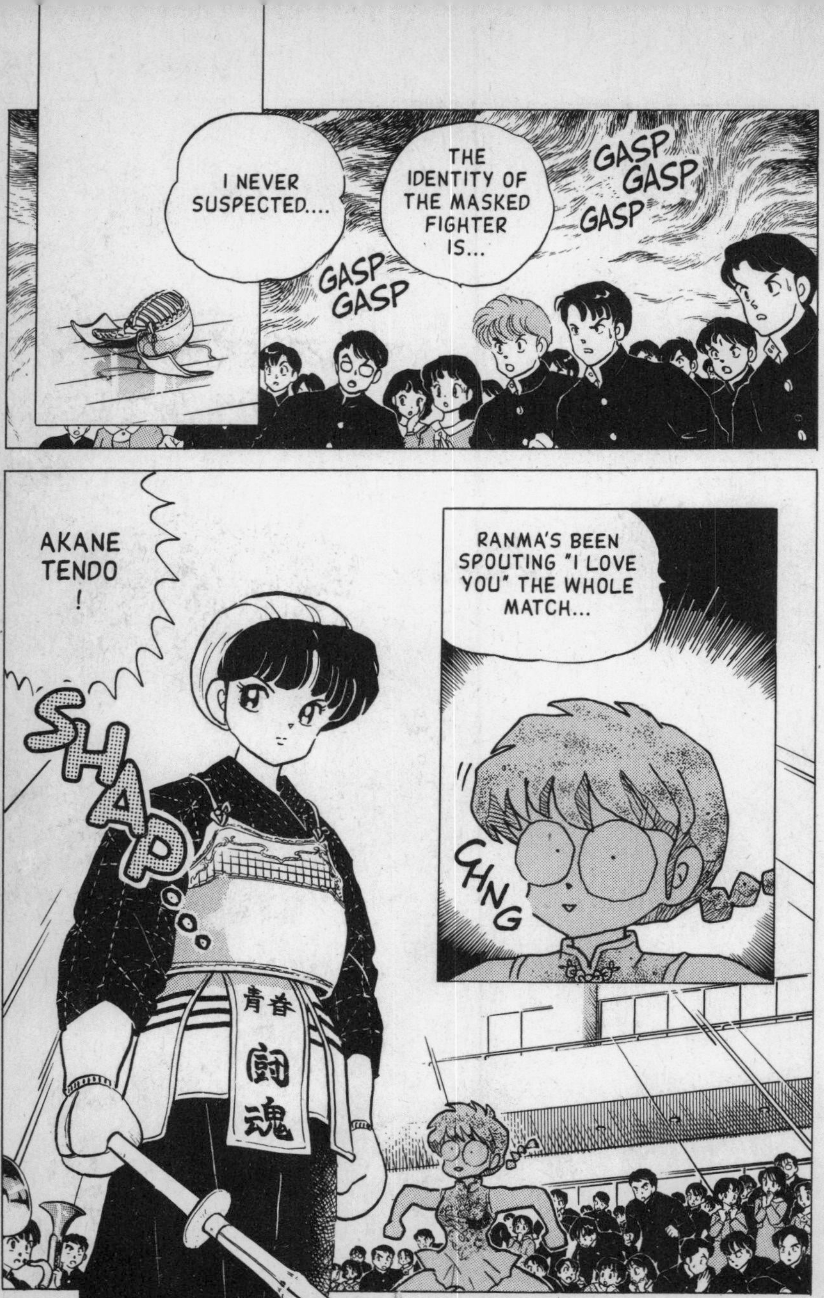
I NEVER SUSPECTED....
THE IDENTITY OF THE MASKED FIGHTER IS...
GASP GASP GASP
GASP GASP
AKANE TENDO !
SHAPOOO
RANMA'S BEEN SPOUTING "I LOVE YOU" THE WHOLE MATCH...
CHNG
青春
闘魂

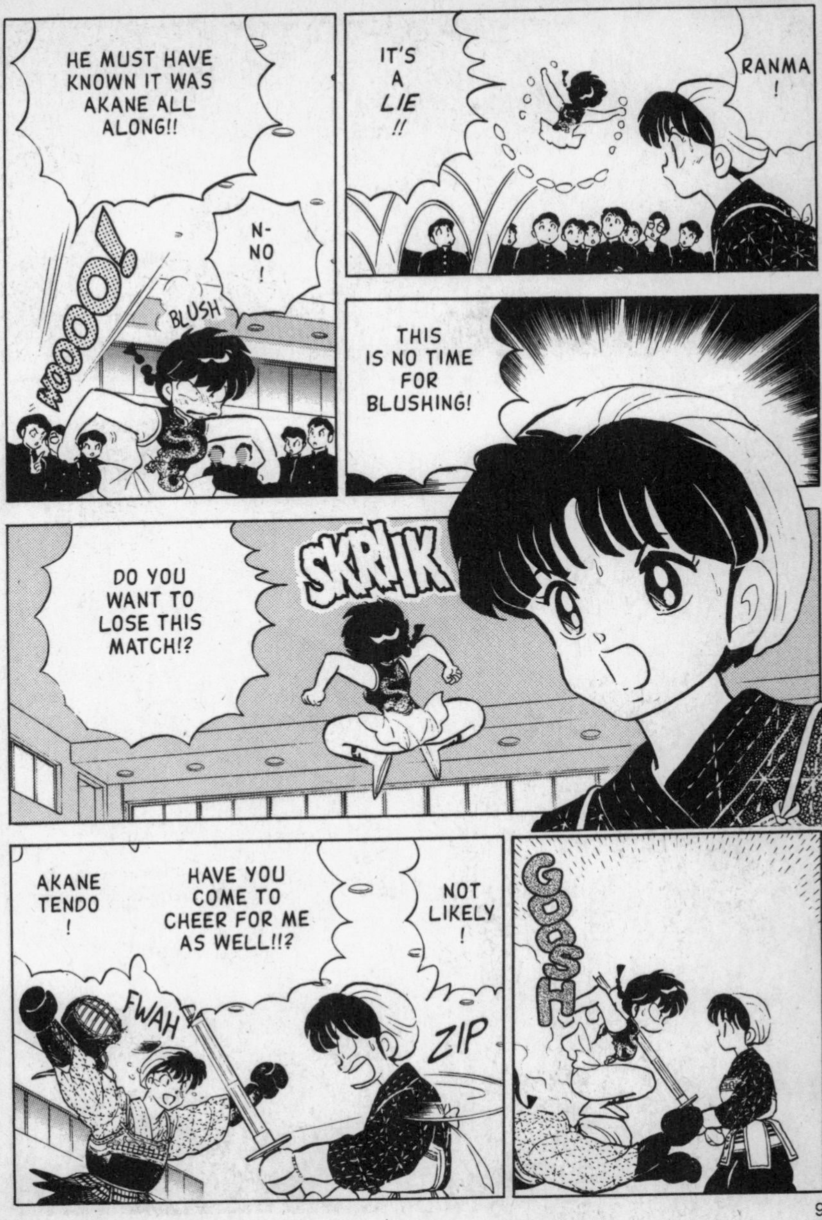
HE MUST HAVE KNOWN IT WAS AKANE ALL ALONG!!
N-NO!
WOOOOO!
BLUSH
IT'S A LIE!!
RANMA!
THIS IS NO TIME FOR BLUSHING!
DO YOU WANT TO LOSE THIS MATCH!?
SKRIIK
AKANE TENDO!
HAVE YOU COME TO CHEER FOR ME AS WELL!!?
NOT LIKELY!
FWAH
ZIP
GOOSH

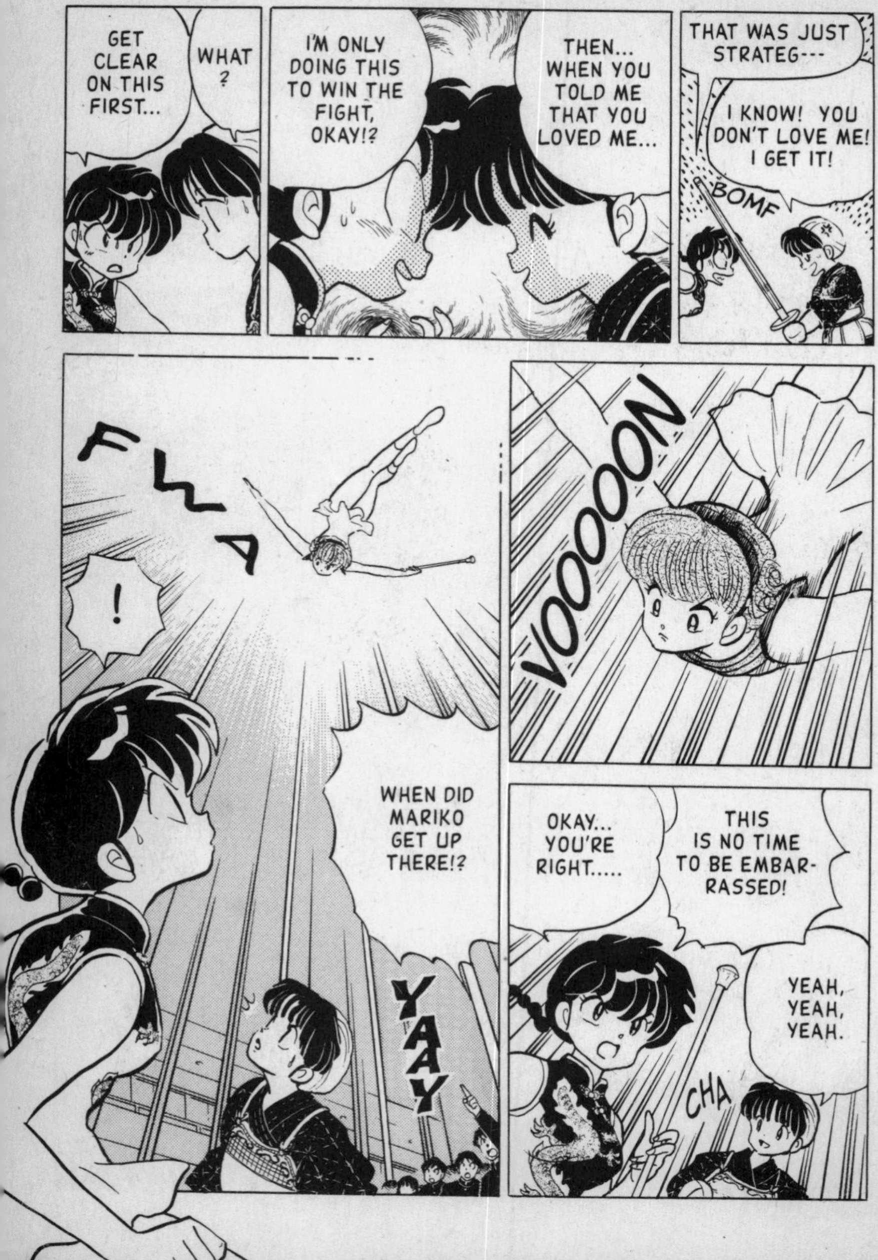
GET CLEAR ON THIS FIRST...
WHAT?
I'M ONLY DOING THIS TO WIN THE FIGHT, OKAY!?
THEN... WHEN YOU TOLD ME THAT YOU LOVED ME...
THAT WAS JUST STRATEG---
I KNOW! YOU DON'T LOVE ME! I GET IT!
BOMF
FWA
!
WHEN DID MARIKO GET UP THERE!?
YAAY
VOOOOON
OKAY... YOU'RE RIGHT.....
THIS IS NO TIME TO BE EMBAR-RASSED!
YEAH, YEAH, YEAH.
CHA

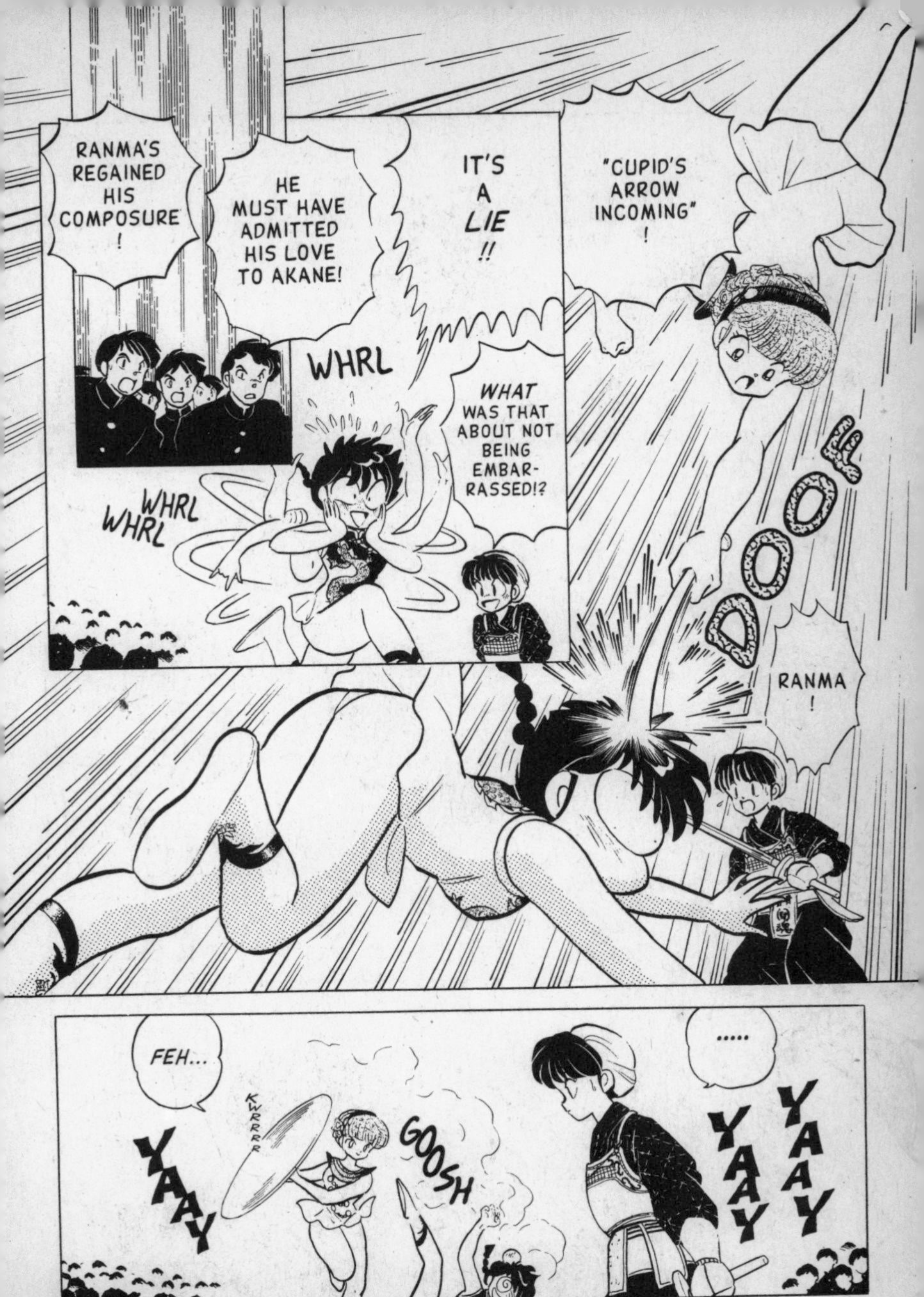
RANMA'S REGAINED HIS COMPOSURE !
HE MUST HAVE ADMITTED HIS LOVE TO AKANE!
IT'S A *LIE* !!
"CUPID'S ARROW INCOMING" !
WHRL
WHRL WHRL
WHAT WAS THAT ABOUT NOT BEING EMBAR-RASSED!?
DOOOM
RANMA !
FEH...
.....
KWRRRR
YAAY
GOOSH
YAAY
YAAY

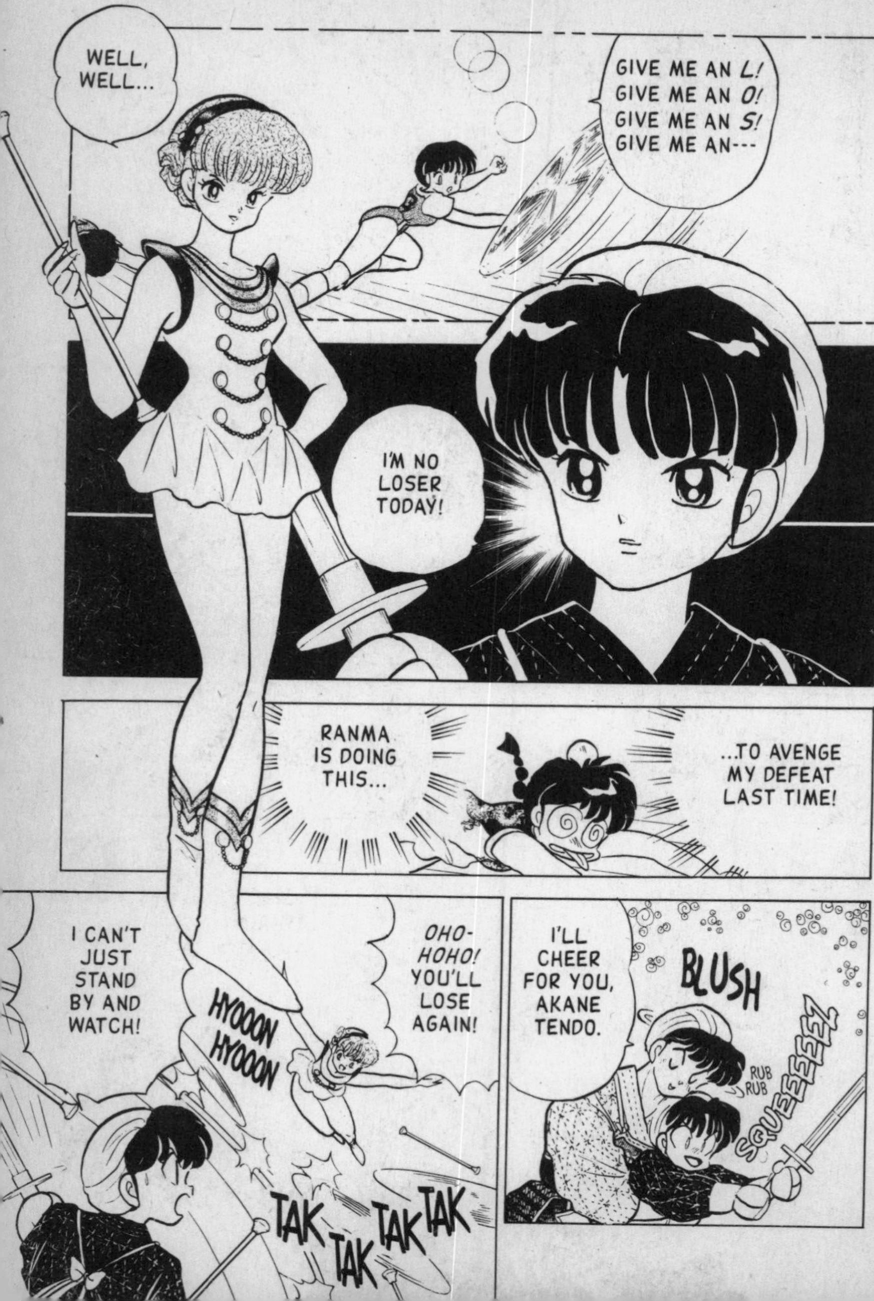
WELL, WELL...
GIVE ME AN L! GIVE ME AN O! GIVE ME AN S! GIVE ME AN---
I'M NO LOSER TODAY!
RANMA IS DOING THIS...
...TO AVENGE MY DEFEAT LAST TIME!
I CAN'T JUST STAND BY AND WATCH!
OHO-HOHO! YOU'LL LOSE AGAIN!
HYOOON HYOOON
TAK TAK TAK TAK
I'LL CHEER FOR YOU, AKANE TENDO.
BLUSH
RUB RUB
SQUEEEEEZ

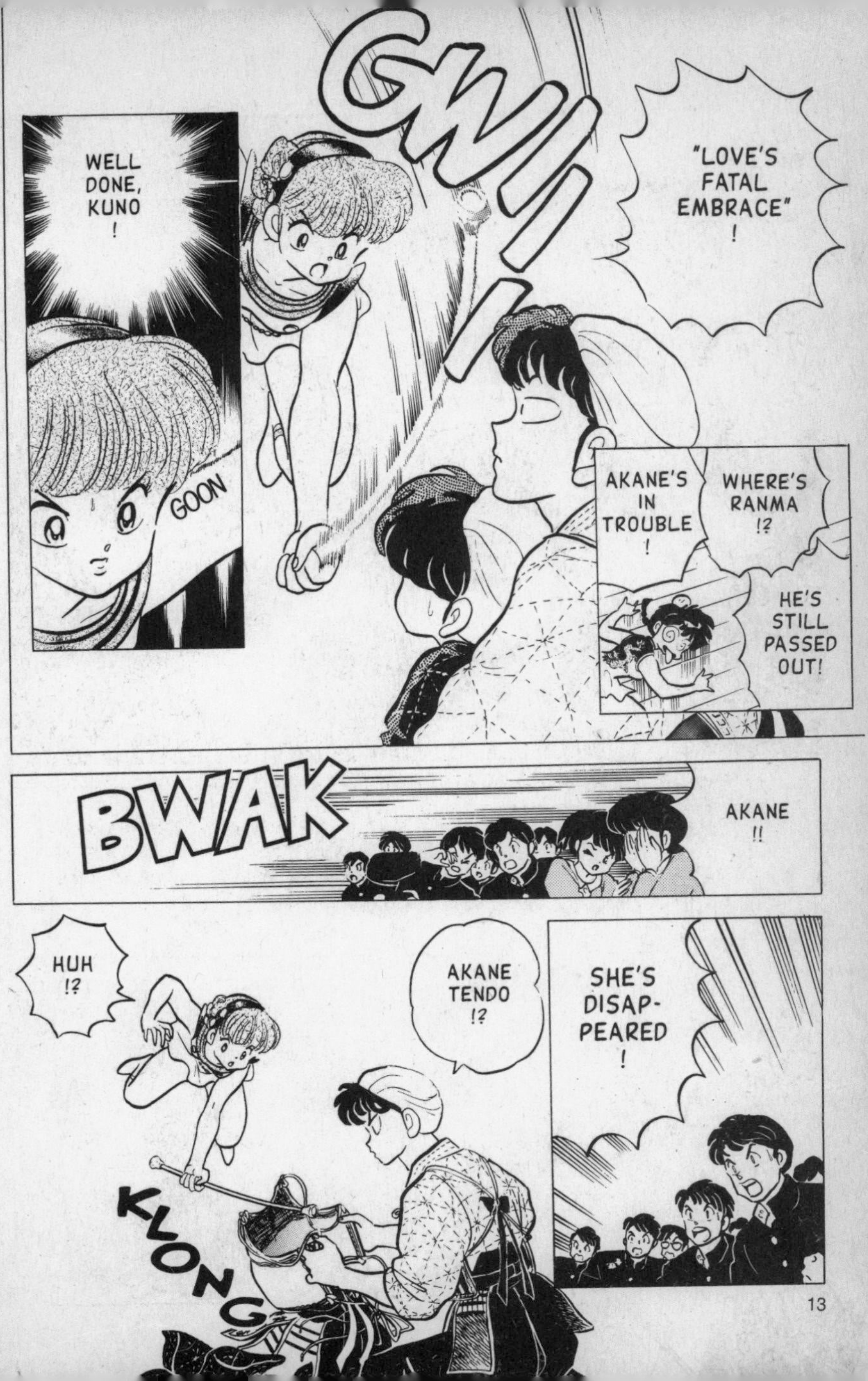
GWIII
WELL DONE, KUNO !
GOON
"LOVE'S FATAL EMBRACE" !
AKANE'S IN TROUBLE !
WHERE'S RANMA !?
HE'S STILL PASSED OUT!
BWAK
AKANE !!
HUH !?
AKANE TENDO !?
KLONG
SHE'S DISAP-PEARED !

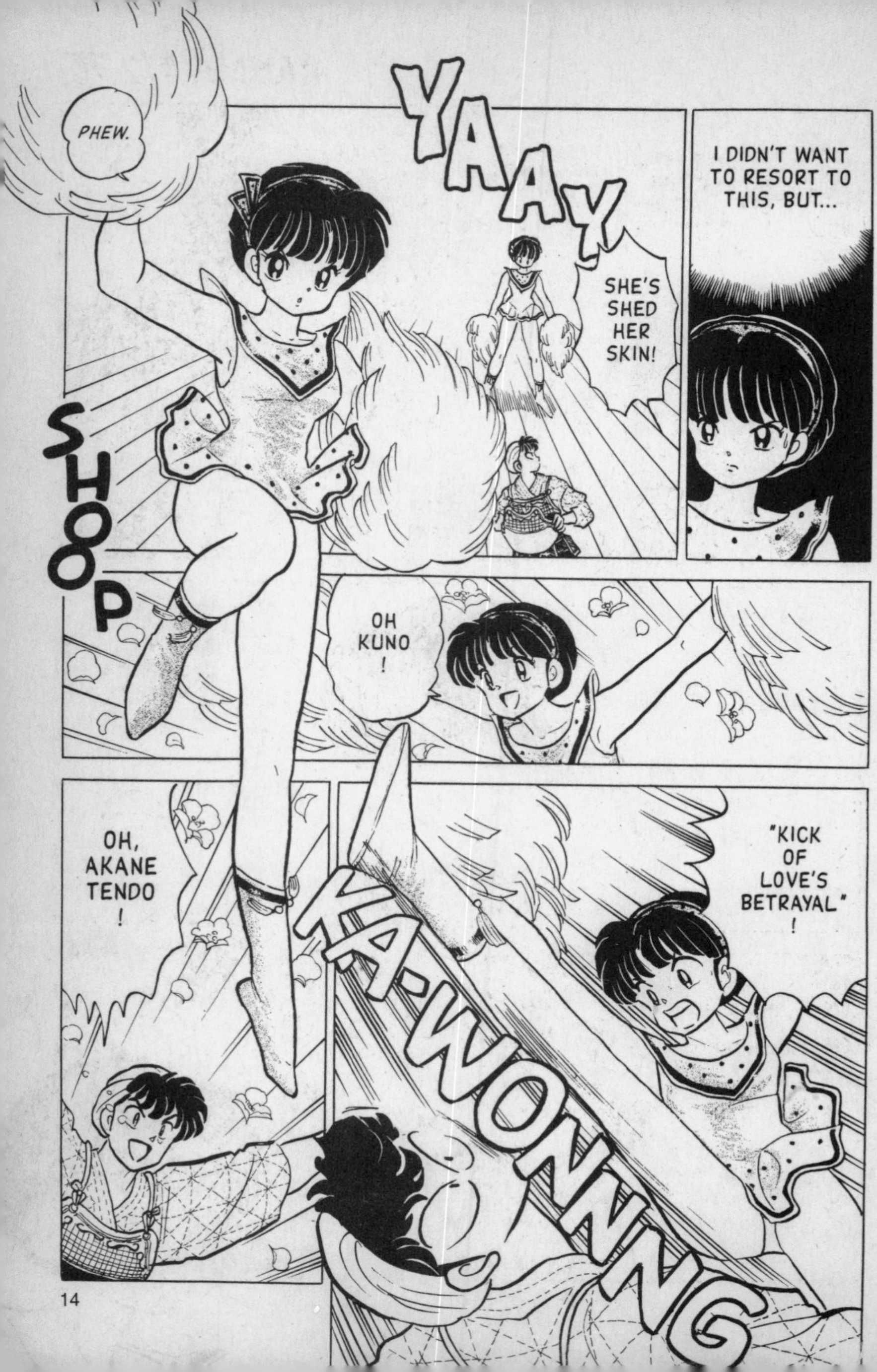
PHEW.
SHOOP
YAAAY
SHE'S SHED HER SKIN!
I DIDN'T WANT TO RESORT TO THIS, BUT...
OH KUNO!
OH, AKANE TENDO!
"KICK OF LOVE'S BETRAYAL"!
KA-WONNG

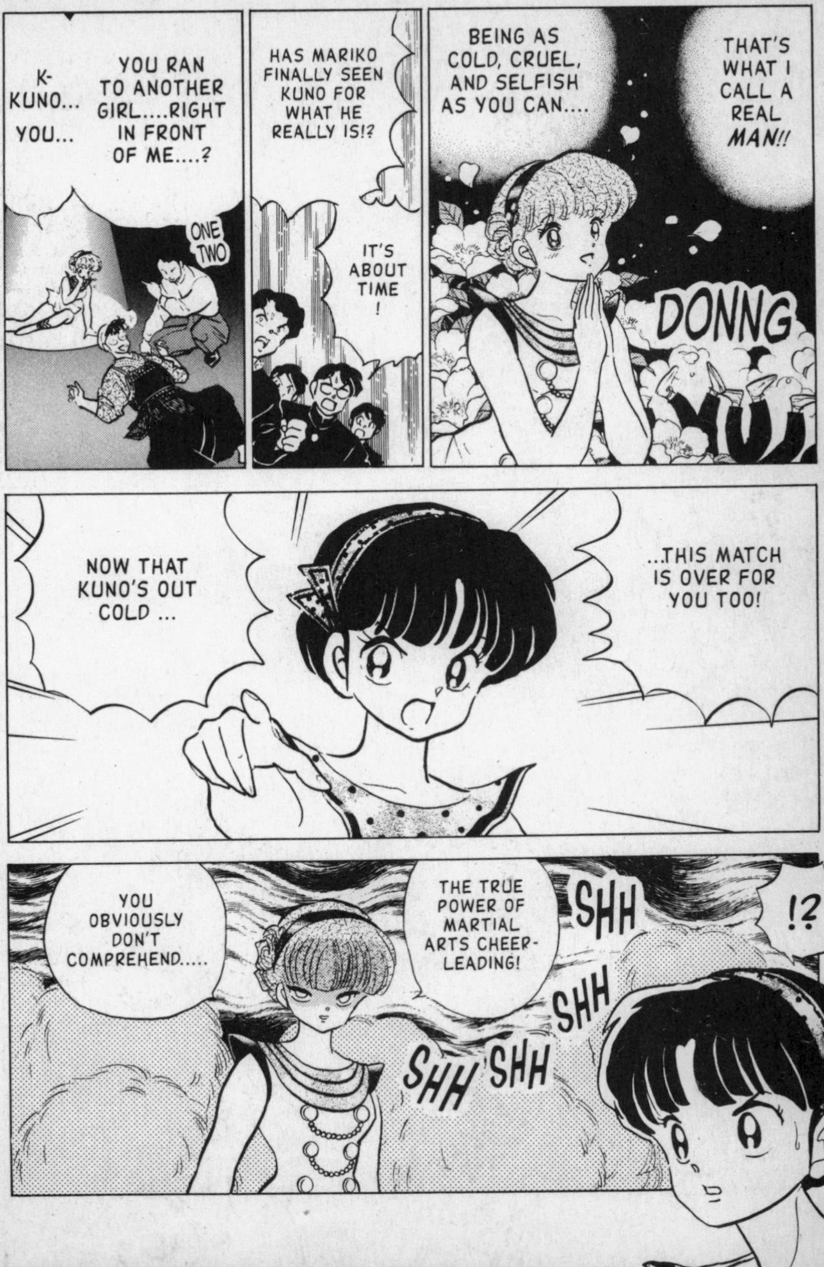
K-
KUNO...
YOU...
YOU RAN TO ANOTHER GIRL....RIGHT IN FRONT OF ME....?
ONE TWO
HAS MARIKO FINALLY SEEN KUNO FOR WHAT HE REALLY IS!?
IT'S ABOUT TIME!
BEING AS COLD, CRUEL, AND SELFISH AS YOU CAN....
THAT'S WHAT I CALL A REAL MAN!!
DONNG
NOW THAT KUNO'S OUT COLD ...
...THIS MATCH IS OVER FOR YOU TOO!
YOU OBVIOUSLY DON'T COMPREHEND.....
THE TRUE POWER OF MARTIAL ARTS CHEER-LEADING!
SHH
!?
SHH
SHH
SHH

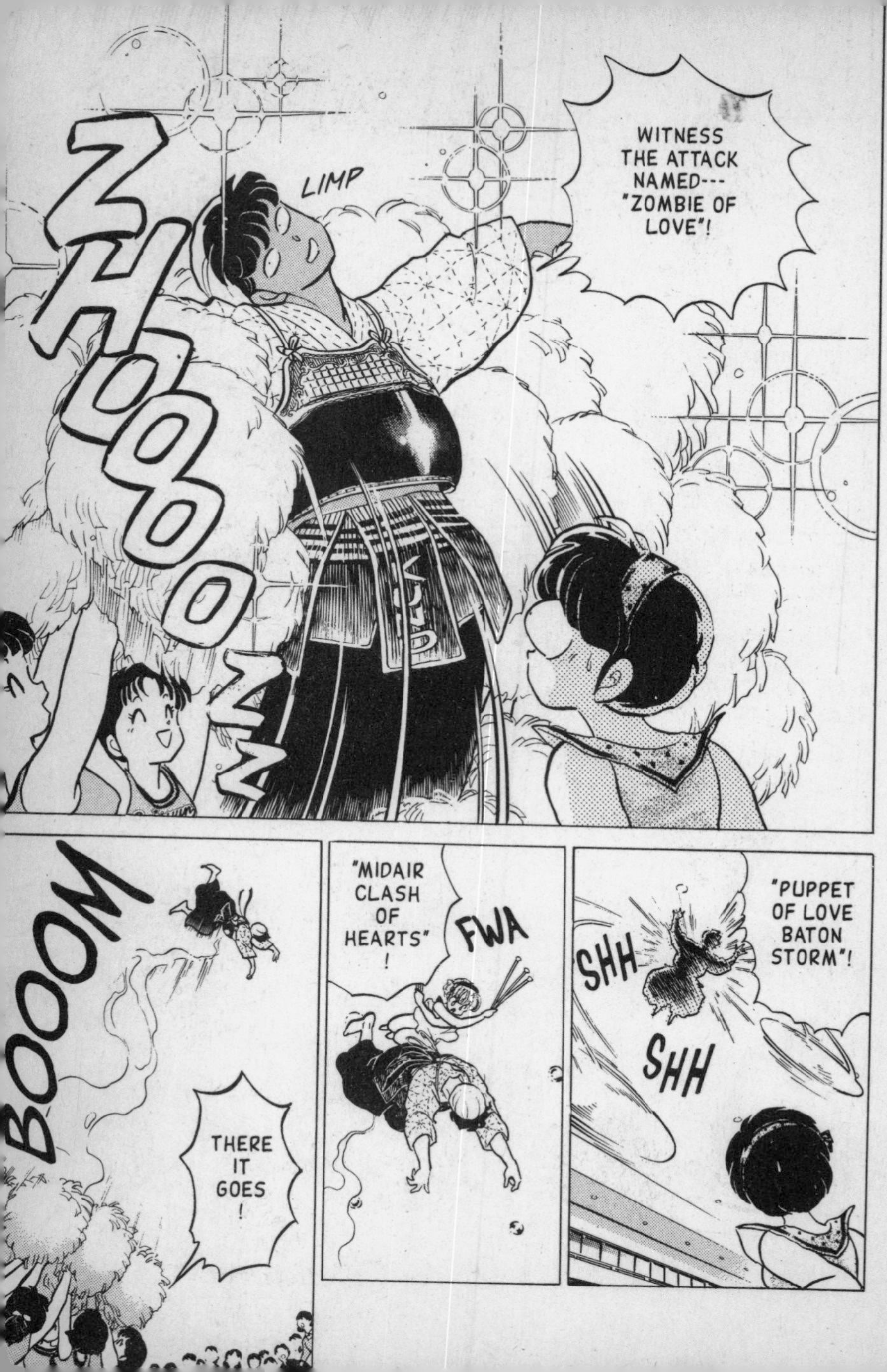
ZHOOOOOM
LIMP
WITNESS THE ATTACK NAMED--- "ZOMBIE OF LOVE"!
BOOOM
THERE IT GOES!
"MIDAIR CLASH OF HEARTS"!
FWA
"PUPPET OF LOVE BATON STORM"!
SHH
SHH

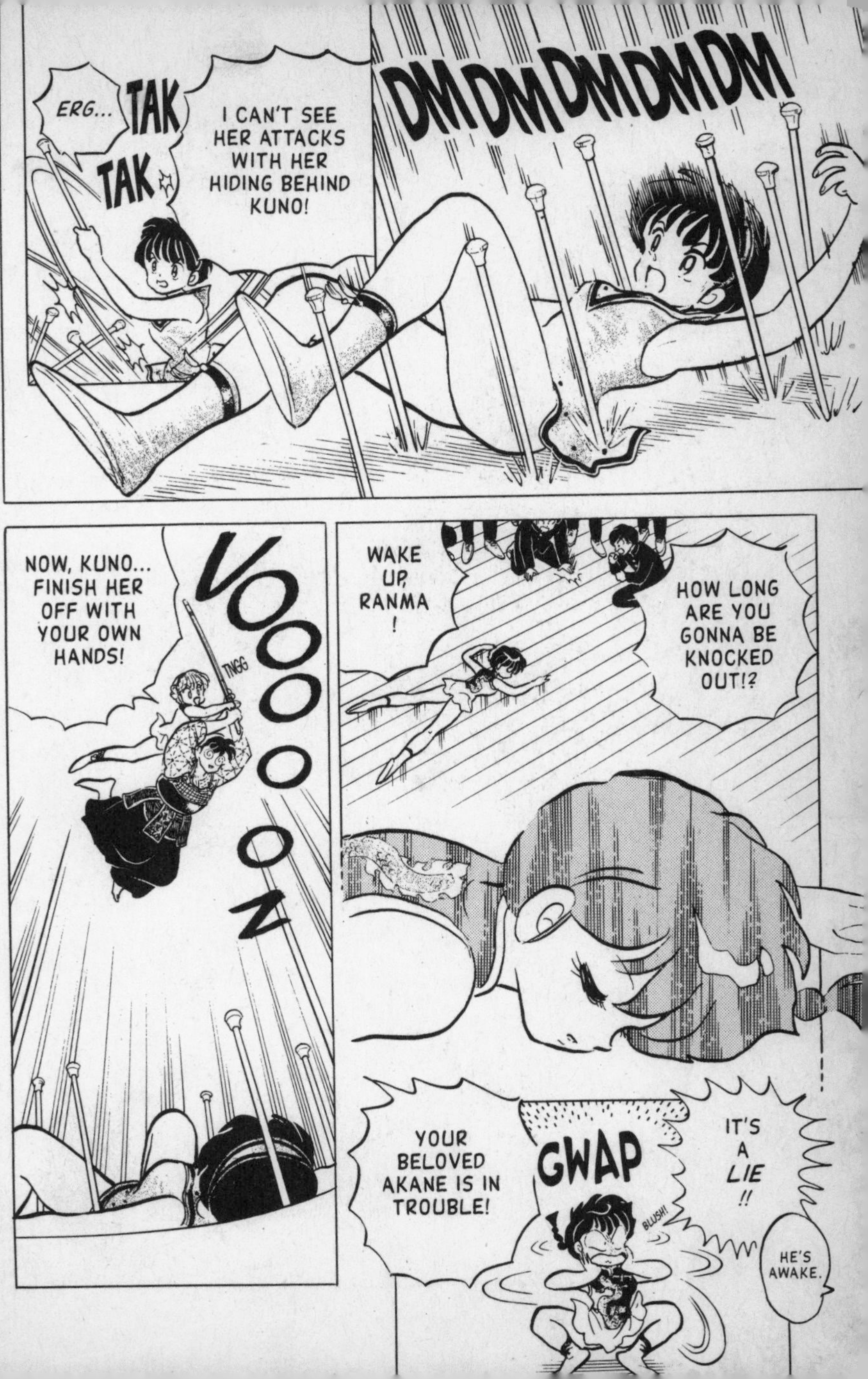
ERG...
TAK
TAK
I CAN'T SEE HER ATTACKS WITH HER HIDING BEHIND KUNO!
DMDMDMDMDM
NOW, KUNO... FINISH HER OFF WITH YOUR OWN HANDS!
VOOOOOON
TNGG
WAKE UP, RANMA!
HOW LONG ARE YOU GONNA BE KNOCKED OUT!?
YOUR BELOVED AKANE IS IN TROUBLE!
GWAP
IT'S A LIE!!
BLUSH!
HE'S AWAKE.

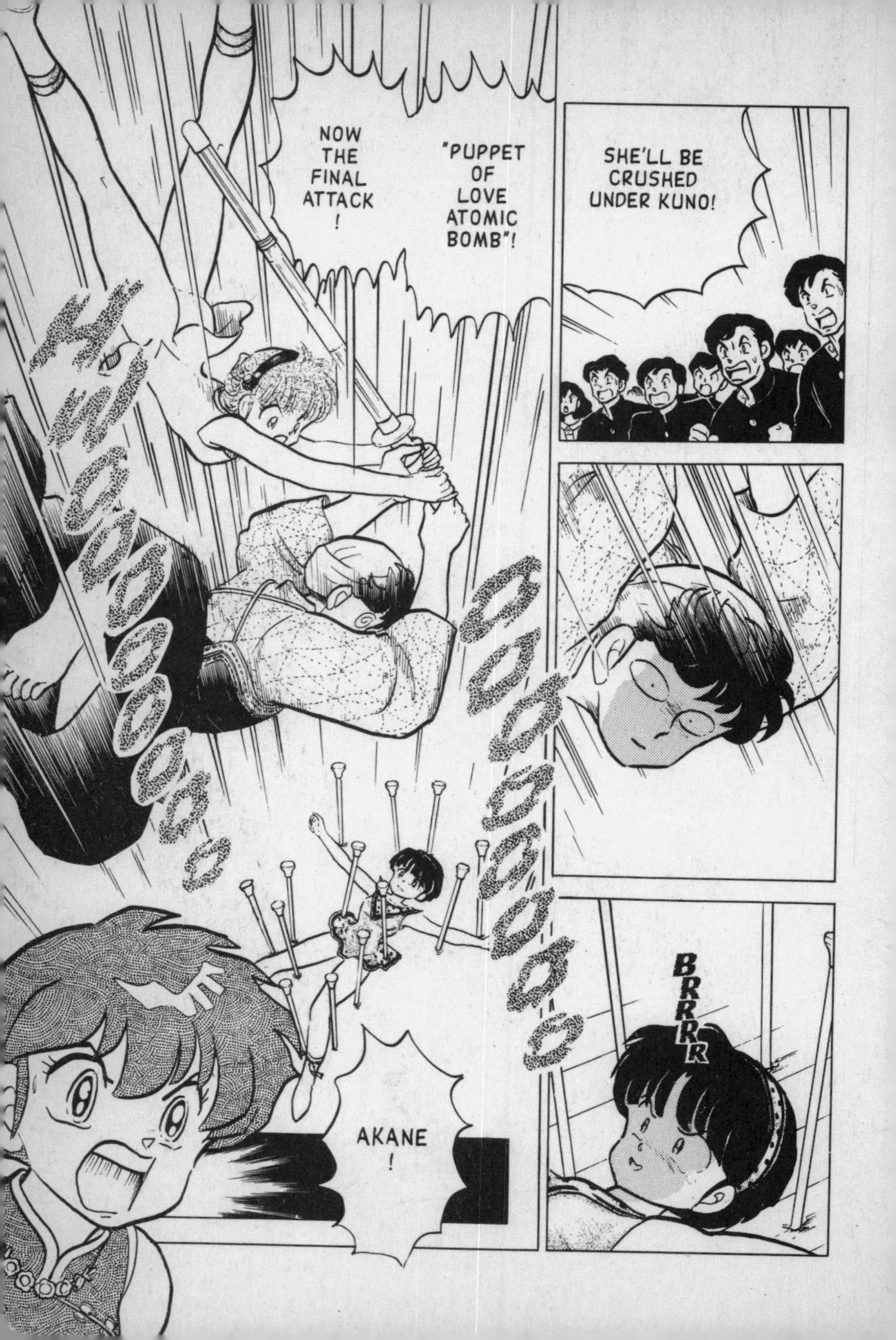
NOW THE FINAL ATTACK!
"PUPPET OF LOVE ATOMIC BOMB"!
AKANE!
SHE'LL BE CRUSHED UNDER KUNO!
BRRRR

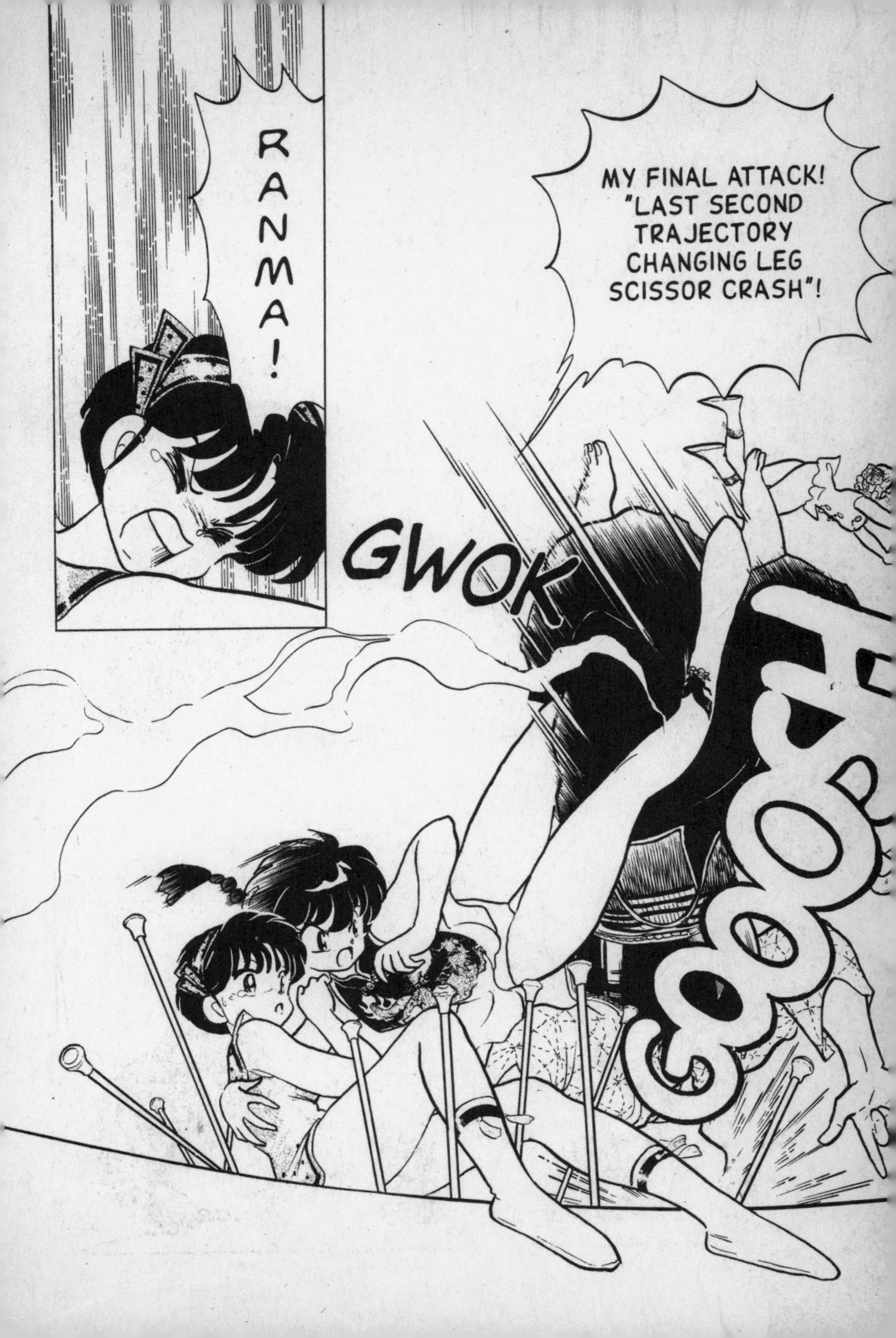
RANMA!
MY FINAL ATTACK! "LAST SECOND TRAJECTORY CHANGING LEG SCISSOR CRASH"!
GWOK
GOOOOOH

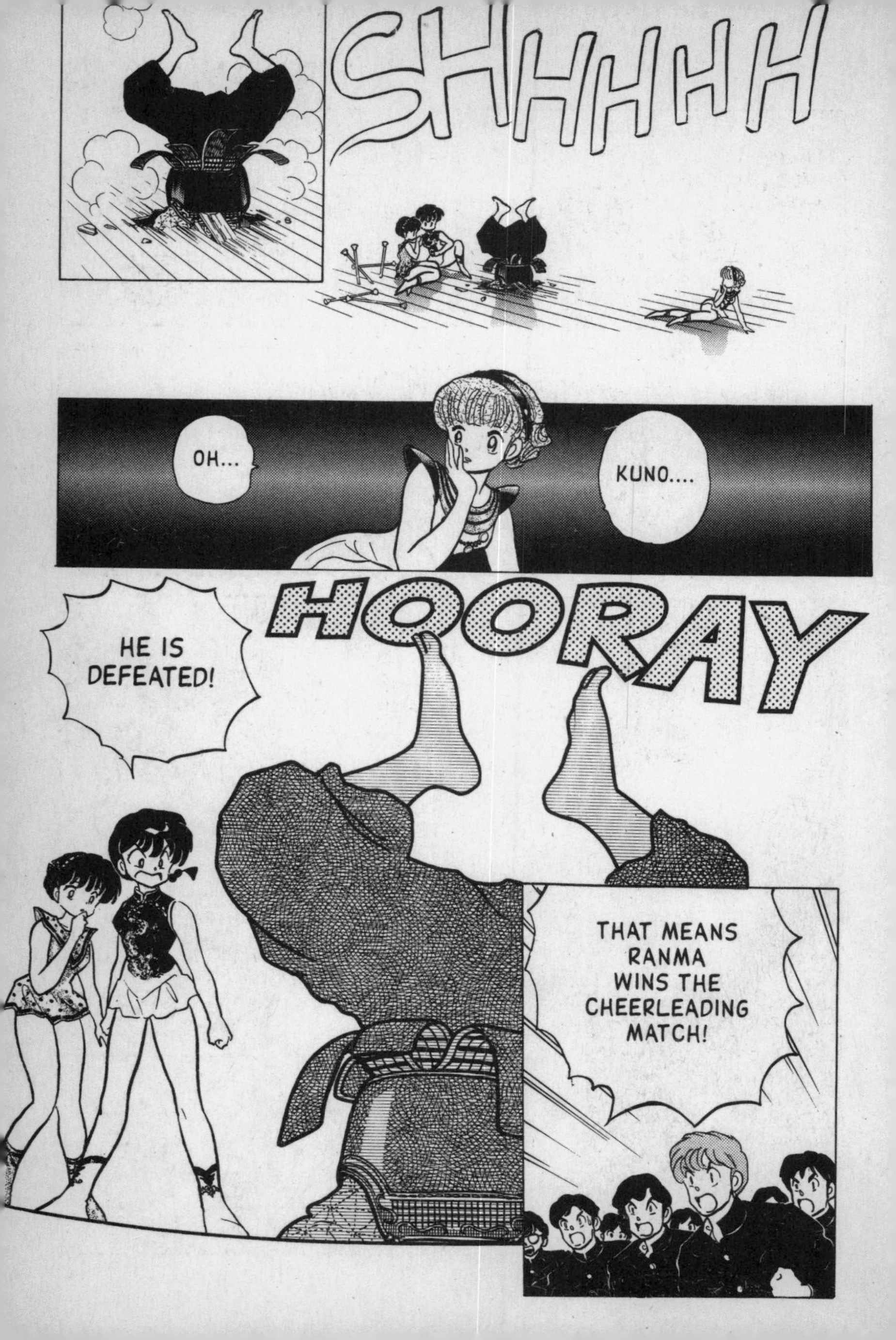
SHHHHH
OH...
KUNO....
HOORAY
HE IS DEFEATED!
THAT MEANS RANMA WINS THE CHEERLEADING MATCH!

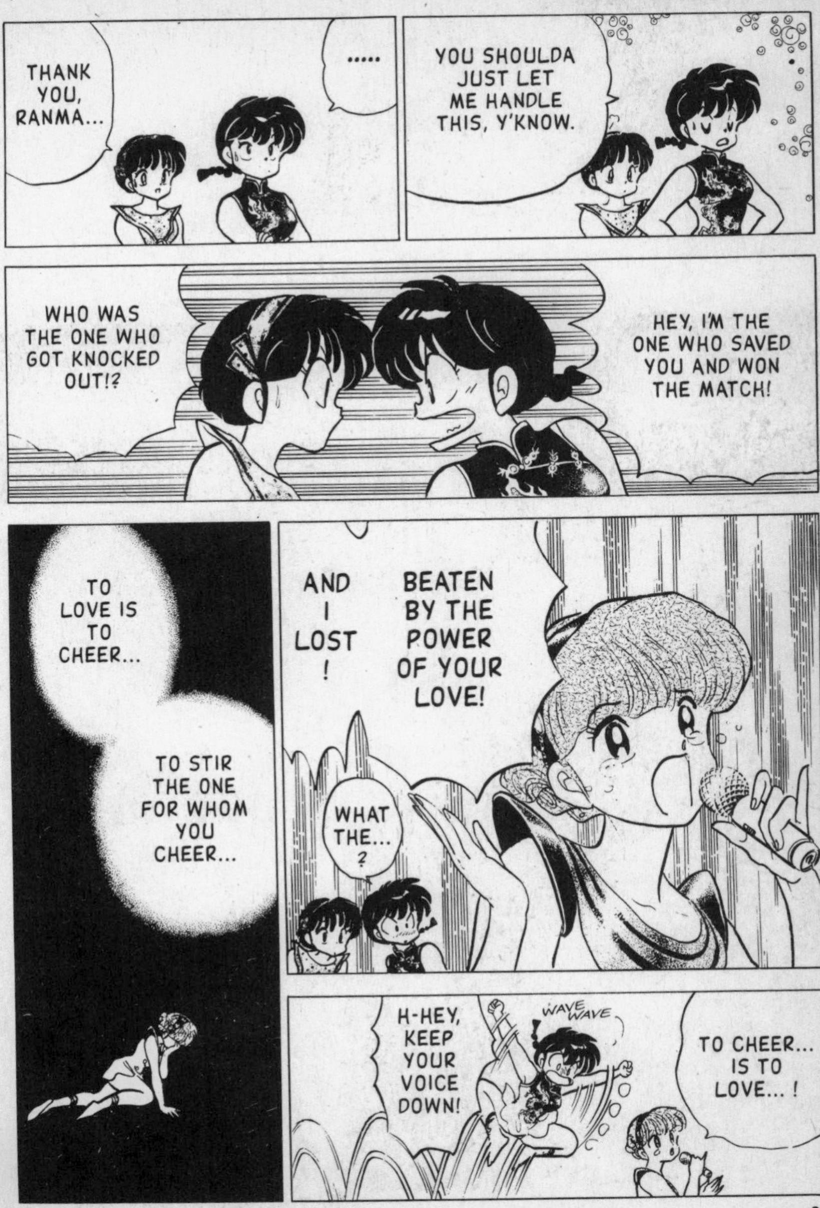
THANK YOU, RANMA...
.....
YOU SHOULDA JUST LET ME HANDLE THIS, Y'KNOW.
WHO WAS THE ONE WHO GOT KNOCKED OUT!?
HEY, I'M THE ONE WHO SAVED YOU AND WON THE MATCH!
TO LOVE IS TO CHEER...
TO STIR THE ONE FOR WHOM YOU CHEER...
AND I LOST!
BEATEN BY THE POWER OF YOUR LOVE!
WHAT THE...?
H-HEY, KEEP YOUR VOICE DOWN!
WAVE WAVE
TO CHEER... IS TO LOVE...!

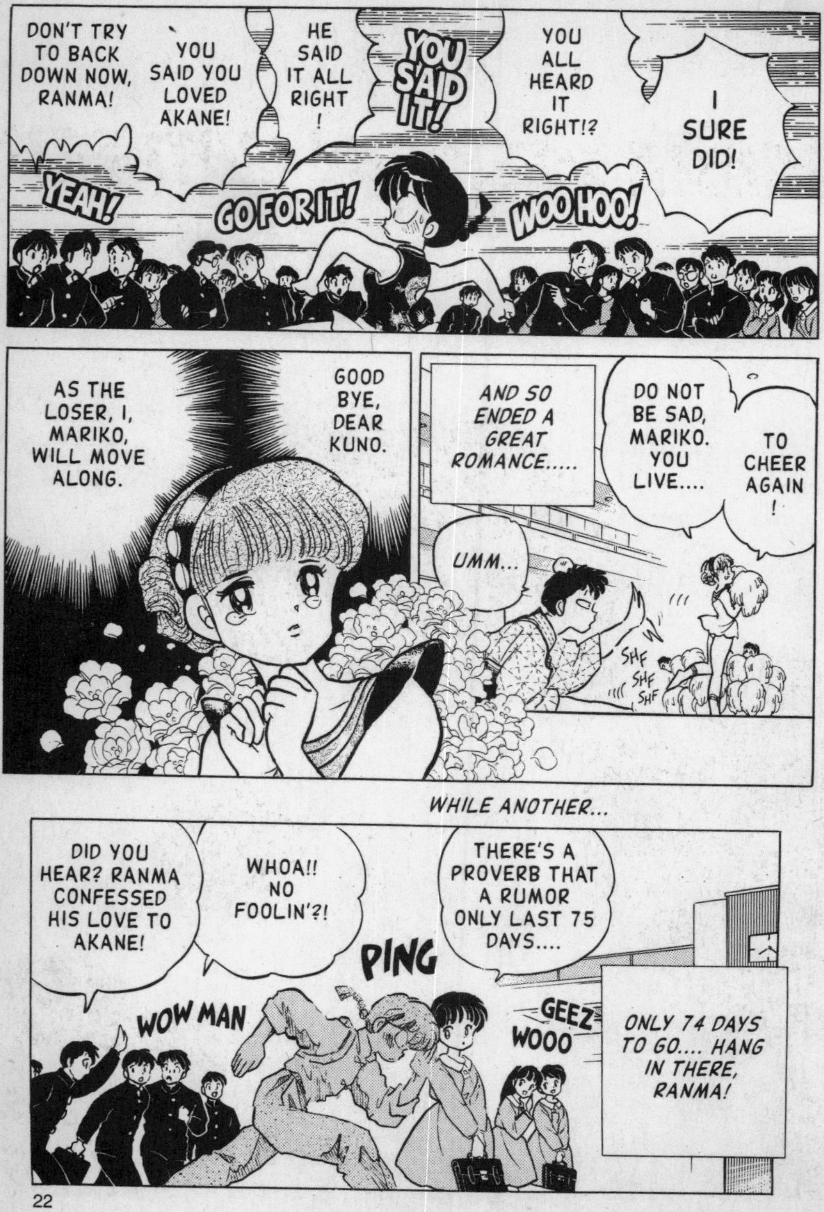
DON'T TRY TO BACK DOWN NOW, RANMA!
YOU SAID YOU LOVED AKANE!
HE SAID IT ALL RIGHT!
YOU SAID IT!
YOU ALL HEARD IT RIGHT!?
I SURE DID!
YEAH!
GO FOR IT!
WOO HOO!
AS THE LOSER, I, MARIKO, WILL MOVE ALONG.
GOOD BYE, DEAR KUNO.
AND SO ENDED A GREAT ROMANCE.....
DO NOT BE SAD, MARIKO. YOU LIVE....
TO CHEER AGAIN!
UMM...
SHF SHF SHF
WHILE ANOTHER...
DID YOU HEAR? RANMA CONFESSED HIS LOVE TO AKANE!
WHOA!! NO FOOLIN'?!
THERE'S A PROVERB THAT A RUMOR ONLY LAST 75 DAYS....
PING
WOW MAN
GEEZ
WOOO
ONLY 74 DAYS TO GO.... HANG IN THERE, RANMA!

Part 2

RANMA MEETS HIS MOTHER!?

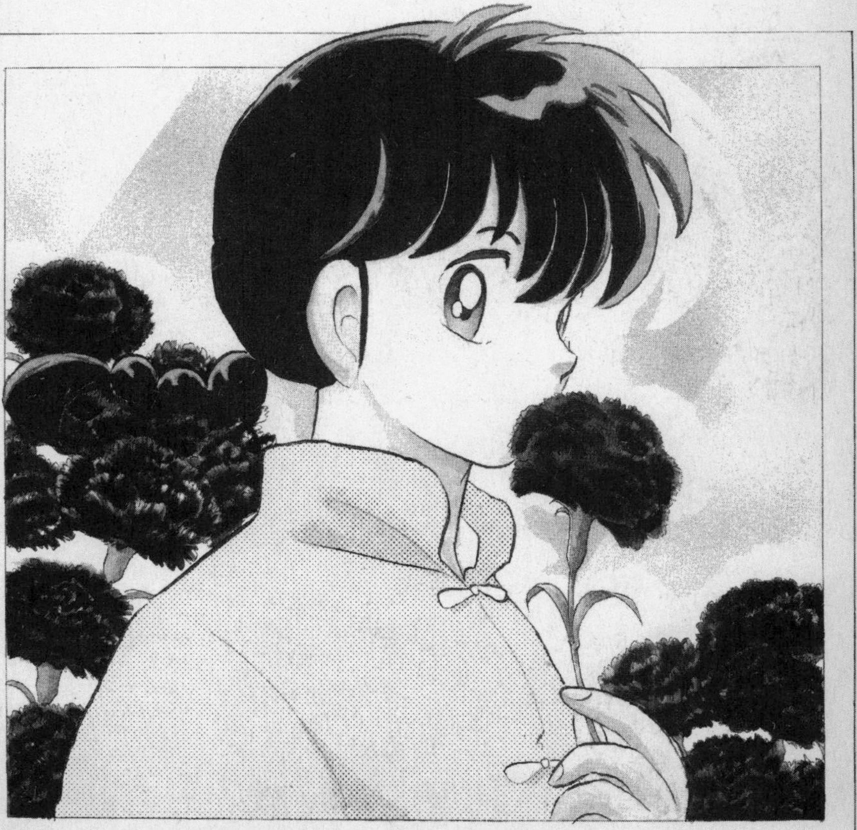

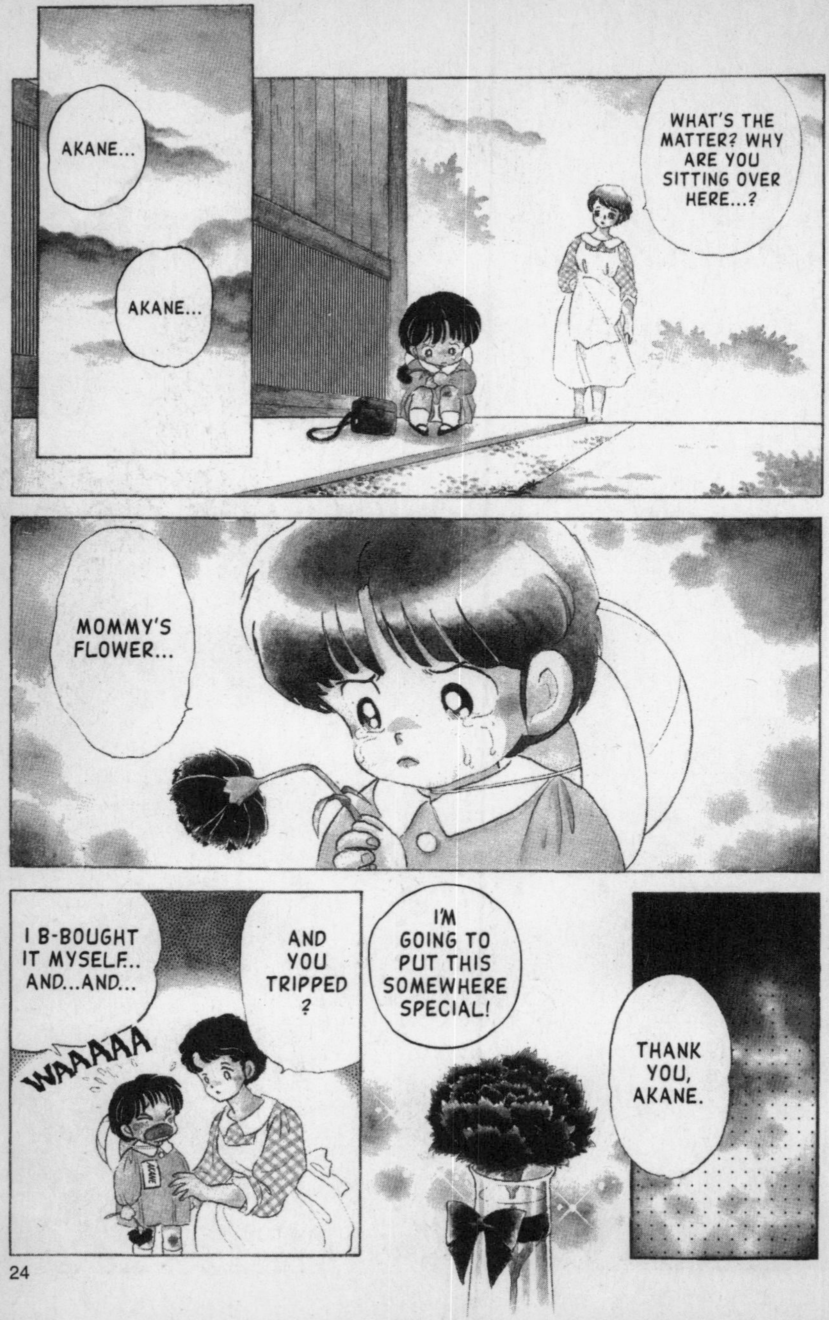
AKANE...
AKANE...
WHAT'S THE MATTER? WHY ARE YOU SITTING OVER HERE...?
MOMMY'S FLOWER...
I B-BOUGHT IT MYSELF... AND...AND...
WAAAAA
AND YOU TRIPPED?
I'M GOING TO PUT THIS SOMEWHERE SPECIAL!
AKANE
THANK YOU, AKANE.

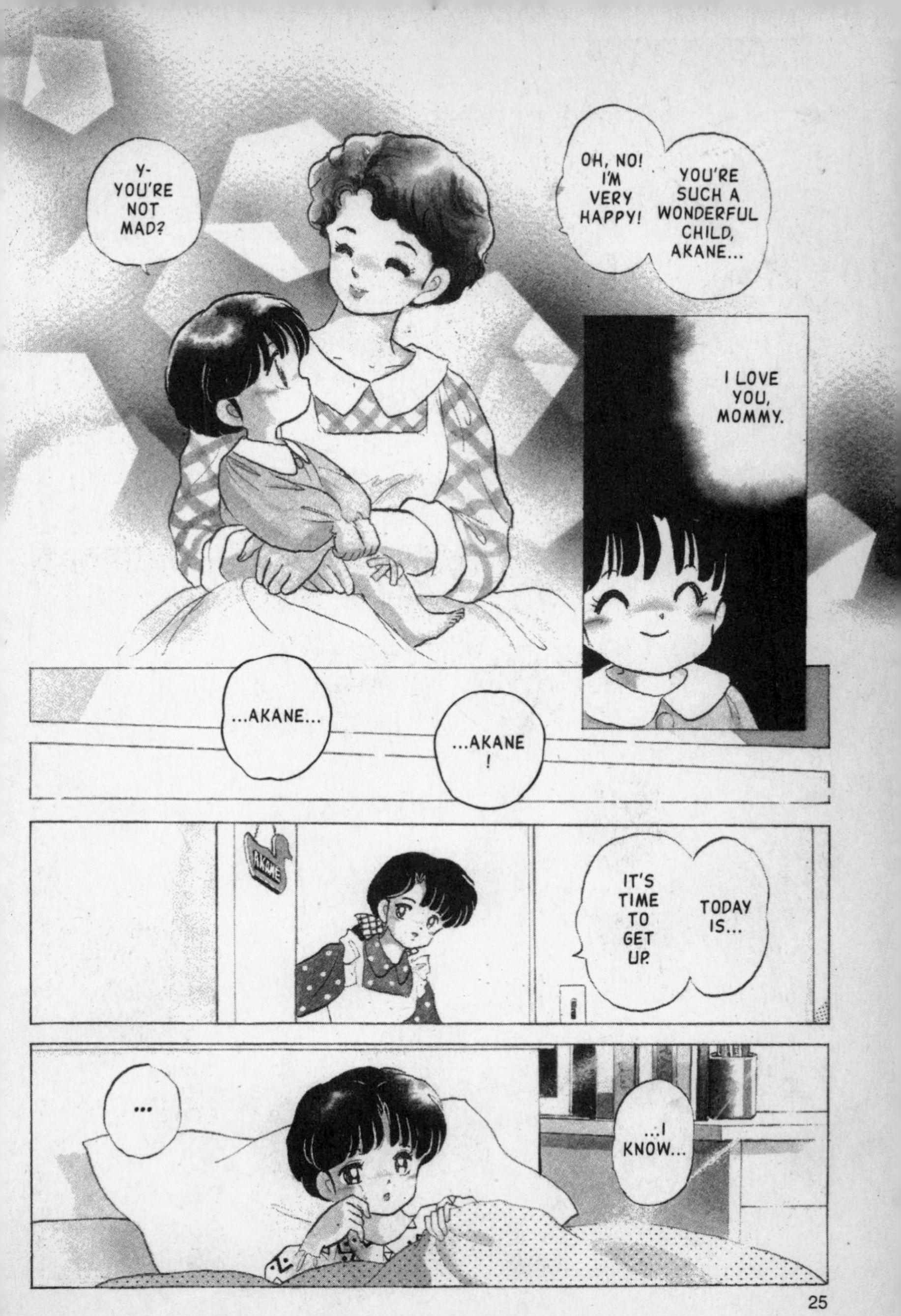
Y- YOU'RE NOT MAD?
OH, NO! I'M VERY HAPPY!
YOU'RE SUCH A WONDERFUL CHILD, AKANE...
I LOVE YOU, MOMMY.
...AKANE...
...AKANE !
IT'S TIME TO GET UP.
TODAY IS...
...
...I KNOW...

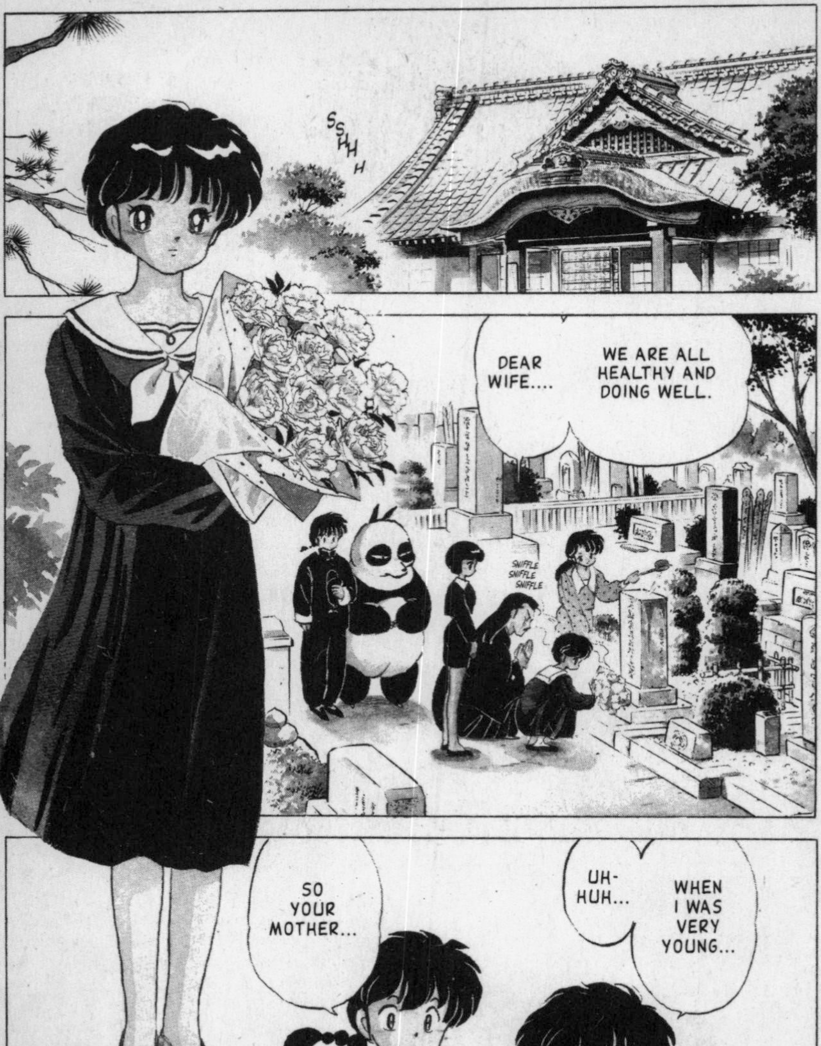
SSHHH
DEAR WIFE....
WE ARE ALL HEALTHY AND DOING WELL.
SNIFFLE SNIFFLE SNIFFLE
SO YOUR MOTHER...
UH-HUH...
WHEN I WAS VERY YOUNG...

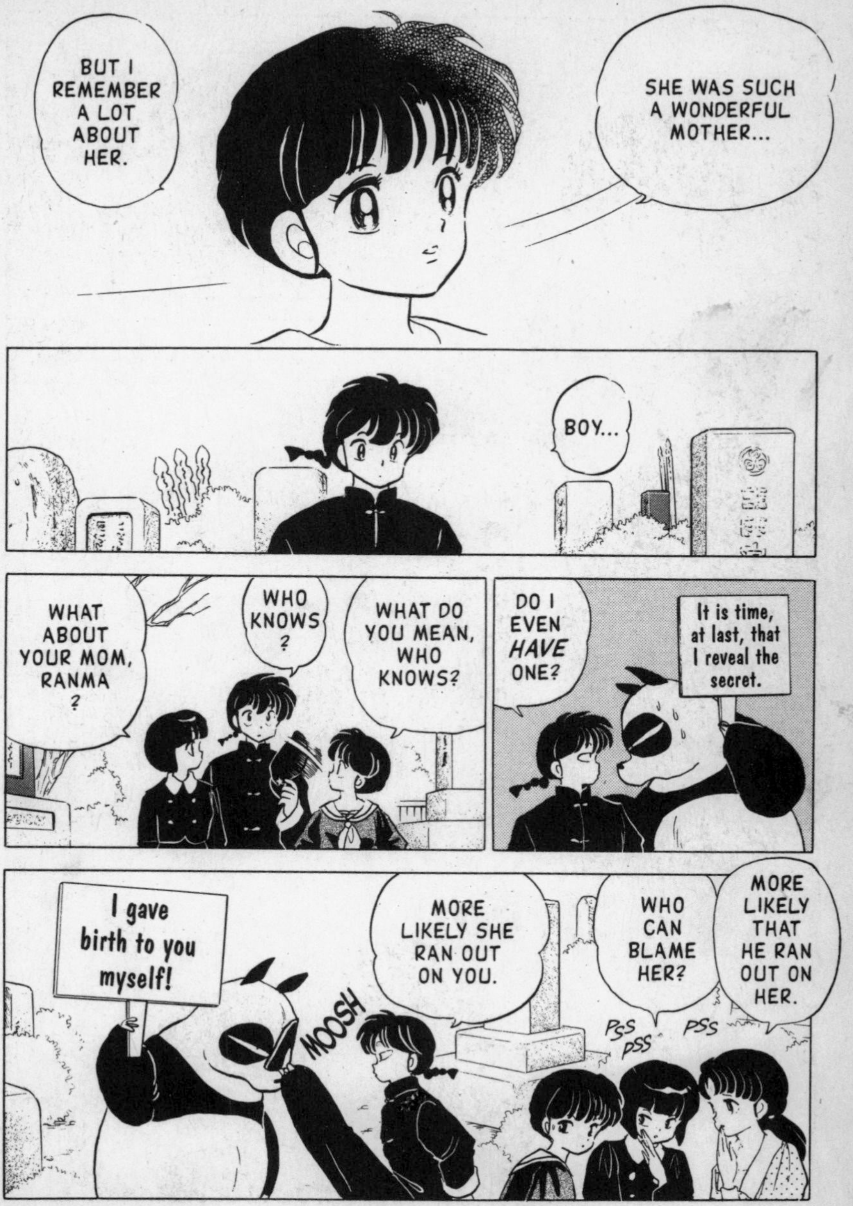
BUT I REMEMBER A LOT ABOUT HER.
SHE WAS SUCH A WONDERFUL MOTHER...
BOY...
WHAT ABOUT YOUR MOM, RANMA?
WHO KNOWS?
WHAT DO YOU MEAN, WHO KNOWS?
DO I EVEN *HAVE* ONE?
It is time, at last, that I reveal the secret.
I gave birth to you myself!
MOOSH
MORE LIKELY SHE RAN OUT ON YOU.
WHO CAN BLAME HER?
PSS PSS
PSS
MORE LIKELY THAT HE RAN OUT ON HER.

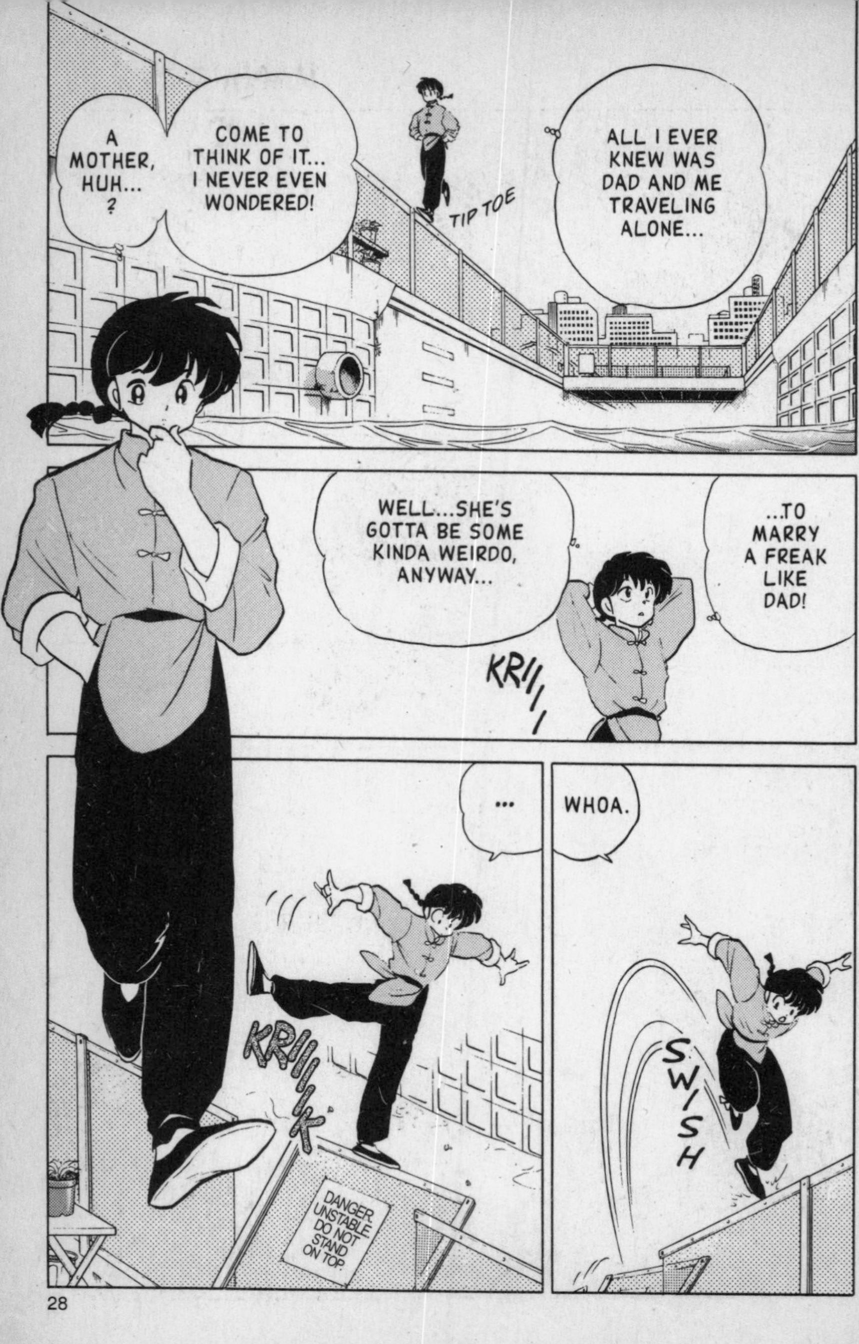
A MOTHER, HUH...?
COME TO THINK OF IT... I NEVER EVEN WONDERED!
TIP TOE
ALL I EVER KNEW WAS DAD AND ME TRAVELING ALONE...
WELL...SHE'S GOTTA BE SOME KINDA WEIRDO, ANYWAY...
...TO MARRY A FREAK LIKE DAD!
KRIII
...
KRIIIIK
DANGER UNSTABLE DO NOT STAND ON TOP
WHOA.
SWISH

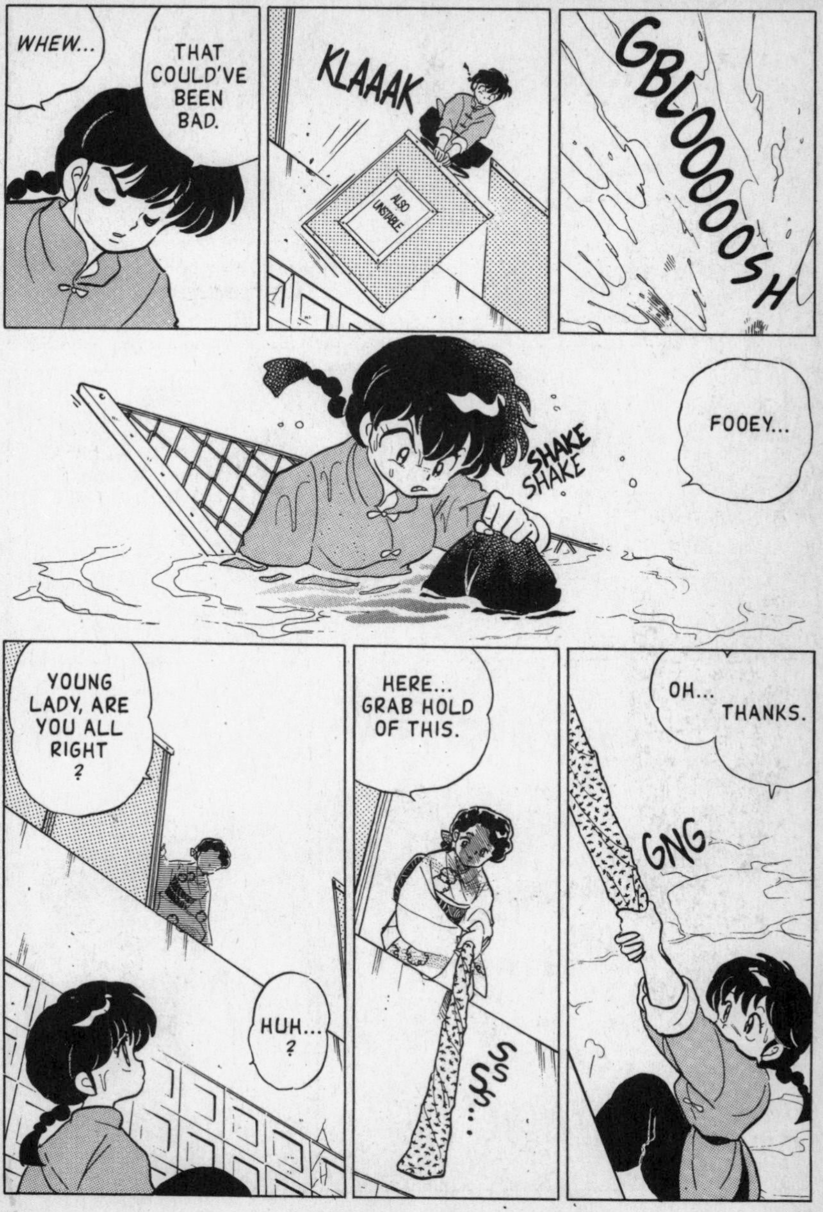
WHEW...
THAT COULD'VE BEEN BAD.
KLAAAK
ALSO UNSTABLE
GBLOOOOOSH
SHAKE SHAKE
FOOEY...
YOUNG LADY, ARE YOU ALL RIGHT ?
HUH... ?
HERE... GRAB HOLD OF THIS.
SSSS...
OH... THANKS.
GNG

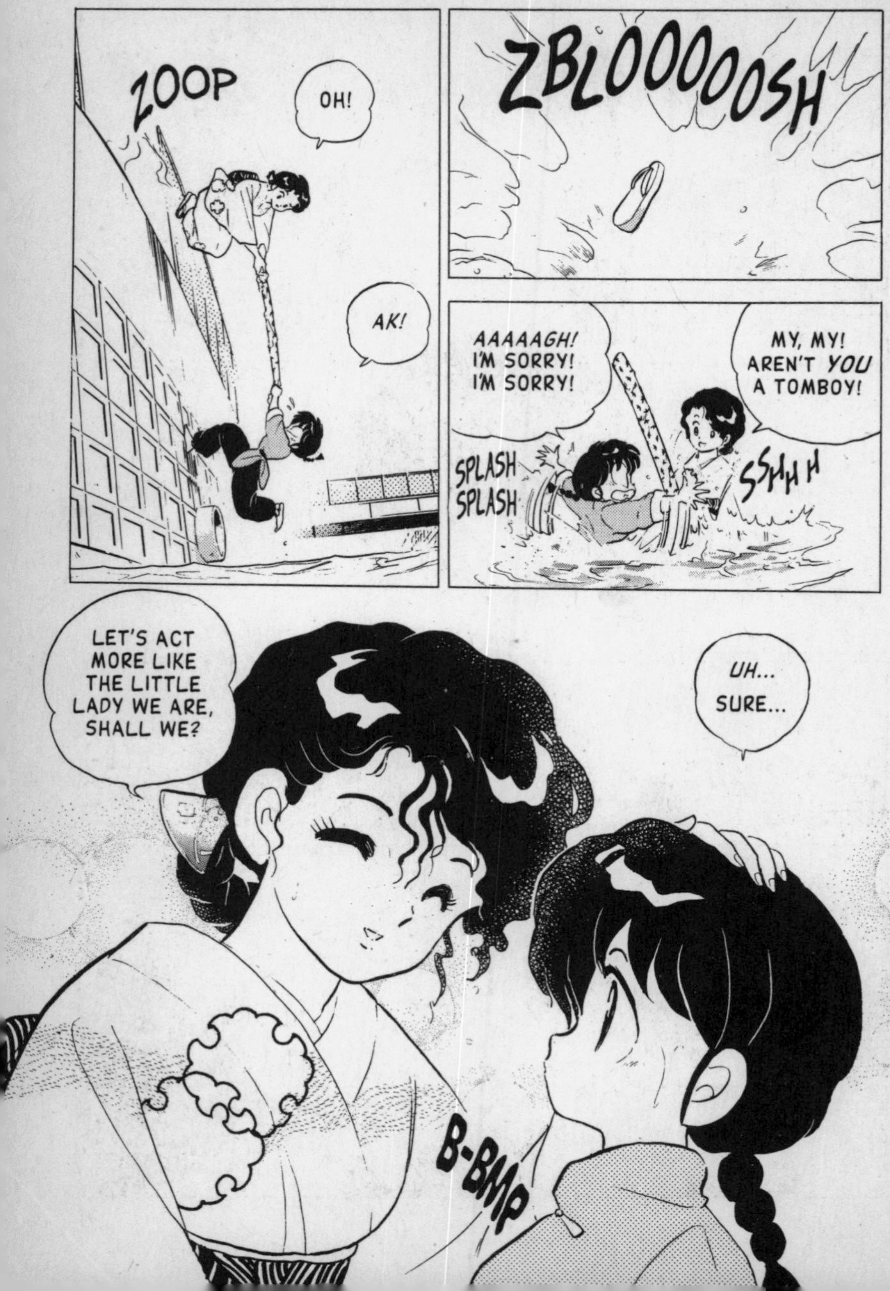
ZOOP
OH!
AK!
ZBLOOOOOOSH
AAAAAGH! I'M SORRY! I'M SORRY!
MY, MY! AREN'T YOU A TOMBOY!
SPLASH SPLASH
SSHHH
LET'S ACT MORE LIKE THE LITTLE LADY WE ARE, SHALL WE?
UH... SURE...
B-BMP

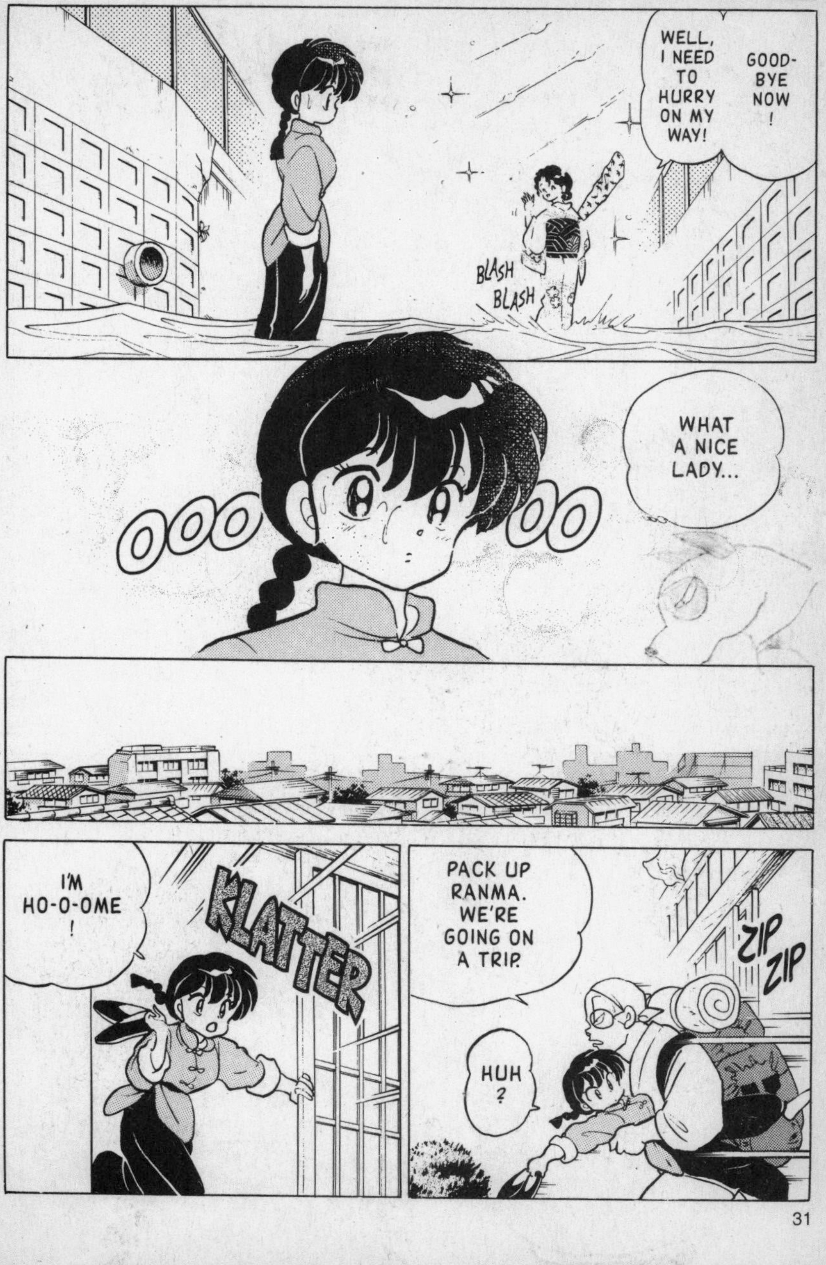
WELL, I NEED TO HURRY ON MY WAY!
GOOD-BYE NOW !
BLASH BLASH
OOO
OO
WHAT A NICE LADY...
I'M HO-O-OME !
KLATTER
PACK UP RANMA. WE'RE GOING ON A TRIP.
ZIP ZIP
HUH ?

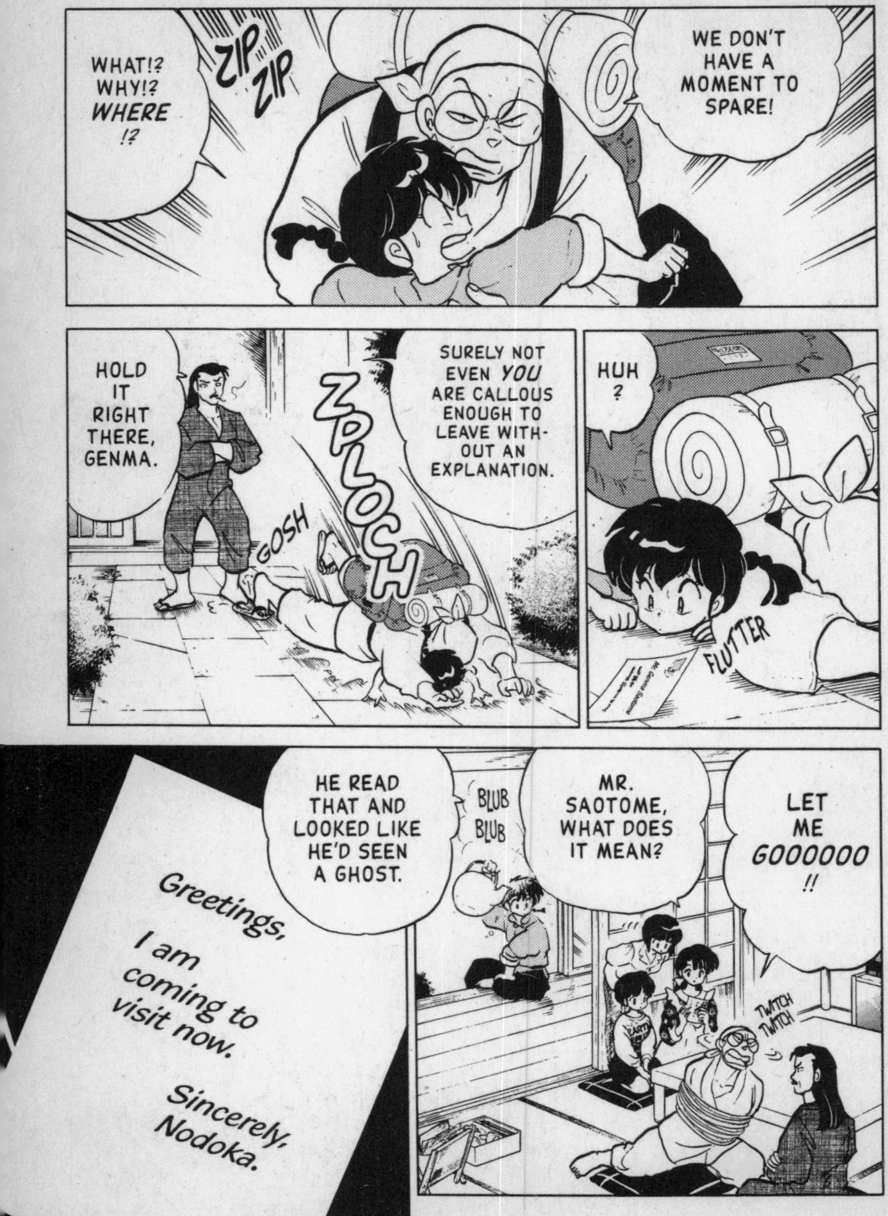
WHAT!? WHY!? WHERE !?
ZIP ZIP
WE DON'T HAVE A MOMENT TO SPARE!
HOLD IT RIGHT THERE, GENMA.
ZPLOCH
GOSH
SURELY NOT EVEN YOU ARE CALLOUS ENOUGH TO LEAVE WITH-OUT AN EXPLANATION.
HUH ?
FLUTTER
Greetings,
I am coming to visit now.
Sincerely, Nodoka.
HE READ THAT AND LOOKED LIKE HE'D SEEN A GHOST.
BLUB BLUB
MR. SAOTOME, WHAT DOES IT MEAN?
LET ME GOOOOOO !!
TWITCH TWITCH

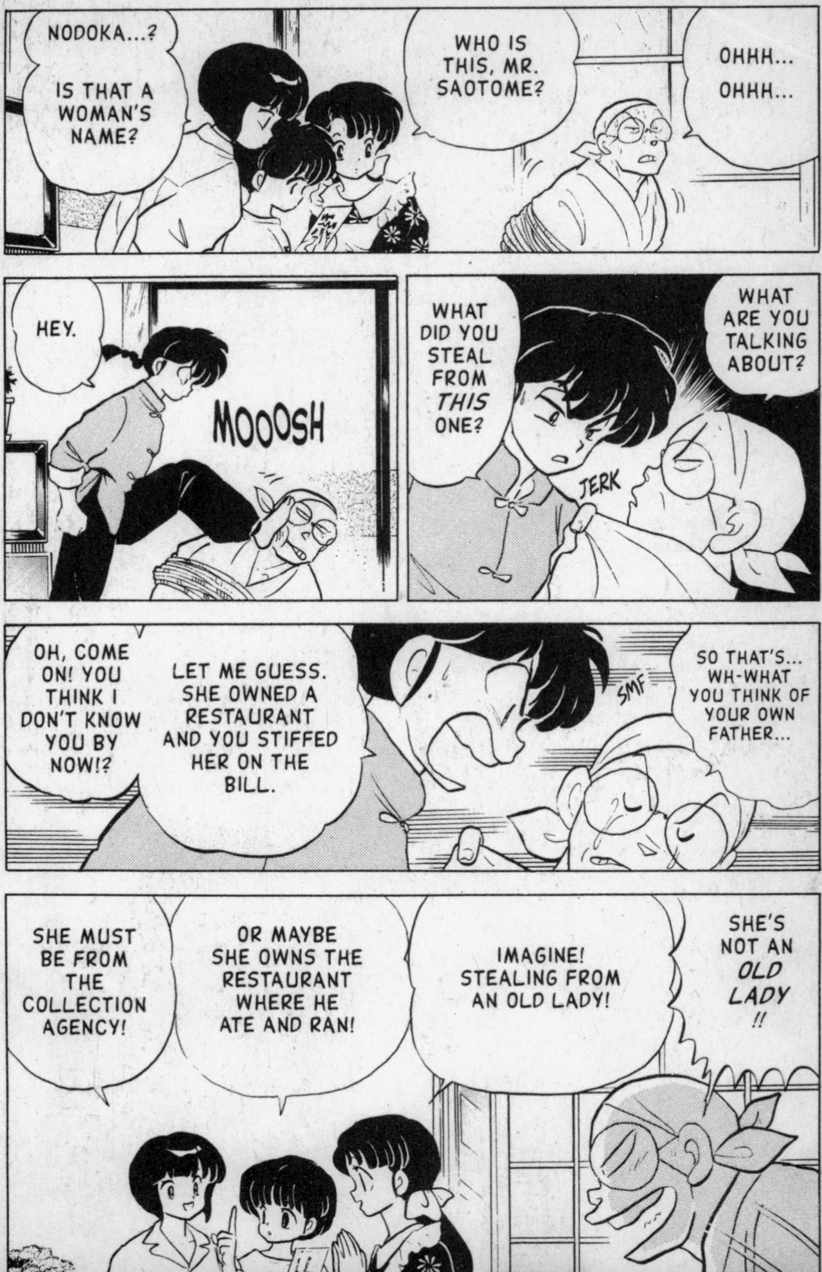
NODOKA...? IS THAT A WOMAN'S NAME?
WHO IS THIS, MR. SAOTOME?
OHHH... OHHH...
HEY.
MOOOSH
WHAT DID YOU STEAL FROM *THIS* ONE?
WHAT ARE YOU TALKING ABOUT?
JERK
OH, COME ON! YOU THINK I DON'T KNOW YOU BY NOW!?
LET ME GUESS. SHE OWNED A RESTAURANT AND YOU STIFFED HER ON THE BILL.
SMF
SO THAT'S... WH-WHAT YOU THINK OF YOUR OWN FATHER...
SHE MUST BE FROM THE COLLECTION AGENCY!
OR MAYBE SHE OWNS THE RESTAURANT WHERE HE ATE AND RAN!
IMAGINE! STEALING FROM AN OLD LADY!
SHE'S NOT AN *OLD LADY* !!

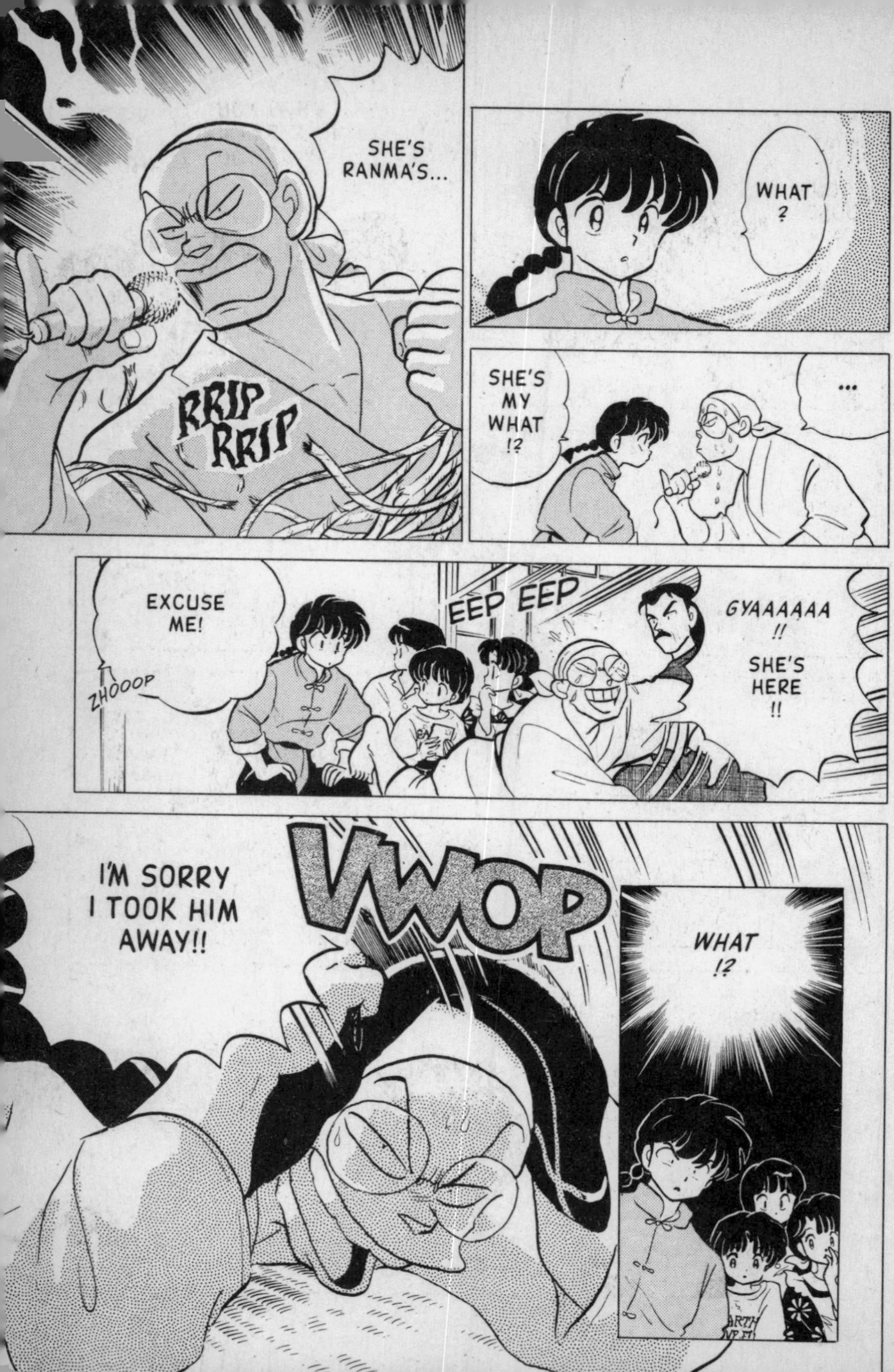
SHE'S RANMA'S...
RRIP RRIP
WHAT ?
SHE'S MY WHAT !?
...
EXCUSE ME!
ZHOOOP
EEP EEP
GYAAAAAA !!
SHE'S HERE !!
I'M SORRY I TOOK HIM AWAY!!
VWOP
WHAT !?

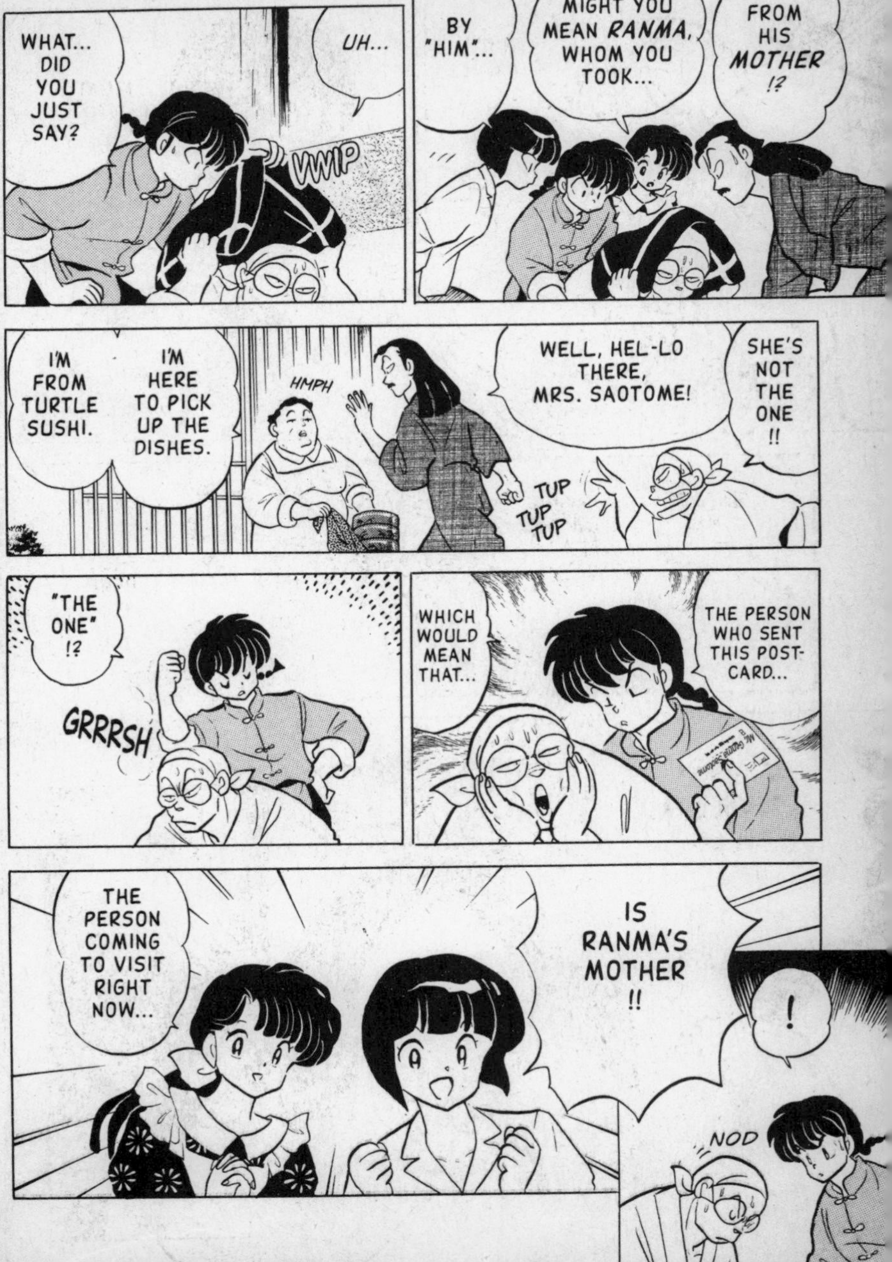

WHAT... DID YOU JUST SAY?
UH...
VWIP
BY "HIM"...
MIGHT YOU MEAN RANMA, WHOM YOU TOOK...
FROM HIS MOTHER !?
I'M FROM TURTLE SUSHI.
I'M HERE TO PICK UP THE DISHES.
HMPH
WELL, HEL-LO THERE, MRS. SAOTOME!
SHE'S NOT THE ONE !!
TUP TUP TUP
"THE ONE" !?
GRRRSH
WHICH WOULD MEAN THAT...
THE PERSON WHO SENT THIS POST-CARD...
THE PERSON COMING TO VISIT RIGHT NOW...
IS RANMA'S MOTHER !!
!
NOD

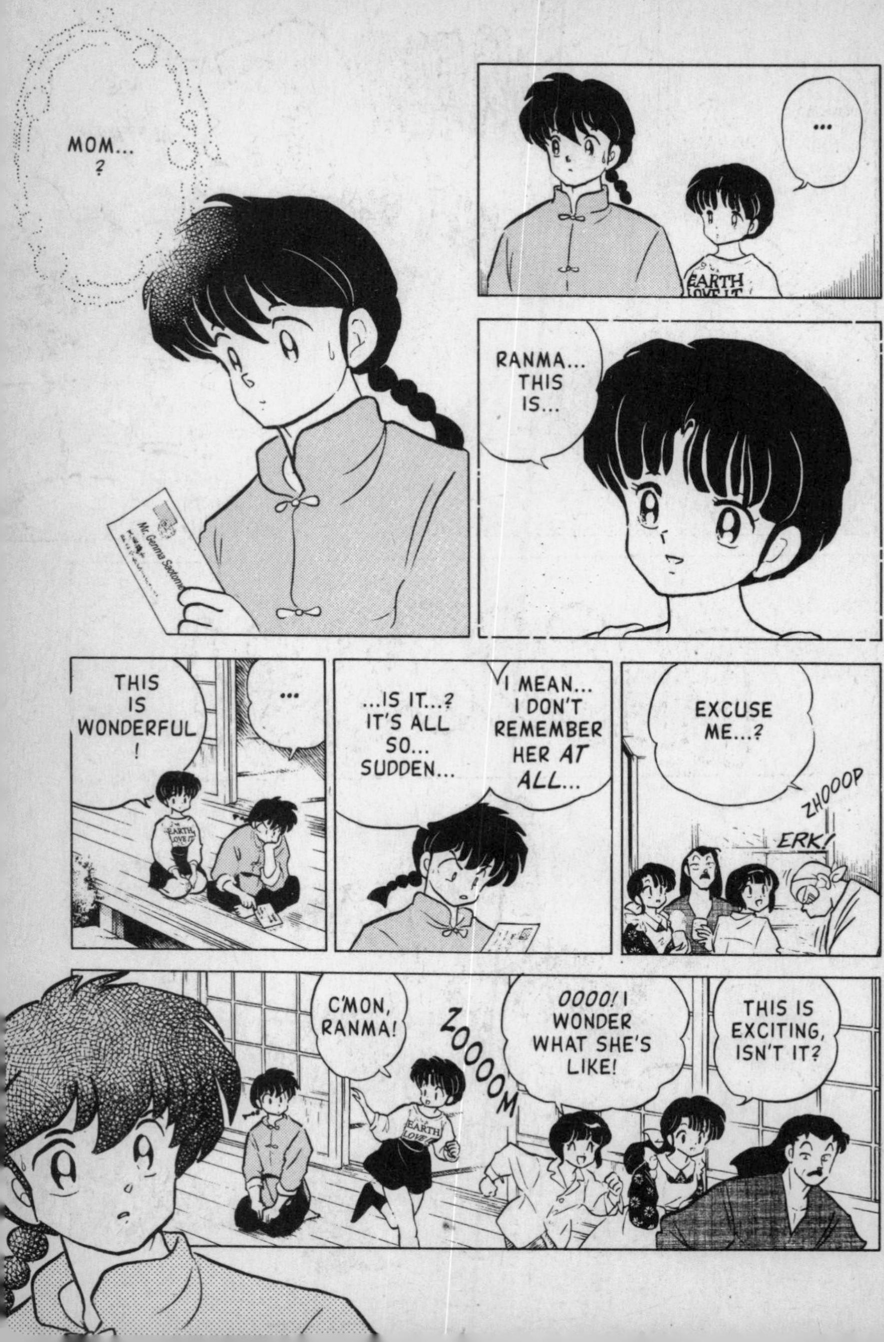
MOM...
?
...
RANMA... THIS IS...
THIS IS WONDERFUL!
...
...IS IT...? IT'S ALL SO... SUDDEN...
I MEAN... I DON'T REMEMBER HER AT ALL...
EXCUSE ME...?
ZHOOOP
ERK!
C'MON, RANMA!
ZOOOOM
OOOO! I WONDER WHAT SHE'S LIKE!
THIS IS EXCITING, ISN'T IT?

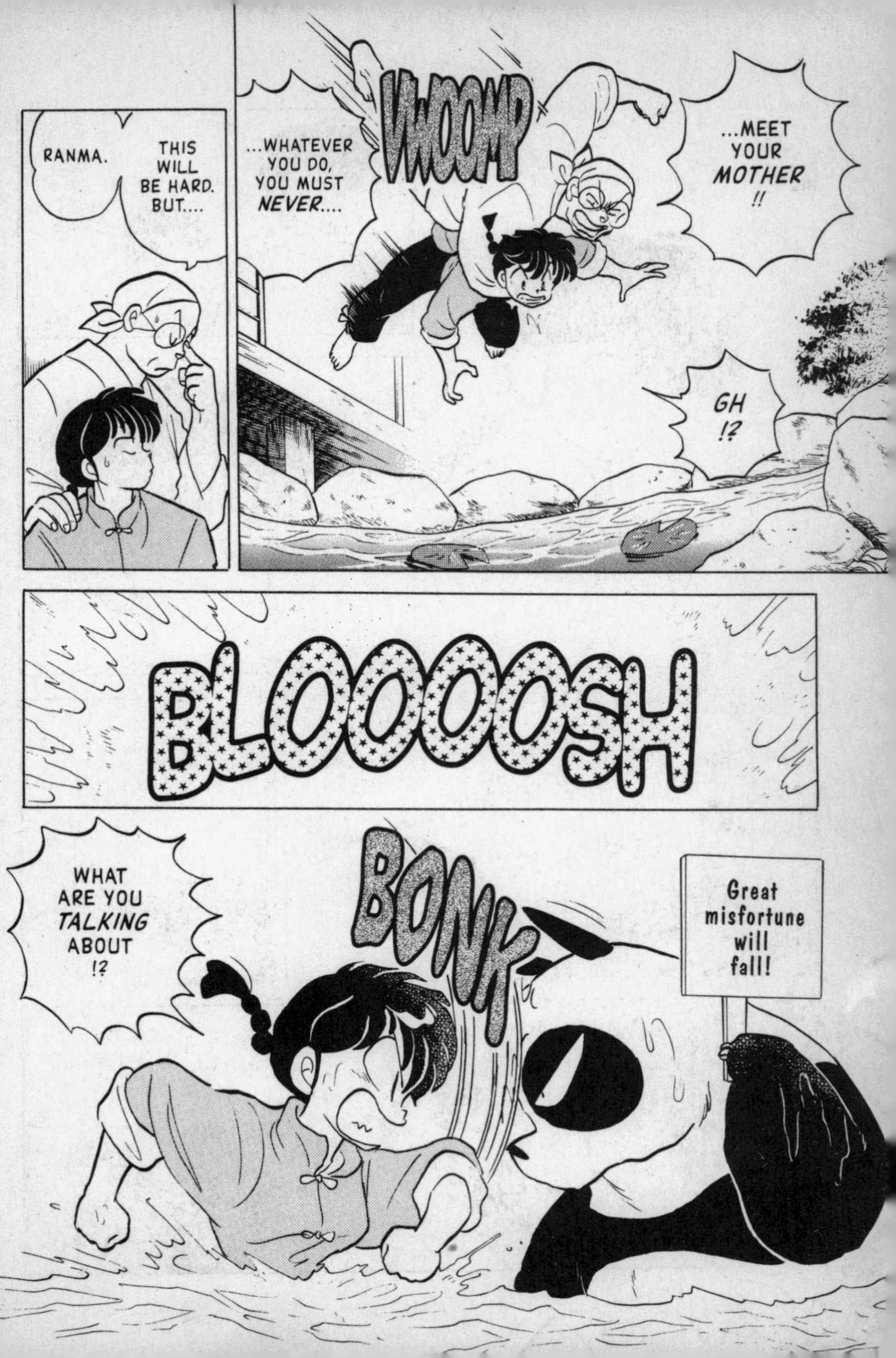
RANMA.
THIS WILL BE HARD. BUT....
...WHATEVER YOU DO, YOU MUST NEVER....
VWOOMP
...MEET YOUR MOTHER !!
GH !?
BLOOOSH
WHAT ARE YOU TALKING ABOUT !?
BONK
Great misfortune will fall!

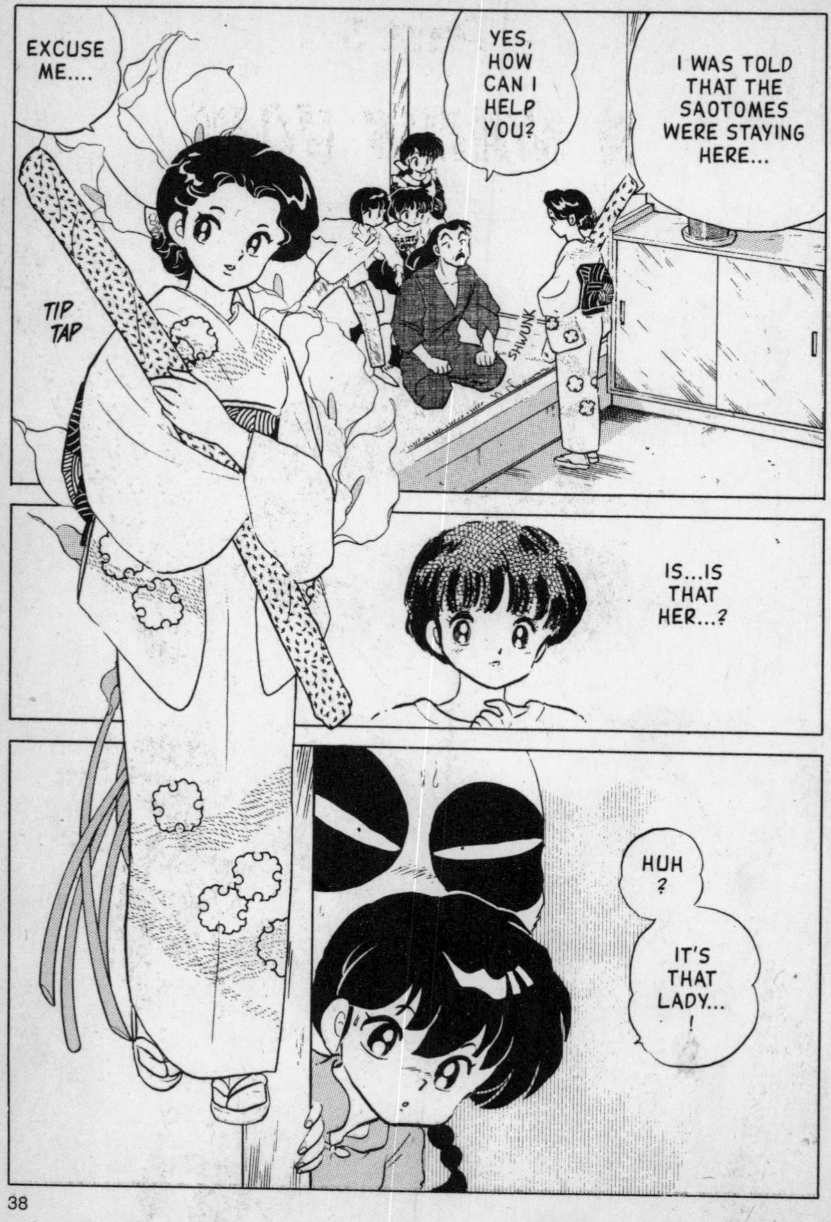
EXCUSE ME....
TIP TAP
YES, HOW CAN I HELP YOU?
SHWUNK
I WAS TOLD THAT THE SAOTOMES WERE STAYING HERE...
IS...IS THAT HER...?
HUH?
IT'S THAT LADY...!

Part 3

A MAN'S VOW

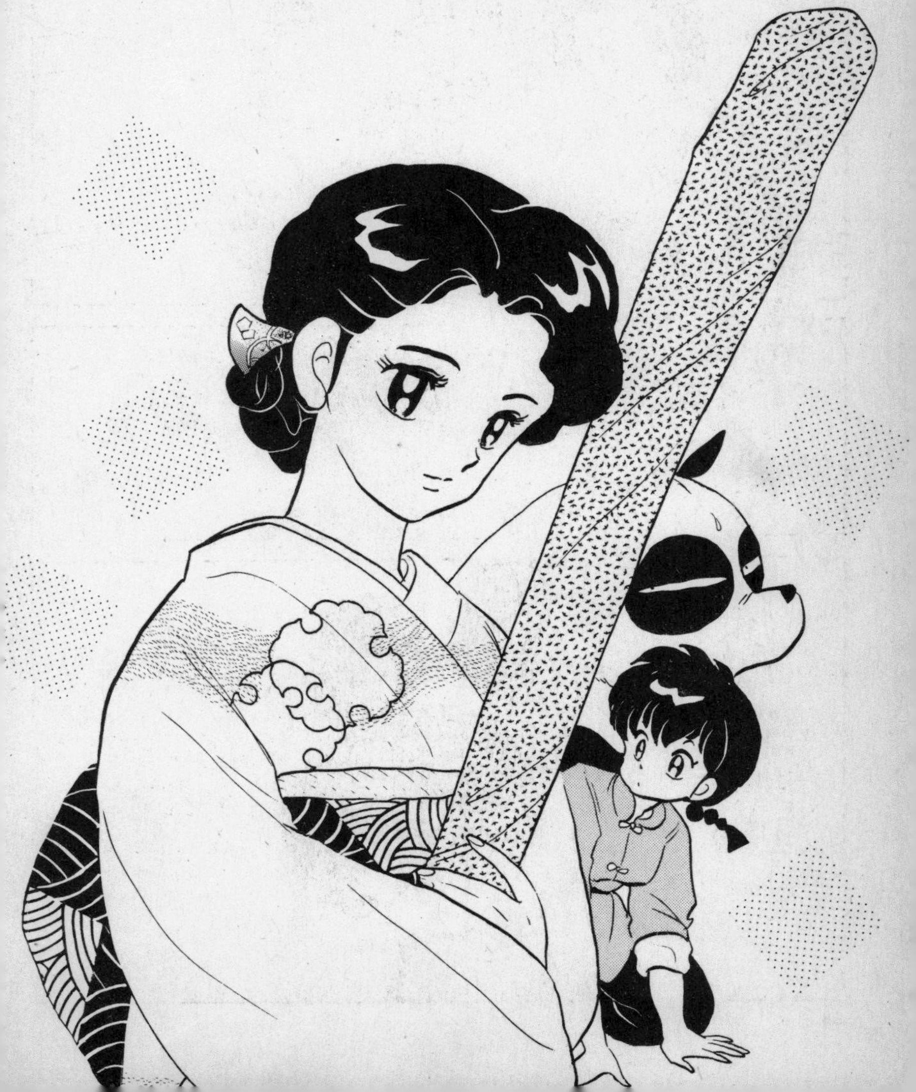

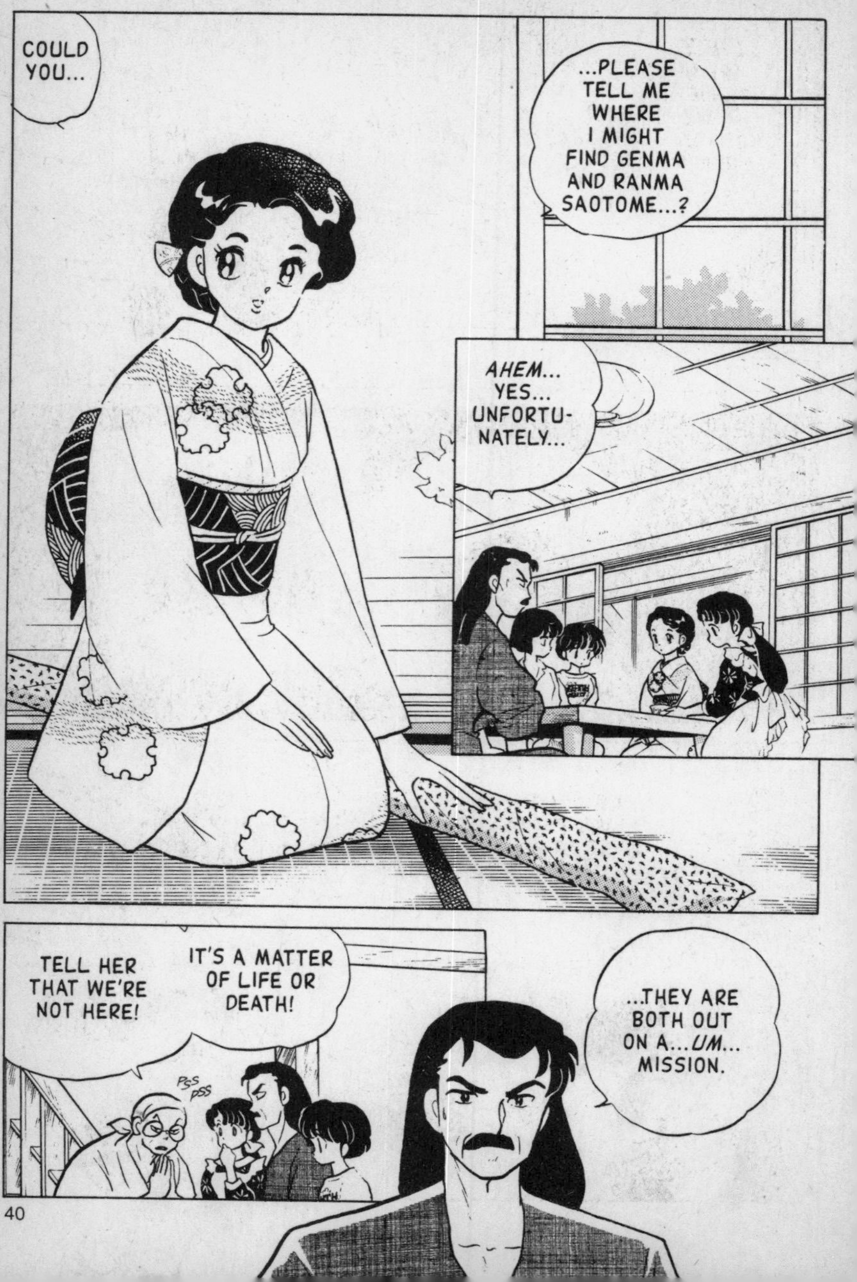
COULD YOU...
...PLEASE TELL ME WHERE I MIGHT FIND GENMA AND RANMA SAOTOME...?
AHEM... YES... UNFORTU-NATELY...
TELL HER THAT WE'RE NOT HERE!
IT'S A MATTER OF LIFE OR DEATH!
PSS PSS
...THEY ARE BOTH OUT ON A...*UM*... MISSION.

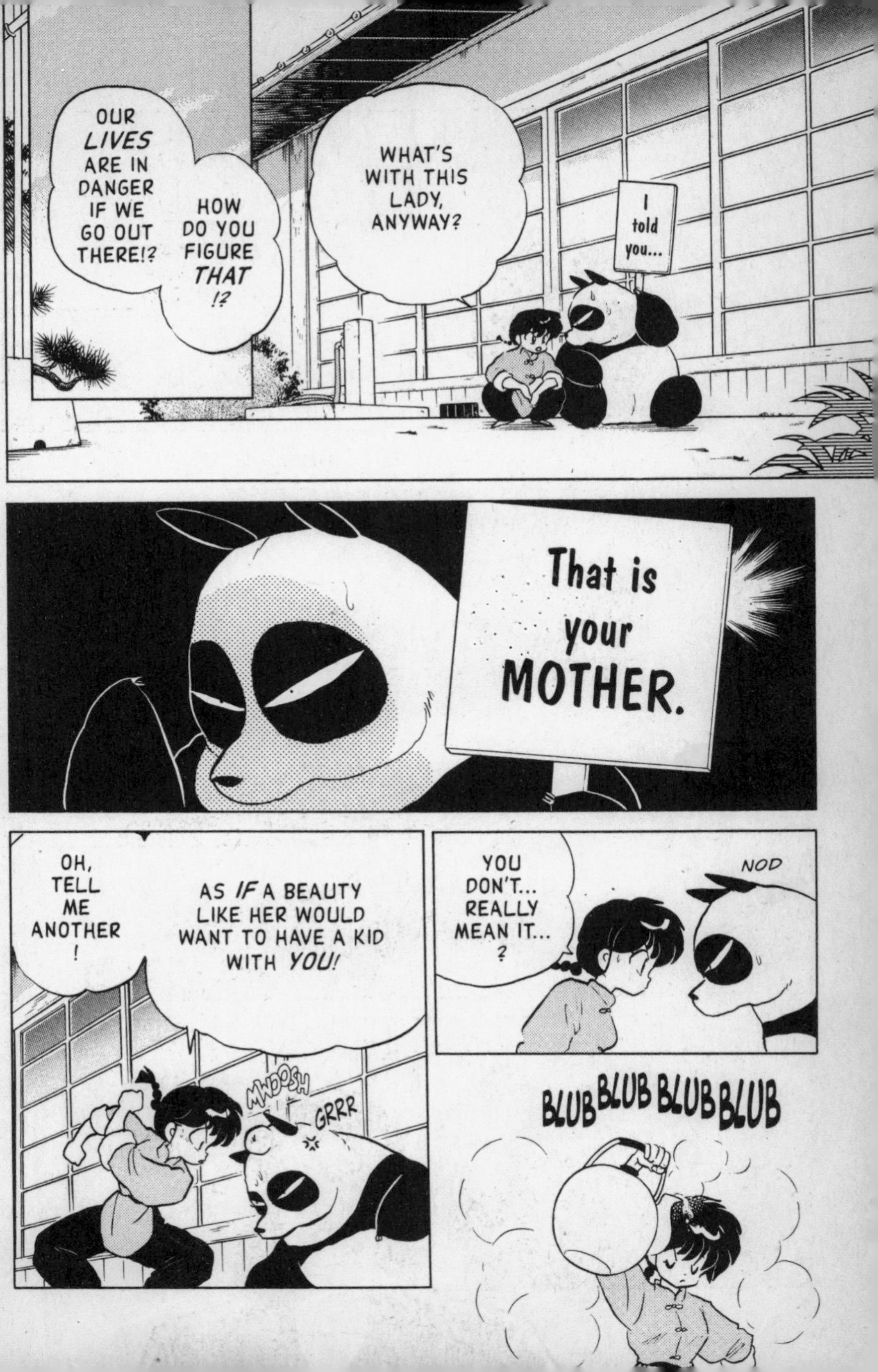
OUR LIVES ARE IN DANGER IF WE GO OUT THERE!?
HOW DO YOU FIGURE THAT !?
WHAT'S WITH THIS LADY, ANYWAY?
I told you...
That is your MOTHER.
OH, TELL ME ANOTHER !
AS IF A BEAUTY LIKE HER WOULD WANT TO HAVE A KID WITH YOU!
MWOOSH
GRRR
YOU DON'T... REALLY MEAN IT... ?
NOD
BLUB BLUB BLUB BLUB

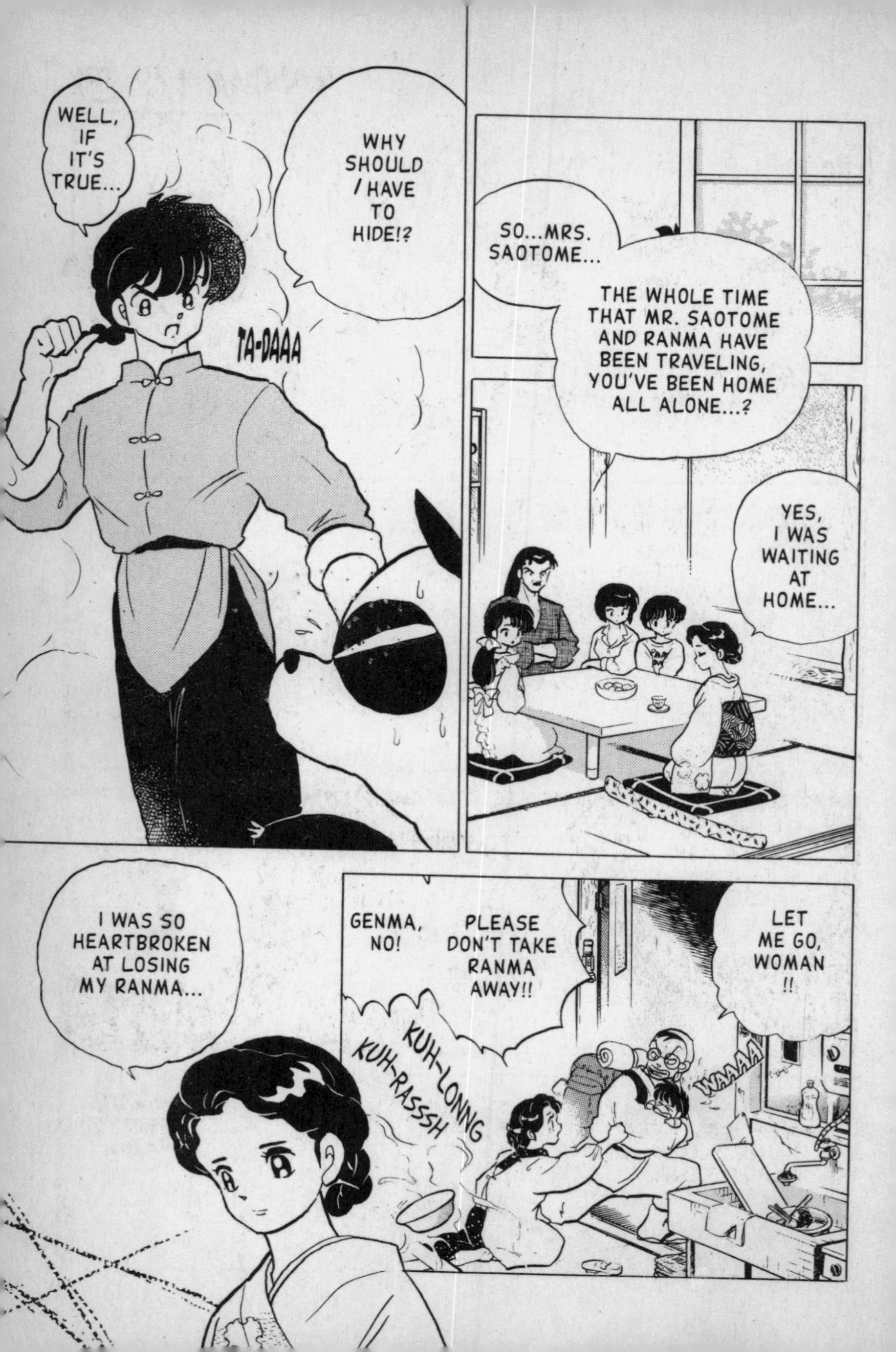
WELL, IF IT'S TRUE...
WHY SHOULD I HAVE TO HIDE!?
TA-DAAA
SO...MRS. SAOTOME...
THE WHOLE TIME THAT MR. SAOTOME AND RANMA HAVE BEEN TRAVELING, YOU'VE BEEN HOME ALL ALONE...?
YES, I WAS WAITING AT HOME...
I WAS SO HEARTBROKEN AT LOSING MY RANMA...
GENMA, NO!
PLEASE DON'T TAKE RANMA AWAY!!
LET ME GO, WOMAN!!
KUH-LONNG
KUH-RASSSH
WAAAA

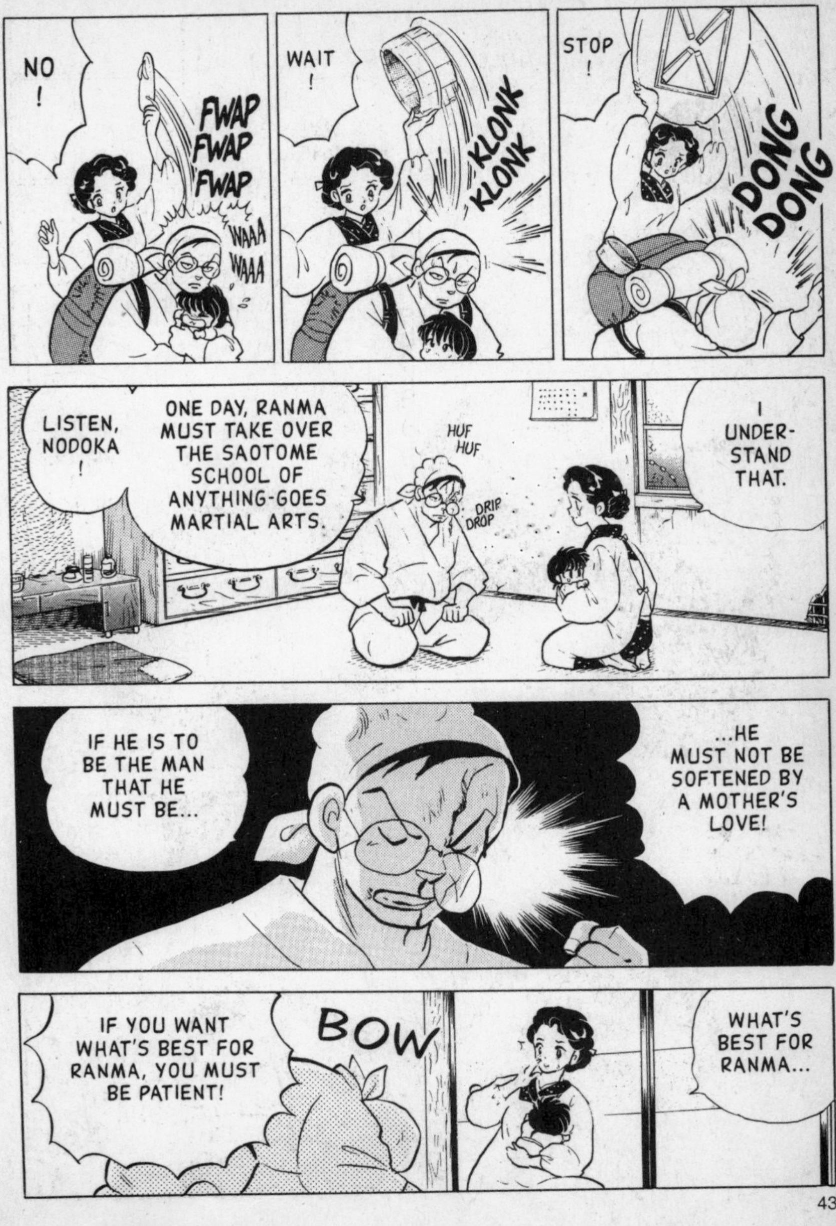
NO !
FWAP FWAP FWAP
WAAA WAAA
WAIT !
KLONK KLONK
STOP !
DONG DONG
LISTEN, NODOKA !
ONE DAY, RANMA MUST TAKE OVER THE SAOTOME SCHOOL OF ANYTHING-GOES MARTIAL ARTS.
HUF HUF
DRIP DROP
I UNDER-STAND THAT.
IF HE IS TO BE THE MAN THAT HE MUST BE...
...HE MUST NOT BE SOFTENED BY A MOTHER'S LOVE!
IF YOU WANT WHAT'S BEST FOR RANMA, YOU MUST BE PATIENT!
BOW
WHAT'S BEST FOR RANMA...

I SEE. SO YOU ENTRUSTED RANMA INTO THE CARE OF HIS FATHER...

WH-WHAT A SACRIFICE....

I HAD FAITH IN MY HUSBAND...

SNFF

BUT BEFORE HE LEFT ON HIS JOURNEY...

...HE ALSO MADE ME A VOW.

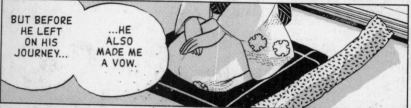

A VOW?

HMM?

WHAT KIND OF...

ARRGH!! LEGGO, YOU OLD JERK!!

WHAM BAM

GASP

A BOY'S VOICE !!

C-COULD IT BE... RANMA... !?

ZIP

BONK

PLASH

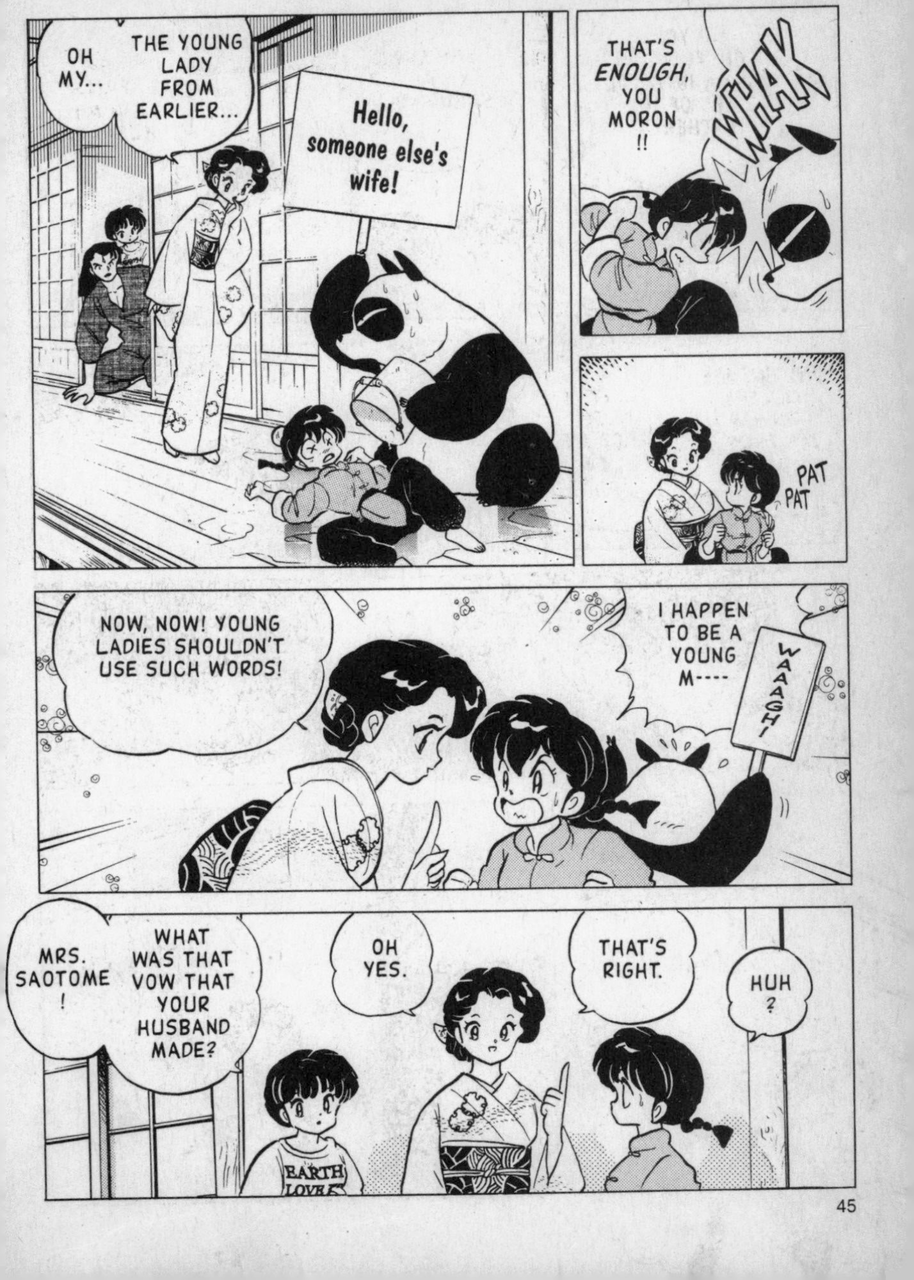
OH MY...
THE YOUNG LADY FROM EARLIER...
Hello, someone else's wife!
THAT'S ENOUGH, YOU MORON !!
WHAK
PAT PAT
NOW, NOW! YOUNG LADIES SHOULDN'T USE SUCH WORDS!
I HAPPEN TO BE A YOUNG M----
WAAAGH!
MRS. SAOTOME !
WHAT WAS THAT VOW THAT YOUR HUSBAND MADE?
OH YES.
THAT'S RIGHT.
HUH ?
EARTH LOVE

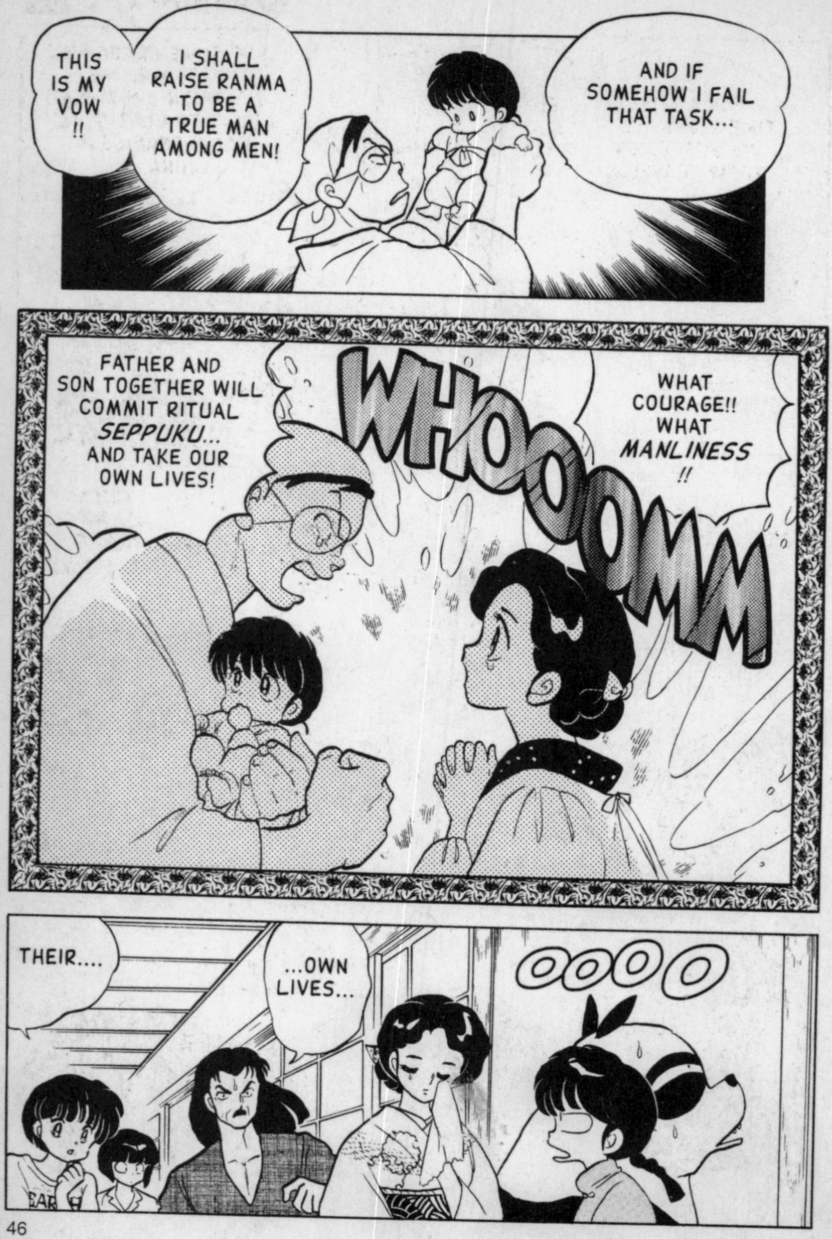
THIS IS MY VOW !!
I SHALL RAISE RANMA TO BE A TRUE MAN AMONG MEN!
AND IF SOMEHOW I FAIL THAT TASK...
FATHER AND SON TOGETHER WILL COMMIT RITUAL *SEPPUKU*... AND TAKE OUR OWN LIVES!
WHOOOOMM
WHAT COURAGE!! WHAT *MANLINESS* !!
THEIR....
...OWN LIVES...
OOOO

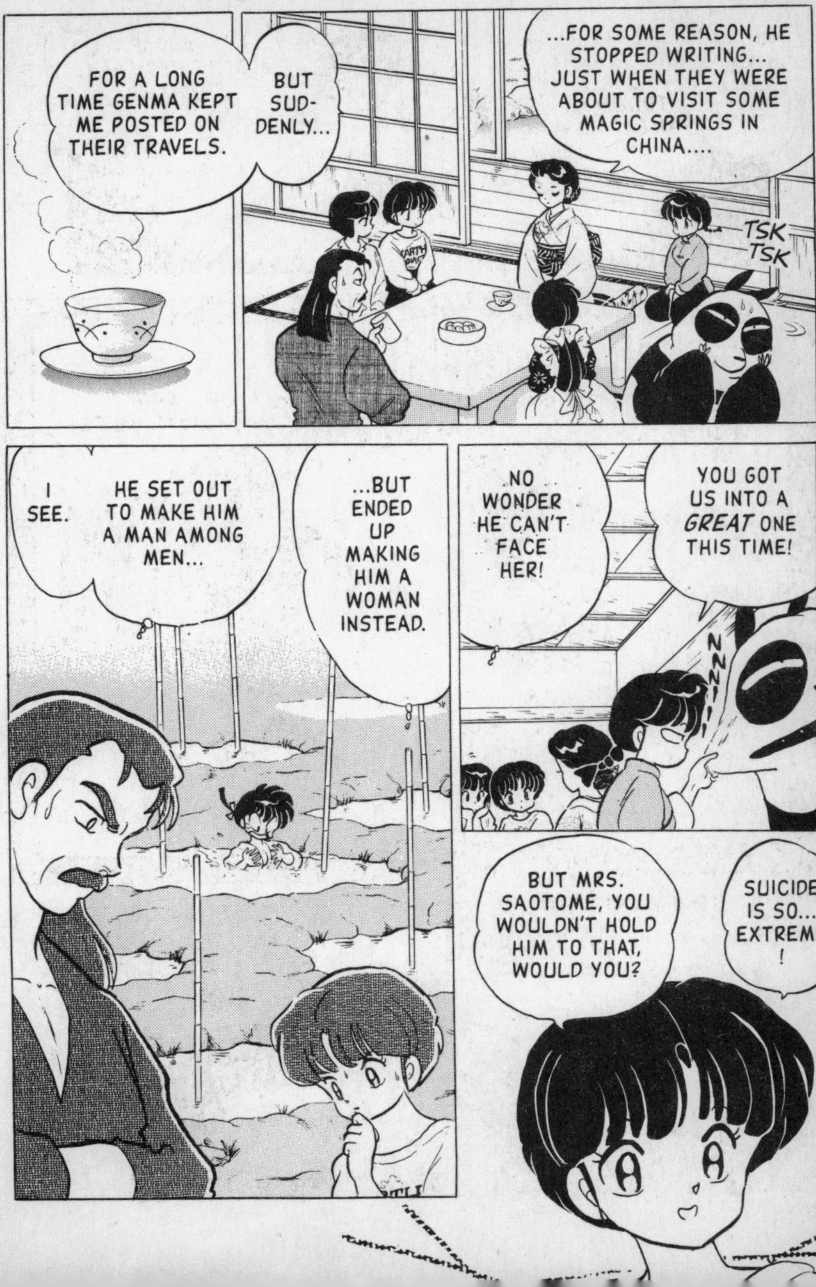
FOR A LONG TIME GENMA KEPT ME POSTED ON THEIR TRAVELS.
BUT SUD-DENLY...
...FOR SOME REASON, HE STOPPED WRITING... JUST WHEN THEY WERE ABOUT TO VISIT SOME MAGIC SPRINGS IN CHINA....
TSK TSK
I SEE.
HE SET OUT TO MAKE HIM A MAN AMONG MEN...
...BUT ENDED UP MAKING HIM A WOMAN INSTEAD.
NO WONDER HE CAN'T FACE HER!
YOU GOT US INTO A *GREAT* ONE THIS TIME!
NNN!!
BUT MRS. SAOTOME, YOU WOULDN'T HOLD HIM TO THAT, WOULD YOU?
SUICIDE IS SO... EXTREME!

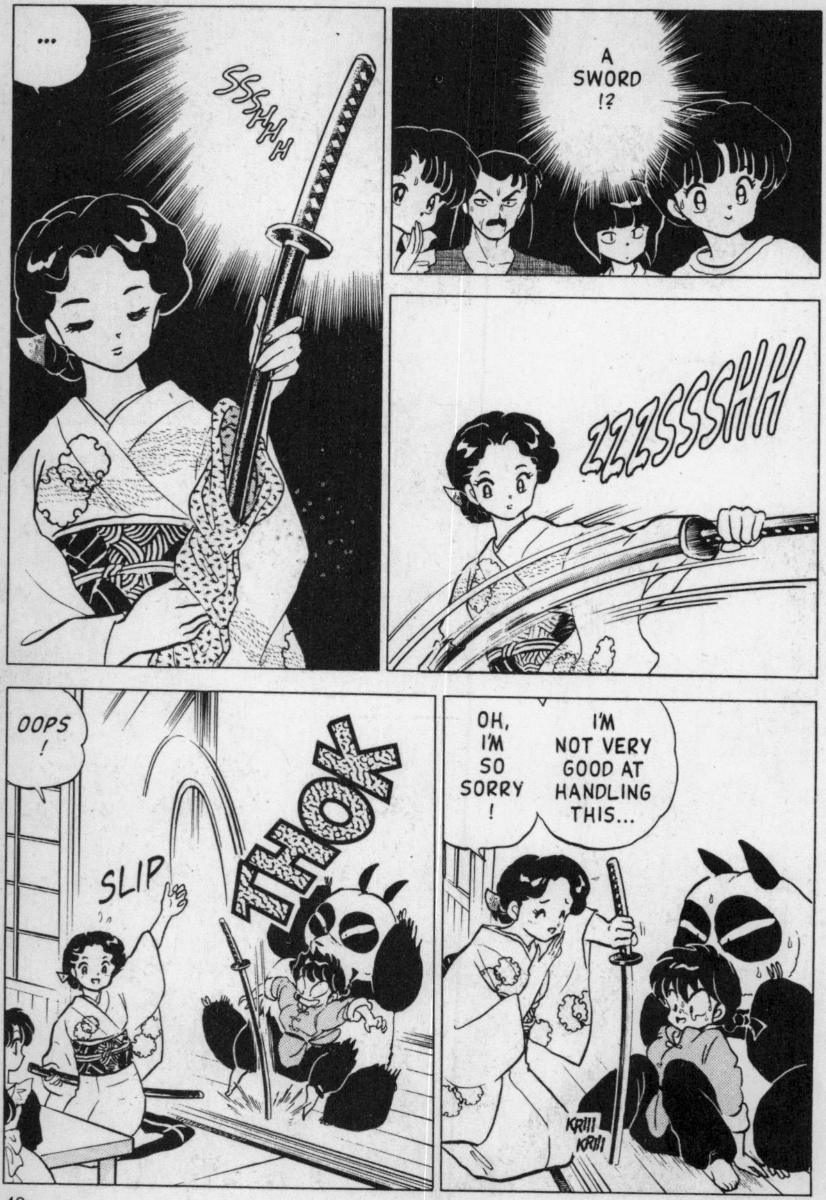
...
SSSHHH
A SWORD !?
ZZZSSSSHH
OOPS !
SLIP
THOK
OH, I'M SO SORRY !
I'M NOT VERY GOOD AT HANDLING THIS...
KRIII KRIII

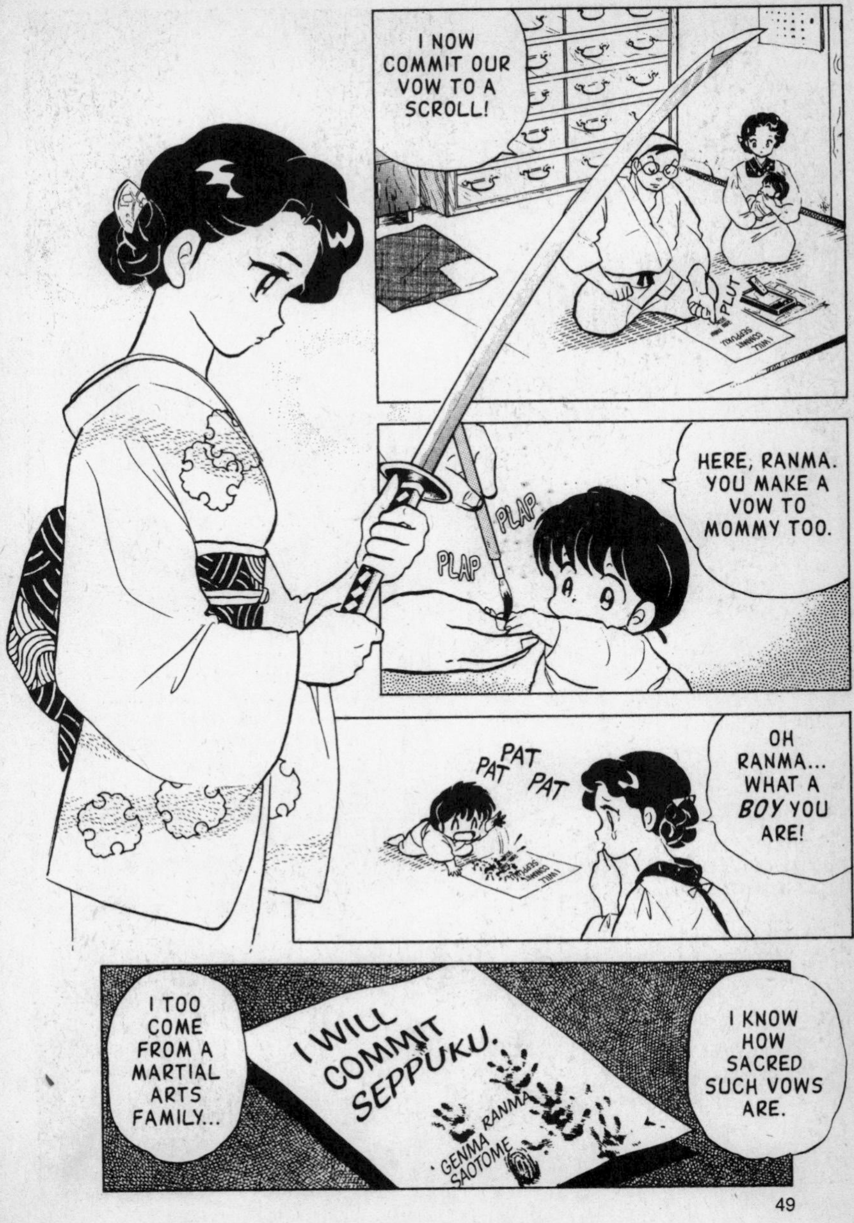
I NOW COMMIT OUR VOW TO A SCROLL!
PLUT
PLAP
PLAP
HERE, RANMA. YOU MAKE A VOW TO MOMMY TOO.
PAT
PAT
PAT
OH RANMA... WHAT A *BOY* YOU ARE!
I TOO COME FROM A MARTIAL ARTS FAMILY...
I WILL COMMIT SEPPUKU.
RANMA
GENMA SAOTOME
I KNOW HOW SACRED SUCH VOWS ARE.

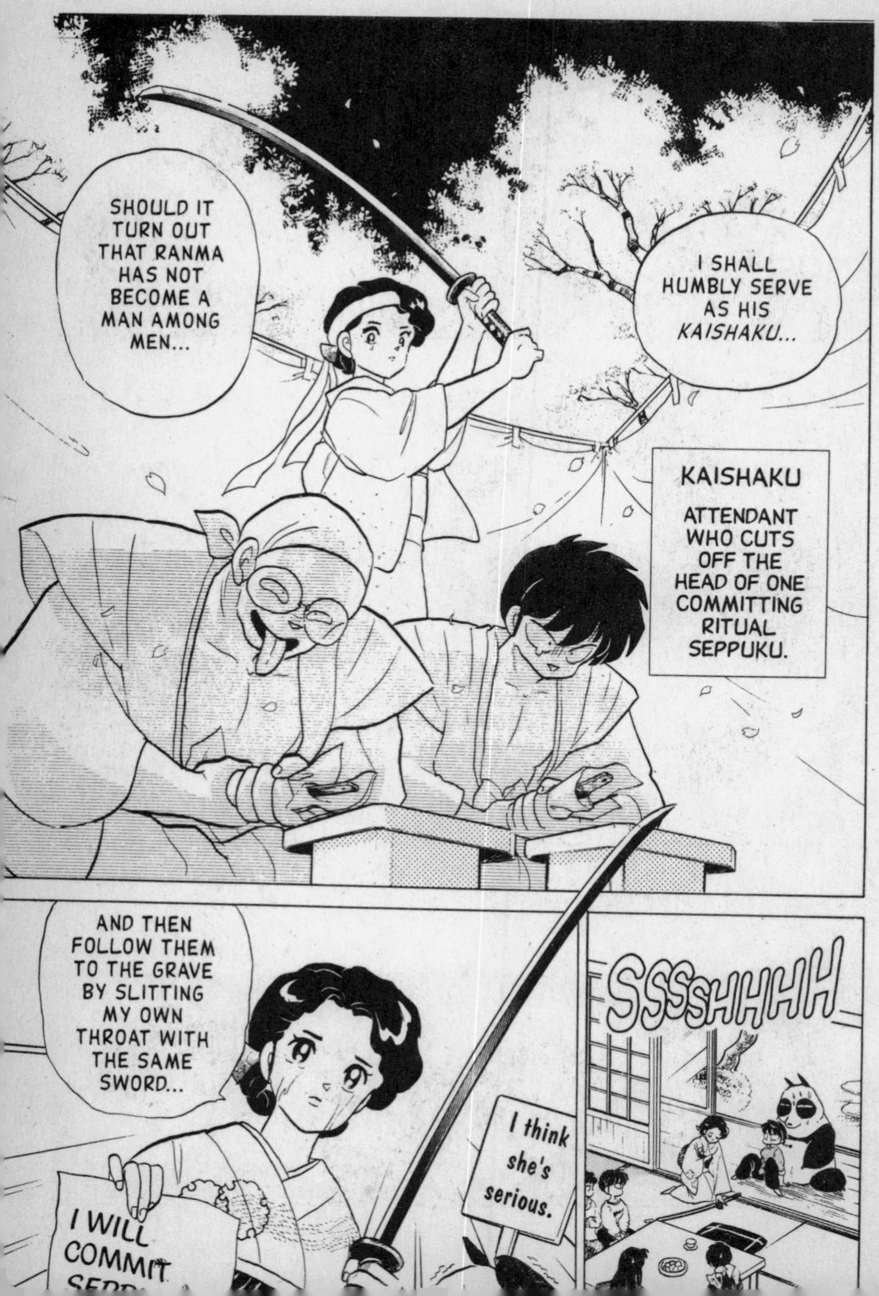
SHOULD IT TURN OUT THAT RANMA HAS NOT BECOME A MAN AMONG MEN...
I SHALL HUMBLY SERVE AS HIS *KAISHAKU*...
KAISHAKU
ATTENDANT WHO CUTS OFF THE HEAD OF ONE COMMITTING RITUAL SEPPUKU.
AND THEN FOLLOW THEM TO THE GRAVE BY SLITTING MY OWN THROAT WITH THE SAME SWORD...
I WILL COMMIT
I think she's serious.
SSSSHHHH

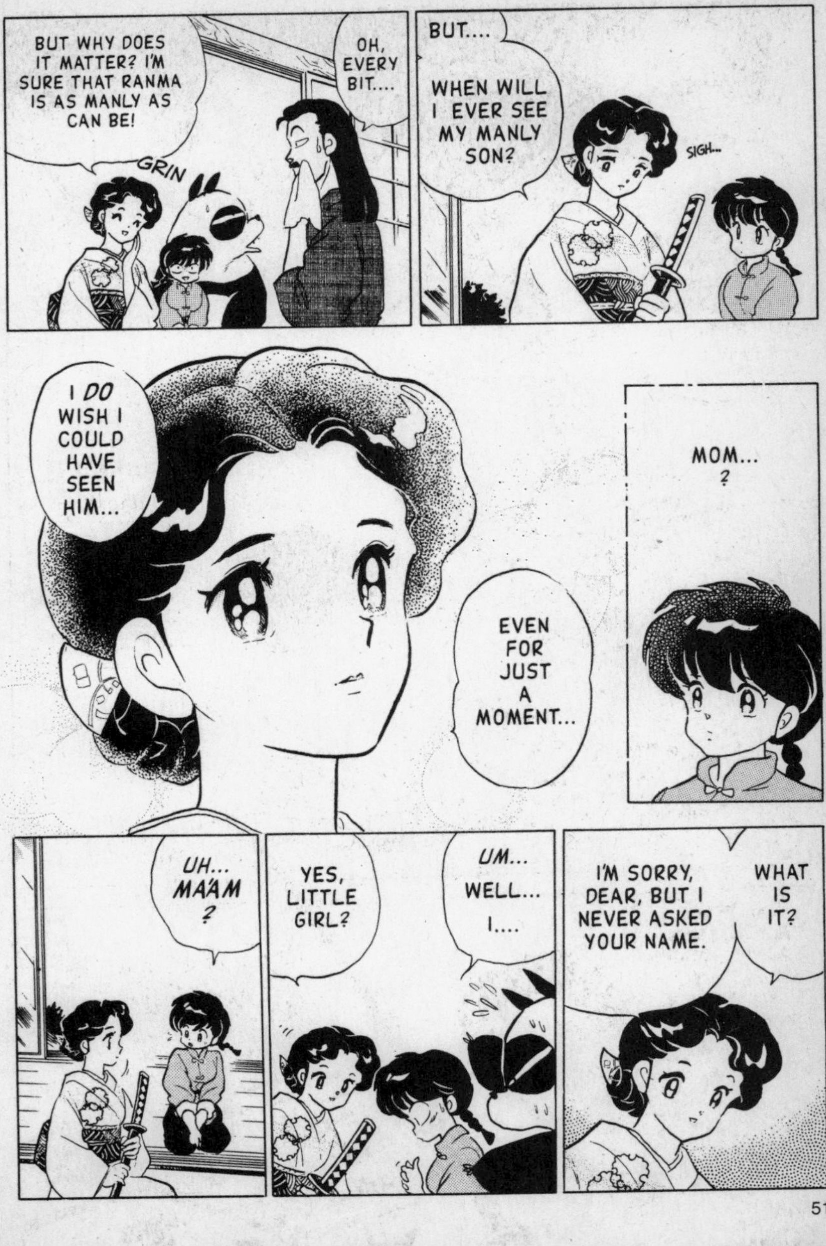
BUT WHY DOES IT MATTER? I'M SURE THAT RANMA IS AS MANLY AS CAN BE!
GRIN
OH, EVERY BIT....
BUT....
WHEN WILL I EVER SEE MY MANLY SON?
SIGH...
I *DO* WISH I COULD HAVE SEEN HIM...
EVEN FOR JUST A MOMENT...
MOM...?
UH... MA'AM?
YES, LITTLE GIRL?
UM... WELL... I....
I'M SORRY, DEAR, BUT I NEVER ASKED YOUR NAME.
WHAT IS IT?

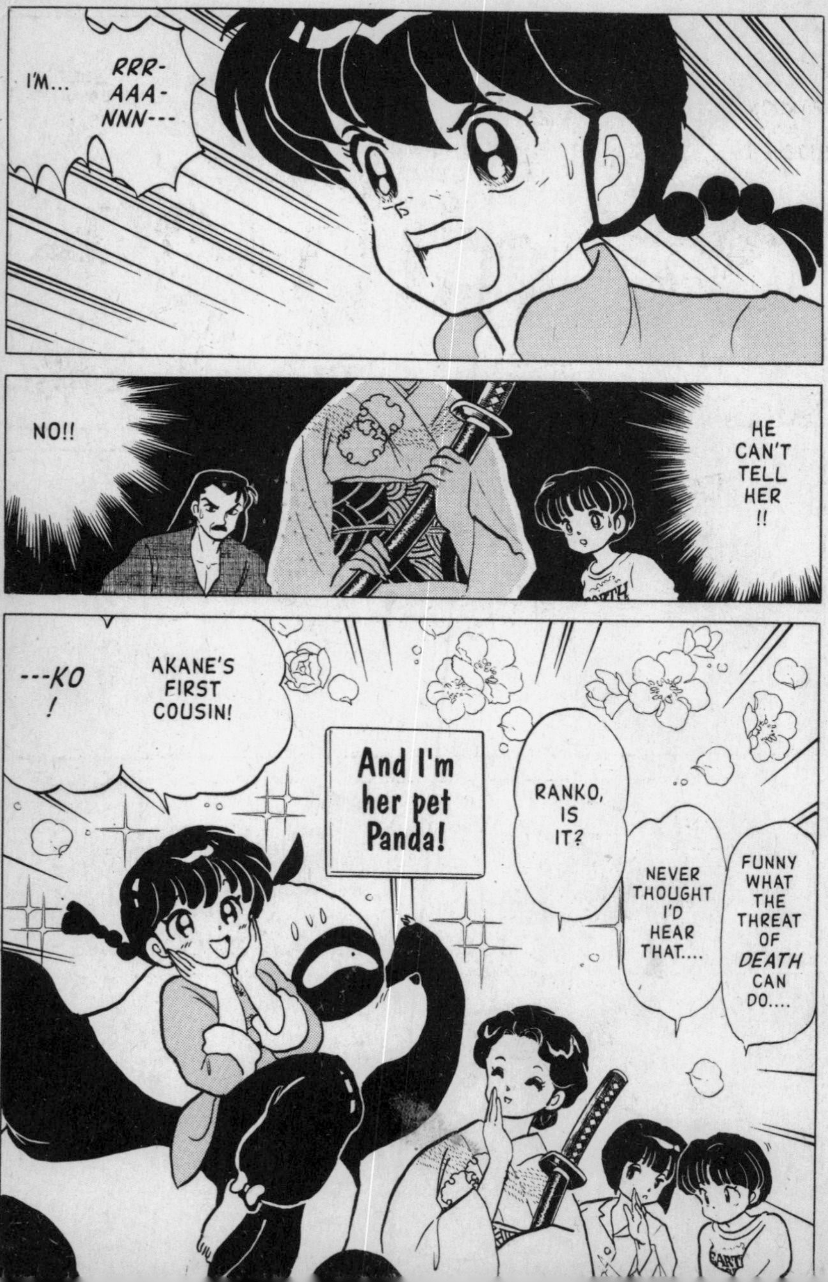
I'M...
RRR-AAA-NNN---
NO!!
HE CAN'T TELL HER !!
---KO !
AKANE'S FIRST COUSIN!
And I'm her pet Panda!
RANKO, IS IT?
NEVER THOUGHT I'D HEAR THAT....
FUNNY WHAT THE THREAT OF DEATH CAN DO....

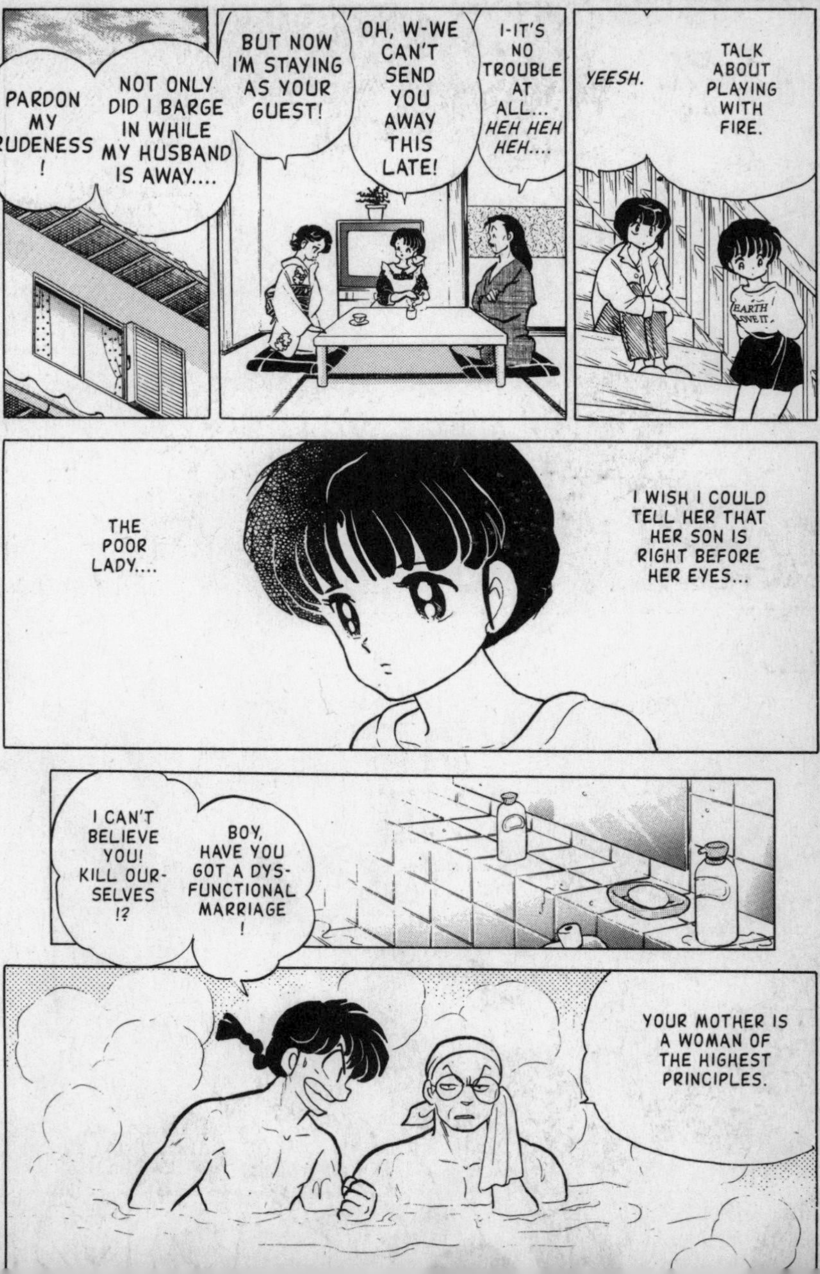
PARDON MY RUDENESS!
NOT ONLY DID I BARGE IN WHILE MY HUSBAND IS AWAY....
BUT NOW I'M STAYING AS YOUR GUEST!
OH, W-WE CAN'T SEND YOU AWAY THIS LATE!
I-IT'S NO TROUBLE AT ALL... *HEH HEH HEH....*
YEESH.
TALK ABOUT PLAYING WITH FIRE.
EARTH LOVE IT
THE POOR LADY....
I WISH I COULD TELL HER THAT HER SON IS RIGHT BEFORE HER EYES...
I CAN'T BELIEVE YOU! KILL OURSELVES !?
BOY, HAVE YOU GOT A DYSFUNCTIONAL MARRIAGE!
YOUR MOTHER IS A WOMAN OF THE HIGHEST PRINCIPLES.

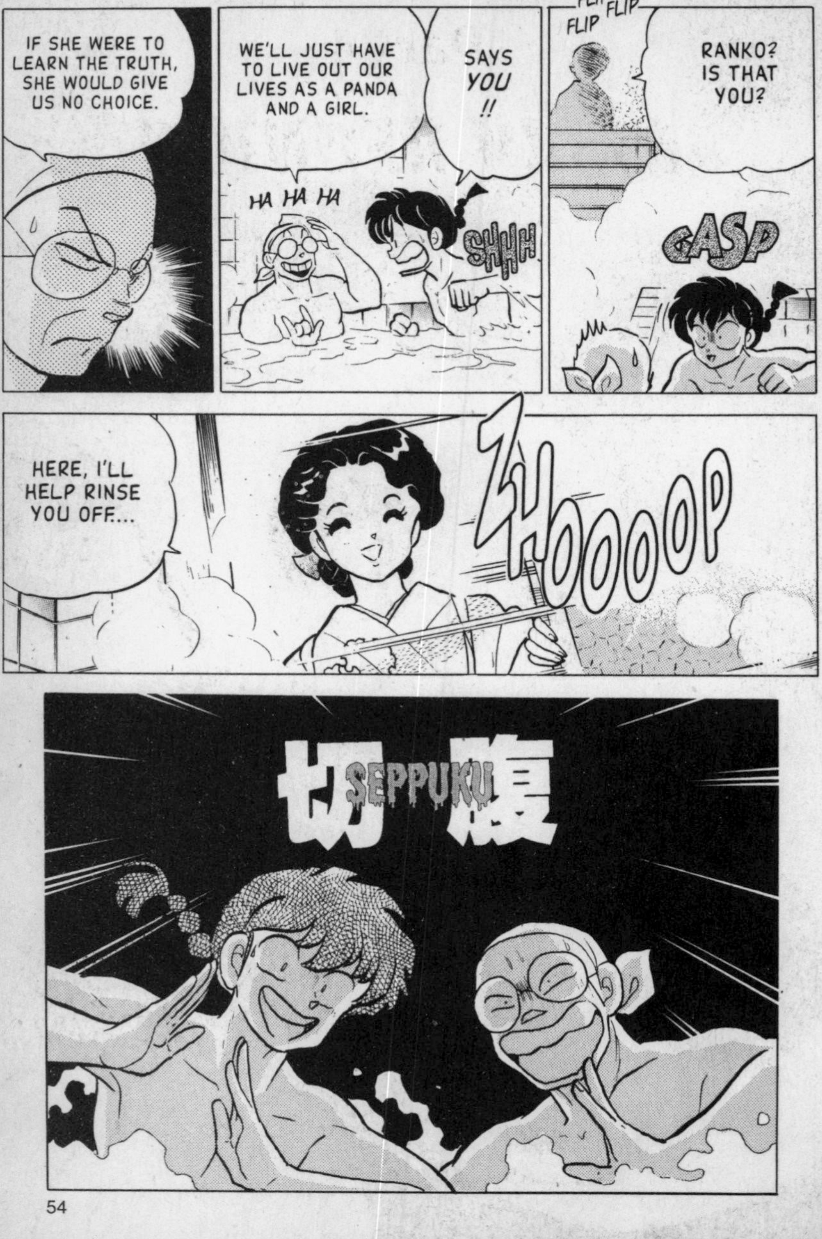
IF SHE WERE TO LEARN THE TRUTH, SHE WOULD GIVE US NO CHOICE.
WE'LL JUST HAVE TO LIVE OUT OUR LIVES AS A PANDA AND A GIRL.
HA HA HA
SAYS YOU !!
SHHH
FLIP FLIP FLIP
RANKO? IS THAT YOU?
GASP
HERE, I'LL HELP RINSE YOU OFF....
ZHOOOOP
切 SEPPUKU 腹

Part 4
RISKY REUNION

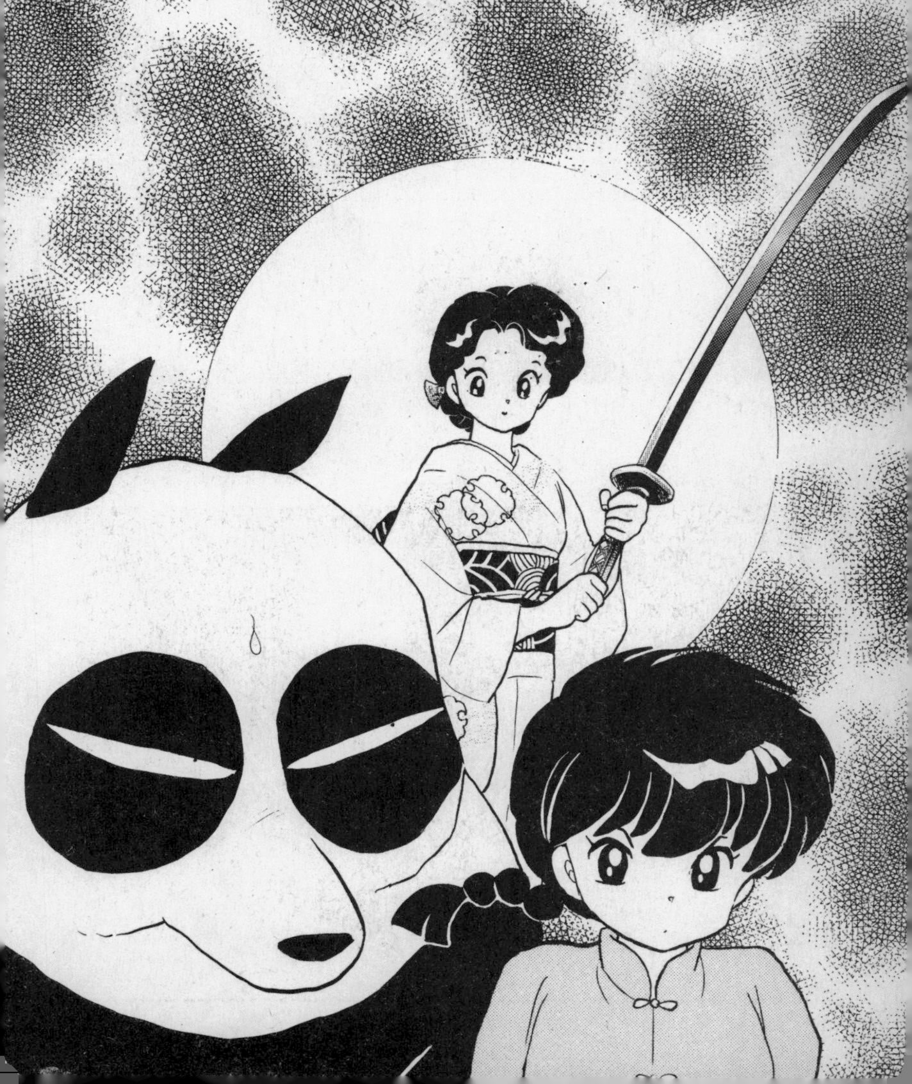

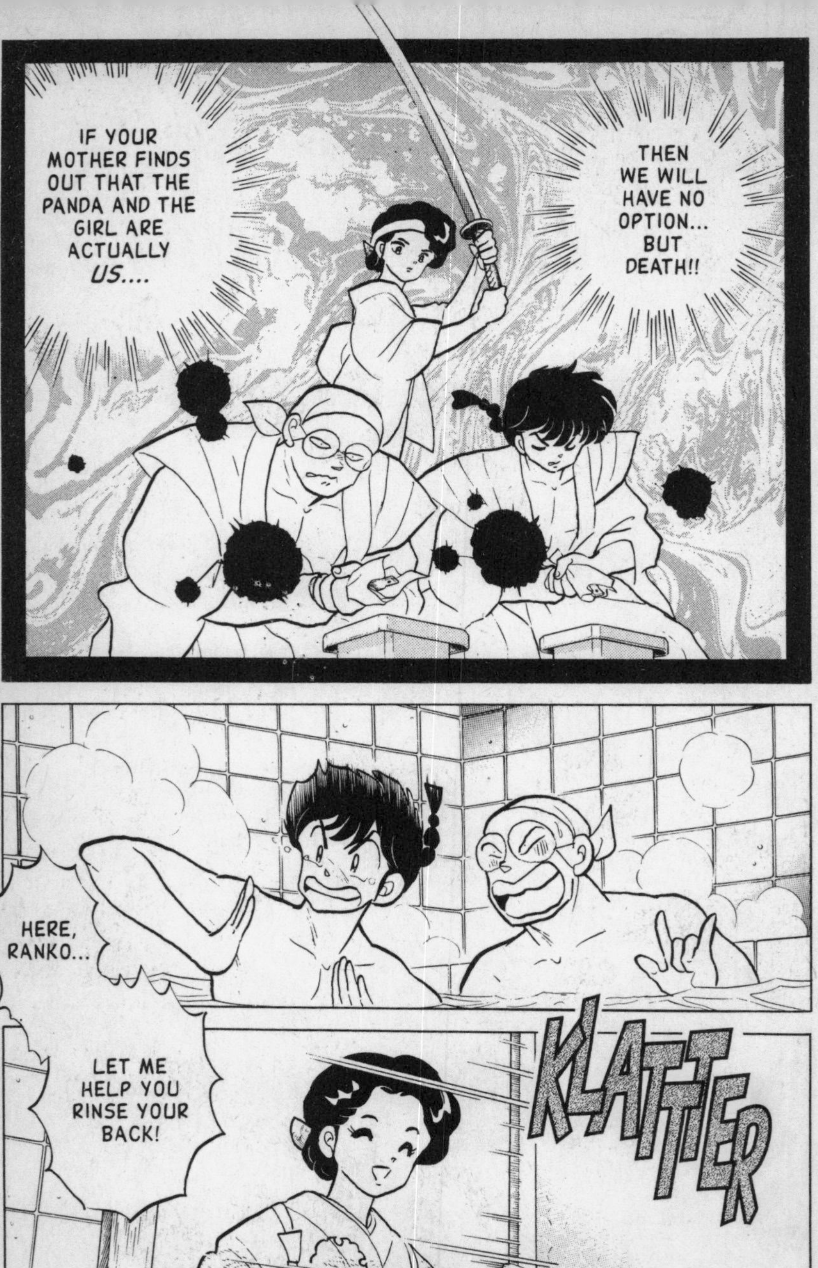
IF YOUR MOTHER FINDS OUT THAT THE PANDA AND THE GIRL ARE ACTUALLY *US*....
THEN WE WILL HAVE NO OPTION... BUT DEATH!!
HERE, RANKO...
LET ME HELP YOU RINSE YOUR BACK!
KLATTER

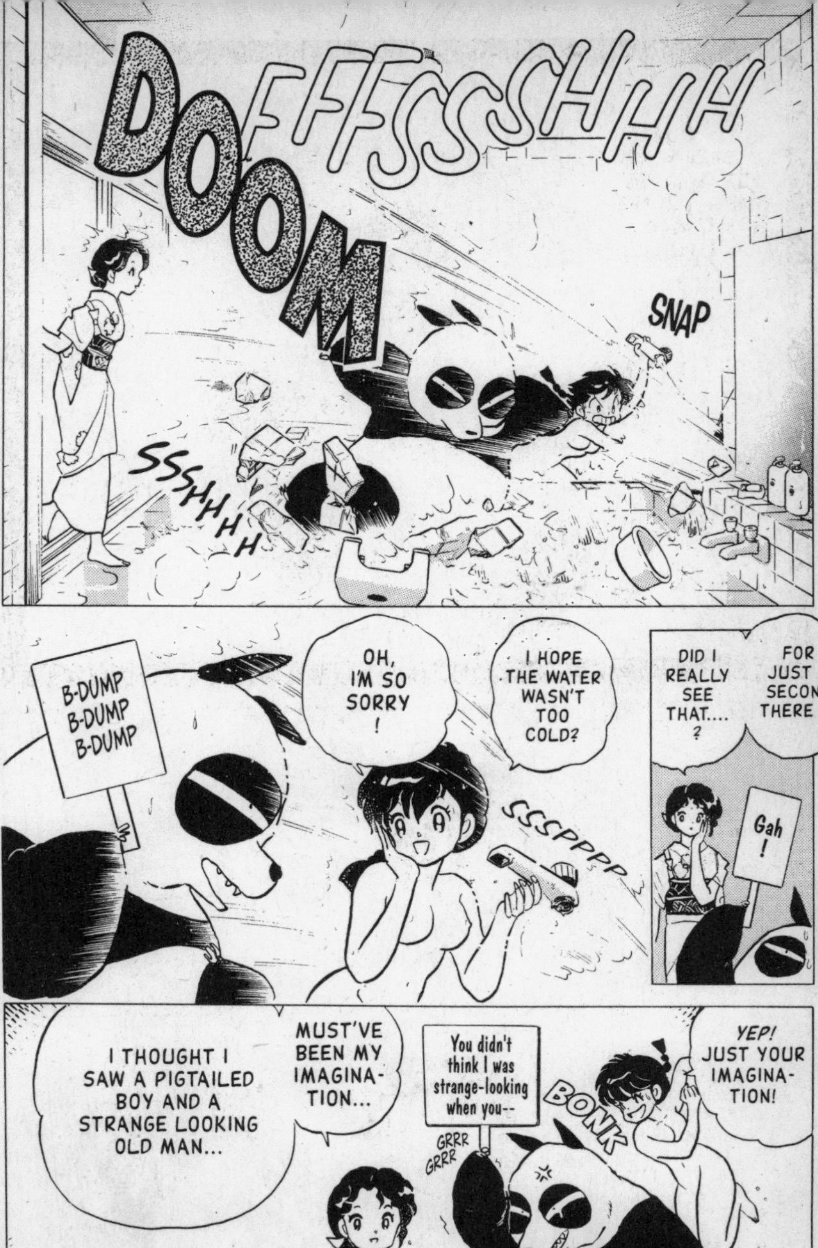

DOOOM
FFFSSSHHHH
SNAP
SSSHHHHH
B-DUMP B-DUMP B-DUMP
OH, I'M SO SORRY!
I HOPE THE WATER WASN'T TOO COLD?
SSSPPPPP
DID I REALLY SEE THAT....?
FOR JUST A SECOND THERE ...
Gah!
I THOUGHT I SAW A PIGTAILED BOY AND A STRANGE LOOKING OLD MAN...
MUST'VE BEEN MY IMAGINA-TION...
You didn't think I was strange-looking when you--
GRRR GRRR
BONK
YEP! JUST YOUR IMAGINA-TION!

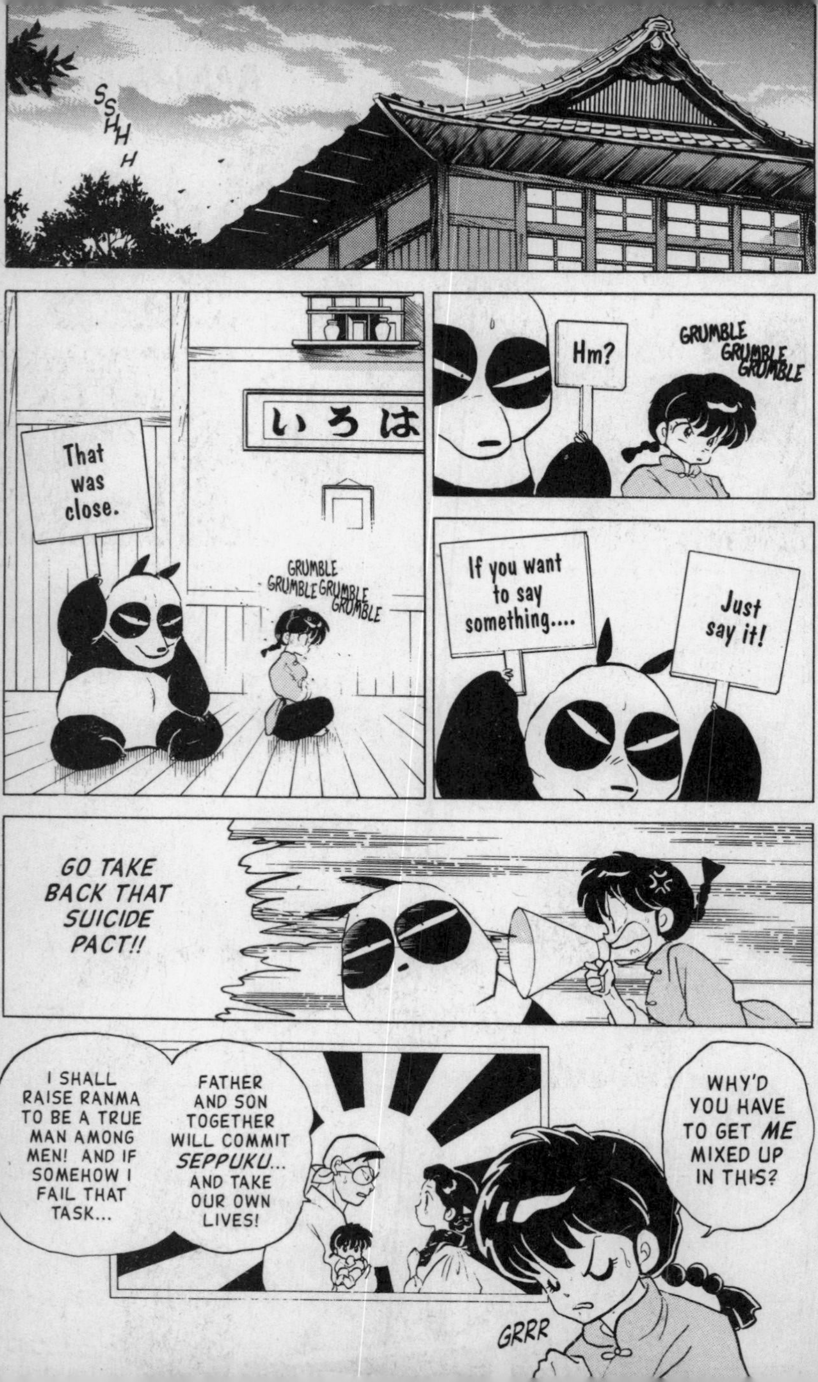
SSHHH
That was close.
いろは
GRUMBLE GRUMBLE GRUMBLE GRUMBLE
Hm?
GRUMBLE GRUMBLE GRUMBLE
If you want to say something....
Just say it!
GO TAKE BACK THAT SUICIDE PACT!!
I SHALL RAISE RANMA TO BE A TRUE MAN AMONG MEN! AND IF SOMEHOW I FAIL THAT TASK...
FATHER AND SON TOGETHER WILL COMMIT *SEPPUKU*... AND TAKE OUR OWN LIVES!
WHY'D YOU HAVE TO GET *ME* MIXED UP IN THIS?
GRRR

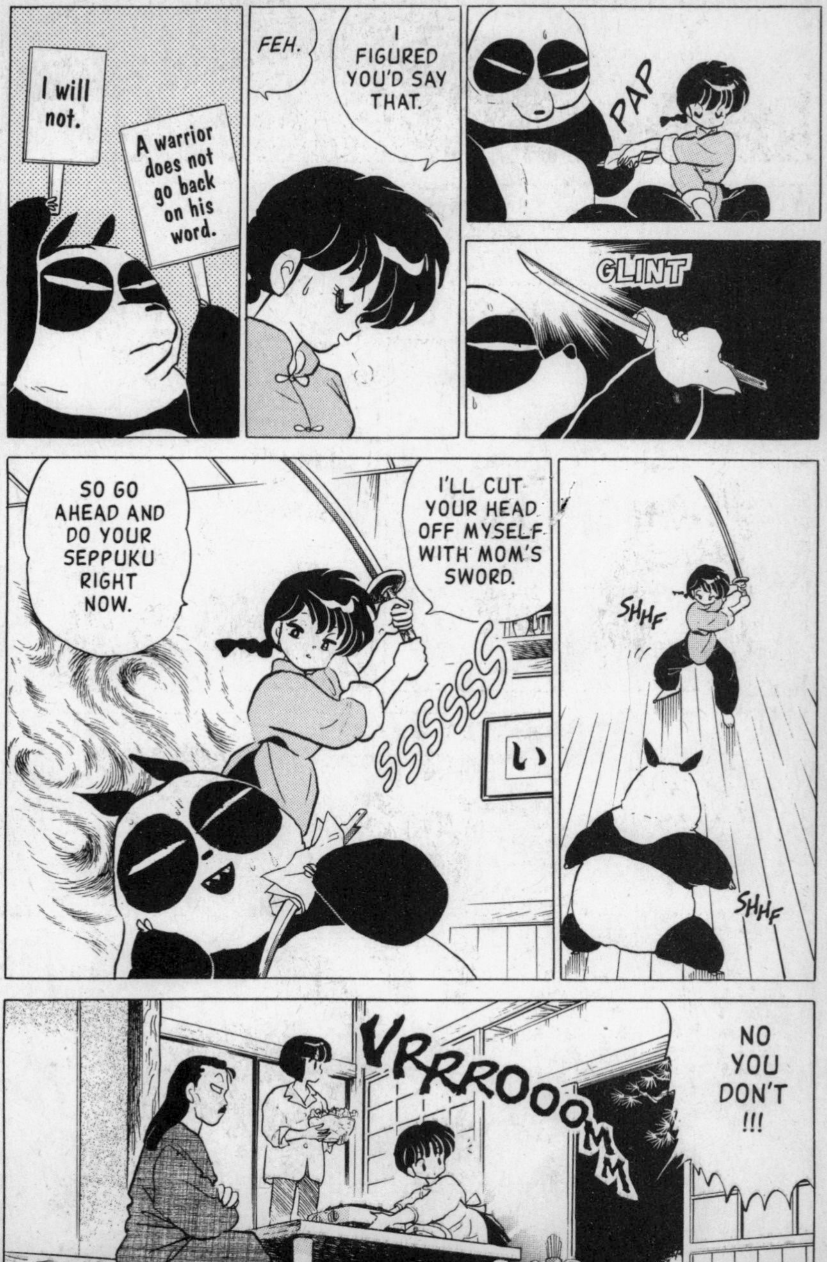
I will not.
A warrior does not go back on his word.
FEH.
I FIGURED YOU'D SAY THAT.
PAP
GLINT
SO GO AHEAD AND DO YOUR SEPPUKU RIGHT NOW.
I'LL CUT YOUR HEAD OFF MYSELF WITH MOM'S SWORD.
SSSSSS
い
SHHF
SHHF
VRRROOOMM
NO YOU DON'T !!!

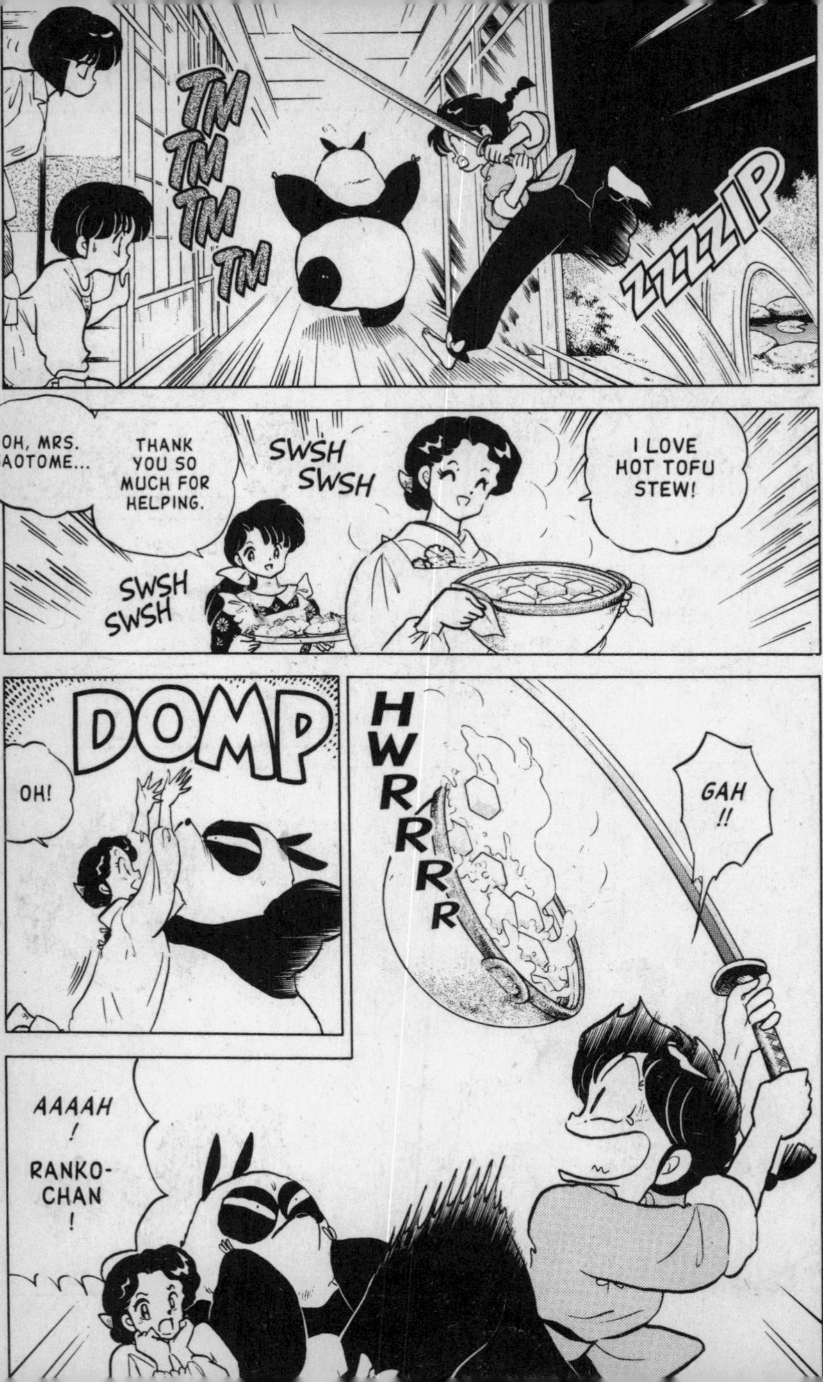
TM TM TM TM
ZZZZIP
OH, MRS. SAOTOME...
THANK YOU SO MUCH FOR HELPING.
SWSH SWSH
SWSH SWSH
I LOVE HOT TOFU STEW!
DOMP
OH!
AAAAH! RANKO-CHAN!
HWRRRR
GAH!!

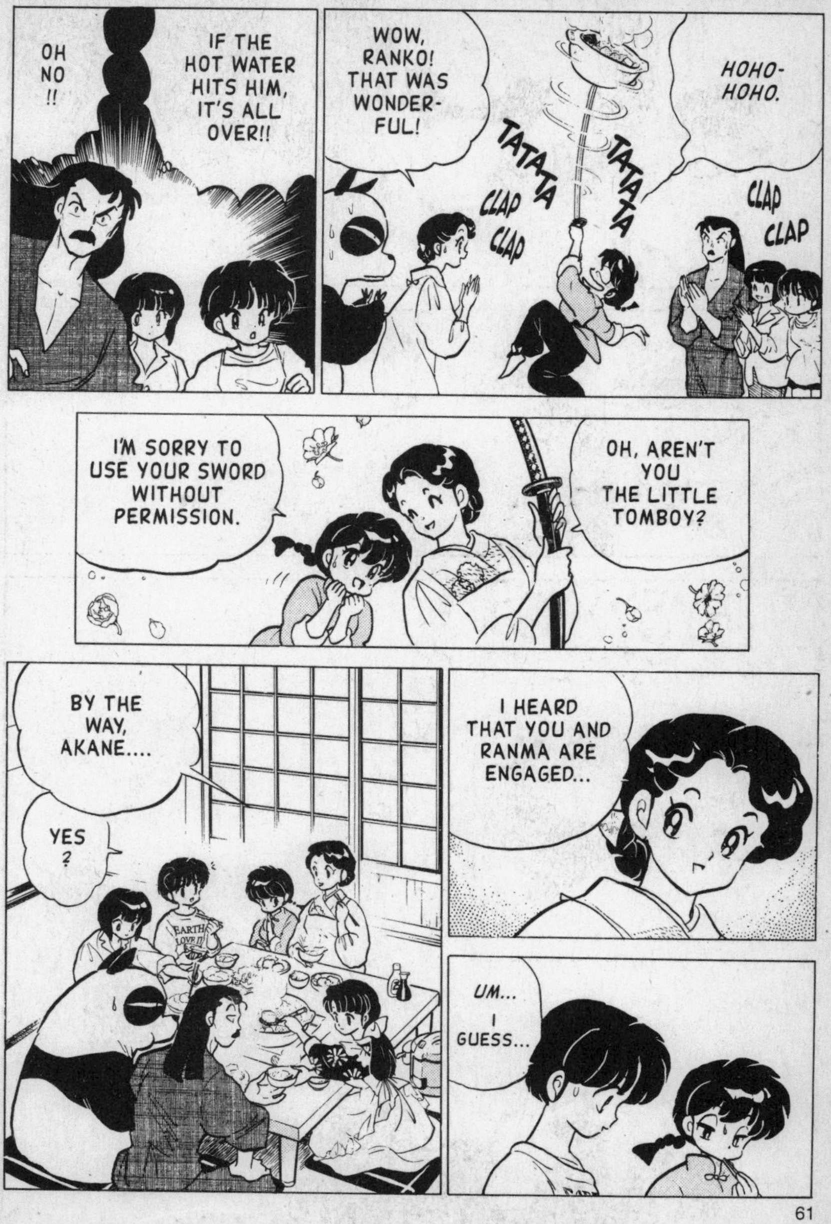
OH NO !!
IF THE HOT WATER HITS HIM, IT'S ALL OVER!!
WOW, RANKO! THAT WAS WONDER-FUL!
TATATA
CLAP CLAP
TATATA
HOHO-HOHO.
CLAP CLAP
I'M SORRY TO USE YOUR SWORD WITHOUT PERMISSION.
OH, AREN'T YOU THE LITTLE TOMBOY?
BY THE WAY, AKANE....
YES ?
I HEARD THAT YOU AND RANMA ARE ENGAGED...
UM... I GUESS...

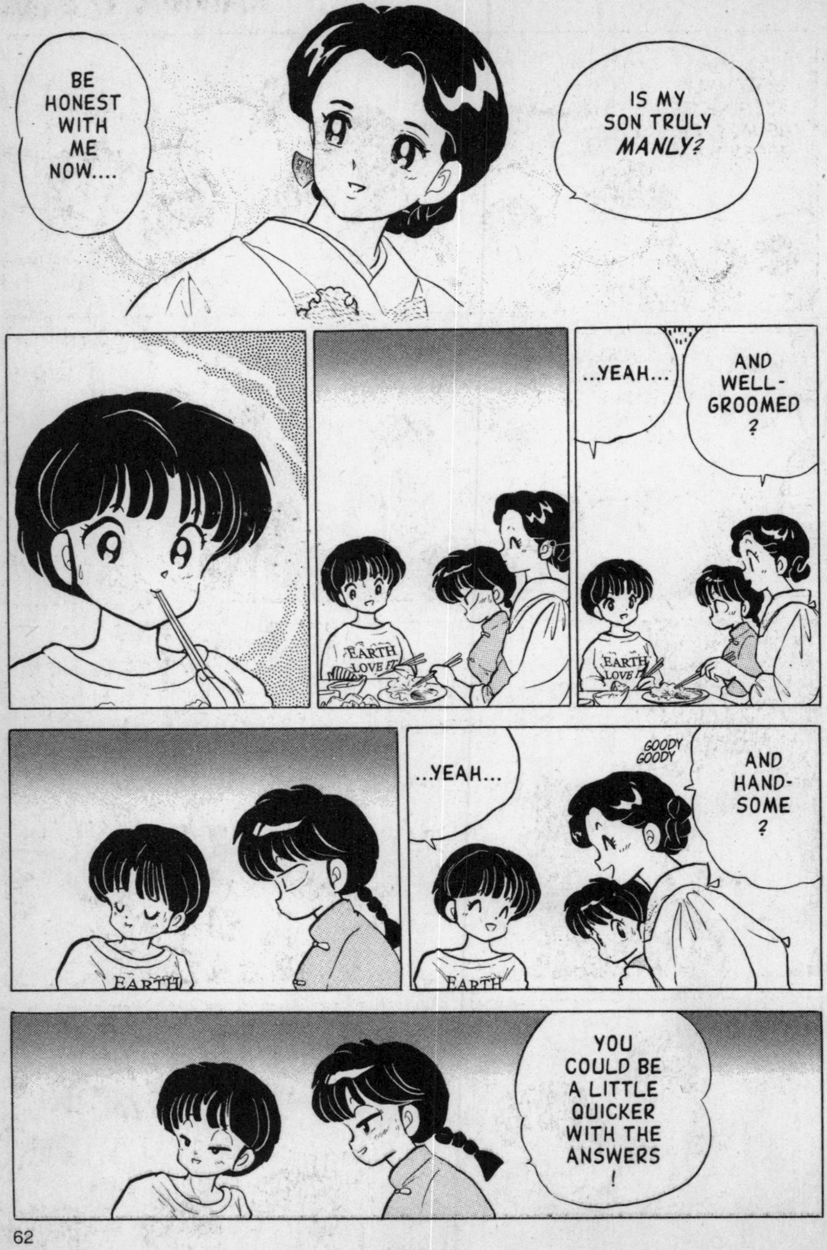
BE HONEST WITH ME NOW....
IS MY SON TRULY *MANLY?*
...YEAH...
AND WELL-GROOMED?
...YEAH...
GOODY GOODY
AND HAND-SOME?
YOU COULD BE A LITTLE QUICKER WITH THE ANSWERS!

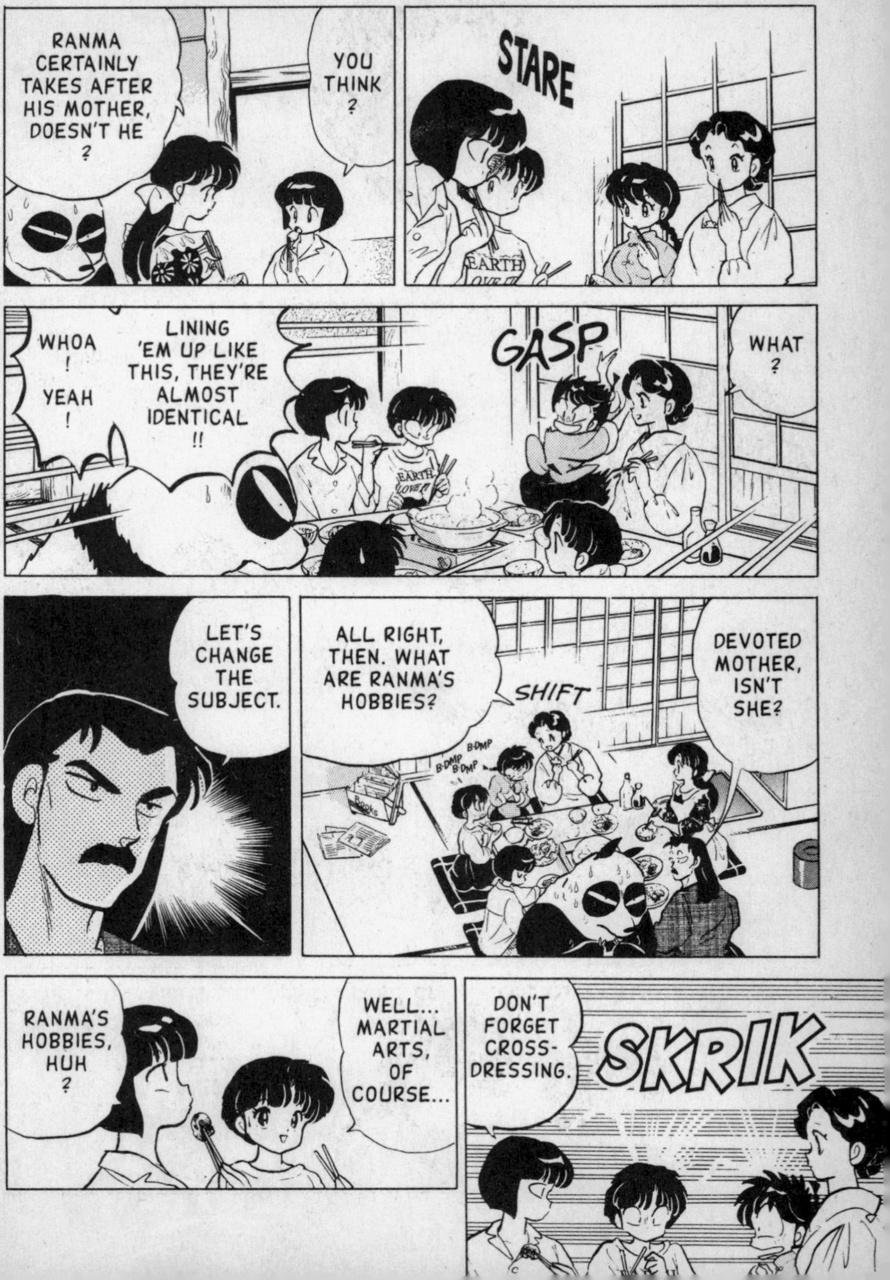
RANMA CERTAINLY TAKES AFTER HIS MOTHER, DOESN'T HE ?
YOU THINK ?
STARE
WHOA ! YEAH !
LINING 'EM UP LIKE THIS, THEY'RE ALMOST IDENTICAL !!
GASP
WHAT ?
LET'S CHANGE THE SUBJECT.
ALL RIGHT, THEN. WHAT ARE RANMA'S HOBBIES?
SHIFT
B-DMP B-DMP B-DMP
DEVOTED MOTHER, ISN'T SHE?
RANMA'S HOBBIES, HUH ?
WELL... MARTIAL ARTS, OF COURSE...
DON'T FORGET CROSS-DRESSING.
SKRIK

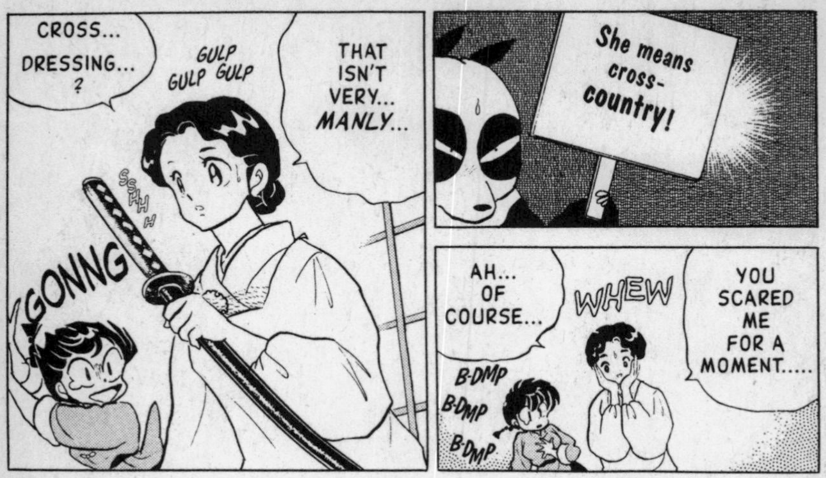
CROSS... DRESSING... ?
GULP GULP GULP
THAT ISN'T VERY... *MANLY*...
SSHHH
GONNG
She means cross-country!
AH... OF COURSE...
WHEW
YOU SCARED ME FOR A MOMENT.....
B-DMP B-DMP B-DMP

NABIKI

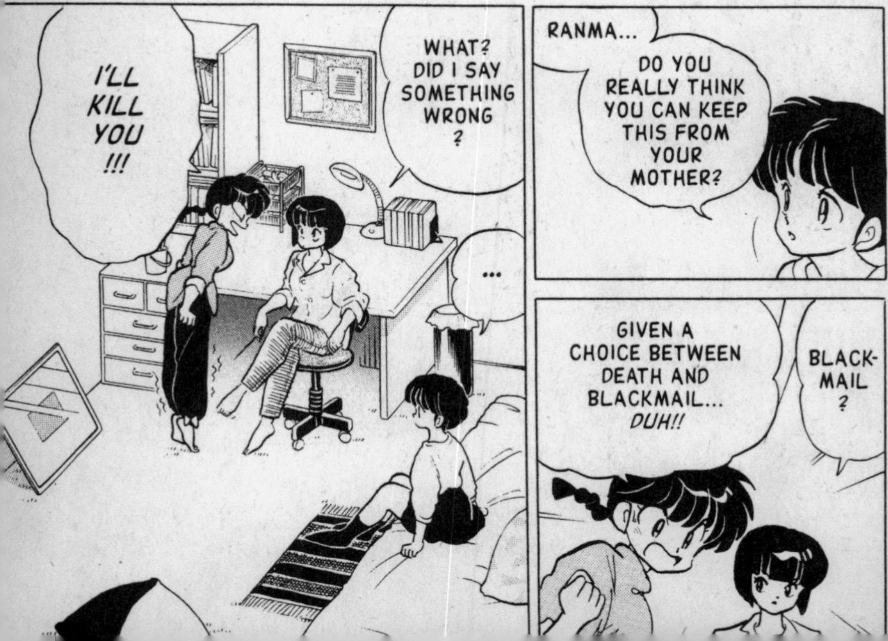
I'LL KILL YOU !!!
WHAT? DID I SAY SOMETHING WRONG ?
...
RANMA...
DO YOU REALLY THINK YOU CAN KEEP THIS FROM YOUR MOTHER?
GIVEN A CHOICE BETWEEN DEATH AND BLACKMAIL... *DUH!!*
BLACK-MAIL ?

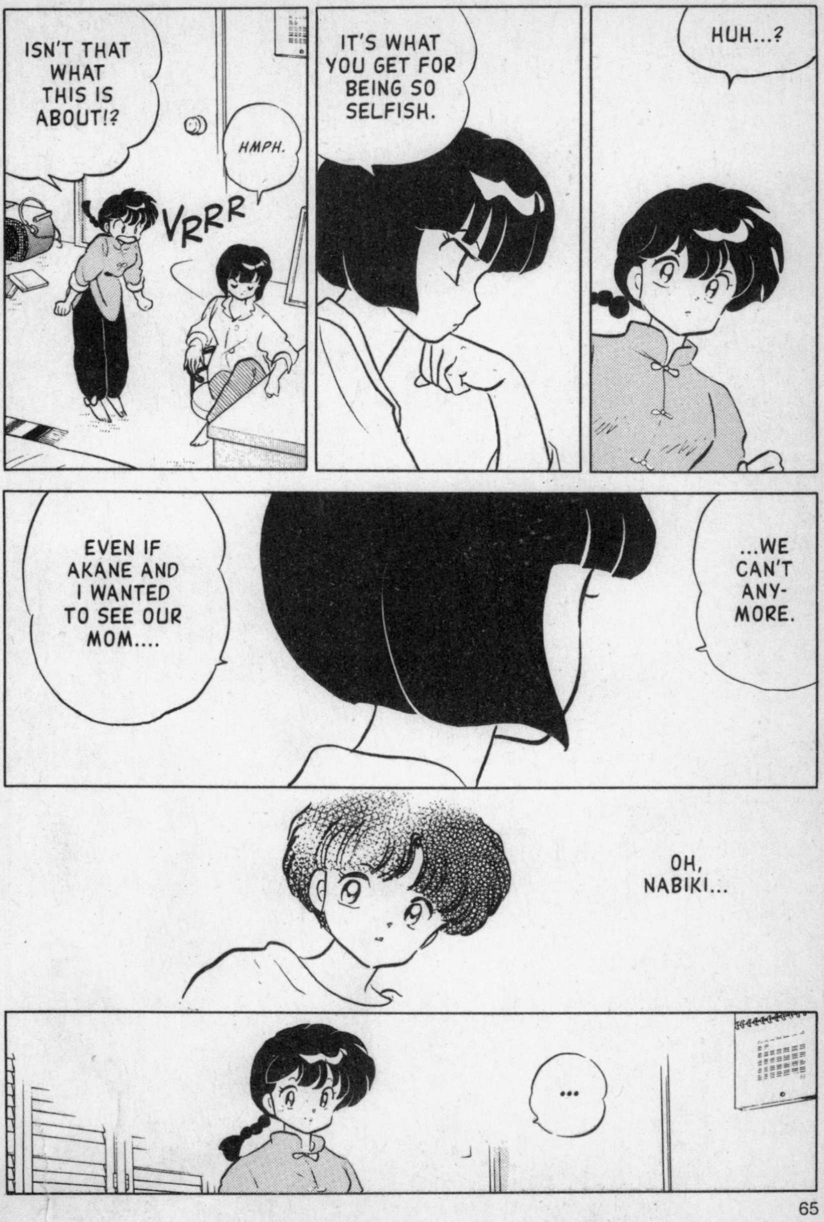
ISN'T THAT WHAT THIS IS ABOUT!?
VRRR
HMPH.
IT'S WHAT YOU GET FOR BEING SO SELFISH.
HUH...?
EVEN IF AKANE AND I WANTED TO SEE OUR MOM....
...WE CAN'T ANYMORE.
OH, NABIKI...
...

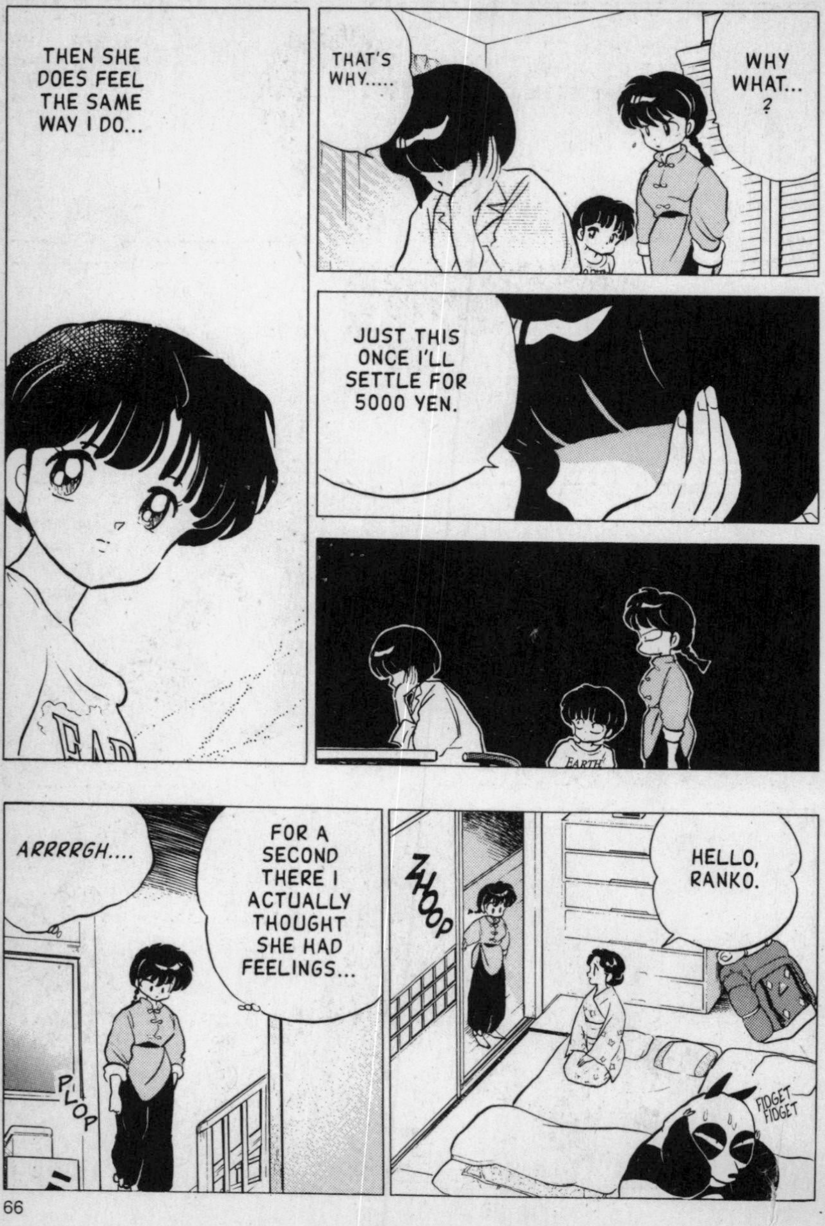
THEN SHE DOES FEEL THE SAME WAY I DO...
THAT'S WHY.....
WHY WHAT... ?
JUST THIS ONCE I'LL SETTLE FOR 5000 YEN.
EARTH
ARRRRGH....
FOR A SECOND THERE I ACTUALLY THOUGHT SHE HAD FEELINGS...
PLOP
ZHOOP
HELLO, RANKO.
FIDGET FIDGET

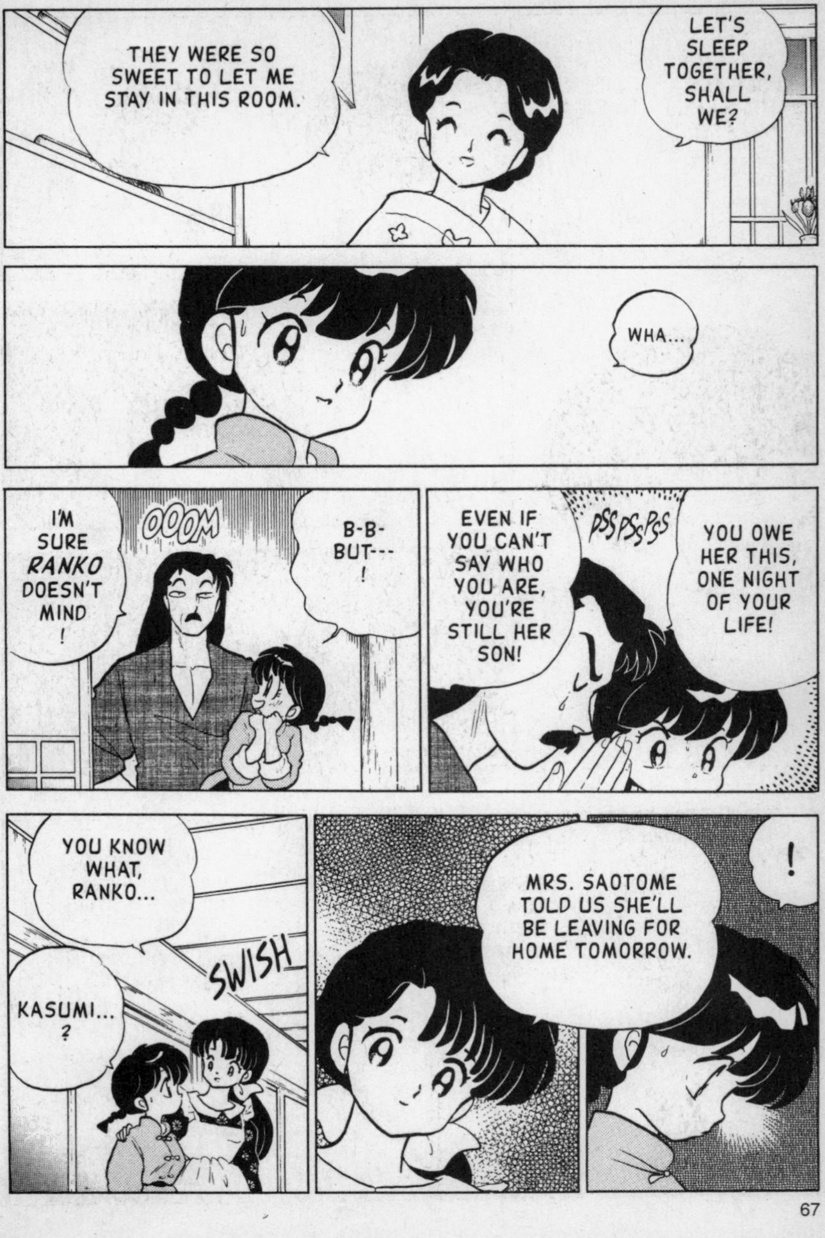
THEY WERE SO SWEET TO LET ME STAY IN THIS ROOM.
LET'S SLEEP TOGETHER, SHALL WE?
WHA...
I'M SURE RANKO DOESN'T MIND!
OOOM
B-B-BUT---!
EVEN IF YOU CAN'T SAY WHO YOU ARE, YOU'RE STILL HER SON!
PSSPSSPSS
YOU OWE HER THIS, ONE NIGHT OF YOUR LIFE!
YOU KNOW WHAT, RANKO...
SWISH
KASUMI...?
MRS. SAOTOME TOLD US SHE'LL BE LEAVING FOR HOME TOMORROW.
!

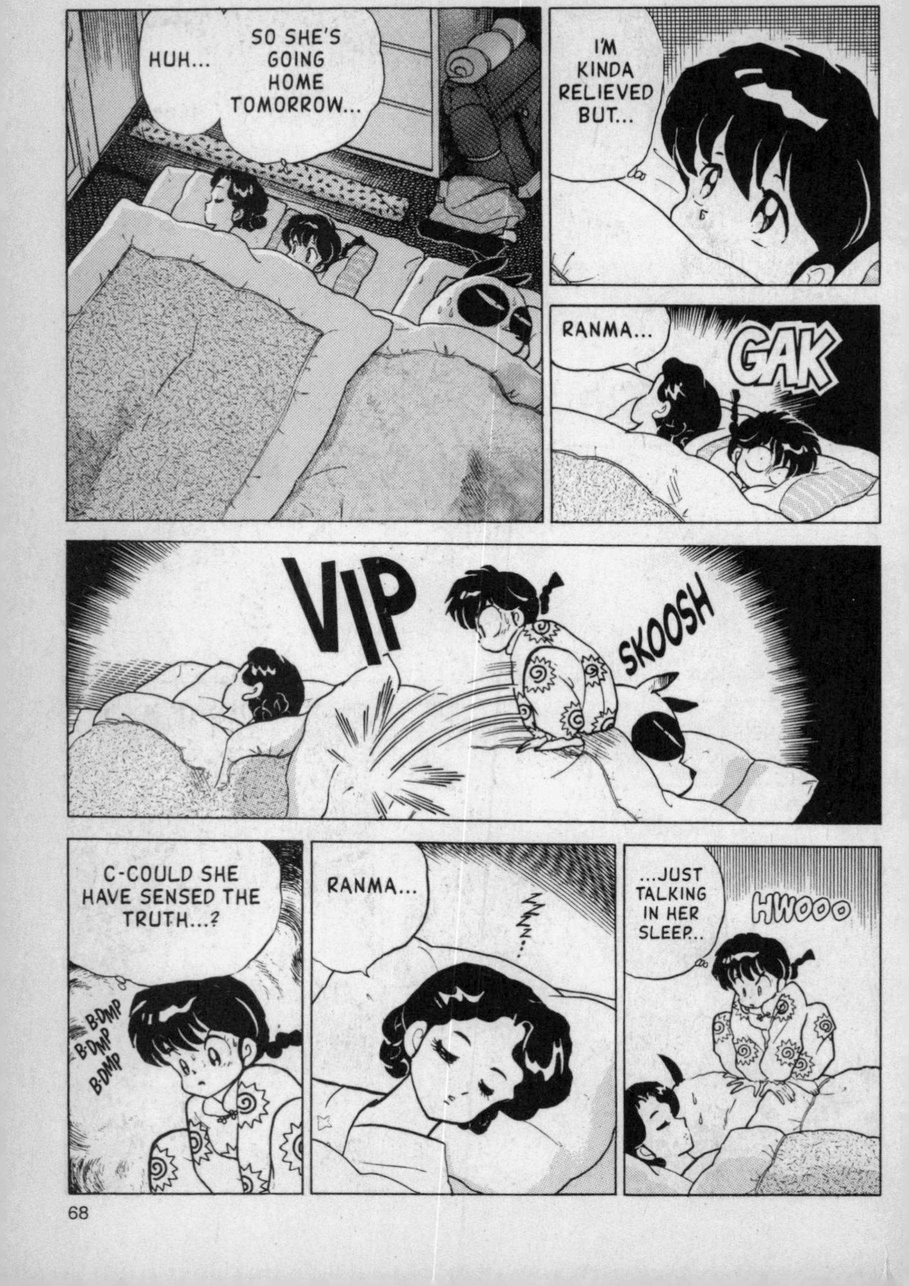
HUH... SO SHE'S GOING HOME TOMORROW...
I'M KINDA RELIEVED BUT...
RANMA...
GAK
VIP
SKOOSH
C-COULD SHE HAVE SENSED THE TRUTH...?
B·DMP B·DMP B·DMP
RANMA...
ZZZZ...
...JUST TALKING IN HER SLEEP...
HWOOO

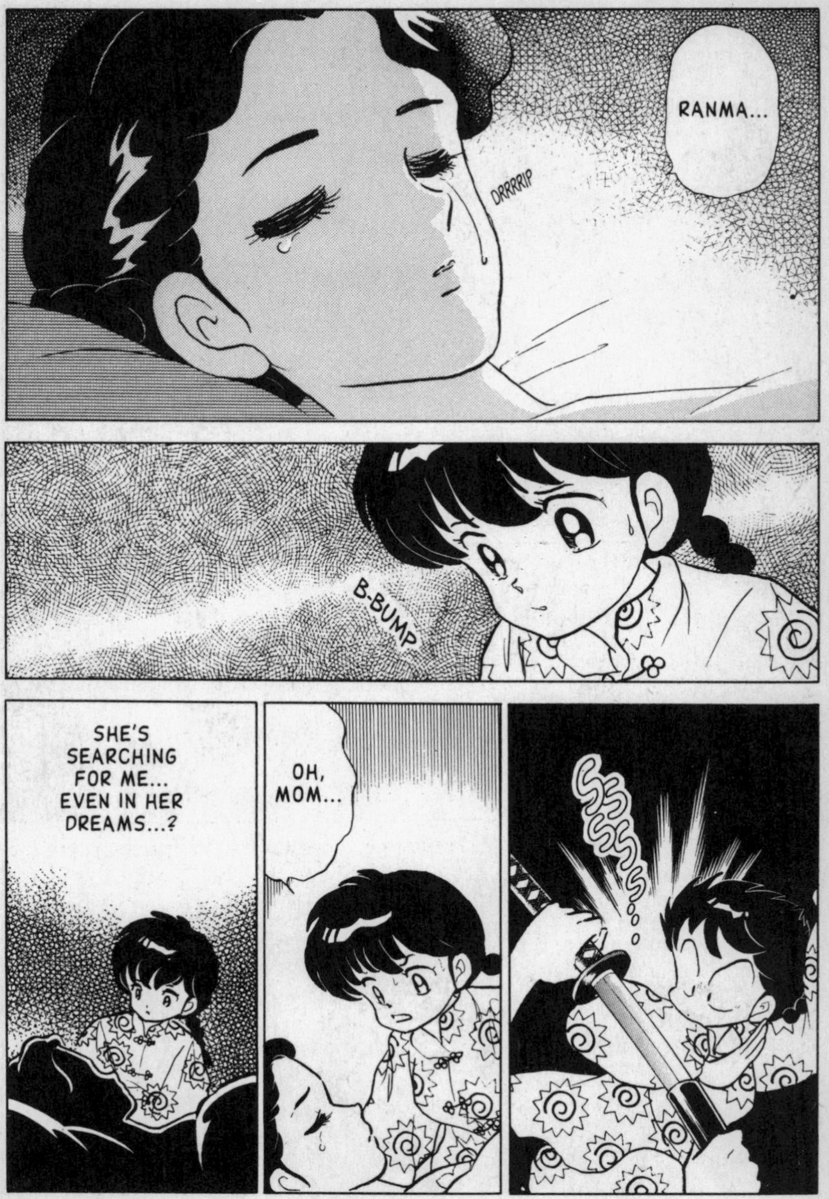
RANMA...
DRRRRIP
B-BUMP
SHE'S SEARCHING FOR ME... EVEN IN HER DREAMS...?
OH, MOM...
SSSS

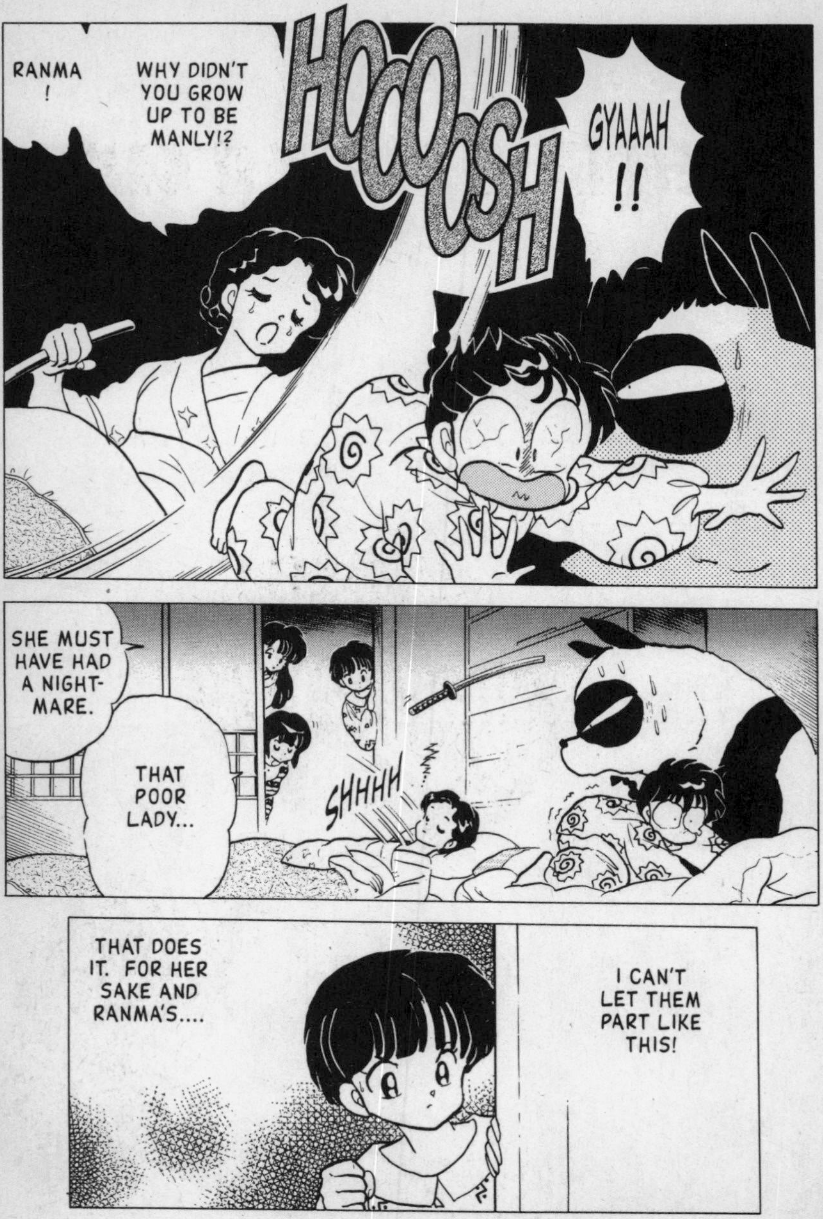
RANMA!
WHY DIDN'T YOU GROW UP TO BE MANLY!?
HOOOOSH
GYAAAH!!
SHE MUST HAVE HAD A NIGHT-MARE.
THAT POOR LADY...
SHHHH
THAT DOES IT. FOR HER SAKE AND RANMA'S....
I CAN'T LET THEM PART LIKE THIS!

Part 5

EVEN IF IT'S JUST A GLANCE

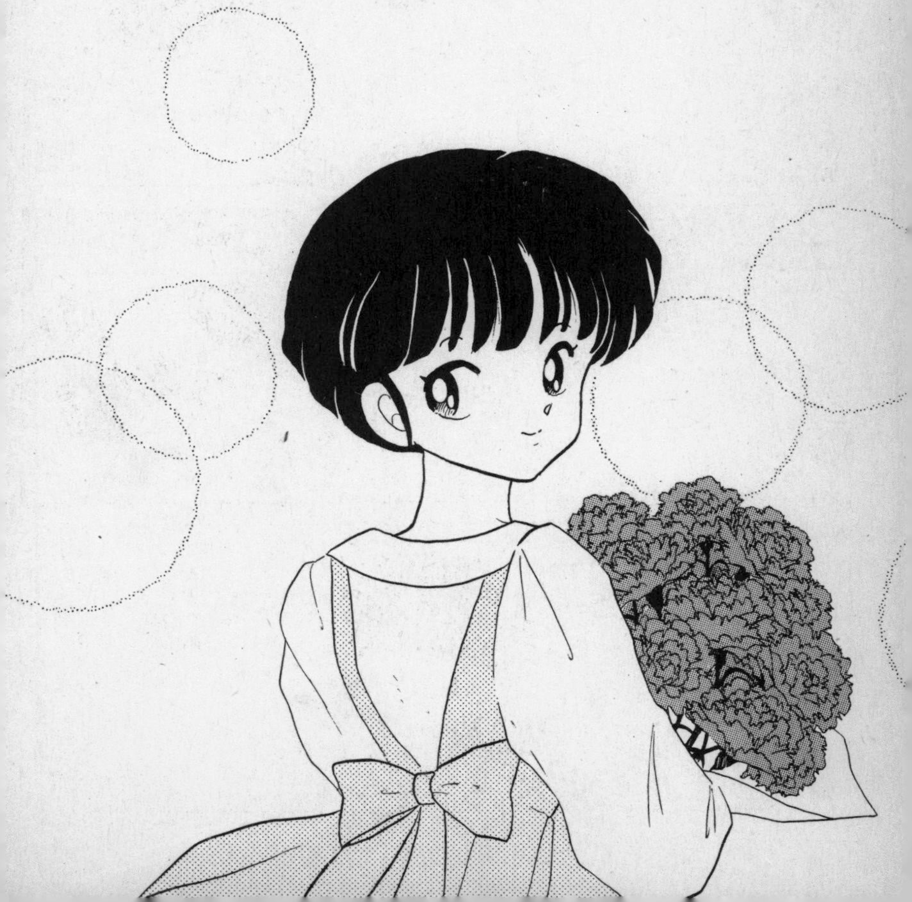

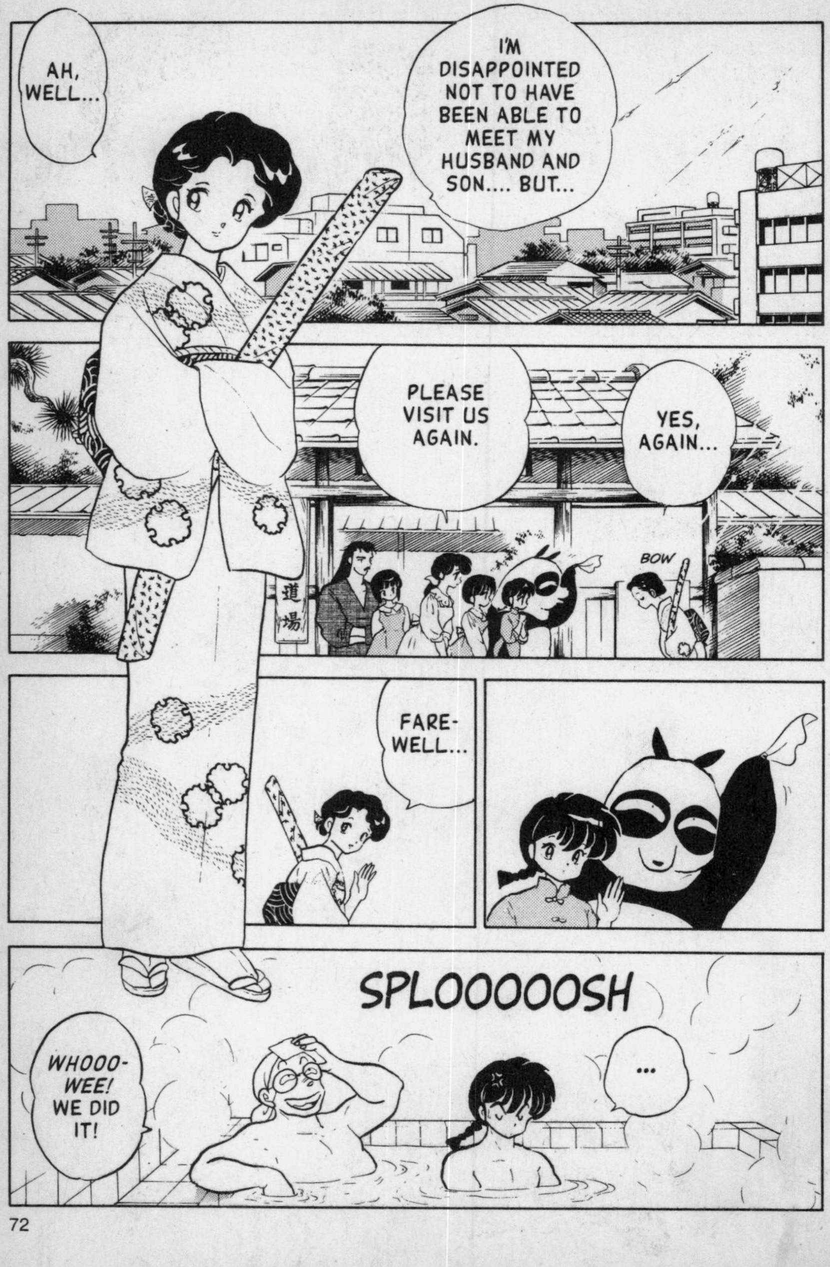
AH, WELL...
I'M DISAPPOINTED NOT TO HAVE BEEN ABLE TO MEET MY HUSBAND AND SON.... BUT...
PLEASE VISIT US AGAIN.
YES, AGAIN...
道場
BOW
FARE-WELL...
SPLOOOOOSH
WHOOO-WEE! WE DID IT!
...

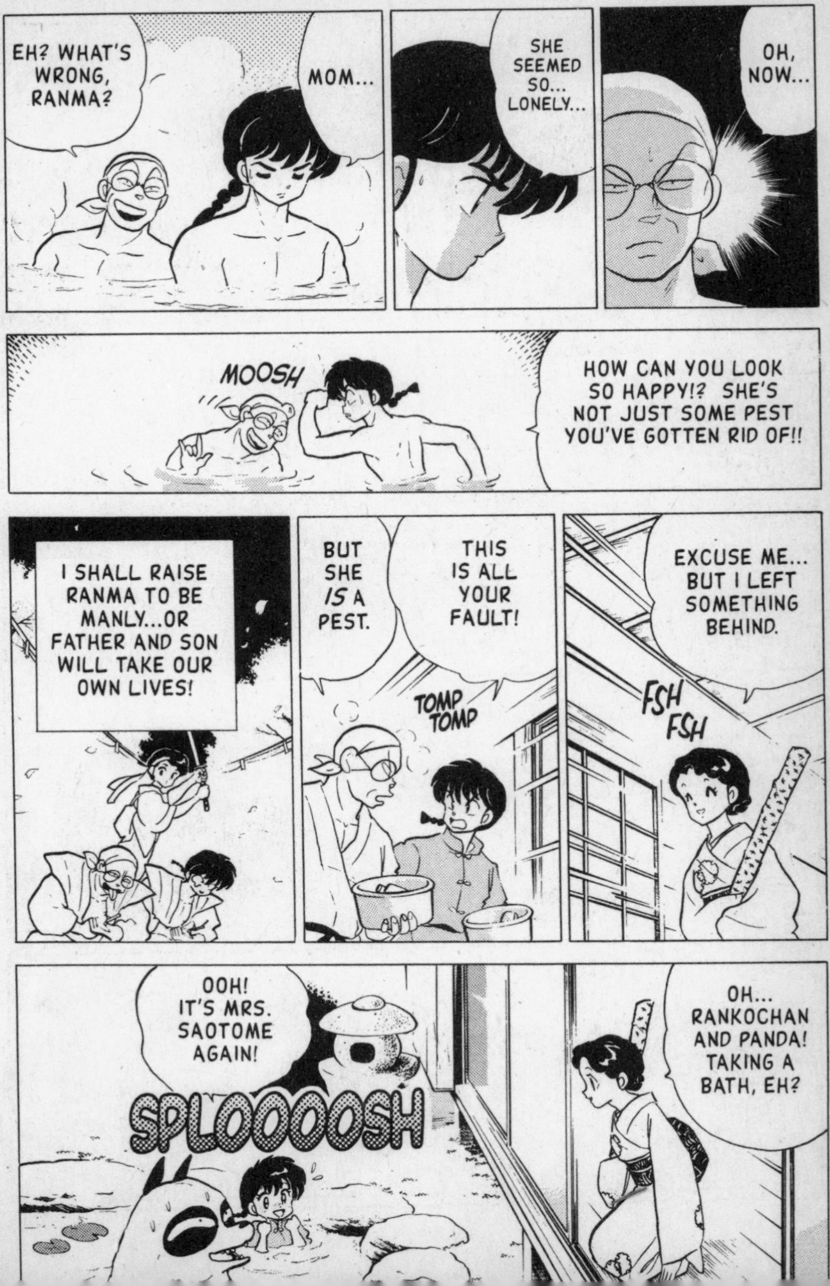
EH? WHAT'S WRONG, RANMA?
MOM...
SHE SEEMED SO... LONELY...
OH, NOW...
MOOSH
HOW CAN YOU LOOK SO HAPPY!? SHE'S NOT JUST SOME PEST YOU'VE GOTTEN RID OF!!
I SHALL RAISE RANMA TO BE MANLY...OR FATHER AND SON WILL TAKE OUR OWN LIVES!
BUT SHE *IS* A PEST.
THIS IS ALL YOUR FAULT!
TOMP TOMP
EXCUSE ME... BUT I LEFT SOMETHING BEHIND.
FSH FSH
OOH! IT'S MRS. SAOTOME AGAIN!
SPLOOOOOSH
OH... RANKOCHAN AND PANDA! TAKING A BATH, EH?

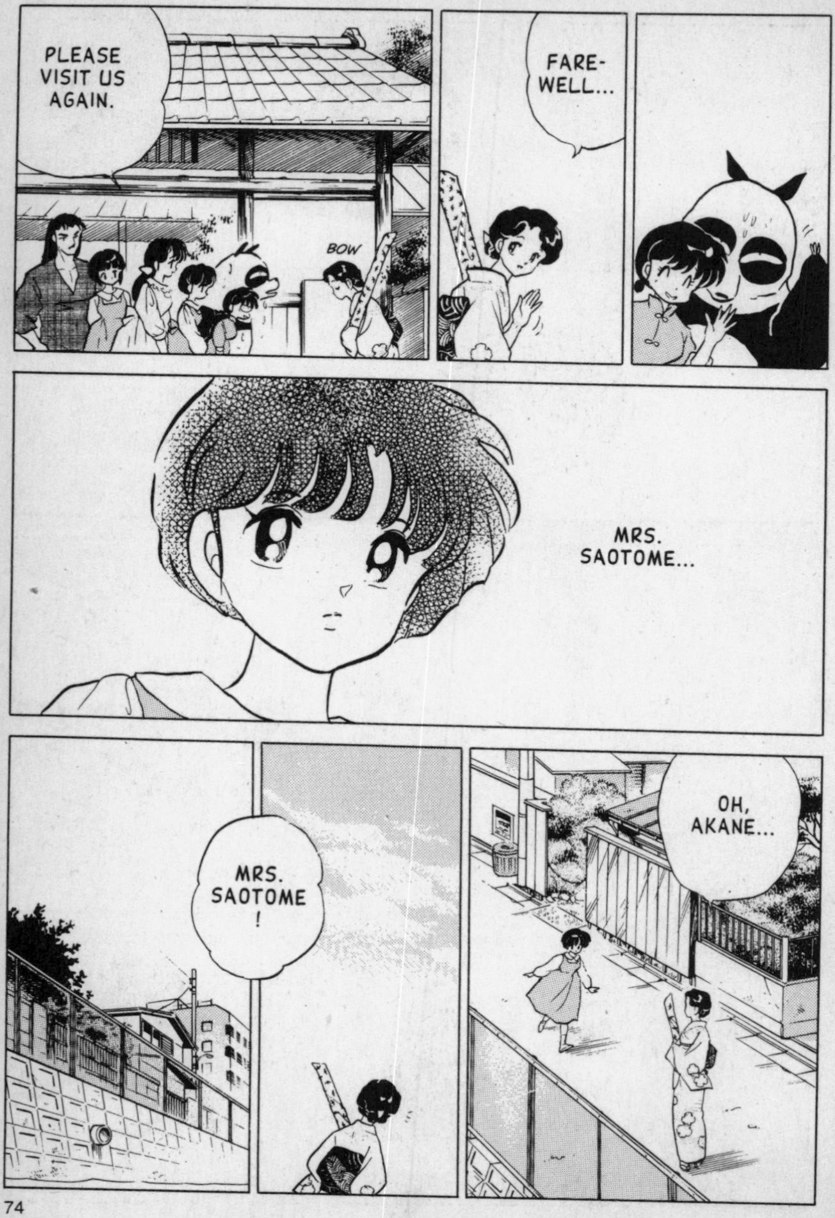

PLEASE VISIT US AGAIN.
BOW
FARE-WELL...
MRS. SAOTOME...
MRS. SAOTOME !
OH, AKANE...

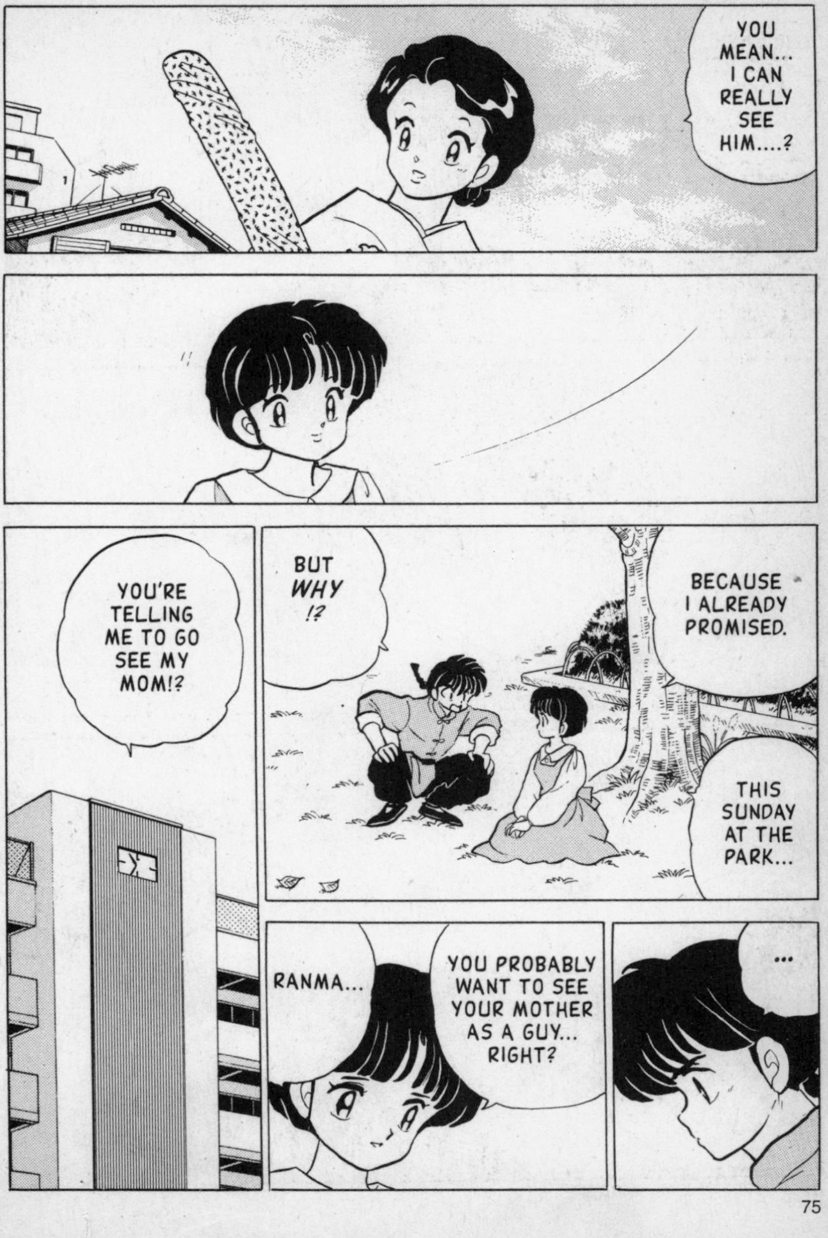
YOU MEAN... I CAN REALLY SEE HIM....?
YOU'RE TELLING ME TO GO SEE MY MOM!?
BUT WHY !?
BECAUSE I ALREADY PROMISED.
THIS SUNDAY AT THE PARK...
RANMA...
YOU PROBABLY WANT TO SEE YOUR MOTHER AS A GUY... RIGHT?
...

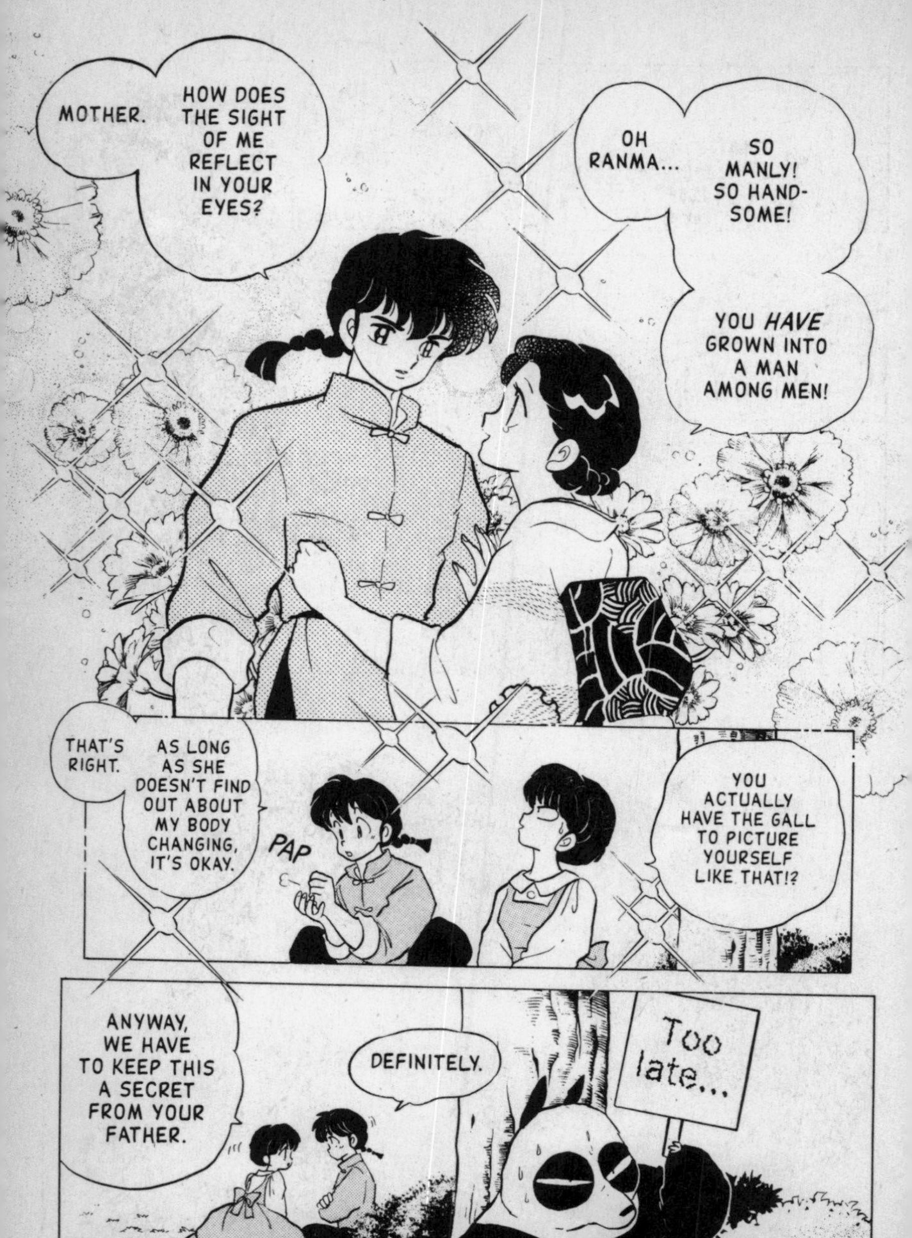
MOTHER.
HOW DOES THE SIGHT OF ME REFLECT IN YOUR EYES?
OH RANMA...
SO MANLY! SO HAND-SOME!
YOU HAVE GROWN INTO A MAN AMONG MEN!
THAT'S RIGHT.
AS LONG AS SHE DOESN'T FIND OUT ABOUT MY BODY CHANGING, IT'S OKAY.
PAP
YOU ACTUALLY HAVE THE GALL TO PICTURE YOURSELF LIKE THAT!?
ANYWAY, WE HAVE TO KEEP THIS A SECRET FROM YOUR FATHER.
DEFINITELY.
Too late...

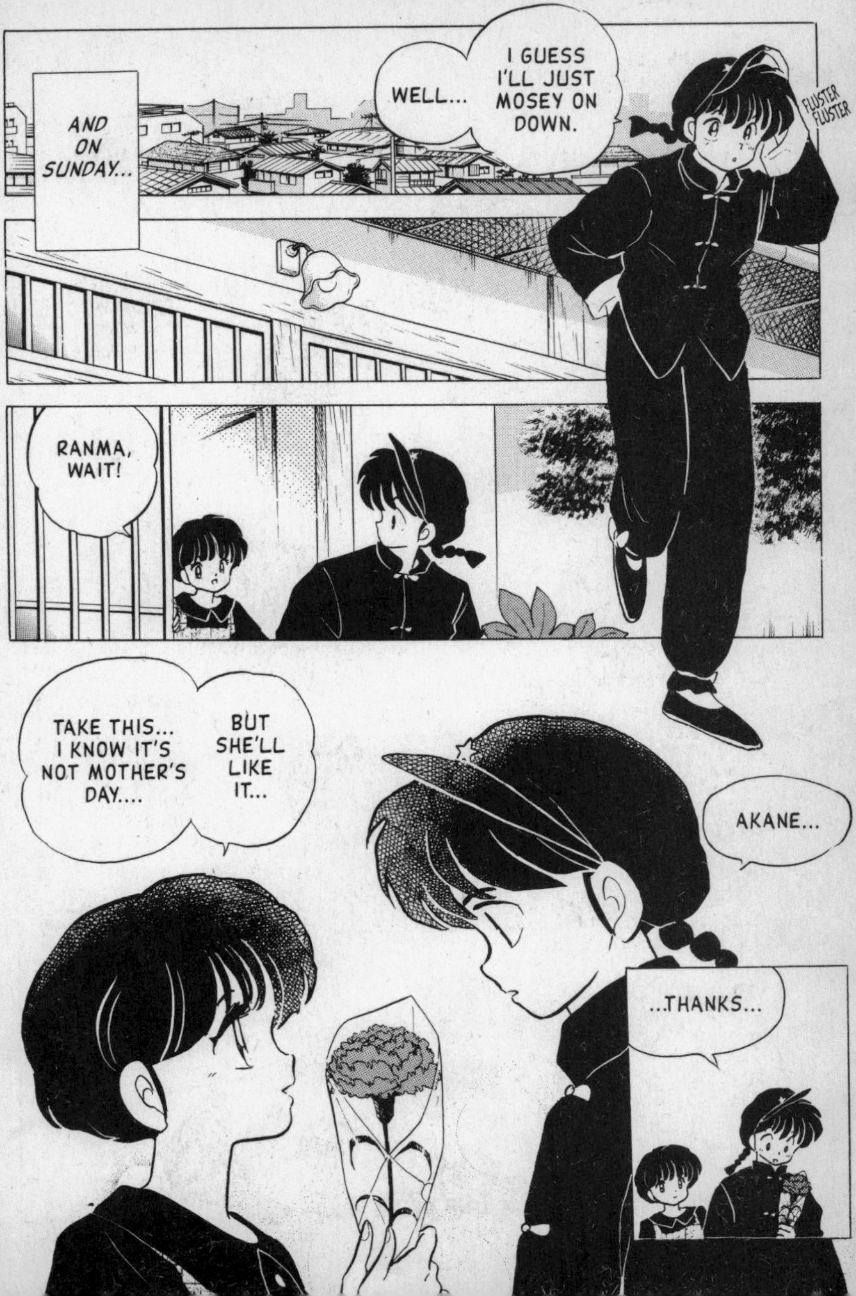
AND ON SUNDAY...
WELL...
I GUESS I'LL JUST MOSEY ON DOWN.
FLUSTER FLUSTER
RANMA, WAIT!
TAKE THIS... I KNOW IT'S NOT MOTHER'S DAY....
BUT SHE'LL LIKE IT...
AKANE...
...THANKS...

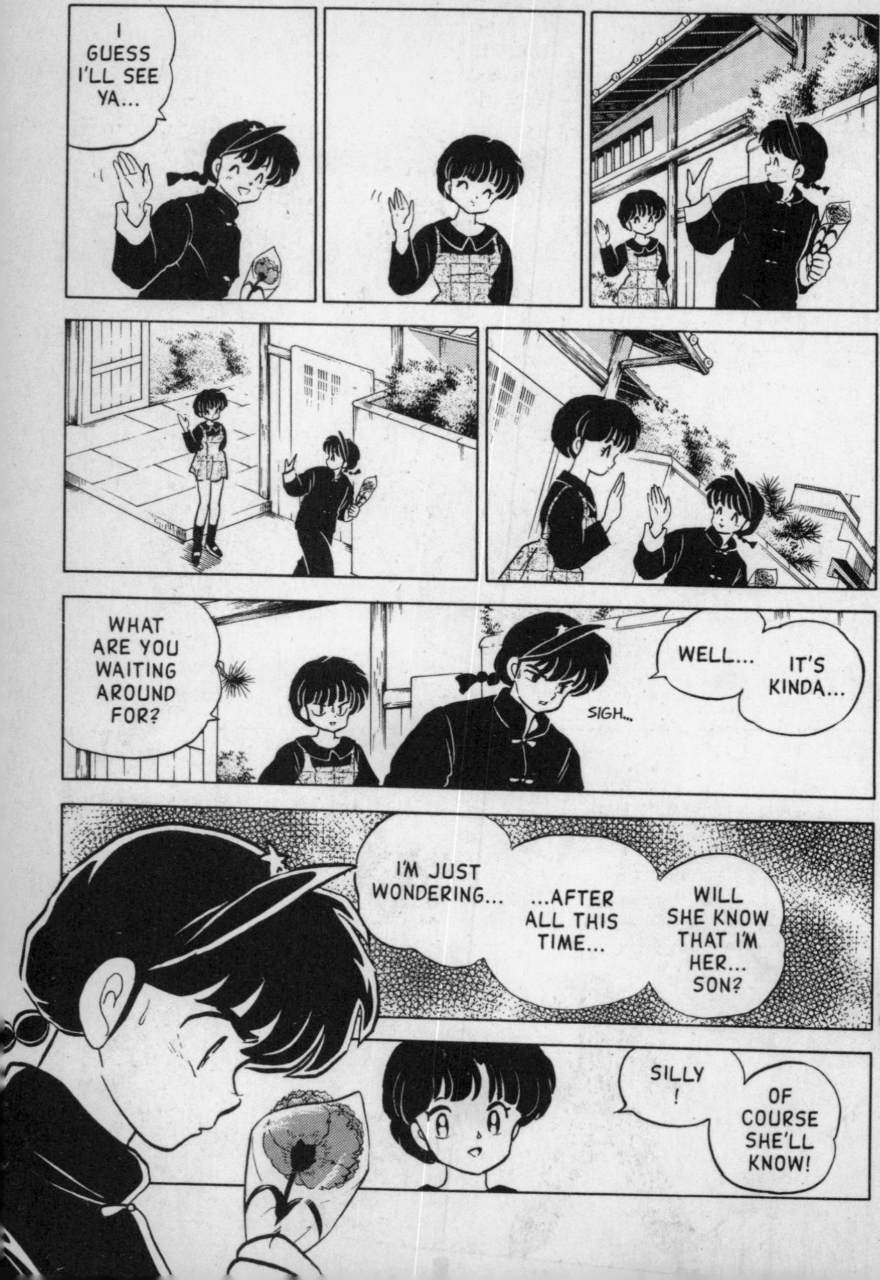
I GUESS I'LL SEE YA...
WHAT ARE YOU WAITING AROUND FOR?
SIGH...
WELL... IT'S KINDA...
I'M JUST WONDERING... ...AFTER ALL THIS TIME... WILL SHE KNOW THAT I'M HER... SON?
SILLY! OF COURSE SHE'LL KNOW!

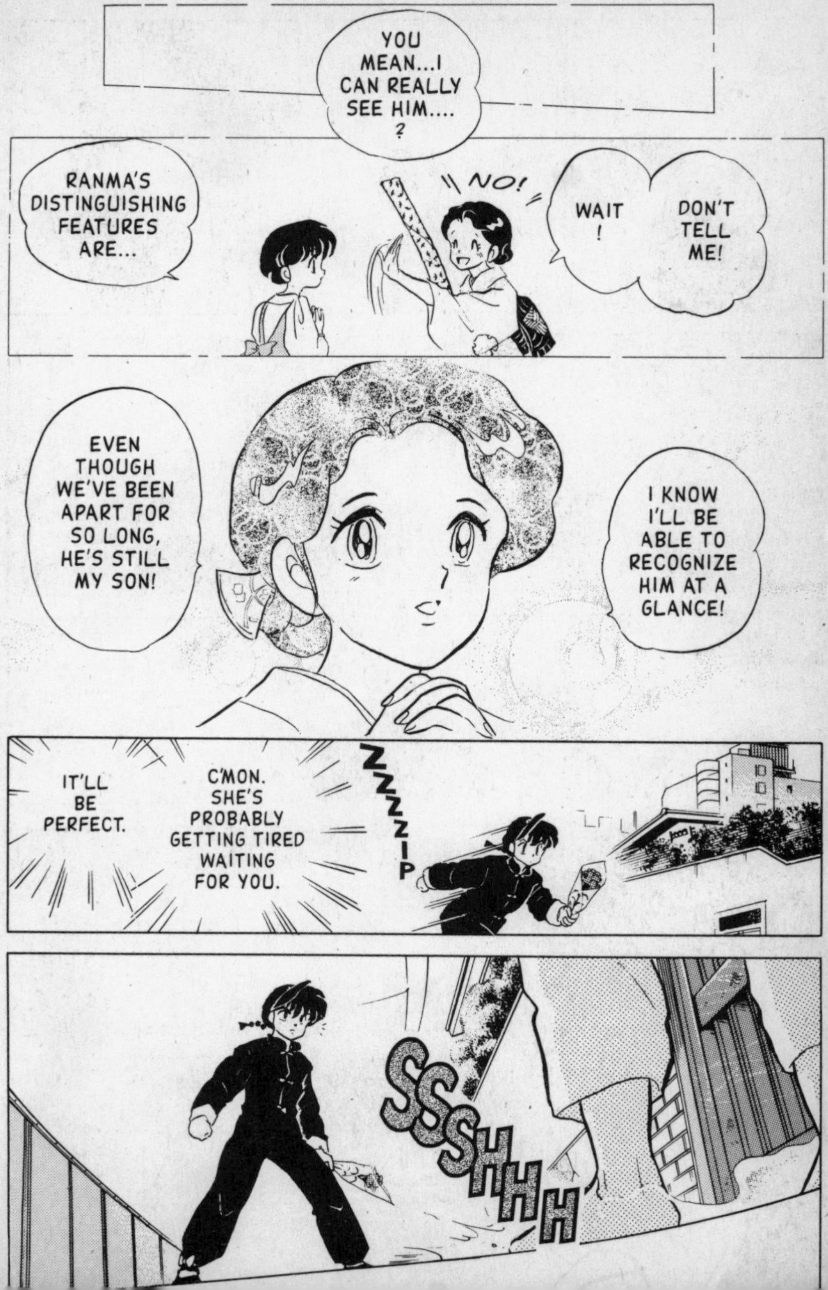
YOU MEAN...I CAN REALLY SEE HIM.... ?
RANMA'S DISTINGUISHING FEATURES ARE...
NO!
WAIT!
DON'T TELL ME!
EVEN THOUGH WE'VE BEEN APART FOR SO LONG, HE'S STILL MY SON!
I KNOW I'LL BE ABLE TO RECOGNIZE HIM AT A GLANCE!
IT'LL BE PERFECT.
C'MON. SHE'S PROBABLY GETTING TIRED WAITING FOR YOU.
ZZZZIP
SSSHHHH

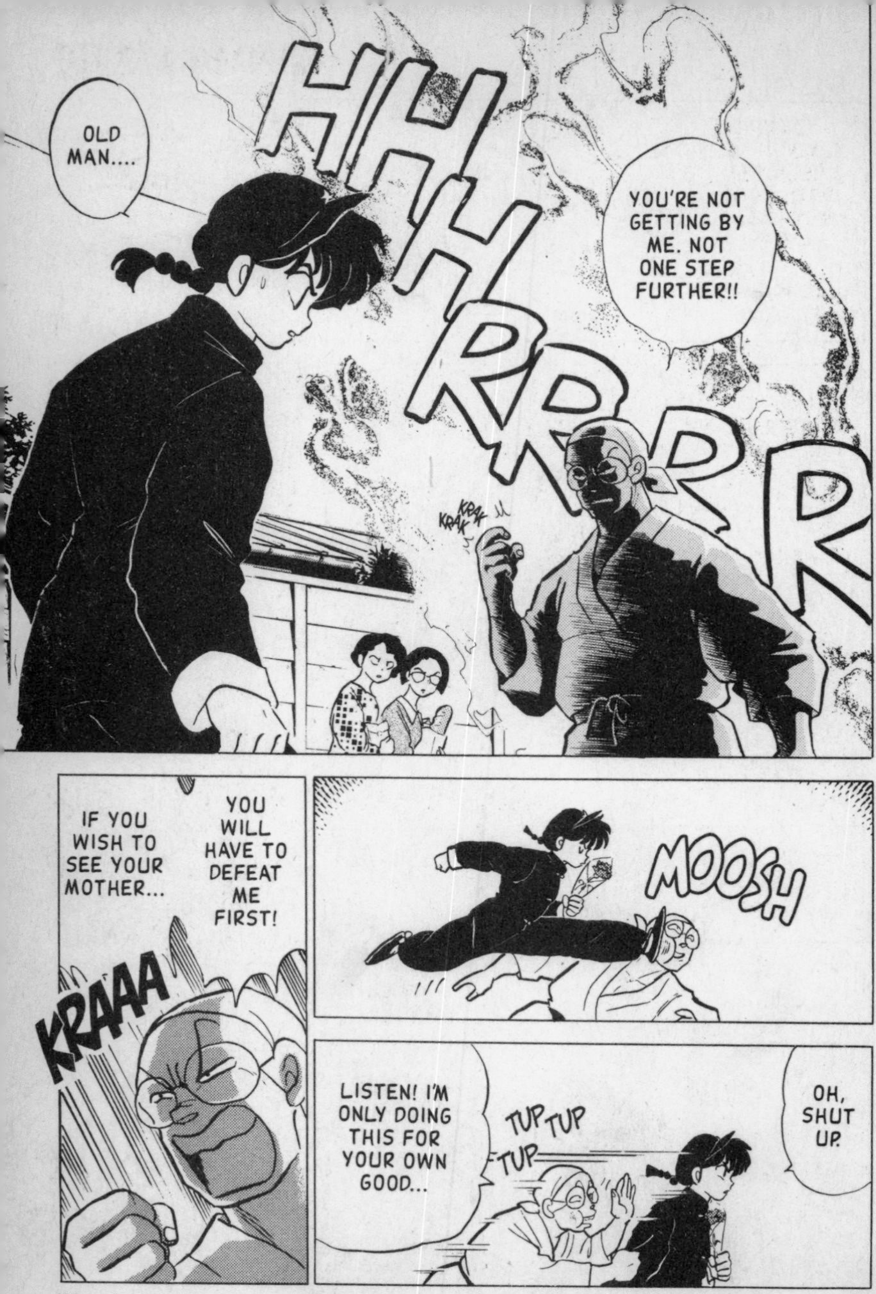

OLD MAN....
HHHHRRRRR
YOU'RE NOT GETTING BY ME. NOT ONE STEP FURTHER!!
KRAK KRAK
IF YOU WISH TO SEE YOUR MOTHER...
YOU WILL HAVE TO DEFEAT ME FIRST!
KRAAA
MOOSH
LISTEN! I'M ONLY DOING THIS FOR YOUR OWN GOOD...
TUP TUP TUP
OH, SHUT UP.

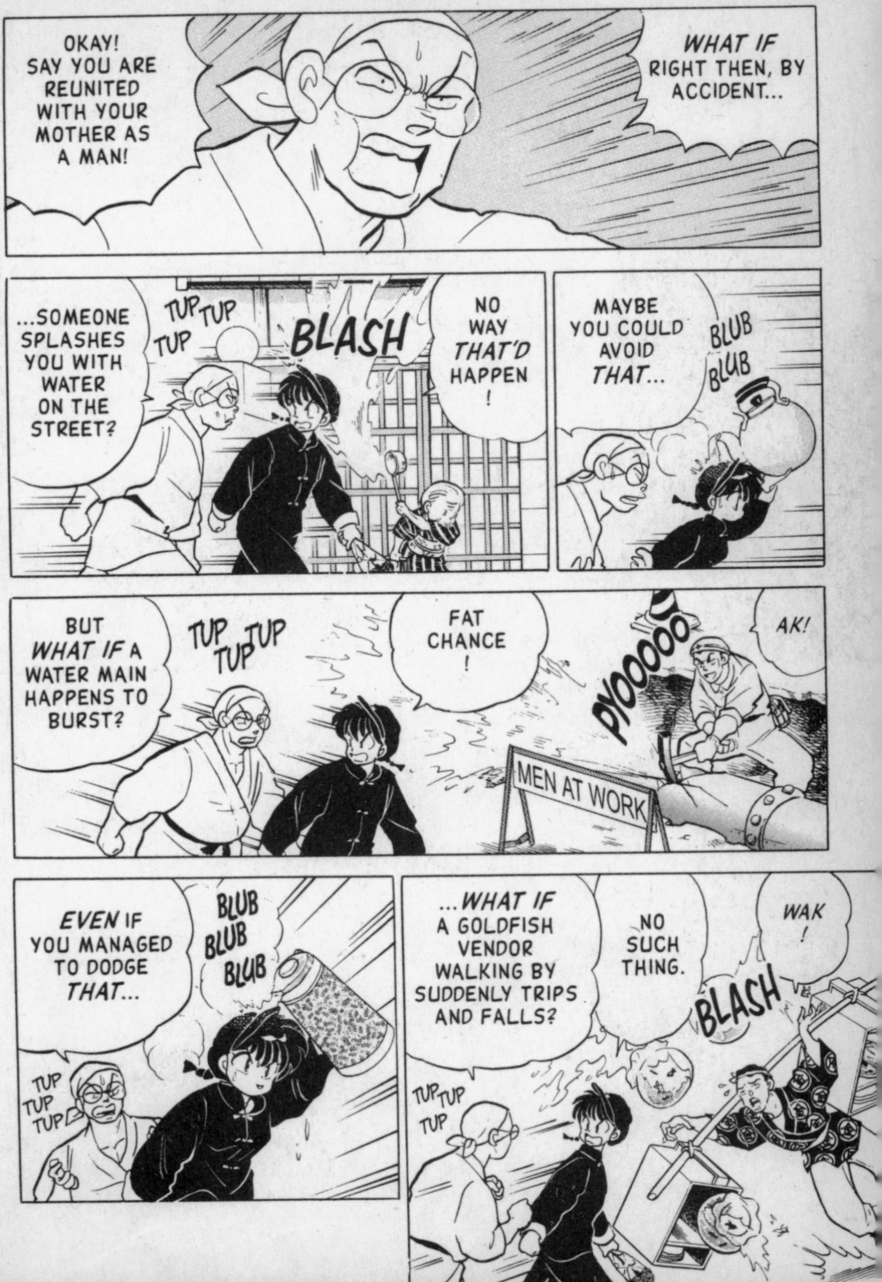
OKAY! SAY YOU ARE REUNITED WITH YOUR MOTHER AS A MAN!
WHAT IF RIGHT THEN, BY ACCIDENT...
...SOMEONE SPLASHES YOU WITH WATER ON THE STREET?
TUP TUP TUP
BLASH
NO WAY THAT'D HAPPEN!
MAYBE YOU COULD AVOID THAT...
BLUB BLUB
BUT WHAT IF A WATER MAIN HAPPENS TO BURST?
TUP TUP TUP
FAT CHANCE!
PYOOOOO
AK!
MEN AT WORK
EVEN IF YOU MANAGED TO DODGE THAT...
BLUB BLUB BLUB
TUP TUP TUP
...WHAT IF A GOLDFISH VENDOR WALKING BY SUDDENLY TRIPS AND FALLS?
NO SUCH THING.
WAK!
BLASH
TUP TUP TUP

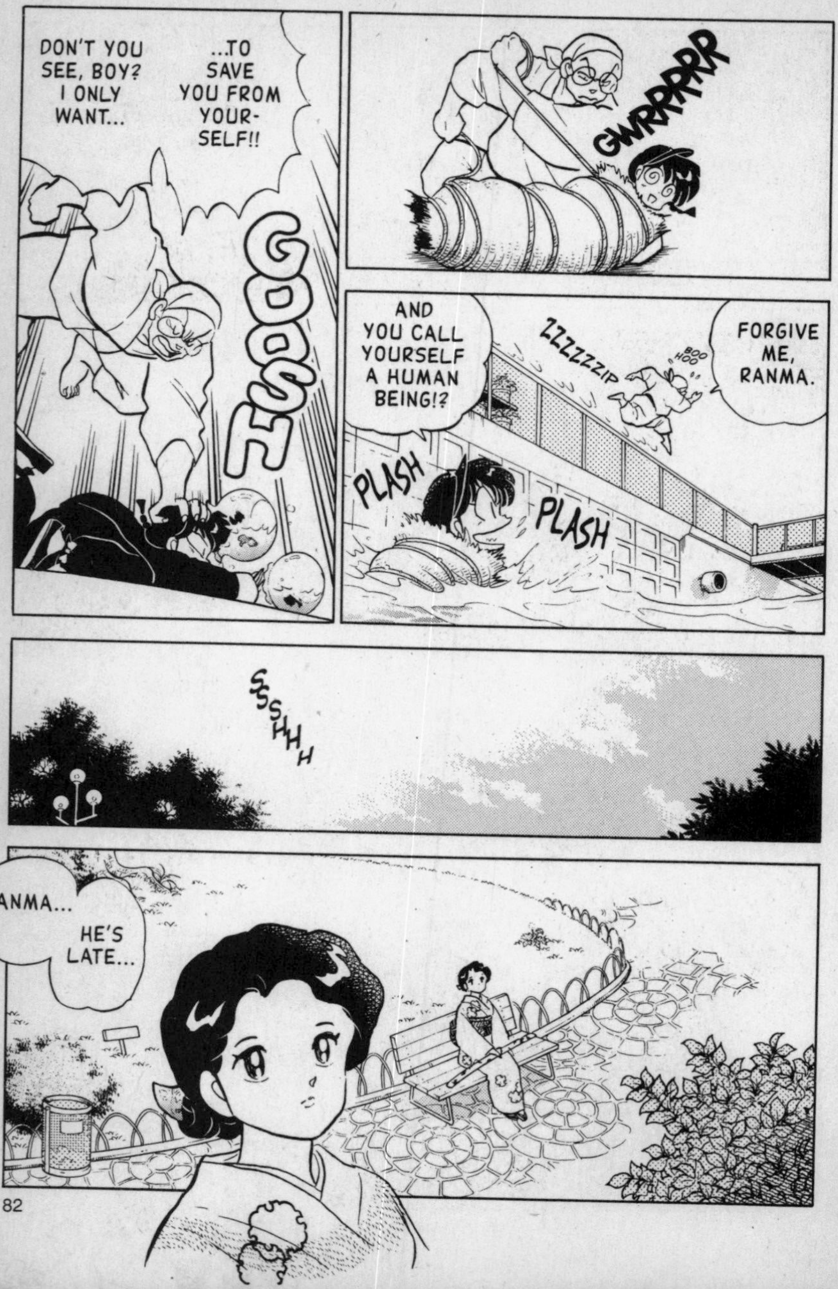
DON'T YOU SEE, BOY? I ONLY WANT...
...TO SAVE YOU FROM YOUR-SELF!!
GOOSH
GWRRRRR
AND YOU CALL YOURSELF A HUMAN BEING!?
ZZZZZZIP
BOO HOO
FORGIVE ME, RANMA.
PLASH
PLASH
SSSHHH
RANMA... HE'S LATE...

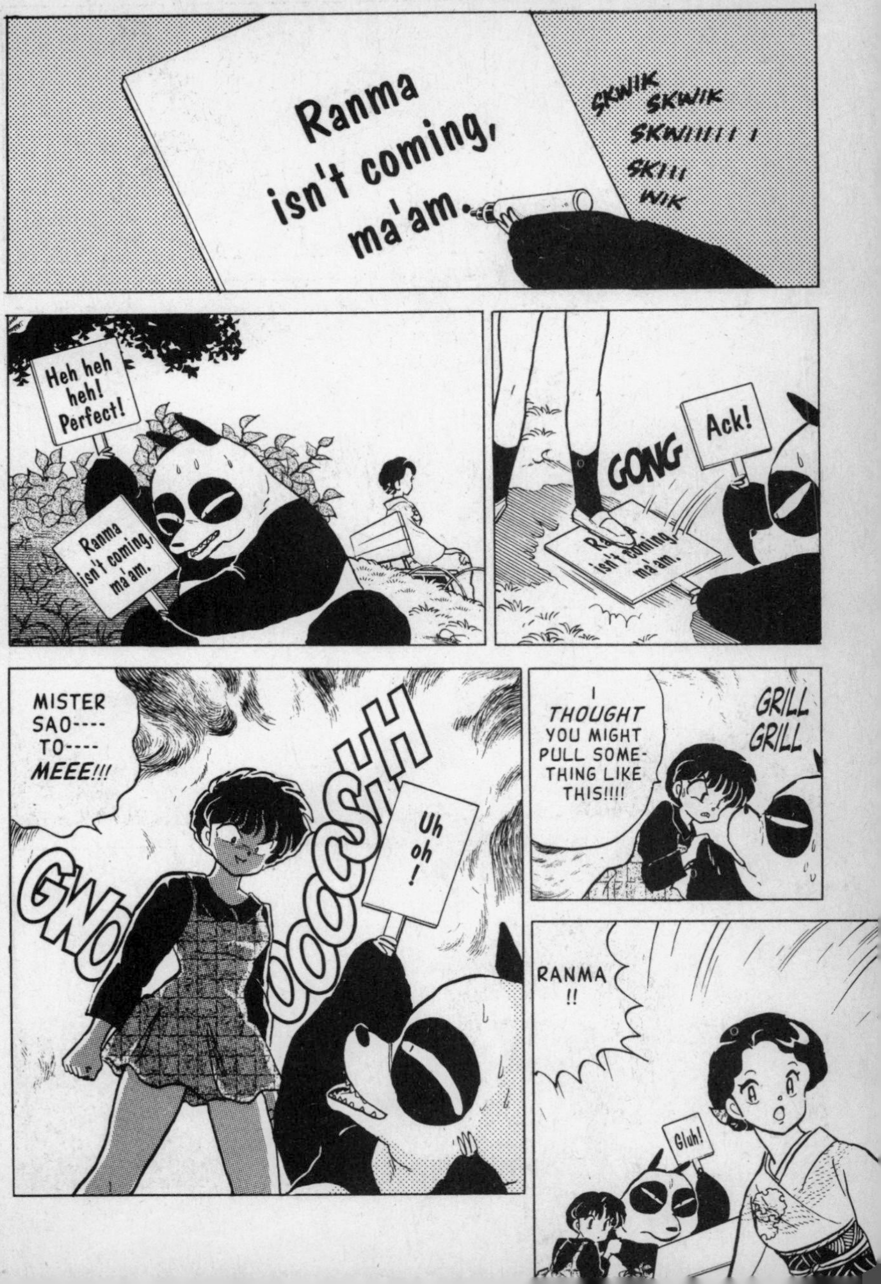
Ranma isn't coming, ma'am.
SKWIK SKWIK
SKWIIIII I
SKIII
WIK
Heh heh heh! Perfect!
Ranma isn't coming, ma'am.
GONG
Ack!
MISTER SAO---- TO---- MEEE!!!
GNOOOOOCSHH
Uh oh!
I THOUGHT YOU MIGHT PULL SOME-THING LIKE THIS!!!!
GRILL GRILL
RANMA !!
Gluh!

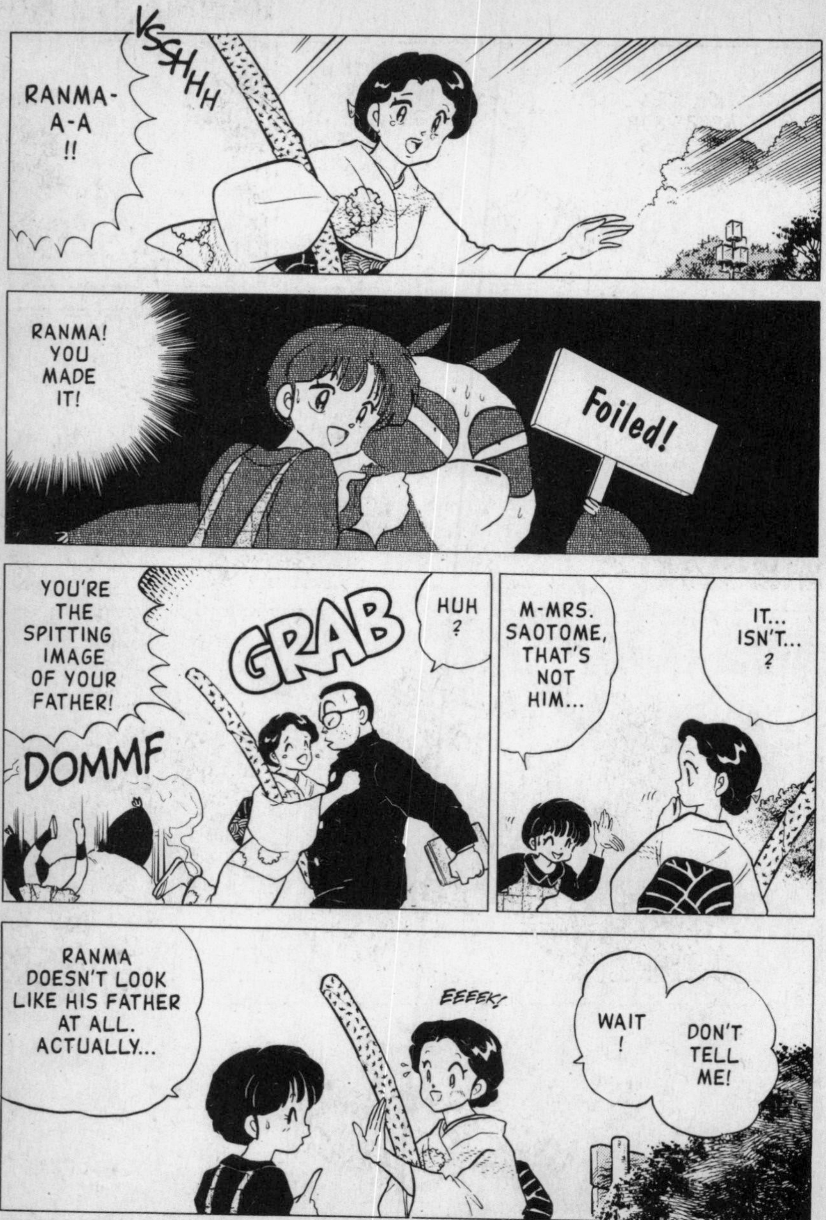
VSSHHH
RANMA-A-A !!
RANMA! YOU MADE IT!
Foiled!
YOU'RE THE SPITTING IMAGE OF YOUR FATHER!
DOMMF
GRAB
HUH?
M-MRS. SAOTOME, THAT'S NOT HIM...
IT... ISN'T...?
RANMA DOESN'T LOOK LIKE HIS FATHER AT ALL. ACTUALLY...
EEEEK!
WAIT!
DON'T TELL ME!

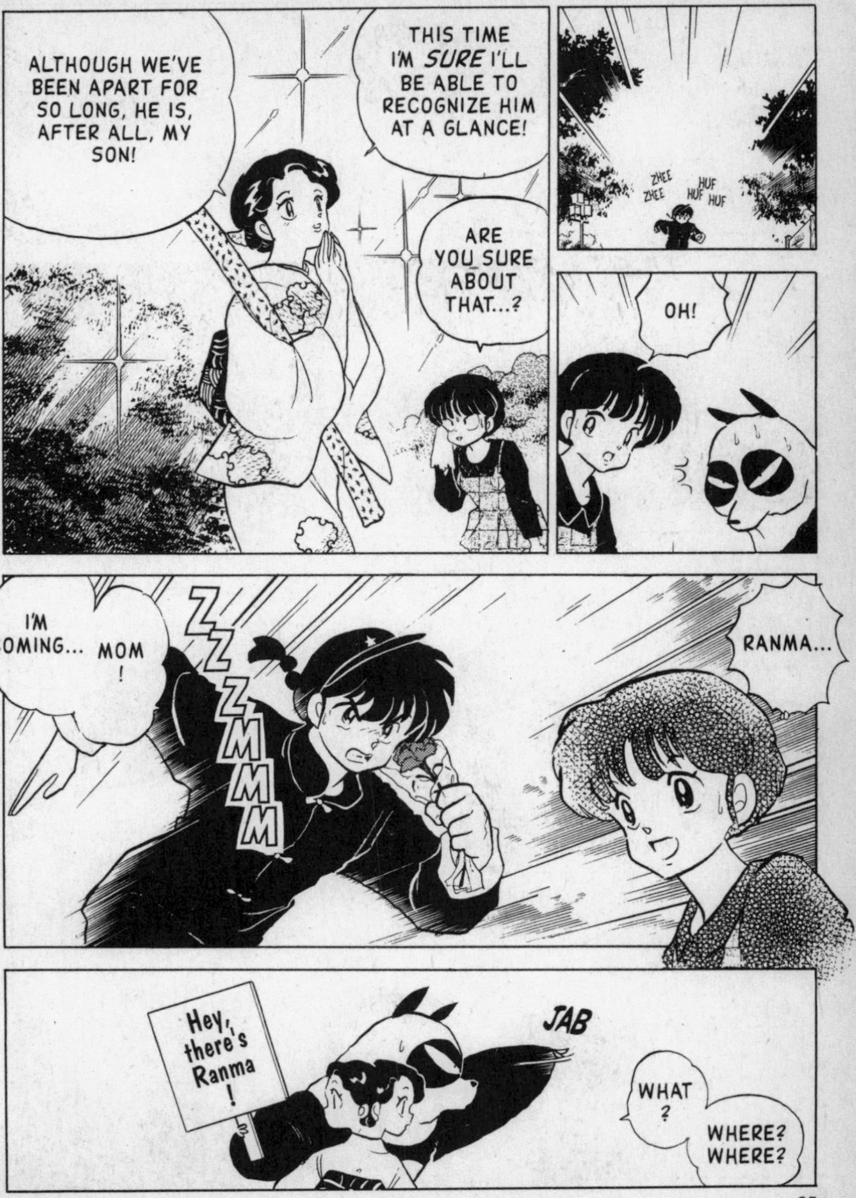
ALTHOUGH WE'VE BEEN APART FOR SO LONG, HE IS, AFTER ALL, MY SON!
THIS TIME I'M *SURE* I'LL BE ABLE TO RECOGNIZE HIM AT A GLANCE!
ARE YOU SURE ABOUT THAT...?
ZHEE ZHEE
HUF HUF HUF
OH!
I'M COMING... MOM!
ZZZMMM
RANMA...
Hey, there's Ranma!
JAB
WHAT?
WHERE? WHERE?

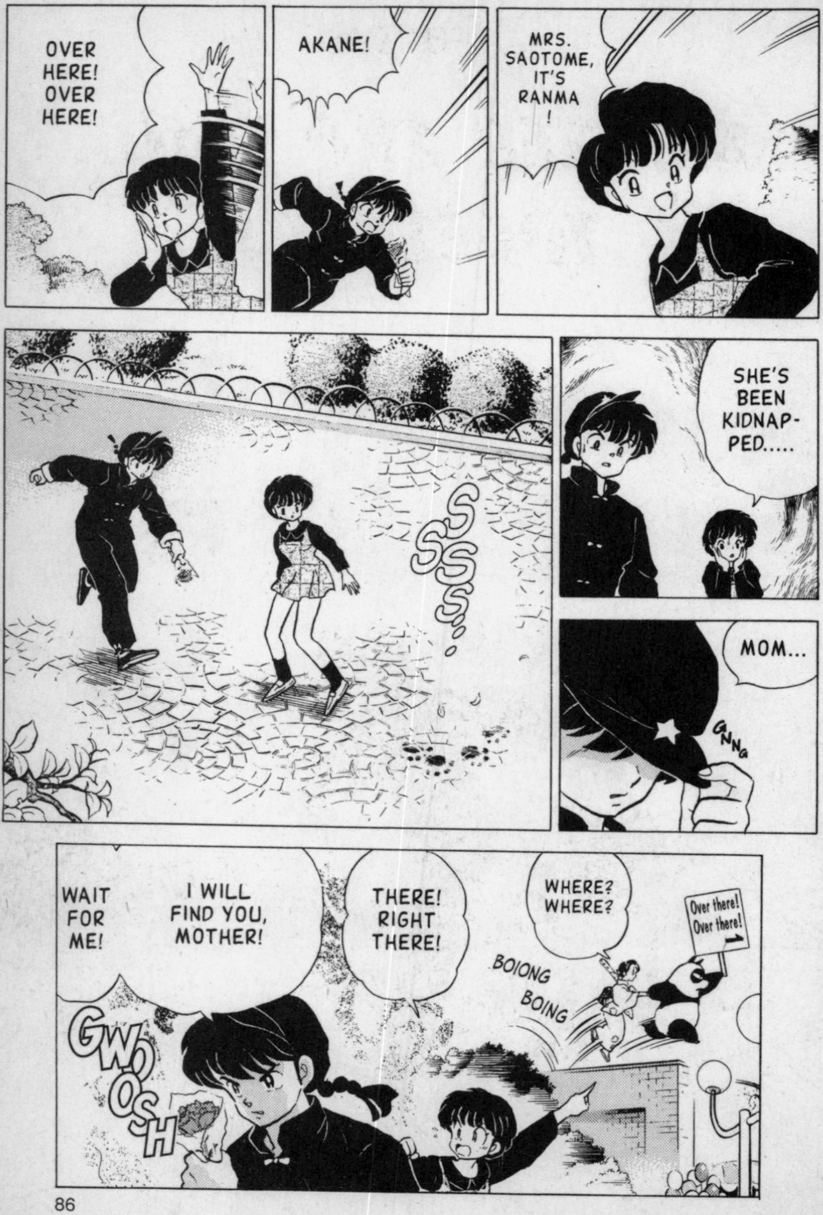
OVER HERE! OVER HERE!
AKANE!
MRS. SAOTOME, IT'S RANMA!
SSSS
SHE'S BEEN KIDNAP-PED.....
MOM...
GNNG
WAIT FOR ME!
I WILL FIND YOU, MOTHER!
THERE! RIGHT THERE!
WHERE? WHERE?
Over there! Over there!
BOIONG
BOING
GWOOSH

Part 6

MOTHER AND SON... TOGETHER!!

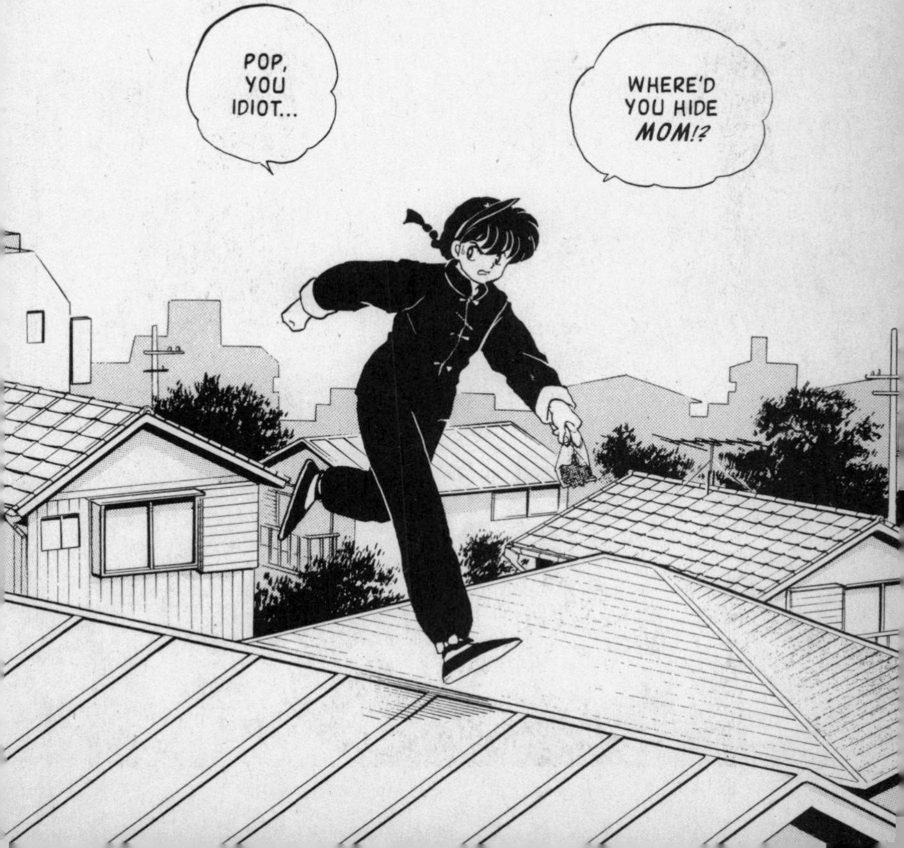
POP, YOU IDIOT...
WHERE'D YOU HIDE *MOM!?*

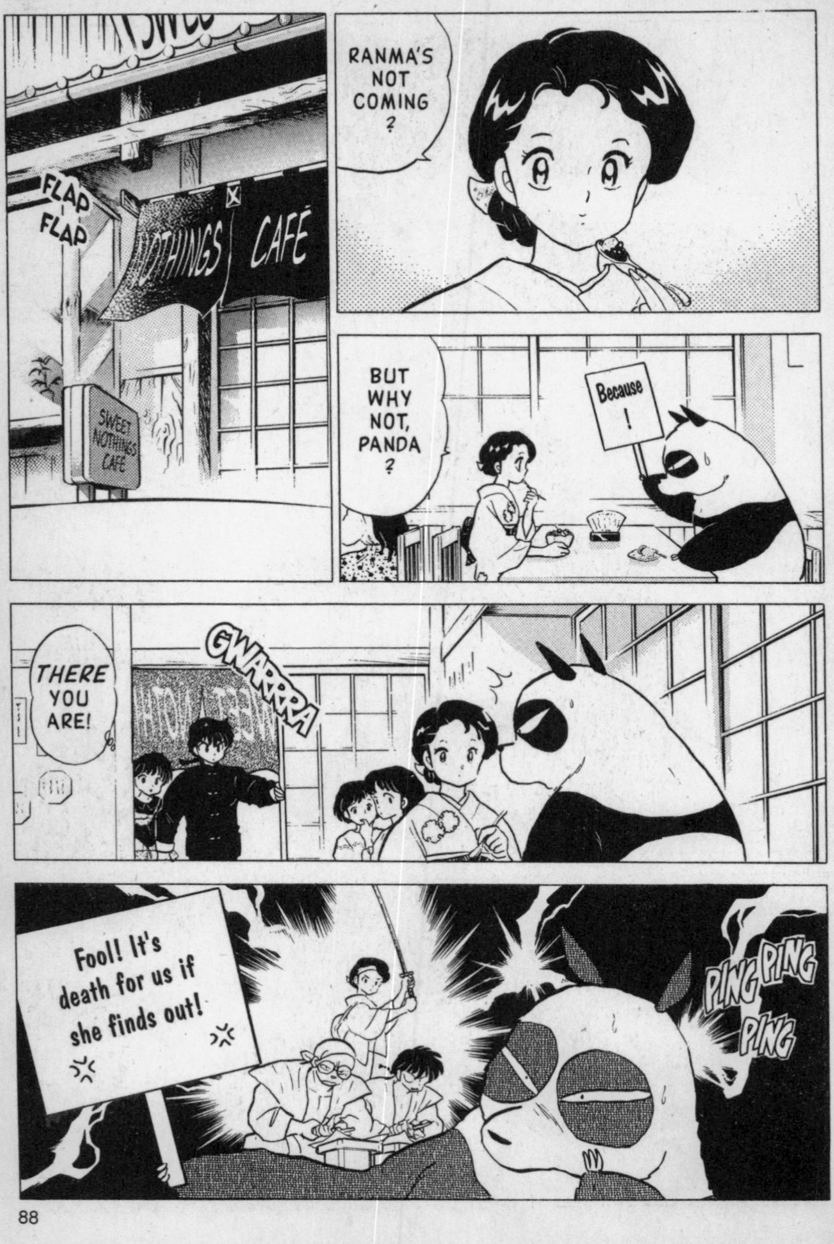
FLAP FLAP
NOTHINGS CAFÉ
SWEET NOTHINGS CAFÉ
RANMA'S NOT COMING?
BUT WHY NOT, PANDA?
Because !
THERE YOU ARE!
GWARRRA
Fool! It's death for us if she finds out!
PING PING PING

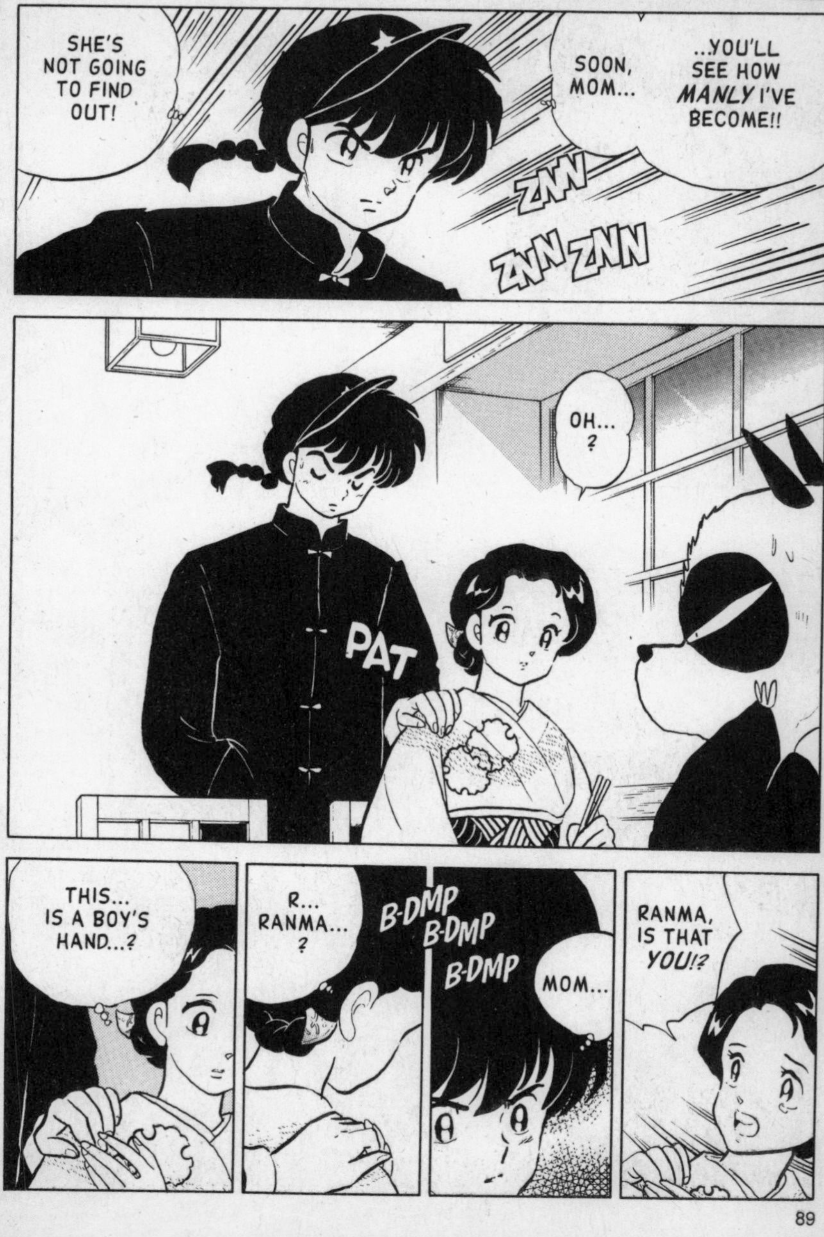
SHE'S NOT GOING TO FIND OUT!
SOON, MOM...
...YOU'LL SEE HOW MANLY I'VE BECOME!!
ZNN
ZNN ZNN
OH... ?
PAT
THIS... IS A BOY'S HAND...?
R... RANMA... ?
B-DMP B-DMP B-DMP
MOM...
RANMA, IS THAT YOU!?

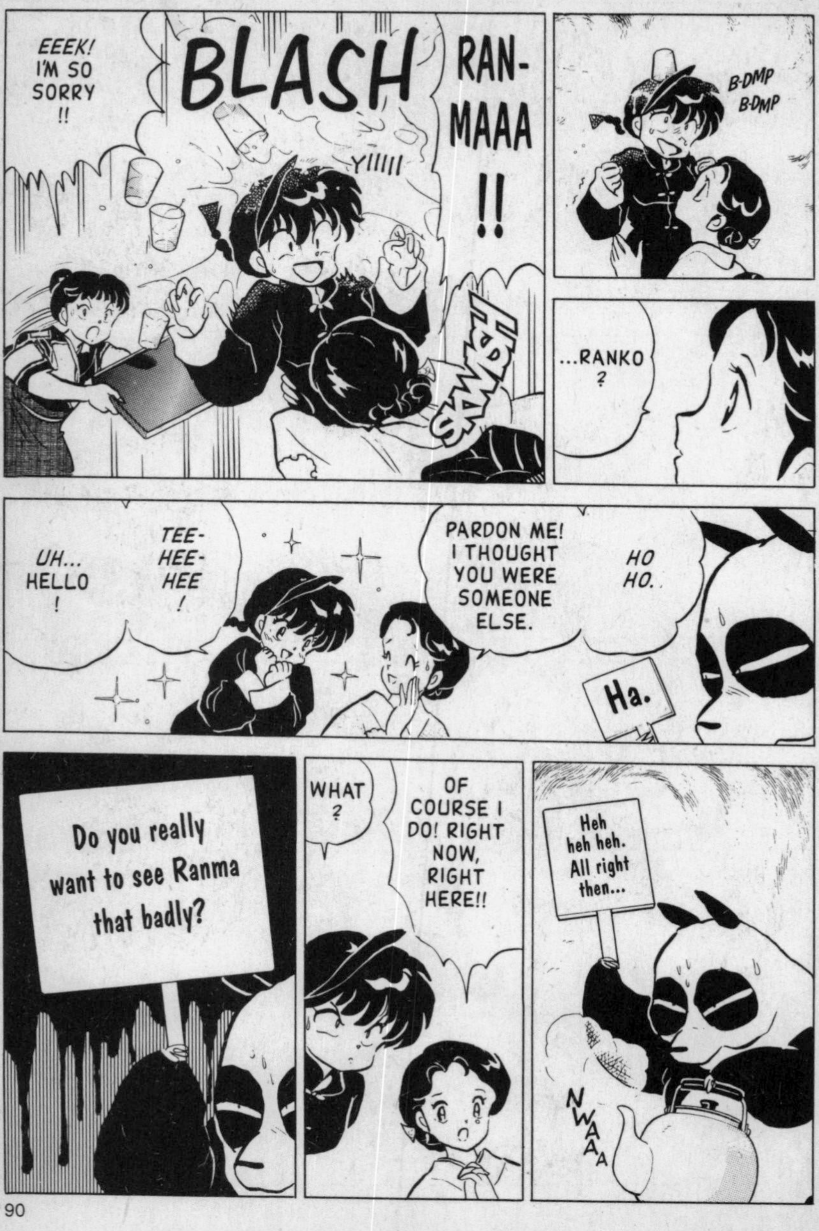
EEEK! I'M SO SORRY !!
BLASH
YIIIII
RAN-MAAA !!
SPLASH
B-DMP B-DMP
...RANKO ?
UH... HELLO !
TEE-HEE-HEE !
PARDON ME! I THOUGHT YOU WERE SOMEONE ELSE.
HO HO..
Ha.
Do you really want to see Ranma that badly?
WHAT ?
OF COURSE I DO! RIGHT NOW, RIGHT HERE!!
Heh heh heh. All right then...
NWAAA

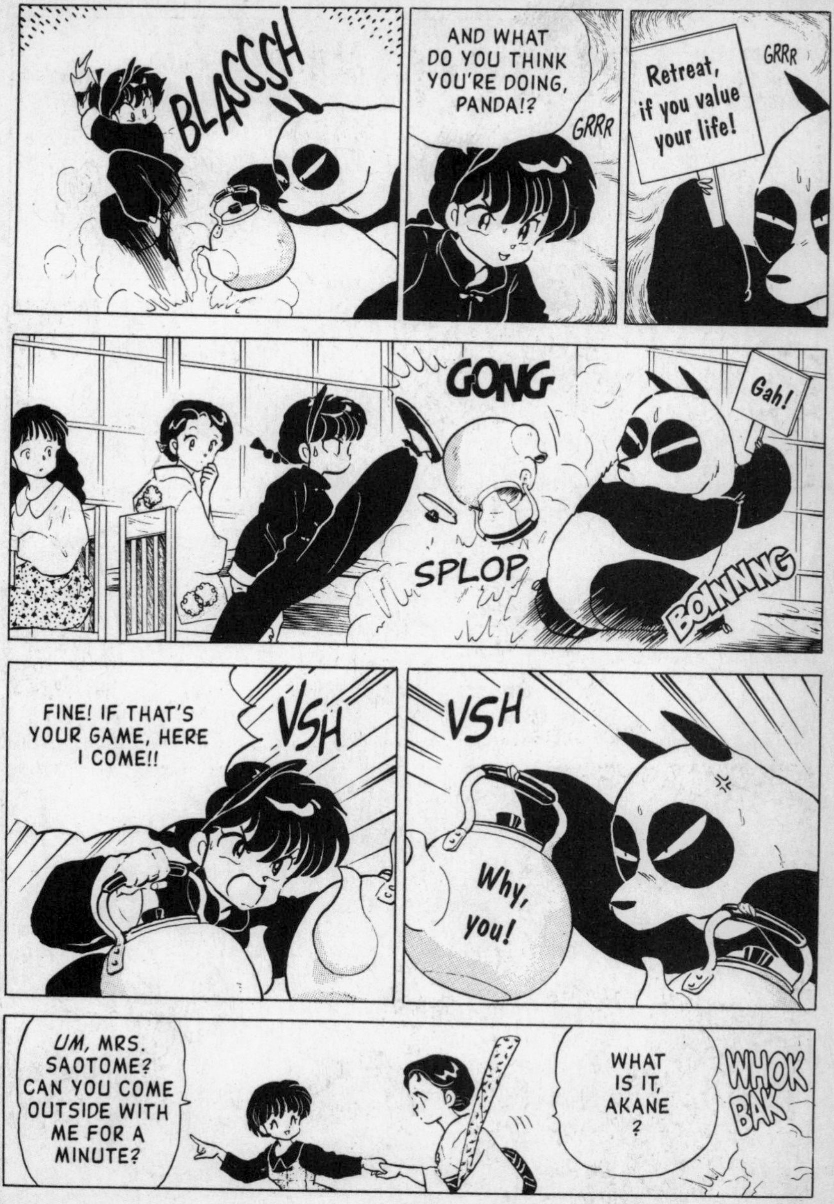
BLASSCH
AND WHAT DO YOU THINK YOU'RE DOING, PANDA!?
GRRR
GRRR
Retreat, if you value your life!
GONG
Gah!
SPLOP
BOINNNG
FINE! IF THAT'S YOUR GAME, HERE I COME!!
VSH
VSH
Why, you!
UM, MRS. SAOTOME? CAN YOU COME OUTSIDE WITH ME FOR A MINUTE?
WHAT IS IT, AKANE ?
WHOK
BAK

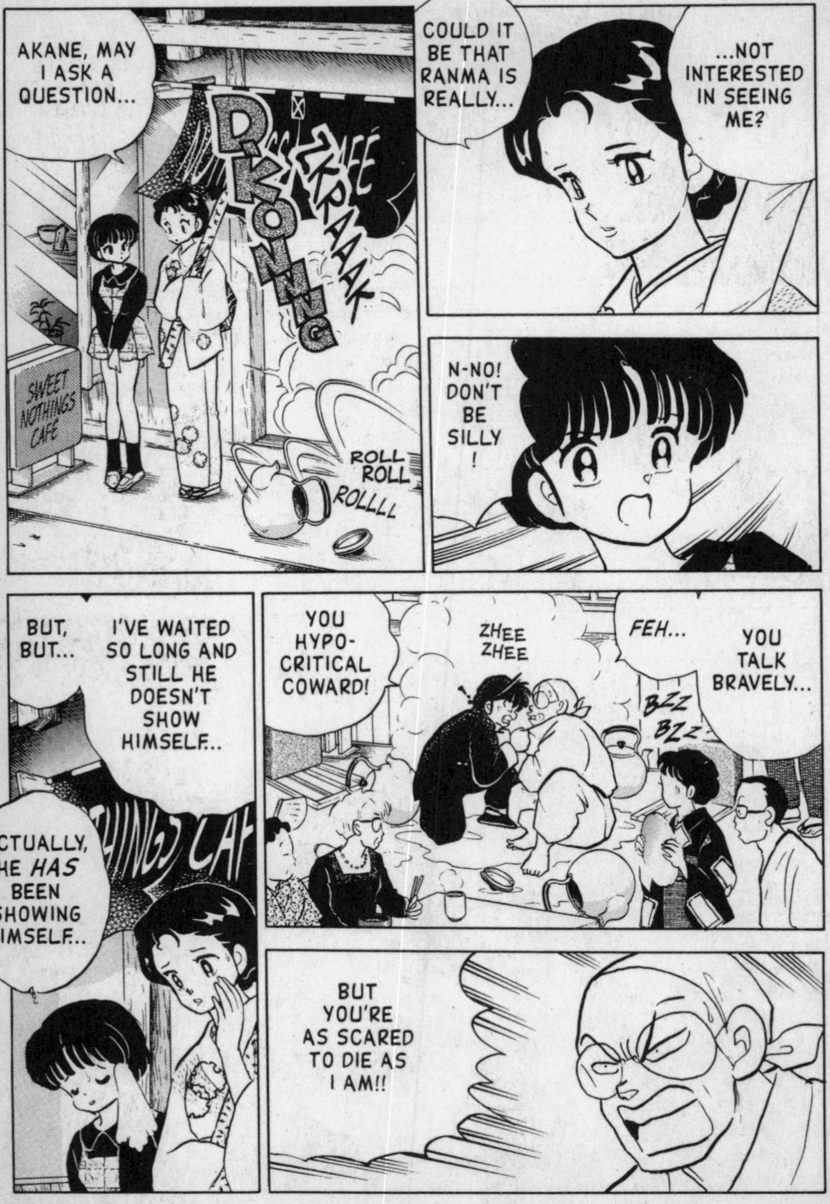

AKANE, MAY I ASK A QUESTION...
D-KONNNG
ZKRAAAK
SWEET NOTHINGS CAFE
ROLL ROLL ROLLLL
COULD IT BE THAT RANMA IS REALLY...
...NOT INTERESTED IN SEEING ME?
N-NO! DON'T BE SILLY!
BUT, BUT...
I'VE WAITED SO LONG AND STILL HE DOESN'T SHOW HIMSELF...
ACTUALLY, HE *HAS* BEEN SHOWING HIMSELF...
YOU HYPO-CRITICAL COWARD!
ZHEE ZHEE
FEH...
YOU TALK BRAVELY...
BZZ BZZ
BUT YOU'RE AS SCARED TO DIE AS I AM!!

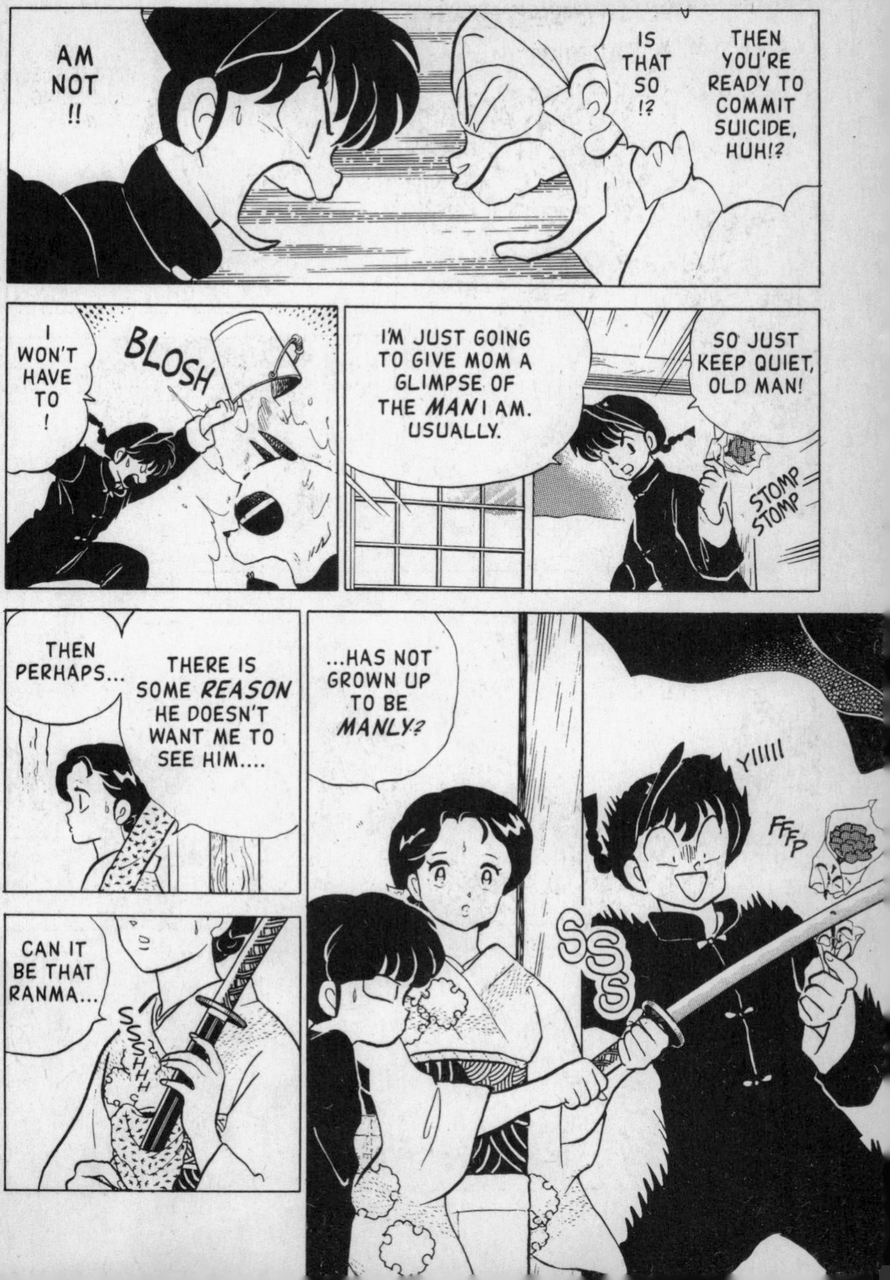
AM NOT !!
IS THAT SO !?
THEN YOU'RE READY TO COMMIT SUICIDE, HUH!?
I WON'T HAVE TO !
BLOSH
I'M JUST GOING TO GIVE MOM A GLIMPSE OF THE MAN I AM. USUALLY.
SO JUST KEEP QUIET, OLD MAN!
STOMP STOMP
THEN PERHAPS...
THERE IS SOME REASON HE DOESN'T WANT ME TO SEE HIM....
CAN IT BE THAT RANMA...
SSSHHH
...HAS NOT GROWN UP TO BE MANLY?
YIIIII
FFFP
SSS

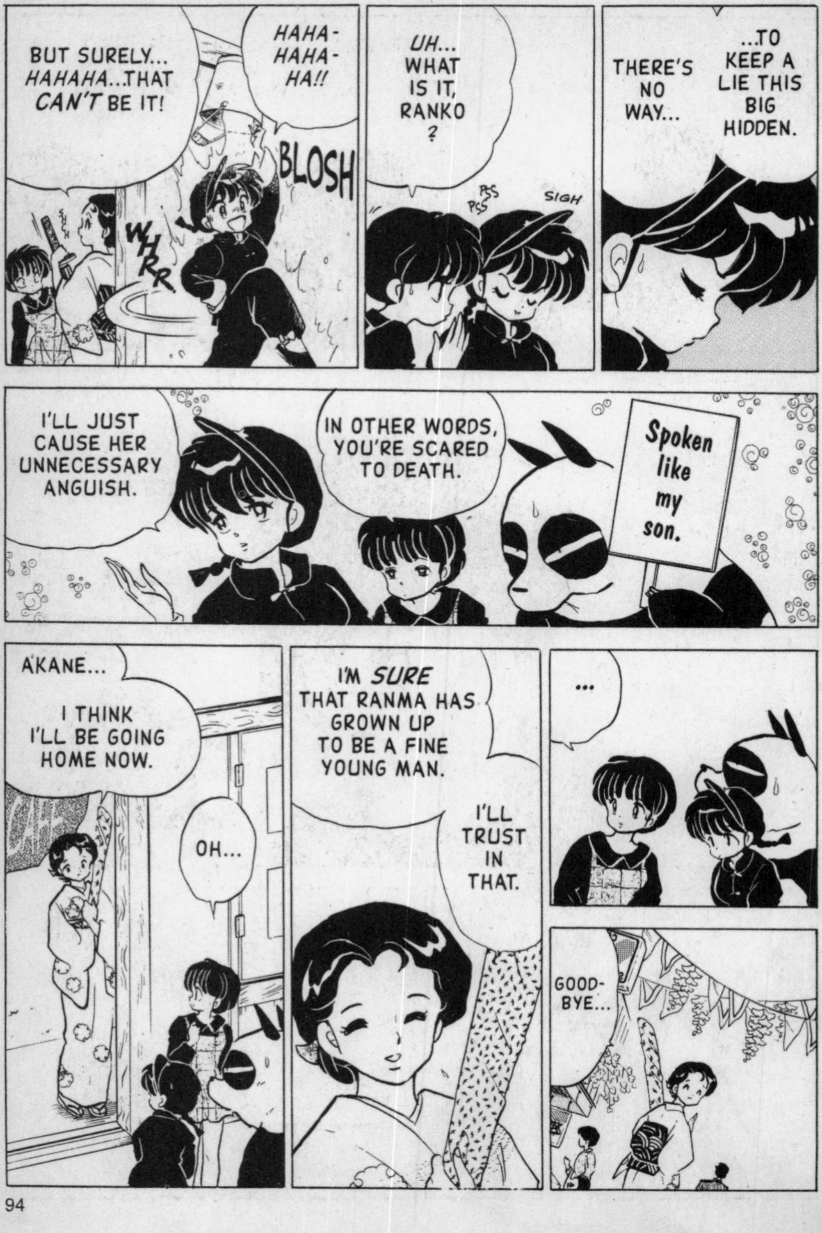
BUT SURELY... *HAHAHA*...THAT *CAN'T* BE IT!
HAHA-HAHAHA-HA!!
BLOSH
WHRR
UH... WHAT IS IT, RANKO ?
PSS PSS
SIGH
THERE'S NO WAY...
...TO KEEP A LIE THIS BIG HIDDEN.
I'LL JUST CAUSE HER UNNECESSARY ANGUISH.
IN OTHER WORDS, YOU'RE SCARED TO DEATH.
Spoken like my son.
AKANE...
I THINK I'LL BE GOING HOME NOW.
OH...
I'M *SURE* THAT RANMA HAS GROWN UP TO BE A FINE YOUNG MAN.
I'LL TRUST IN THAT.
...
GOOD-BYE...

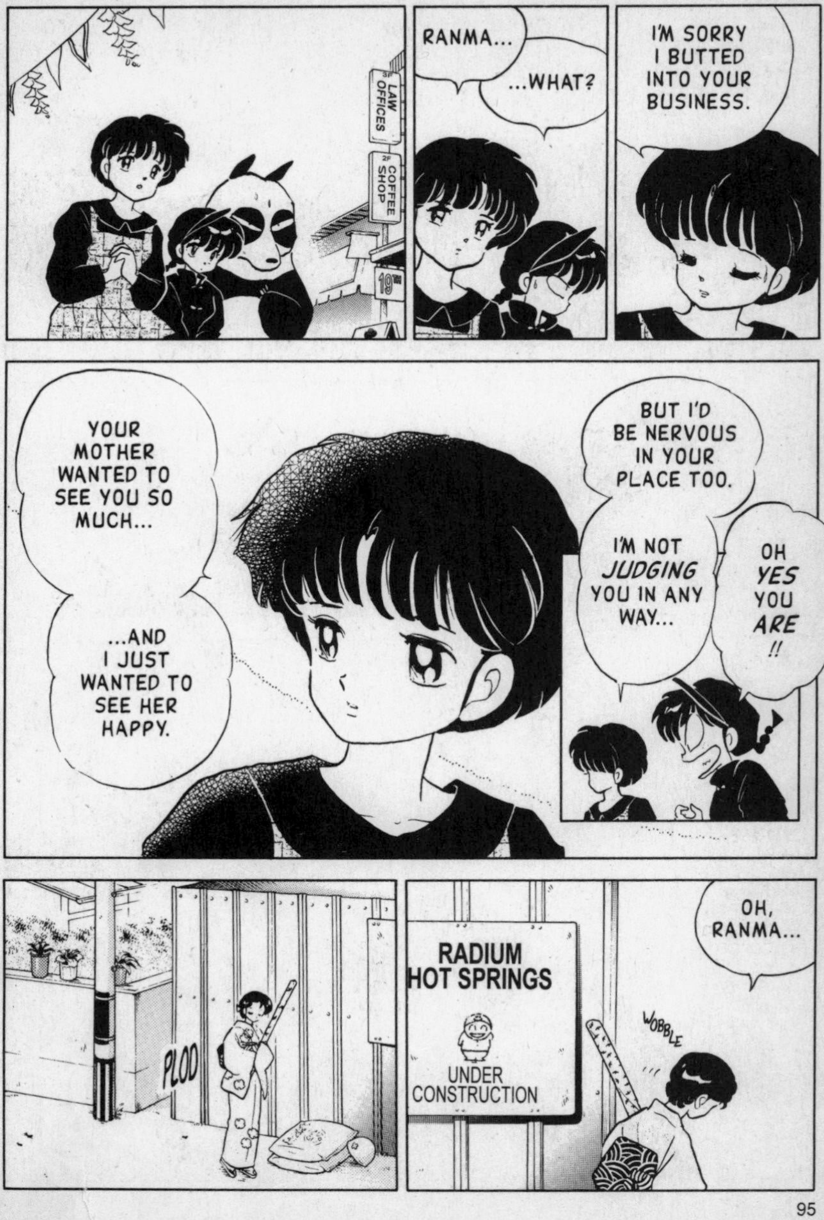
LAW OFFICES
COFFEE SHOP
RANMA...
...WHAT?
I'M SORRY I BUTTED INTO YOUR BUSINESS.
YOUR MOTHER WANTED TO SEE YOU SO MUCH...
...AND I JUST WANTED TO SEE HER HAPPY.
BUT I'D BE NERVOUS IN YOUR PLACE TOO.
I'M NOT *JUDGING* YOU IN ANY WAY...
OH *YES* YOU *ARE* !!
PLOD
RADIUM HOT SPRINGS
UNDER CONSTRUCTION
WOBBLE
OH, RANMA...

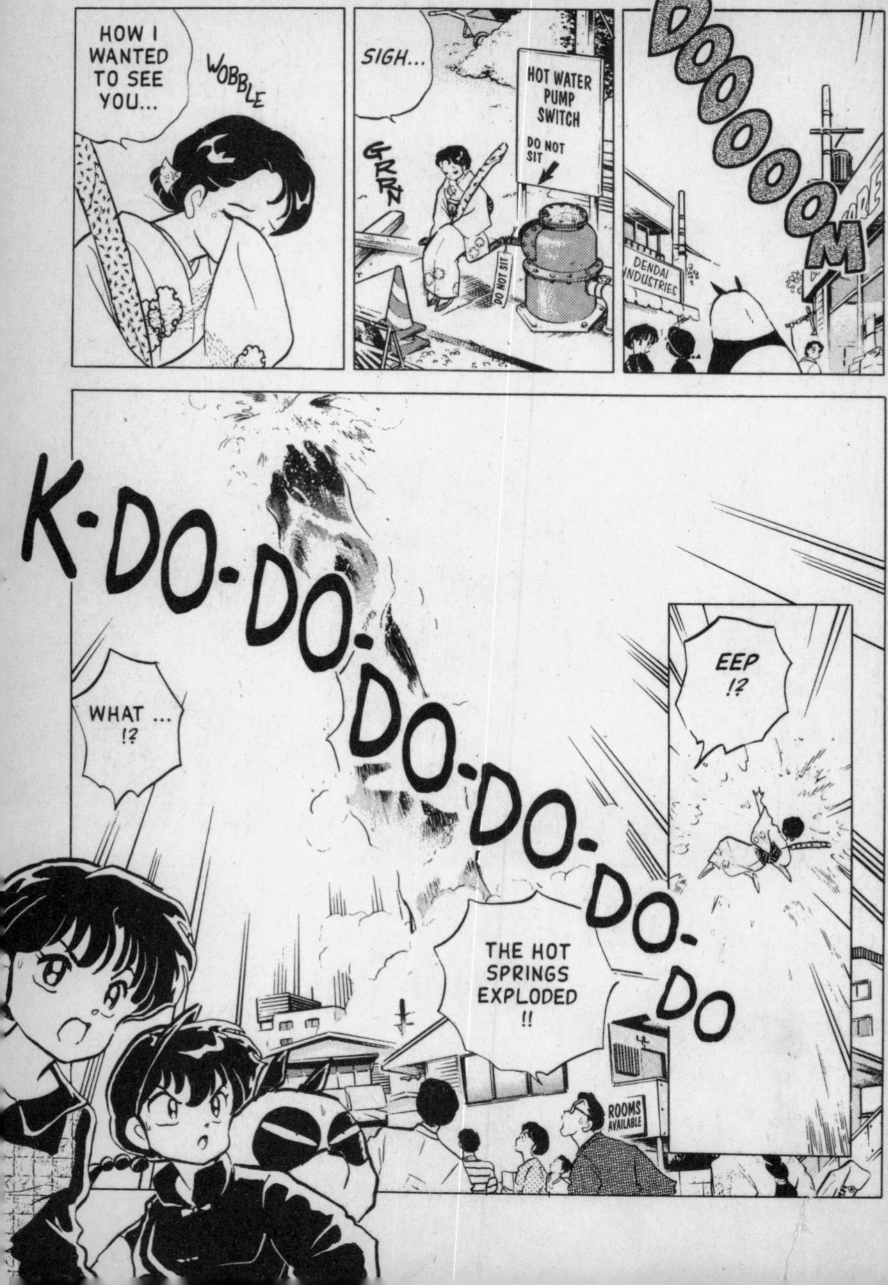

HOW I WANTED TO SEE YOU...
WOBBLE
SIGH...
HOT WATER PUMP SWITCH
DO NOT SIT
GRRN
DO NOT SIT
DOOOOOOM
DENDAI INDUSTRIES
K-DO-DO-DO-DO-DO-DO-DO-DO
WHAT ... !?
EEP !?
THE HOT SPRINGS EXPLODED !!
ROOMS AVAILABLE

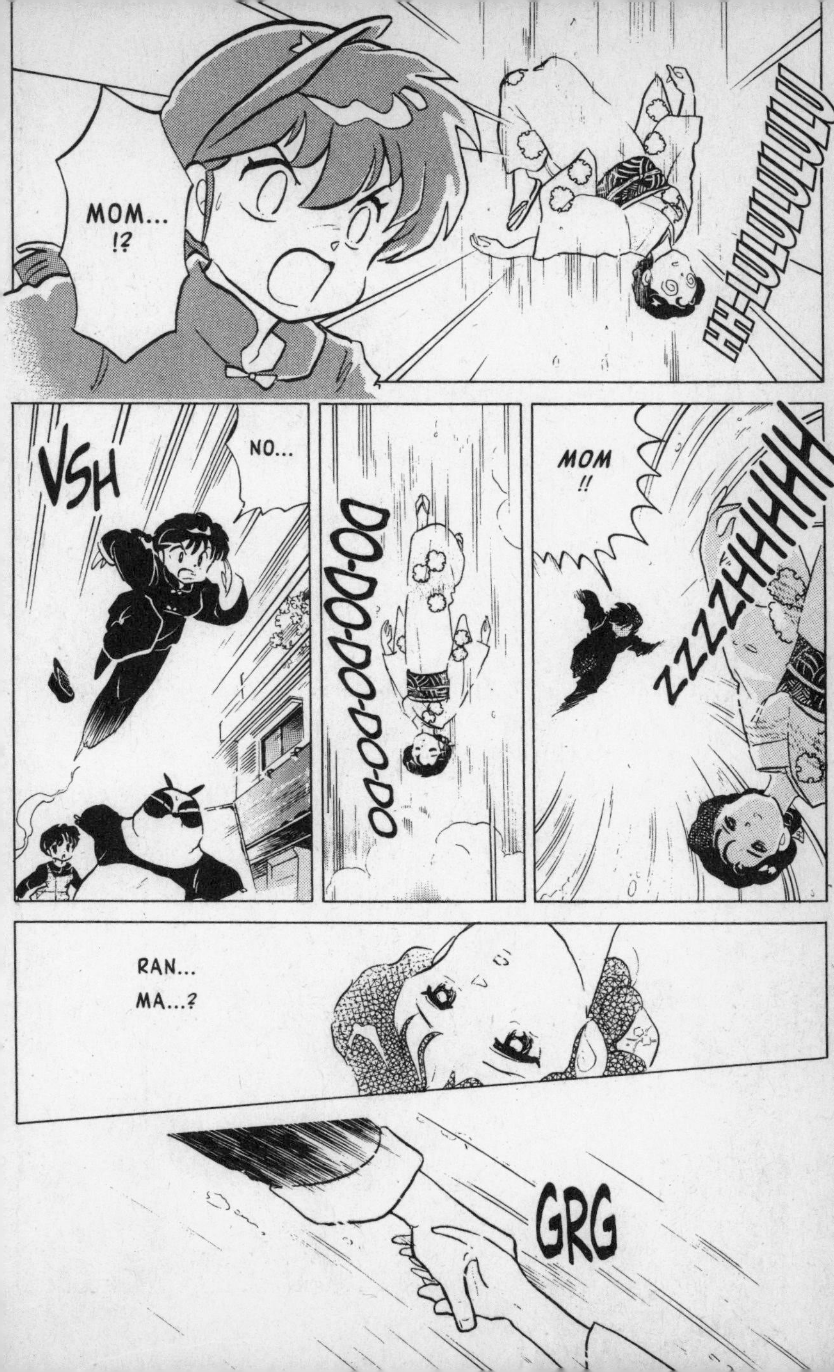
MOM... !?
HH-LULULULULU
VSH
NO...
DO-DO-DO-DO-DO-DO-DO-DO
MOM !!
ZZZZHHHHHH
RAN... MA...?
GRG

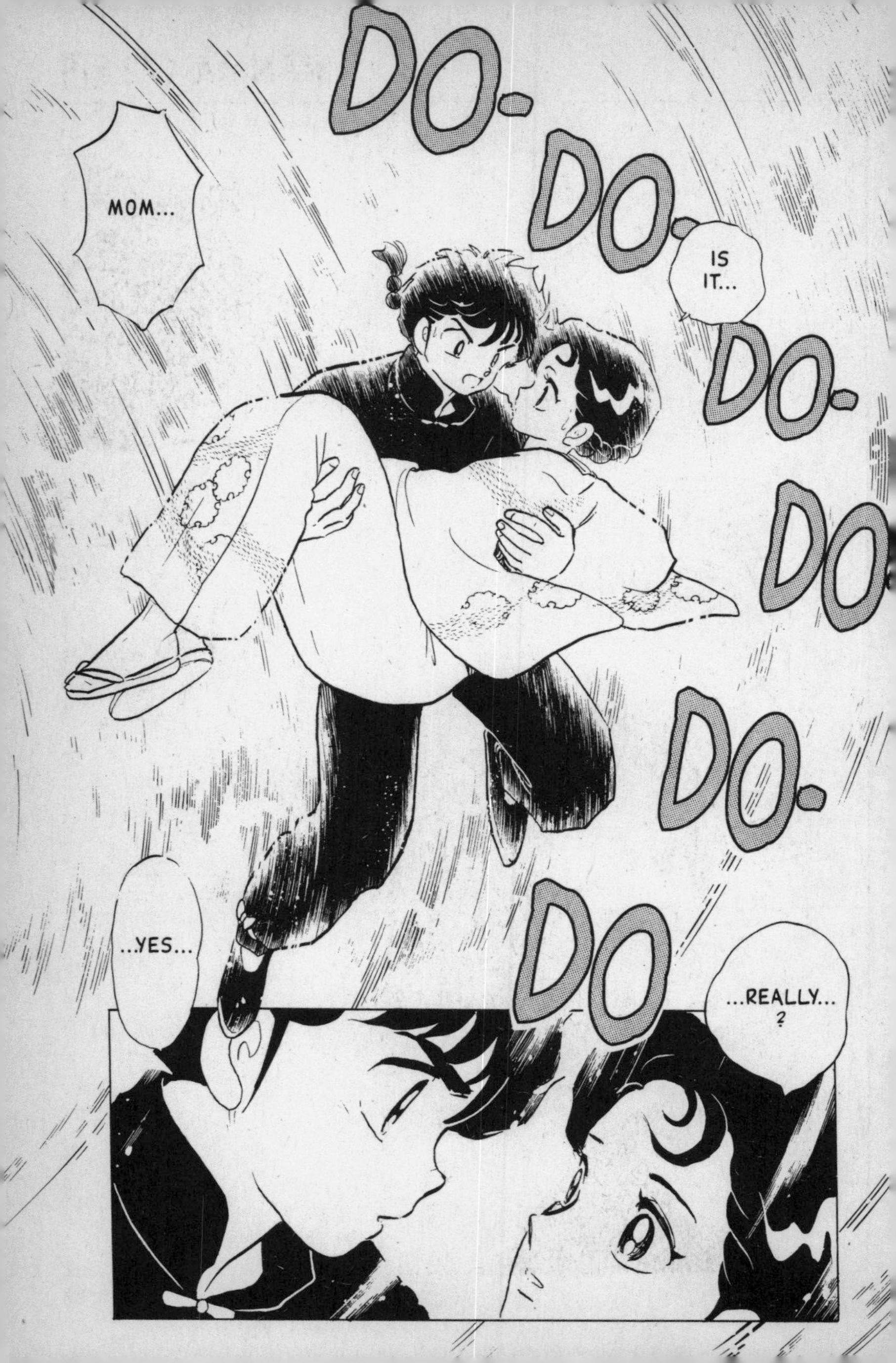
MOM...
DO-DO-DO-
IS IT...
DO-DO-DO-DO-
...YES...
DO
...REALLY...?

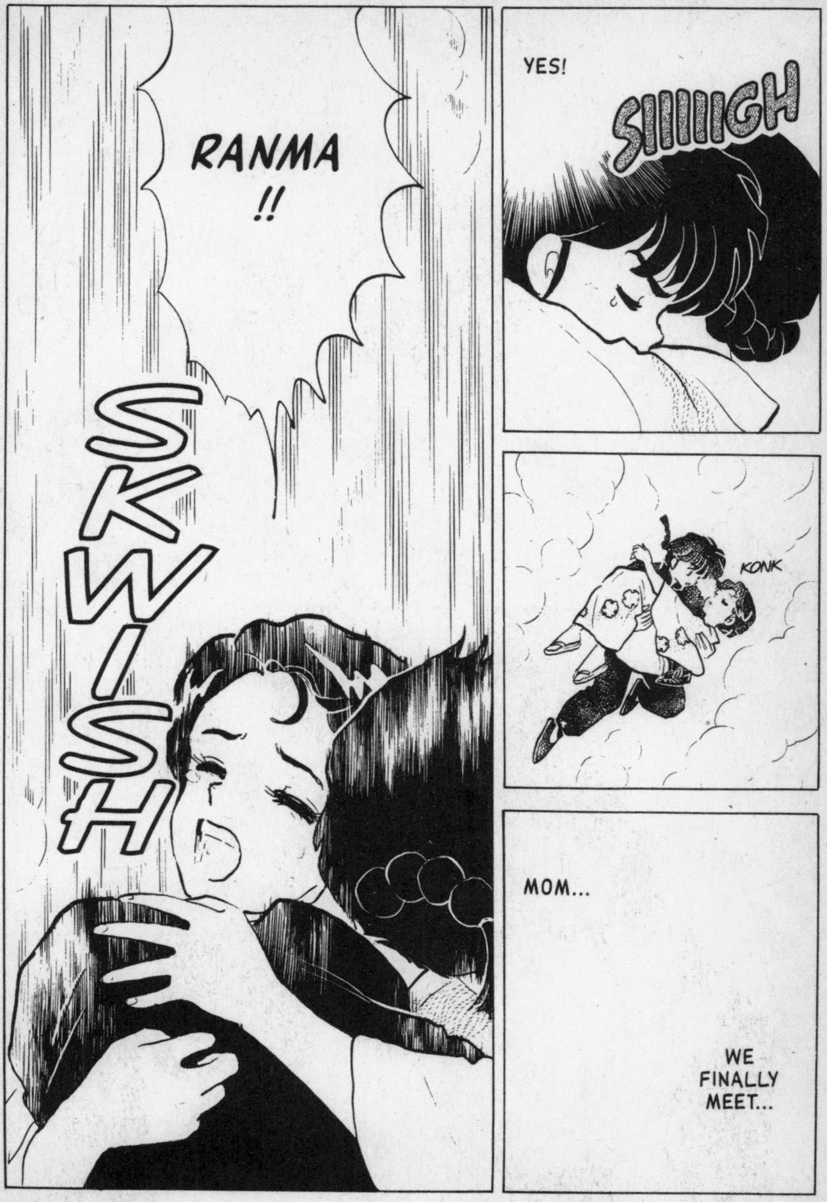
RANMA !!
SKWISH
YES!
SIIIIIGH
KONK
MOM...
WE FINALLY MEET...

NOW THAT SHE'S SEEN ME...

I WONDER IF SHE'S BE DISAPPOINTED...

KAW KAW
KAW KAW

HOW COULD SHE BE?

YOU WERE SO BRAVE AND MANLY...

YEAH

N....
N...

!

MOM...

RRRRRMMM

GASP

SSSHHHHH

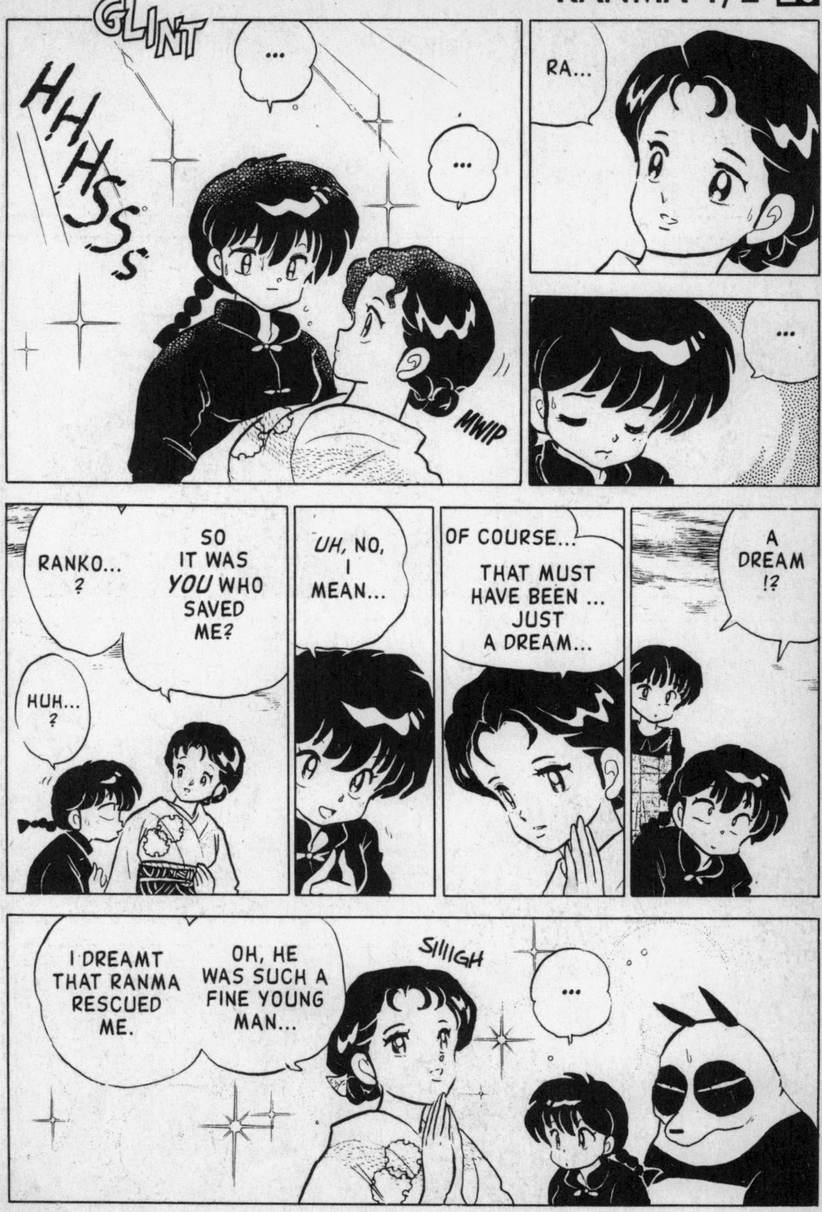
GLINT
HHHSSSS
...
...
MWIP
RA...
...
RANKO... ?
SO IT WAS *YOU* WHO SAVED ME?
HUH... ?
UH, NO, I MEAN...
OF COURSE...
THAT MUST HAVE BEEN ... JUST A DREAM...
A DREAM !?
I DREAMT THAT RANMA RESCUED ME.
OH, HE WAS SUCH A FINE YOUNG MAN...
SIIIIGH
...

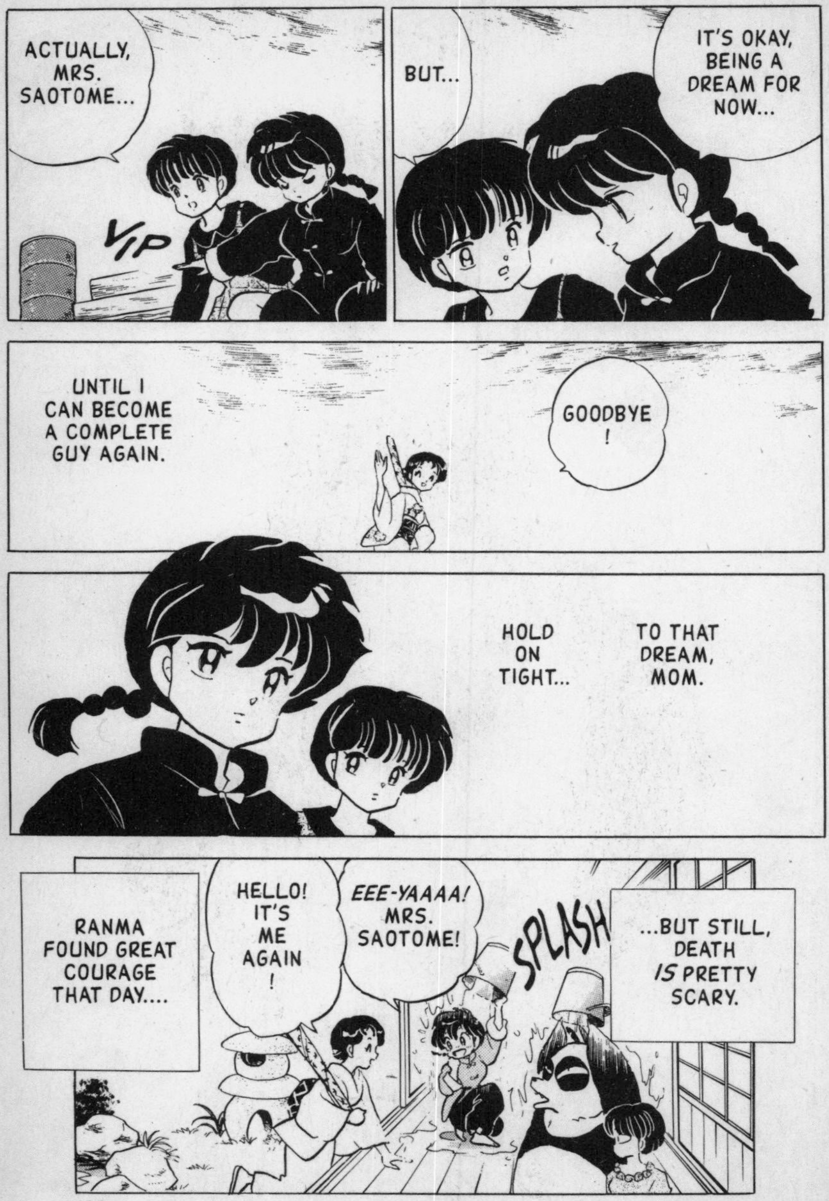
ACTUALLY, MRS. SAOTOME...
VIP
BUT...
IT'S OKAY, BEING A DREAM FOR NOW...
UNTIL I CAN BECOME A COMPLETE GUY AGAIN.
GOODBYE!
HOLD ON TIGHT...
TO THAT DREAM, MOM.
RANMA FOUND GREAT COURAGE THAT DAY....
HELLO! IT'S ME AGAIN!
EEE-YAAAA! MRS. SAOTOME!
SPLASH
...BUT STILL, DEATH *IS* PRETTY SCARY.

Part 7
SUDDEN HATE!!

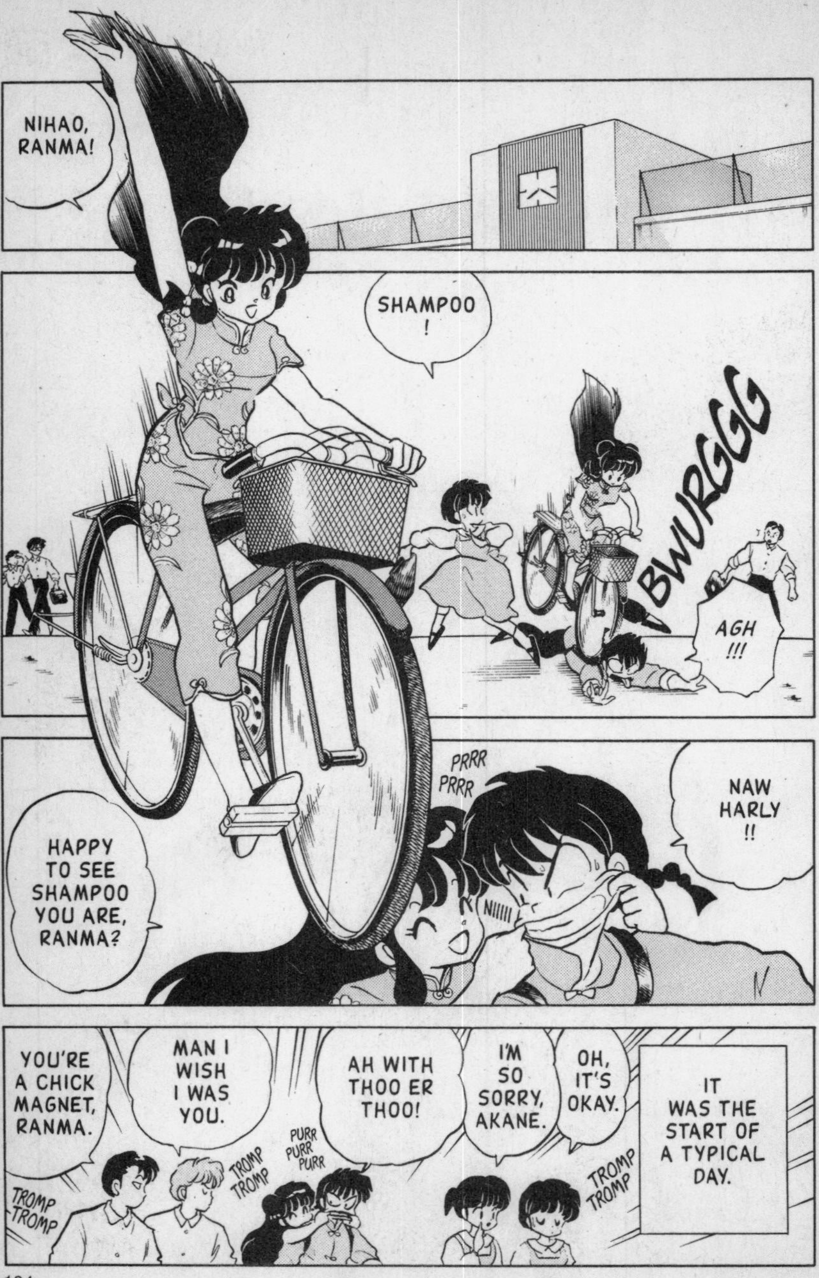
NIHAO, RANMA!
SHAMPOO !
BWURGGG
AGH !!!
PRRR PRRR
HAPPY TO SEE SHAMPOO YOU ARE, RANMA?
NIIIII
NAW HARLY !!
YOU'RE A CHICK MAGNET, RANMA.
MAN I WISH I WAS YOU.
TROMP TROMP
TROMP TROMP
PURR PURR PURR
AH WITH THOO ER THOO!
I'M SO SORRY, AKANE.
OH, IT'S OKAY.
TROMP TROMP
IT WAS THE START OF A TYPICAL DAY.

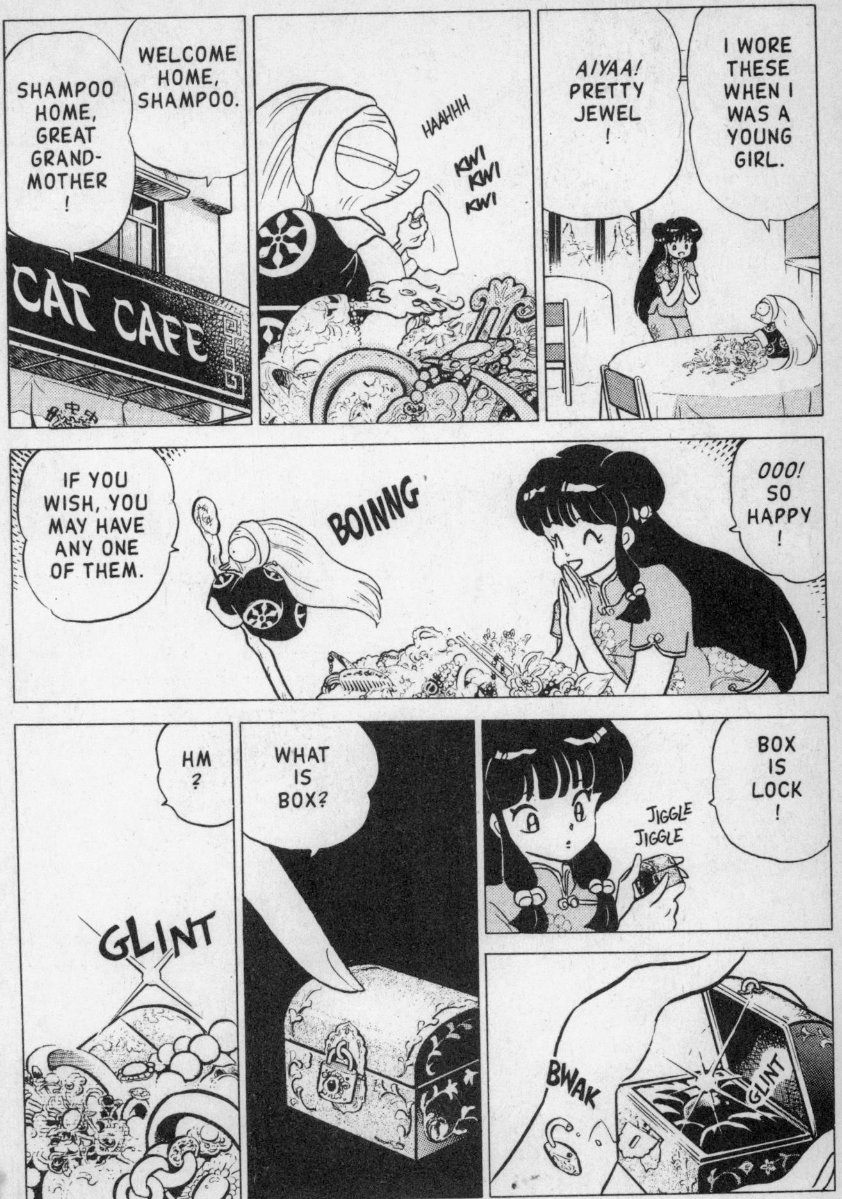
SHAMPOO HOME, GREAT GRAND-MOTHER !
WELCOME HOME, SHAMPOO.
CAT CAFE
HAAHHH
KWI KWI KWI
AIYAA! PRETTY JEWEL !
I WORE THESE WHEN I WAS A YOUNG GIRL.
IF YOU WISH, YOU MAY HAVE ANY ONE OF THEM.
BOINNG
OOO! SO HAPPY !
HM ?
GLINT
WHAT IS BOX?
JIGGLE JIGGLE
BOX IS LOCK !
BWAK
GLINT

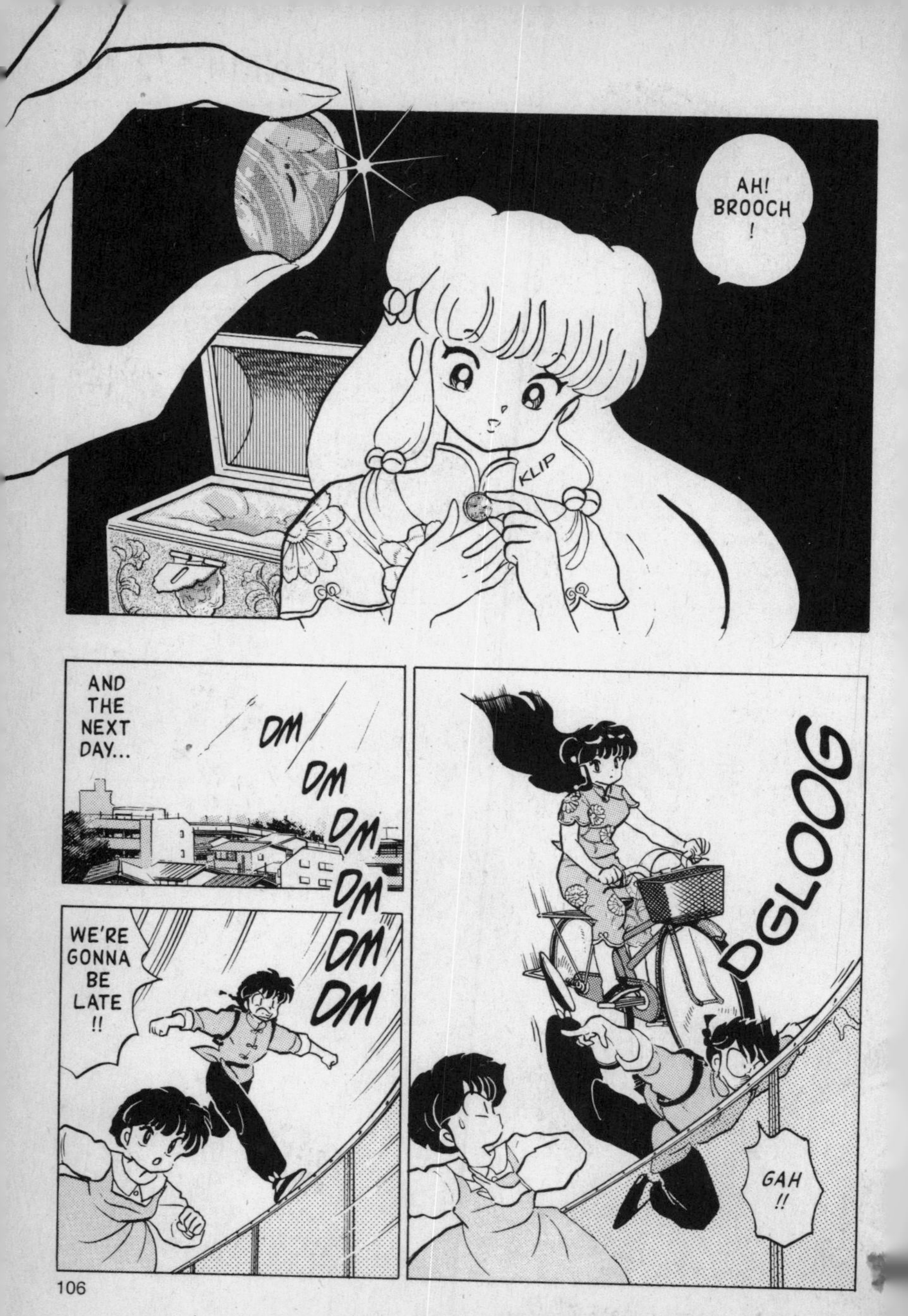
AH! BROOCH !
KLIP
AND THE NEXT DAY...
DM DM DM DM DM DM
DGLOOG
WE'RE GONNA BE LATE !!
GAH !!

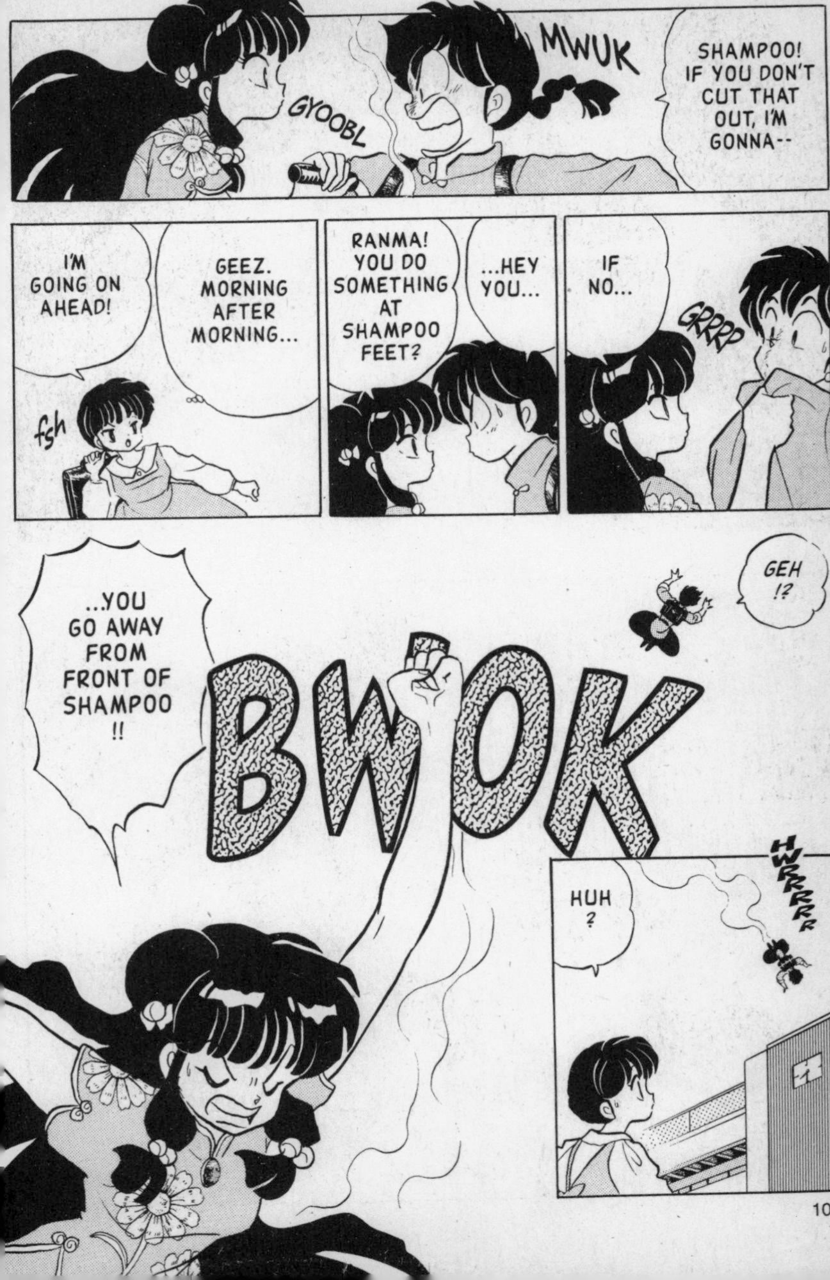
GYOOBL
MWUK
SHAMPOO! IF YOU DON'T CUT THAT OUT, I'M GONNA--
I'M GOING ON AHEAD!
GEEZ. MORNING AFTER MORNING...
fsh
RANMA! YOU DO SOMETHING AT SHAMPOO FEET?
...HEY YOU...
IF NO...
GRRRP
...YOU GO AWAY FROM FRONT OF SHAMPOO !!
BWOK
GEH !?
HUH ?
HWRRRRR

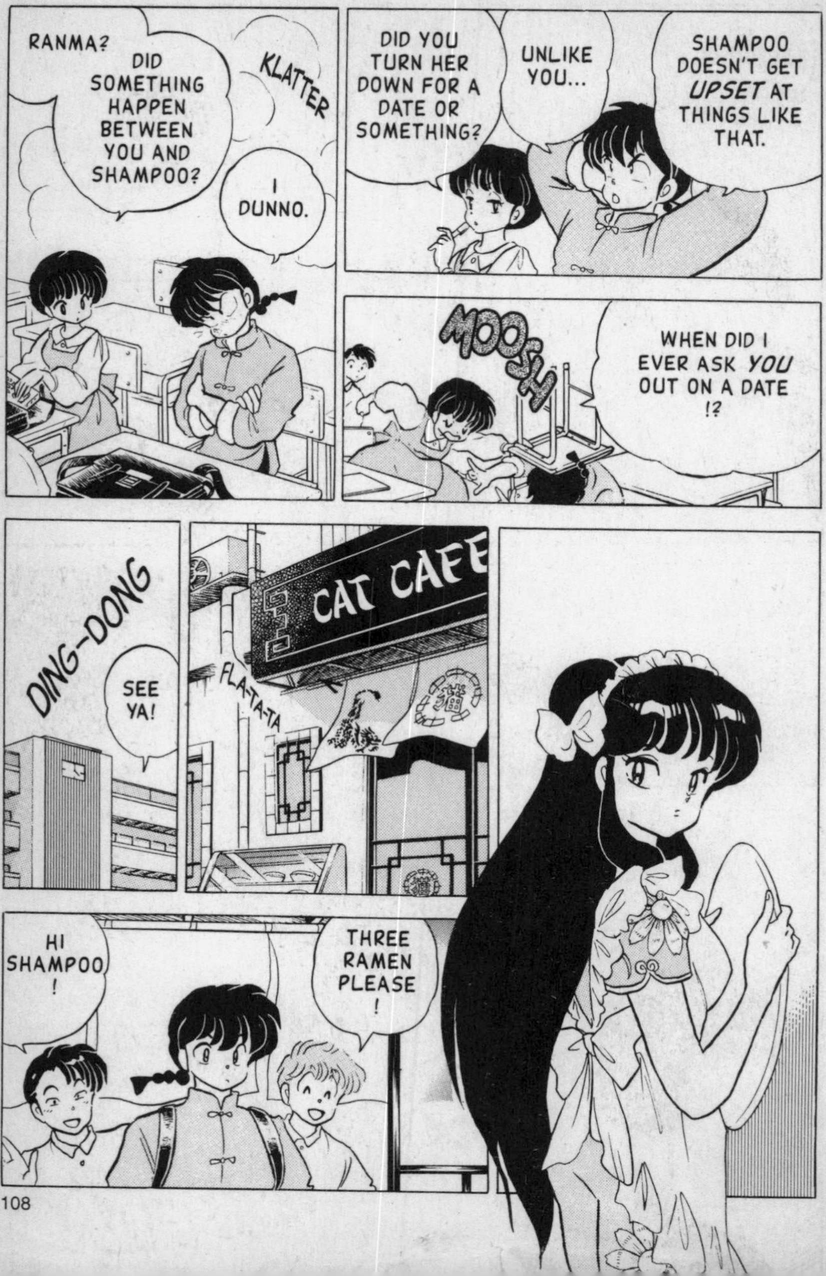
RANMA? DID SOMETHING HAPPEN BETWEEN YOU AND SHAMPOO?
KLATTER
I DUNNO.
DID YOU TURN HER DOWN FOR A DATE OR SOMETHING?
UNLIKE YOU...
SHAMPOO DOESN'T GET UPSET AT THINGS LIKE THAT.
MOOSH
WHEN DID I EVER ASK YOU OUT ON A DATE !?
DING-DONG
SEE YA!
CAT CAFE
FLA-TA-TA
HI SHAMPOO !
THREE RAMEN PLEASE !

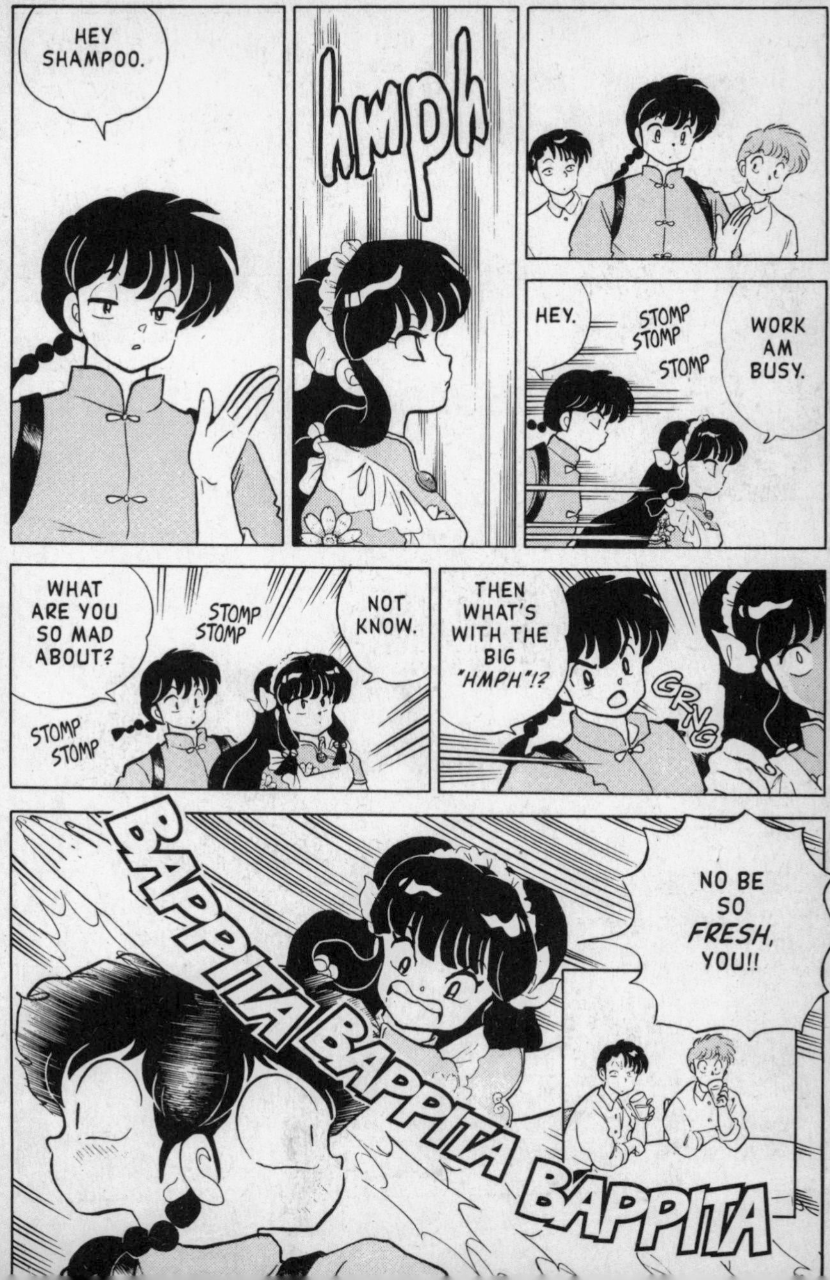
HEY SHAMPOO.
hmph
HEY.
STOMP STOMP
STOMP
WORK AM BUSY.
WHAT ARE YOU SO MAD ABOUT?
STOMP STOMP
STOMP STOMP
NOT KNOW.
THEN WHAT'S WITH THE BIG "HMPH"!?
GRNG
BAPPITA BAPPITA BAPPITA BAPPITA
NO BE SO *FRESH,* YOU!!

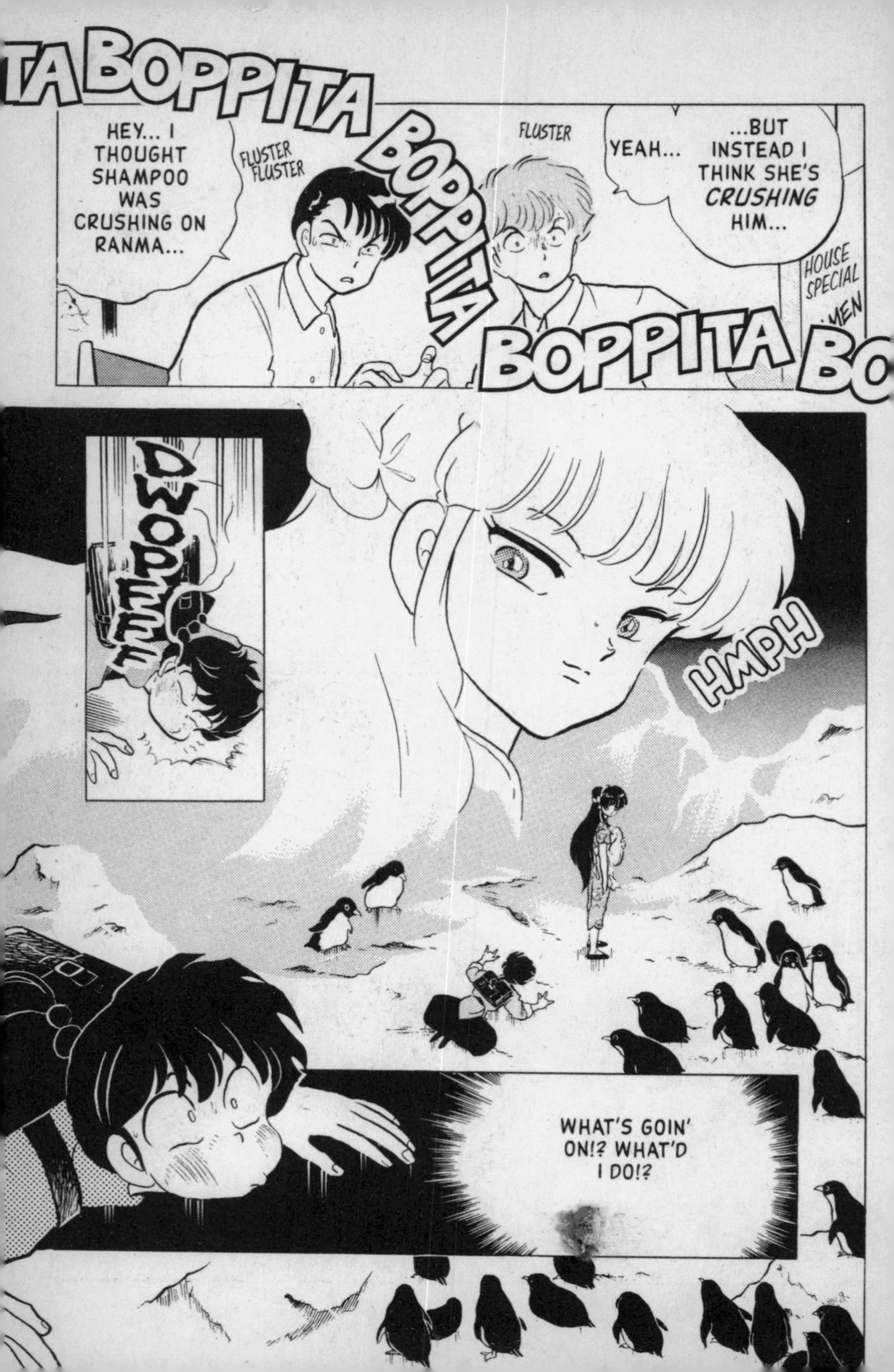
BOPPITA BOPPITA
...BUT INSTEAD I THINK SHE'S CRUSHING HIM...
YEAH...
FLUSTER
HOUSE SPECIAL
MEN
BOPPITA
FLUSTER FLUSTER
HEY... I THOUGHT SHAMPOO WAS CRUSHING ON RANMA...
BOPPITA BO
HMPH
DWOPEEE
WHAT'S GOIN' ON!? WHAT'D I DO!?

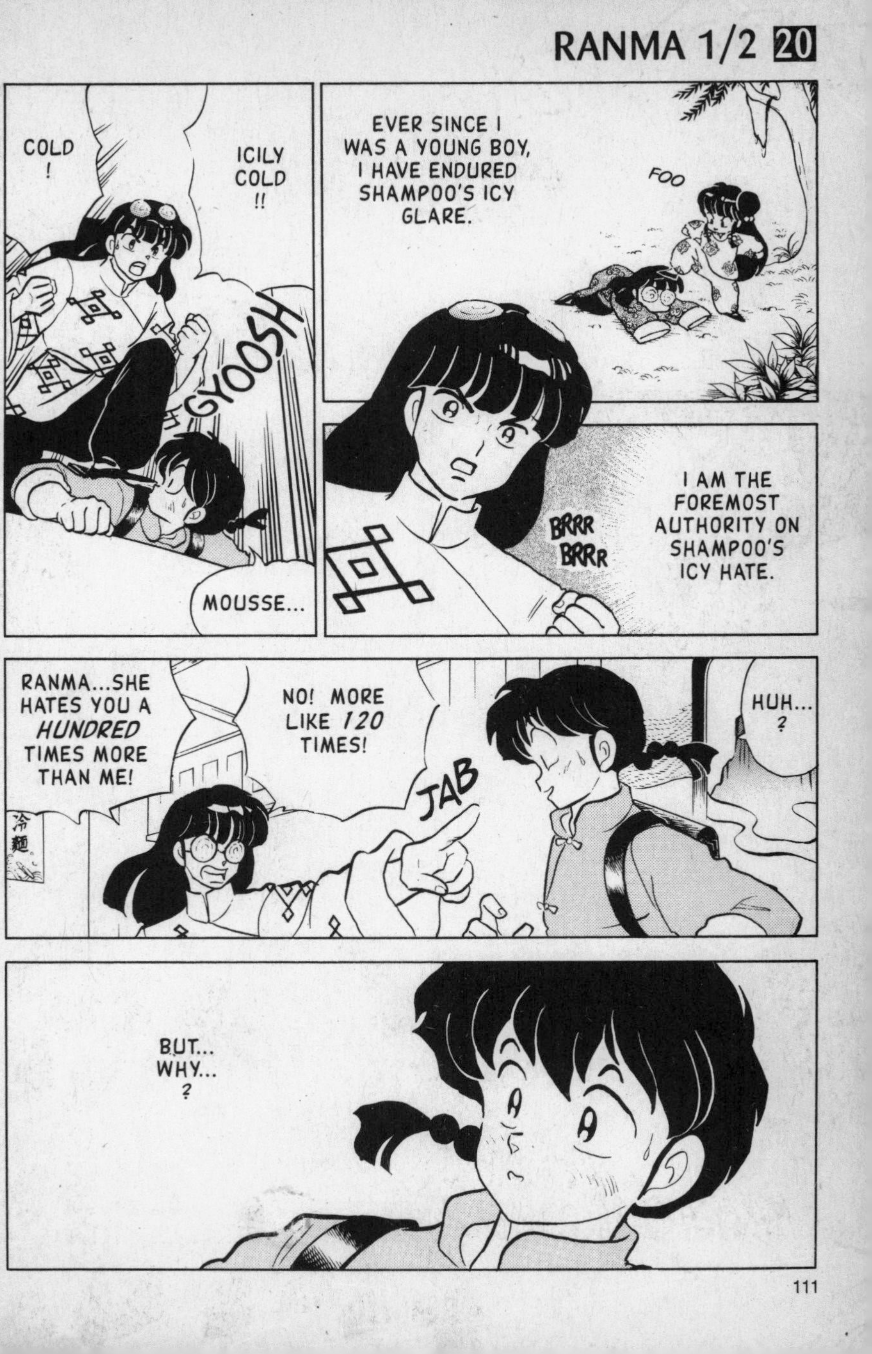
COLD !
ICILY COLD !!
GYOOSH
MOUSSE...
EVER SINCE I WAS A YOUNG BOY, I HAVE ENDURED SHAMPOO'S ICY GLARE.
FOO
BRRR BRRR
I AM THE FOREMOST AUTHORITY ON SHAMPOO'S ICY HATE.
RANMA...SHE HATES YOU A *HUNDRED* TIMES MORE THAN ME!
NO! MORE LIKE *120* TIMES!
JAB
HUH... ?
BUT... WHY... ?

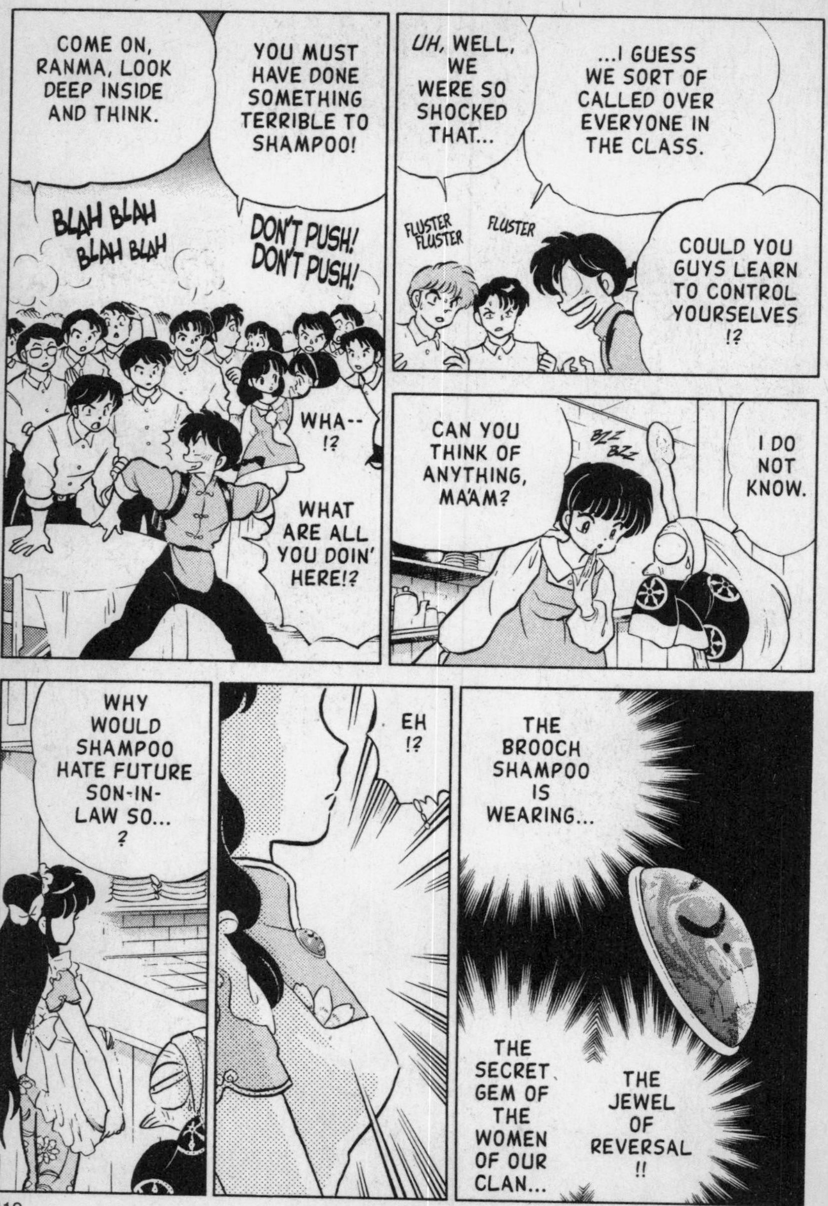
COME ON, RANMA, LOOK DEEP INSIDE AND THINK.
YOU MUST HAVE DONE SOMETHING TERRIBLE TO SHAMPOO!
BLAH BLAH BLAH BLAH
DON'T PUSH! DON'T PUSH!
WHA-- !?
WHAT ARE ALL YOU DOIN' HERE!?
UH, WELL, WE WERE SO SHOCKED THAT...
...I GUESS WE SORT OF CALLED OVER EVERYONE IN THE CLASS.
FLUSTER FLUSTER
FLUSTER
COULD YOU GUYS LEARN TO CONTROL YOURSELVES !?
CAN YOU THINK OF ANYTHING, MA'AM?
BZZ BZZ
I DO NOT KNOW.
WHY WOULD SHAMPOO HATE FUTURE SON-IN-LAW SO... ?
EH !?
THE BROOCH SHAMPOO IS WEARING...
THE SECRET GEM OF THE WOMEN OF OUR CLAN...
THE JEWEL OF REVERSAL !!

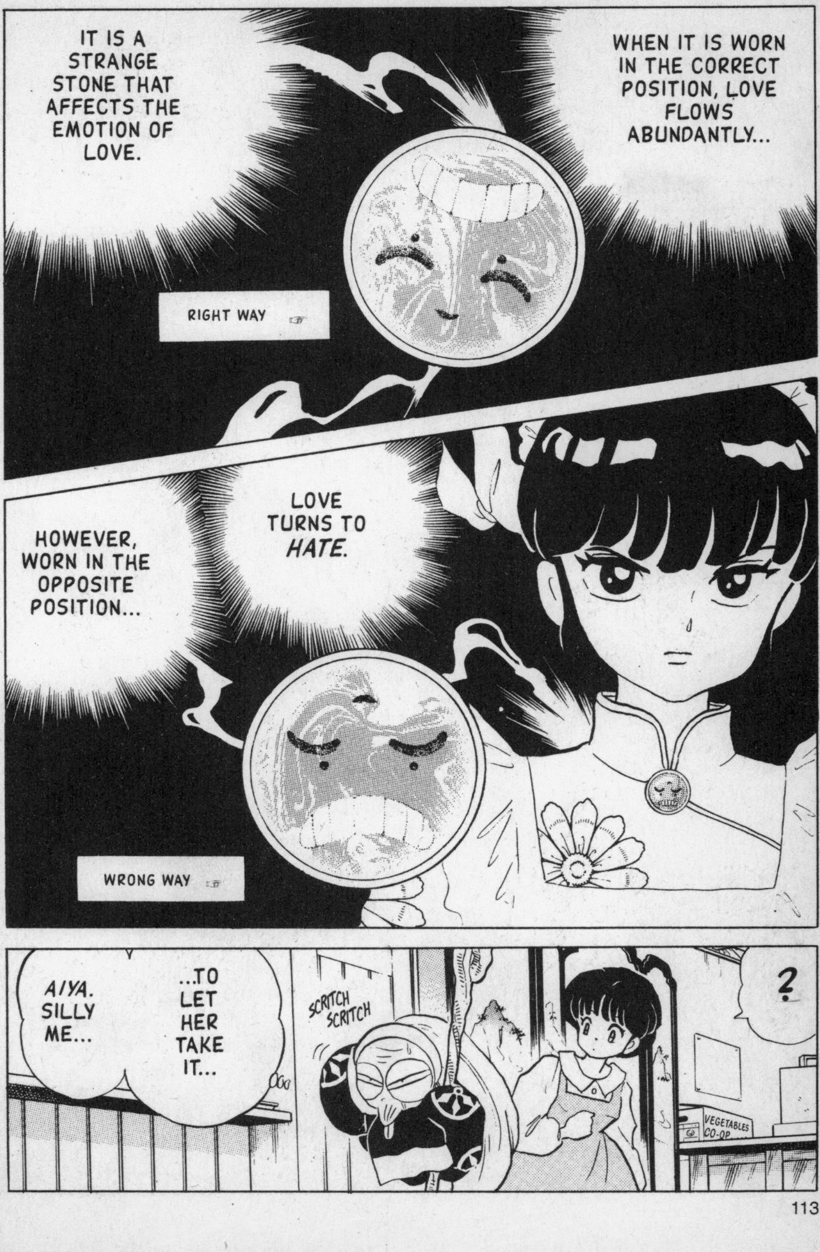
IT IS A STRANGE STONE THAT AFFECTS THE EMOTION OF LOVE.
WHEN IT IS WORN IN THE CORRECT POSITION, LOVE FLOWS ABUNDANTLY...
RIGHT WAY
HOWEVER, WORN IN THE OPPOSITE POSITION...
LOVE TURNS TO *HATE*.
WRONG WAY
AIYA. SILLY ME...
...TO LET HER TAKE IT...
SCRITCH SCRITCH
?
VEGETABLES CO-OP

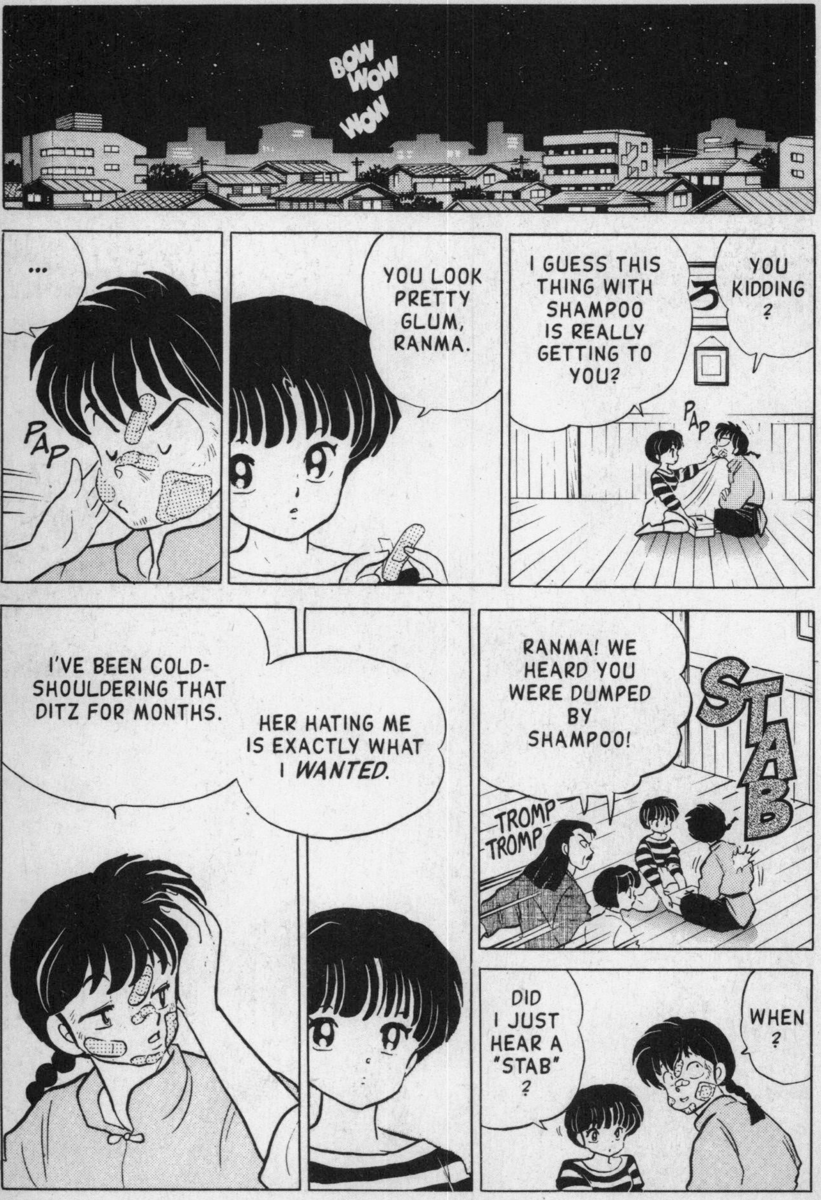
BOW WOW WOW
...
PAP
YOU LOOK PRETTY GLUM, RANMA.
I GUESS THIS THING WITH SHAMPOO IS REALLY GETTING TO YOU?
YOU KIDDING?
PAP
I'VE BEEN COLD-SHOULDERING THAT DITZ FOR MONTHS.
HER HATING ME IS EXACTLY WHAT I *WANTED*.
RANMA! WE HEARD YOU WERE DUMPED BY SHAMPOO!
STAB
TROMP TROMP
DID I JUST HEAR A "STAB"?
WHEN?

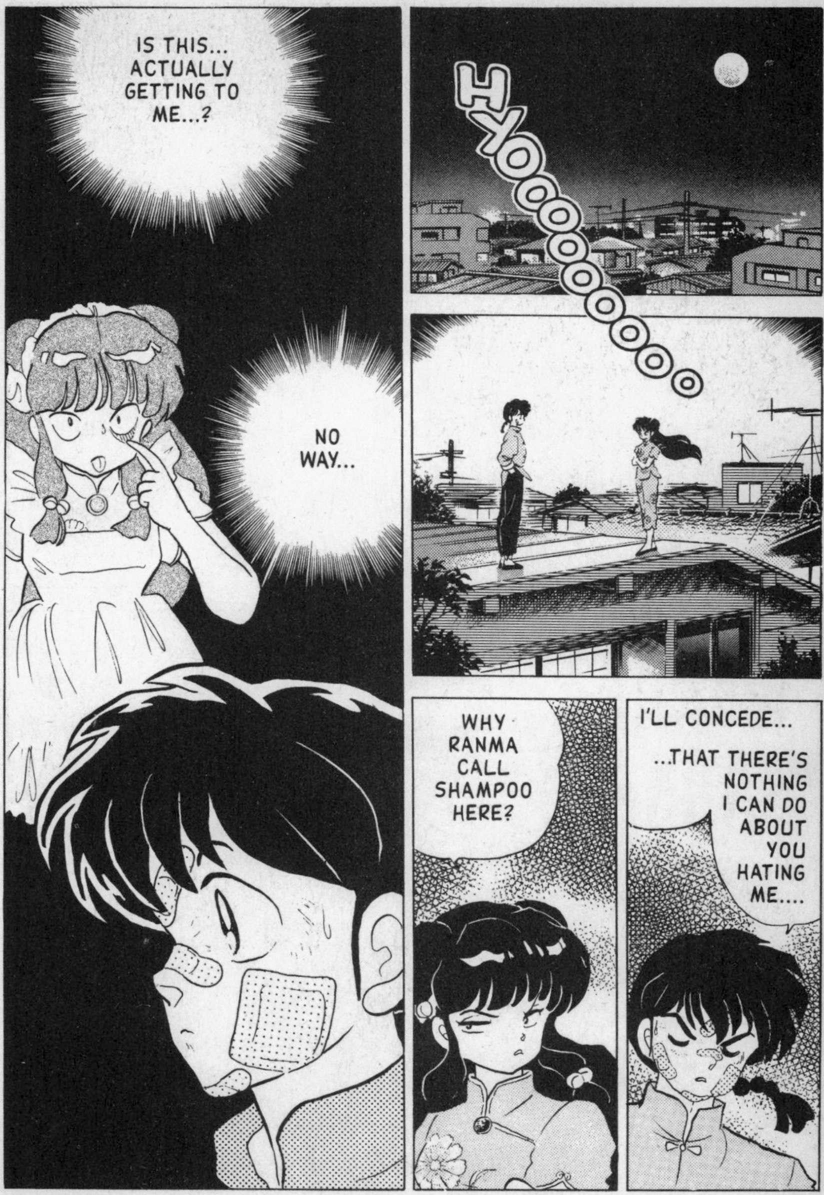
IS THIS... ACTUALLY GETTING TO ME...?
NO WAY...
HYOOOOOOOOOOO
WHY RANMA CALL SHAMPOO HERE?
I'LL CONCEDE...
...THAT THERE'S NOTHING I CAN DO ABOUT YOU HATING ME....

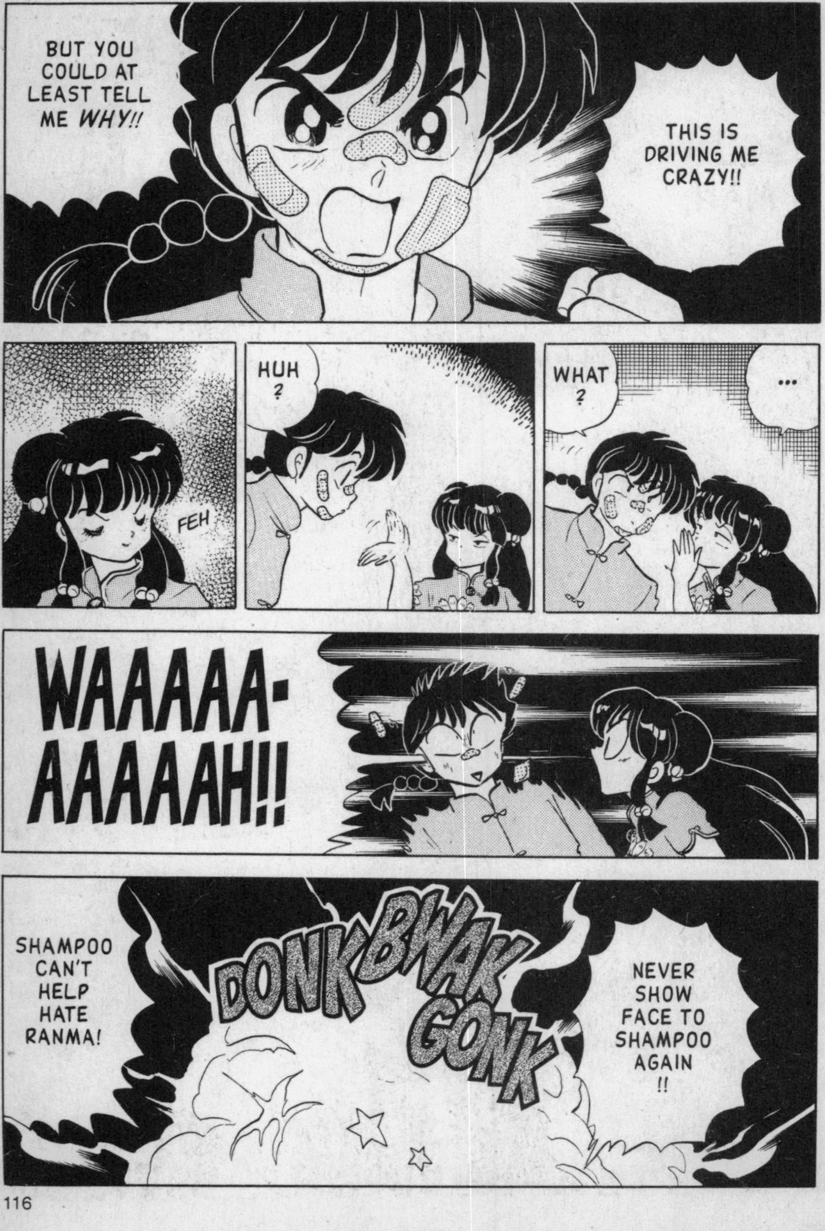
BUT YOU COULD AT LEAST TELL ME *WHY!!*
THIS IS DRIVING ME CRAZY!!
FEH
HUH?
WHAT?
...
WAAAAA-AAAAAH!!
SHAMPOO CAN'T HELP HATE RANMA!
DONK BWAK GONK
NEVER SHOW FACE TO SHAMPOO AGAIN!!

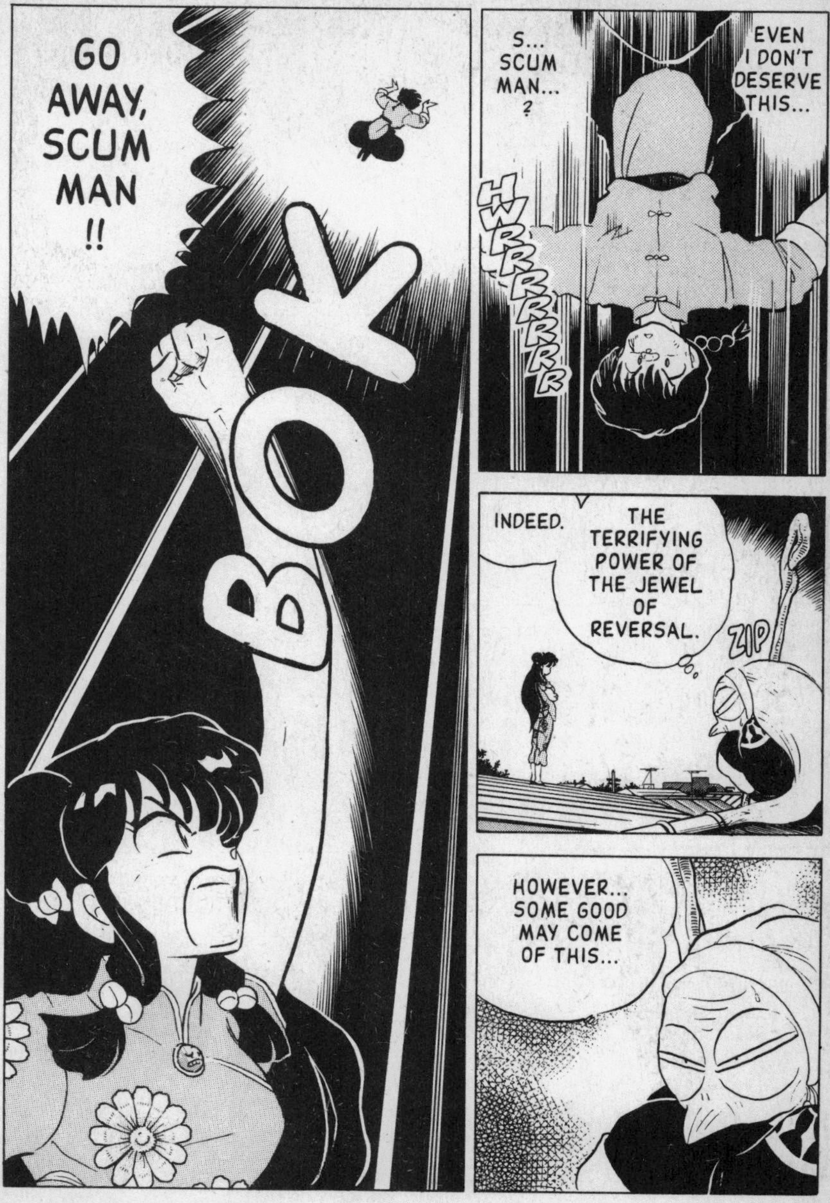
EVEN I DON'T DESERVE THIS...
S... SCUM MAN...?
HWRRRRRR
INDEED. THE TERRIFYING POWER OF THE JEWEL OF REVERSAL.
ZIP
HOWEVER... SOME GOOD MAY COME OF THIS...
GO AWAY, SCUM MAN!!
BOK

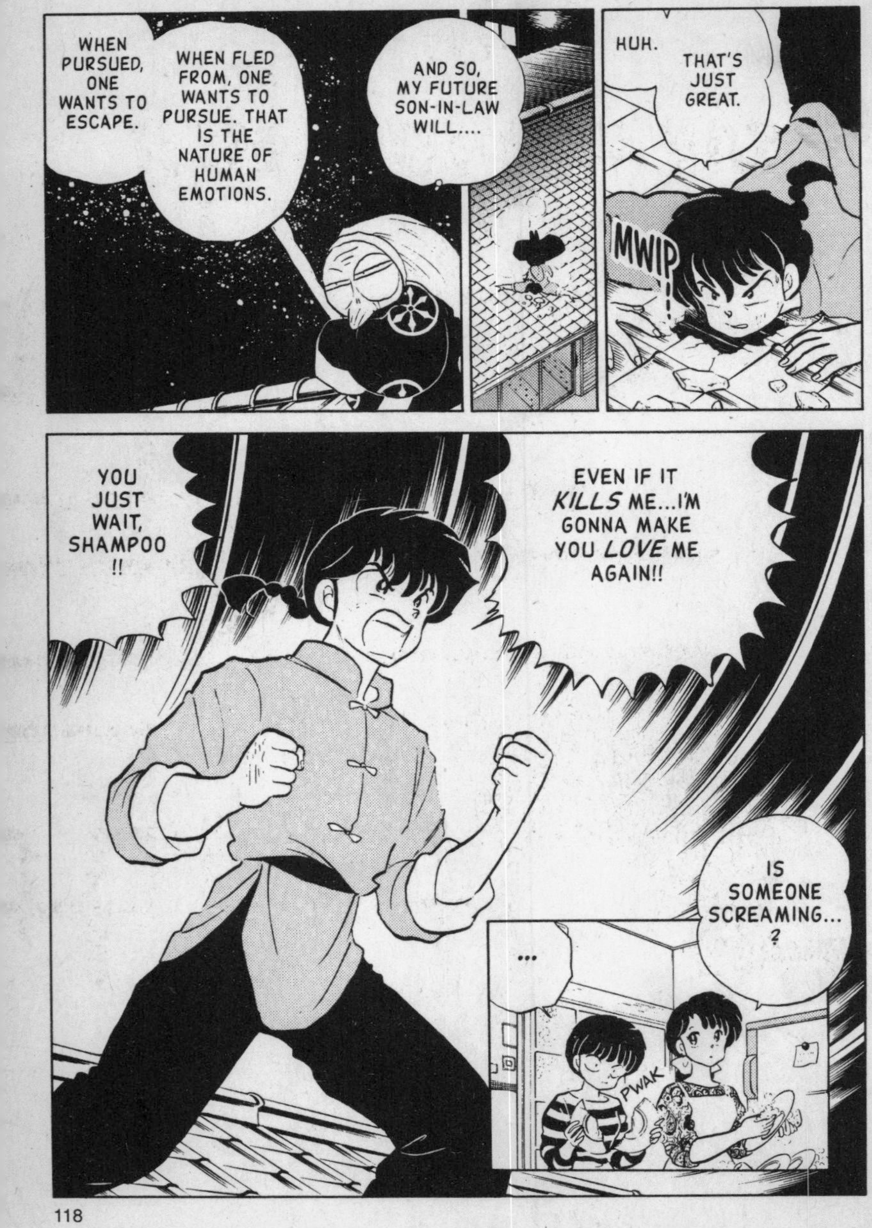
WHEN PURSUED, ONE WANTS TO ESCAPE.
WHEN FLED FROM, ONE WANTS TO PURSUE. THAT IS THE NATURE OF HUMAN EMOTIONS.
AND SO, MY FUTURE SON-IN-LAW WILL....
HUH.
THAT'S JUST GREAT.
MWIP
YOU JUST WAIT, SHAMPOO !!
EVEN IF IT *KILLS* ME...I'M GONNA MAKE YOU *LOVE* ME AGAIN!!
...
IS SOMEONE SCREAMING... ?
PWAK

Part 8

SAY YOU LOVE ME!!

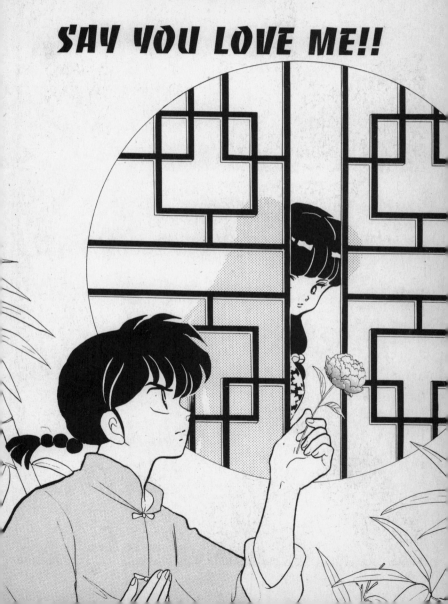

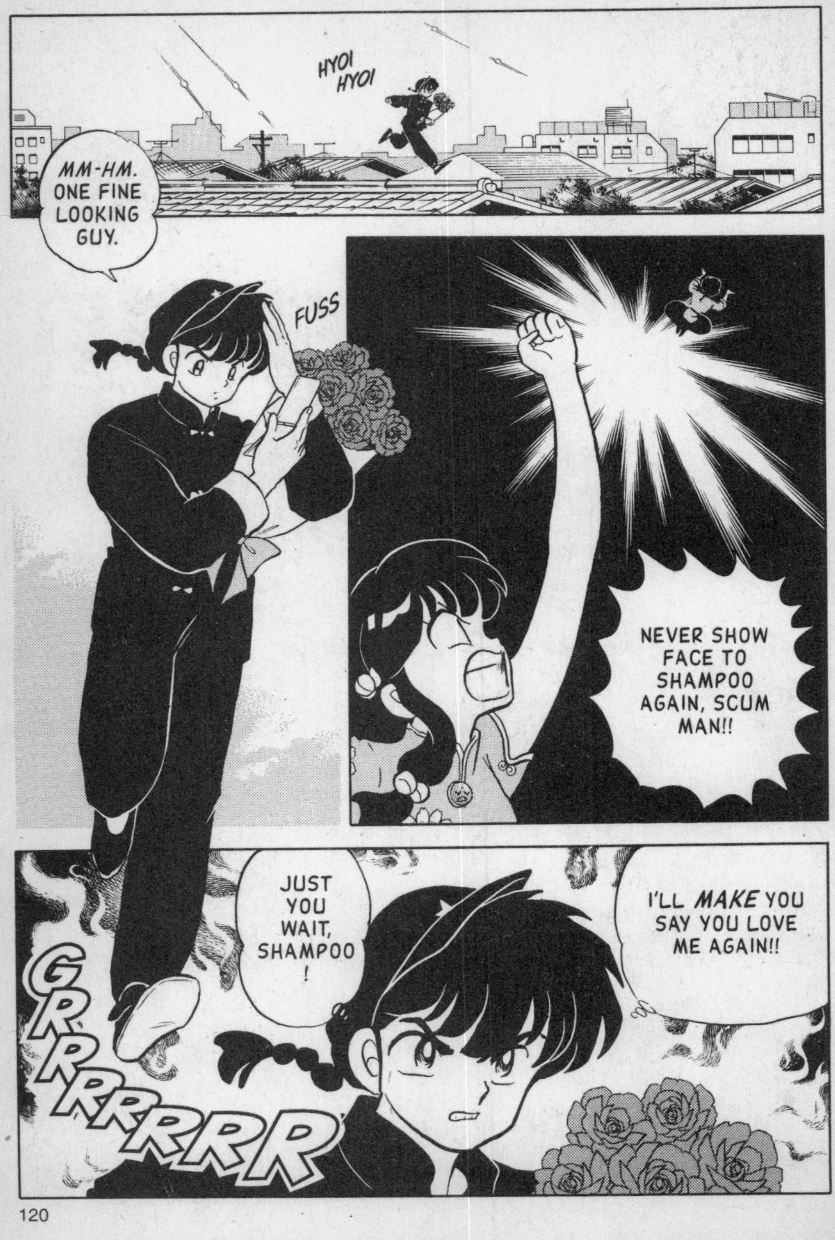
HYOI HYOI
MM-HM. ONE FINE LOOKING GUY.
FUSS
NEVER SHOW FACE TO SHAMPOO AGAIN, SCUM MAN!!
GRRRRRRR
JUST YOU WAIT, SHAMPOO!
I'LL *MAKE* YOU SAY YOU LOVE ME AGAIN!!

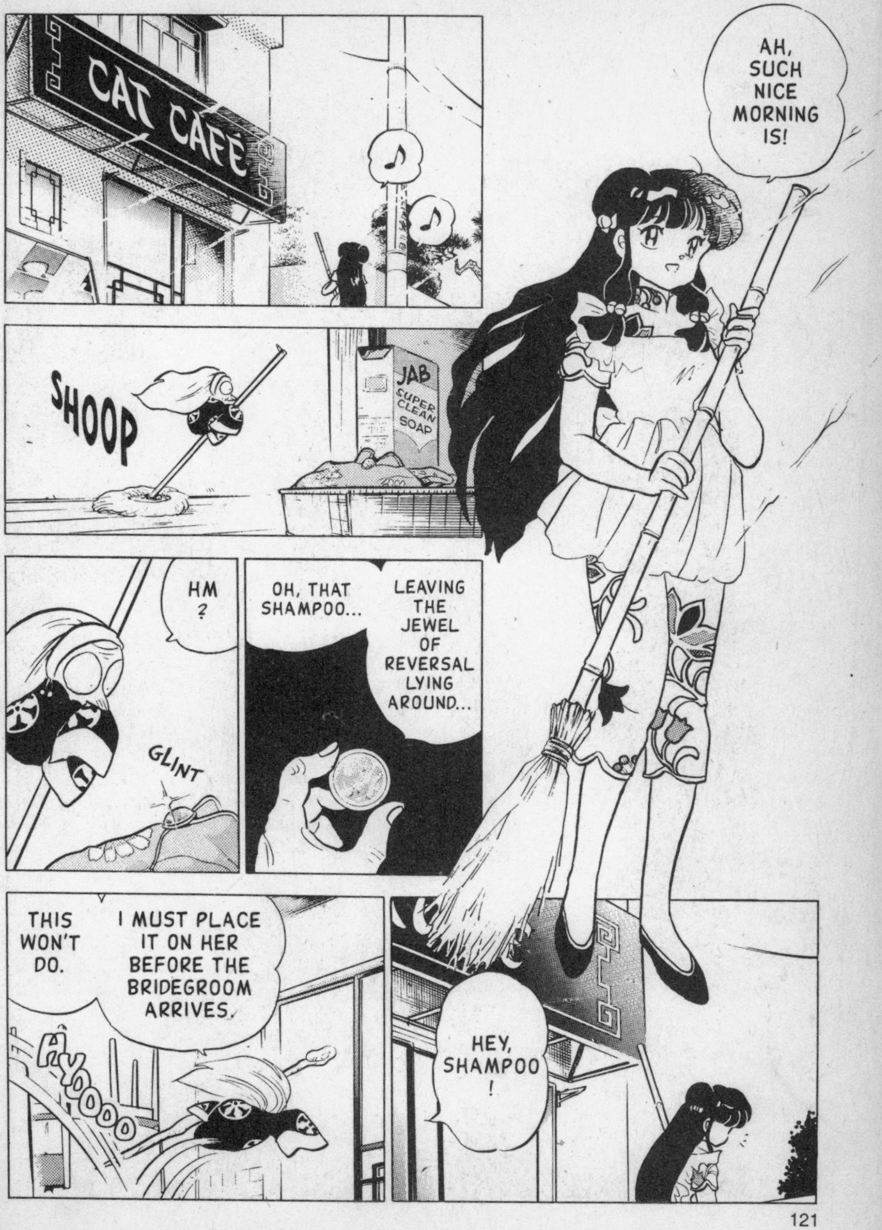
CAT CAFÉ
♪
♪
AH, SUCH NICE MORNING IS!
SHOOP
JAB SUPER CLEAN SOAP
HM ?
GLINT
OH, THAT SHAMPOO...
LEAVING THE JEWEL OF REVERSAL LYING AROUND...
THIS WON'T DO.
I MUST PLACE IT ON HER BEFORE THE BRIDEGROOM ARRIVES.
HYOOOO
HEY, SHAMPOO !

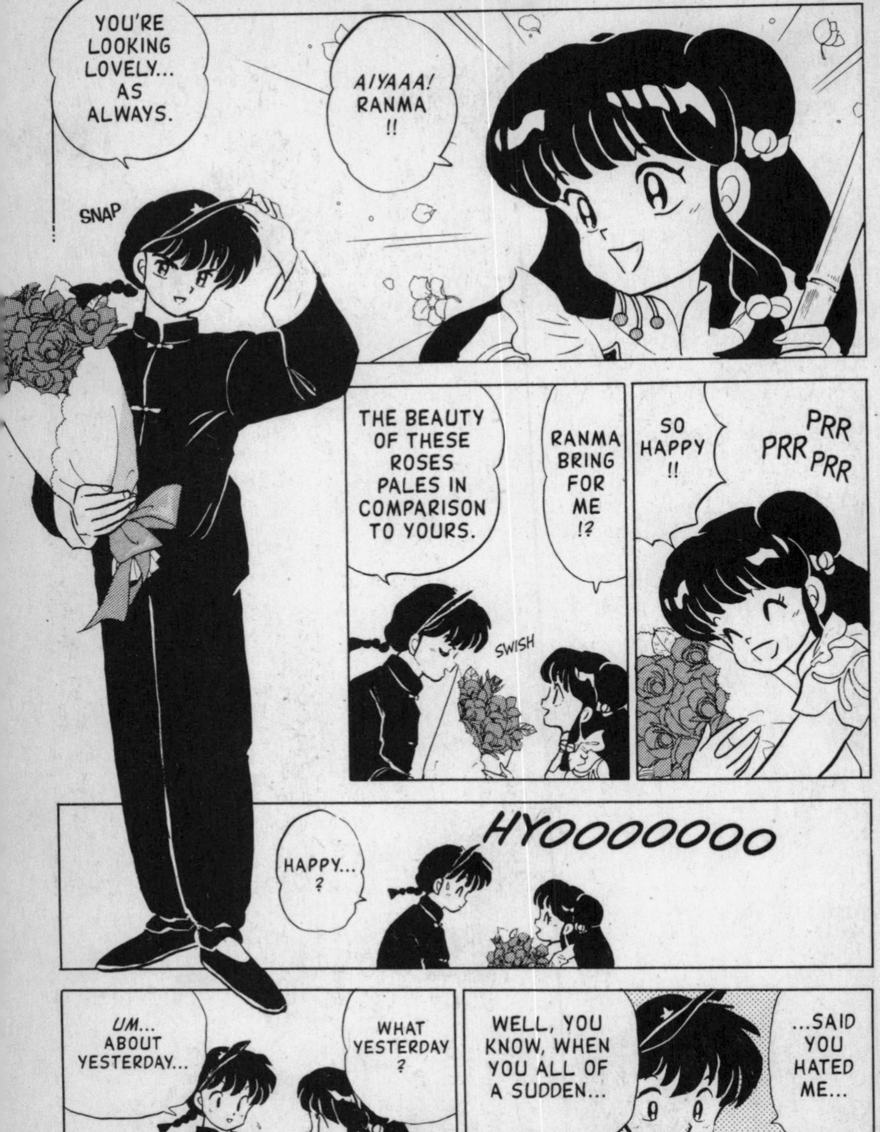

YOU'RE LOOKING LOVELY... AS ALWAYS.
SNAP
AIYAAA! RANMA !!
THE BEAUTY OF THESE ROSES PALES IN COMPARISON TO YOURS.
RANMA BRING FOR ME !?
SWISH
SO HAPPY !!
PRR PRR PRR
HAPPY... ?
HYOOOOOOO
UM... ABOUT YESTERDAY...
WHAT YESTERDAY ?
WELL, YOU KNOW, WHEN YOU ALL OF A SUDDEN...
...SAID YOU HATED ME...

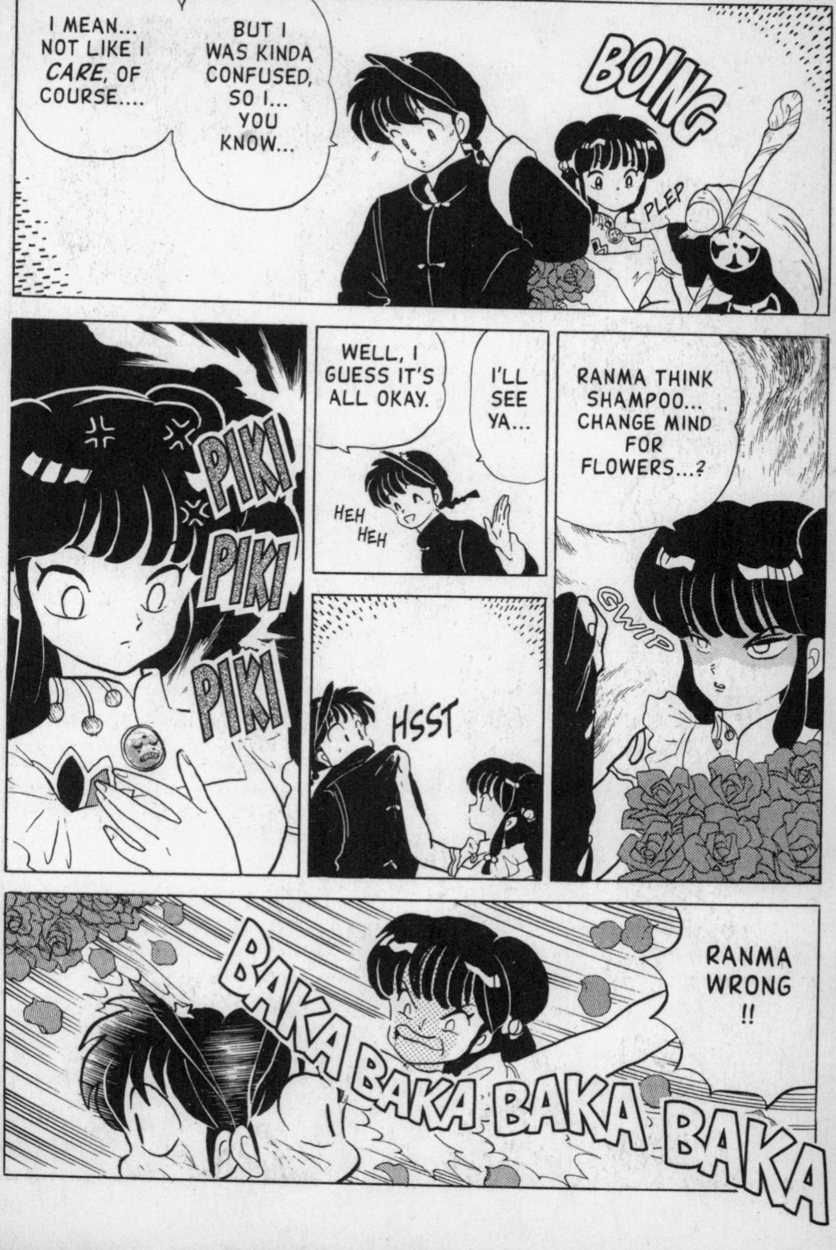
I MEAN... NOT LIKE I *CARE*, OF COURSE....
BUT I WAS KINDA CONFUSED, SO I... YOU KNOW...
BOING
PLEP
PIKI
PIKI
PIKI
WELL, I GUESS IT'S ALL OKAY.
I'LL SEE YA...
HEH HEH
HSST
RANMA THINK SHAMPOO... CHANGE MIND FOR FLOWERS...?
GWIP
BAKA BAKA BAKA BAKA BAKA
RANMA WRONG !!

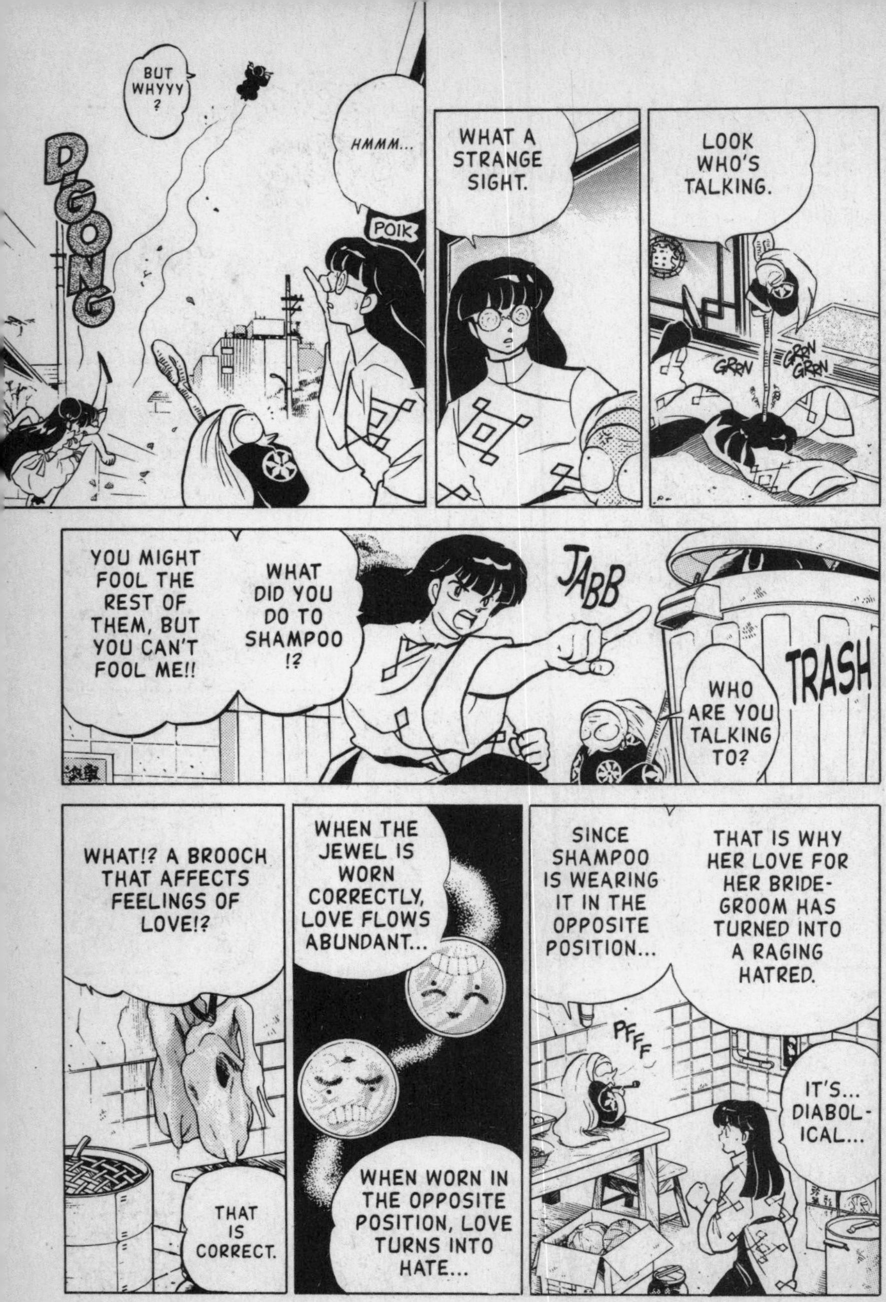

DGONG
BUT WHYYY?
HMMM...
POIK
WHAT A STRANGE SIGHT.
LOOK WHO'S TALKING.
GRRN
GRRN GRRN
YOU MIGHT FOOL THE REST OF THEM, BUT YOU CAN'T FOOL ME!!
WHAT DID YOU DO TO SHAMPOO!?
JABB
WHO ARE YOU TALKING TO?
TRASH
WHAT!? A BROOCH THAT AFFECTS FEELINGS OF LOVE!?
THAT IS CORRECT.
WHEN THE JEWEL IS WORN CORRECTLY, LOVE FLOWS ABUNDANT...
WHEN WORN IN THE OPPOSITE POSITION, LOVE TURNS INTO HATE...
SINCE SHAMPOO IS WEARING IT IN THE OPPOSITE POSITION...
THAT IS WHY HER LOVE FOR HER BRIDE-GROOM HAS TURNED INTO A RAGING HATRED.
PFFF
IT'S... DIABOL-ICAL...

BUT THAT MEANS... THAT THE SHAMPOO WHO IS USUALLY ICE COLD TO ME WOULD NOW ...

SHAMPOO!!

TREMBLE TREMBLE

WAK WAK

BOPP

I'M HAPPY FOR YOU, MOUSSE.

LOOKS LIKE SHE DIDN'T HATE YOU SO MUCH AFTER ALL.

SPLASH

QUAK

CLANNNG

QUAK QUAK QUAK

I NEED TO KEEP THE TRUTH OF THE JEWEL SECRET.

QUAK QUAK

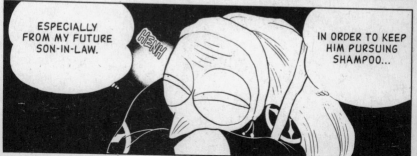

ESPECIALLY FROM MY FUTURE SON-IN-LAW.

HENH

IN ORDER TO KEEP HIM PURSUING SHAMPOO...

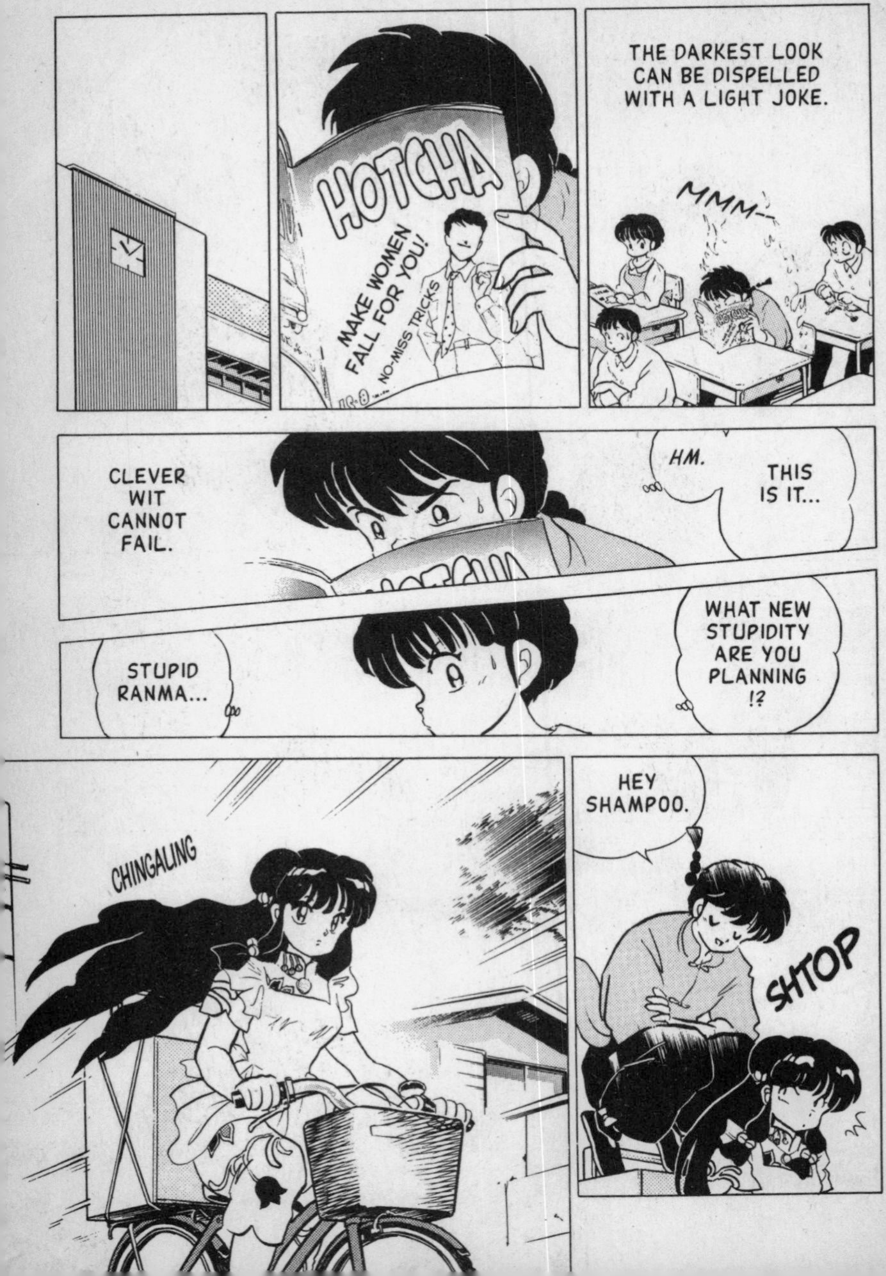
HOTCHA
MAKE WOMEN FALL FOR YOU!
NO-MISS TRICKS
THE DARKEST LOOK CAN BE DISPELLED WITH A LIGHT JOKE.
MMM--
CLEVER WIT CANNOT FAIL.
HM.
THIS IS IT...
STUPID RANMA...
WHAT NEW STUPIDITY ARE YOU PLANNING !?
CHINGALING
HEY SHAMPOO.
SHTOP

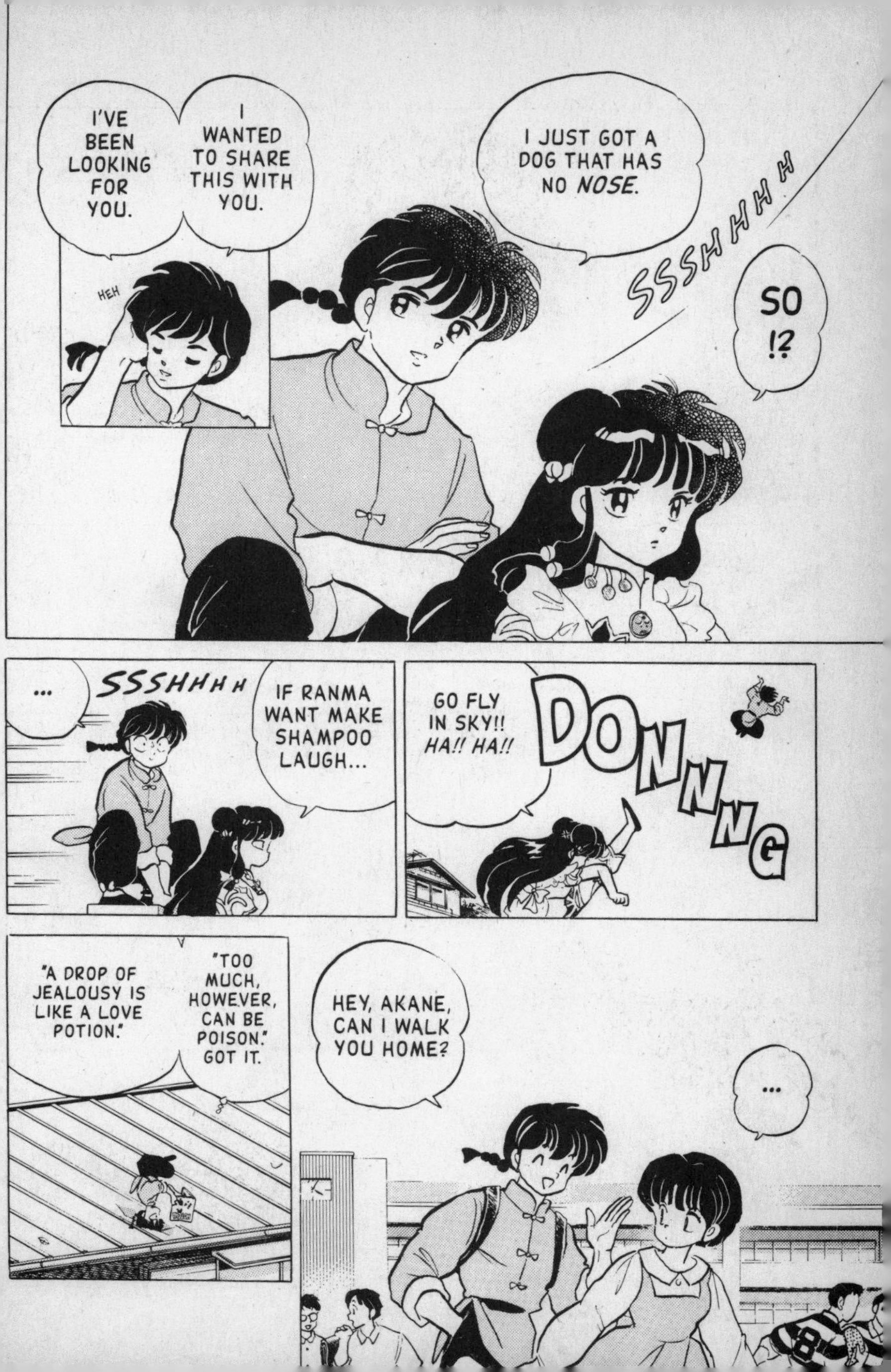
I'VE BEEN LOOKING FOR YOU.
I WANTED TO SHARE THIS WITH YOU.
HEH
I JUST GOT A DOG THAT HAS NO *NOSE*.
SSSHHHH
SO !?
...
SSSHHHH
IF RANMA WANT MAKE SHAMPOO LAUGH...
GO FLY IN SKY!! *HA!! HA!!*
DONNNNG
"A DROP OF JEALOUSY IS LIKE A LOVE POTION."
"TOO MUCH, HOWEVER, CAN BE POISON." GOT IT.
HEY, AKANE, CAN I WALK YOU HOME?
...

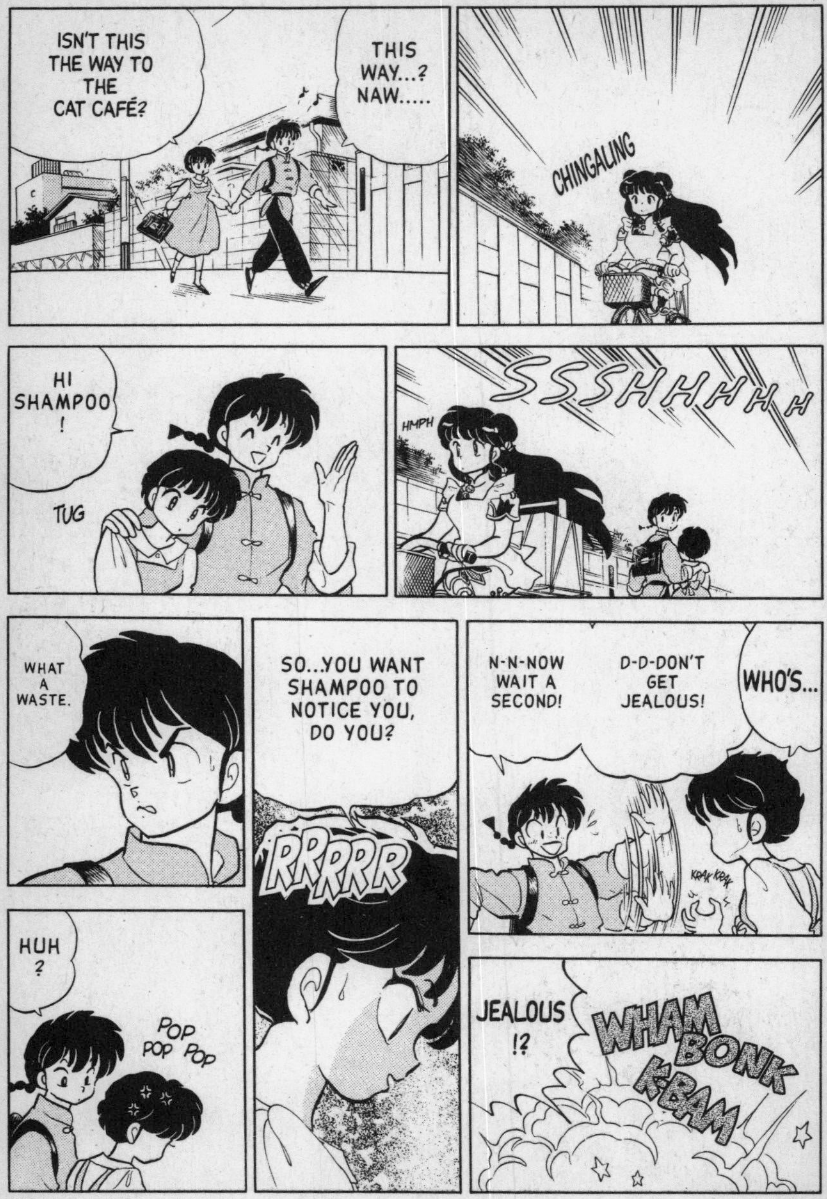
ISN'T THIS THE WAY TO THE CAT CAFÉ?
THIS WAY...? NAW.....
CHINGALING
HI SHAMPOO!
TUG
SSSHHHHHH
HMPH
WHAT A WASTE.
HUH?
POP POP POP
SO...YOU WANT SHAMPOO TO NOTICE YOU, DO YOU?
RRRRR
N-N-NOW WAIT A SECOND!
D-D-DON'T GET JEALOUS!
WHO'S...
KRAK KRAK
JEALOUS!?
WHAM BONK K-BAM

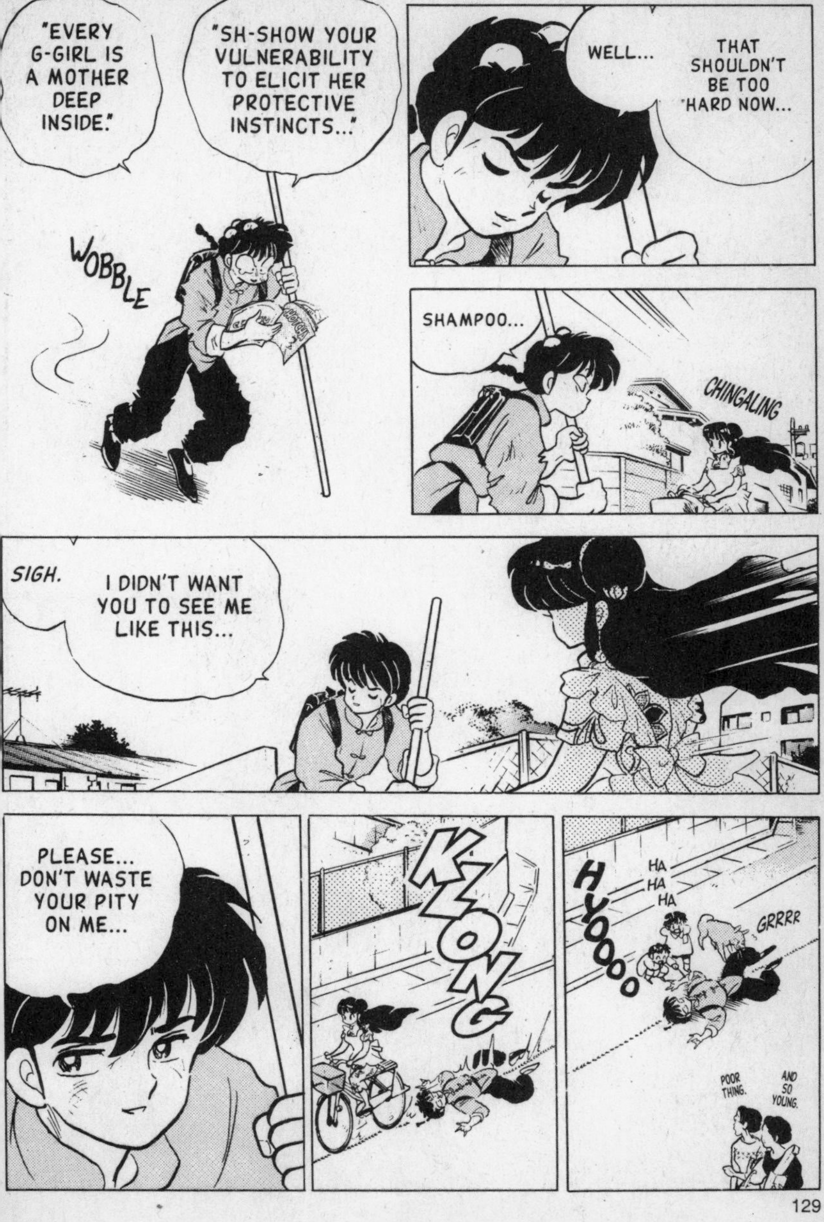
"EVERY G-GIRL IS A MOTHER DEEP INSIDE."
"SH-SHOW YOUR VULNERABILITY TO ELICIT HER PROTECTIVE INSTINCTS..."
WOBBLE
WELL...
THAT SHOULDN'T BE TOO HARD NOW...
SHAMPOO...
CHINGALING
SIGH.
I DIDN'T WANT YOU TO SEE ME LIKE THIS...
PLEASE... DON'T WASTE YOUR PITY ON ME...
KLONG
HYOOOOO
HA HA HA
GRRRR
POOR THING.
AND SO YOUNG.

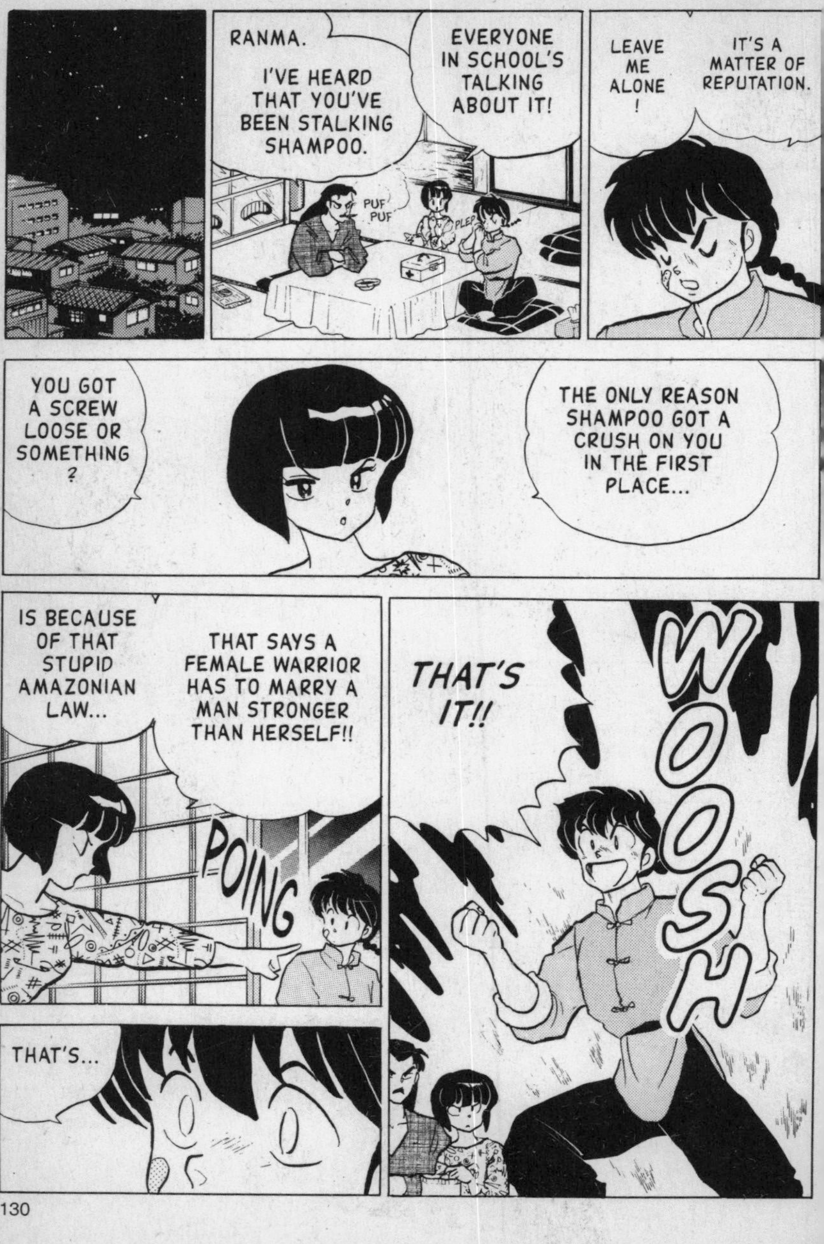
RANMA.
I'VE HEARD THAT YOU'VE BEEN STALKING SHAMPOO.
EVERYONE IN SCHOOL'S TALKING ABOUT IT!
PUF PUF
PLEP
LEAVE ME ALONE!
IT'S A MATTER OF REPUTATION.
YOU GOT A SCREW LOOSE OR SOMETHING?
THE ONLY REASON SHAMPOO GOT A CRUSH ON YOU IN THE FIRST PLACE...
IS BECAUSE OF THAT STUPID AMAZONIAN LAW...
THAT SAYS A FEMALE WARRIOR HAS TO MARRY A MAN STRONGER THAN HERSELF!!
POING
THAT'S...
THAT'S IT!!
WOOOSH

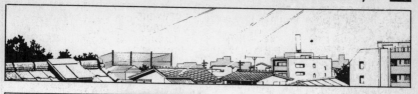

AGAIN YOU.

HEH HEH HEH.

THE LAWS OF YOUR VILLAGE ARE ABSOLUTE, YES?

!

I CHALLENGE YOU TO BATTLE, SHAMPOO!!

MAN WHO NO LEARN NO IS ANSWER....

KRAK

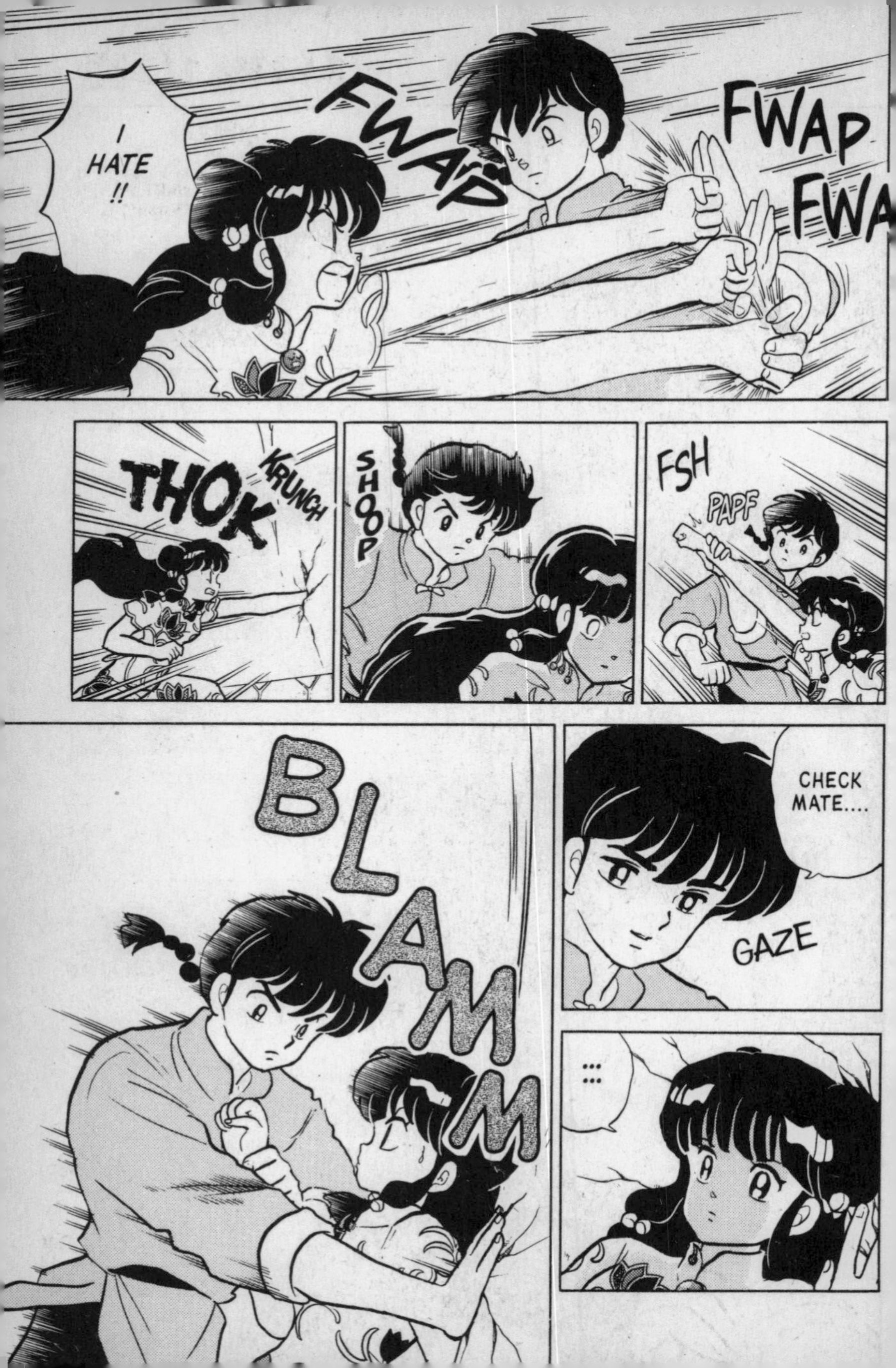

I HATE !!
FWAP
FWAP
FWA
THOK
KRUNCH
SHOOP
FSH
PAPF
BLAMM
CHECK MATE....
GAZE
...

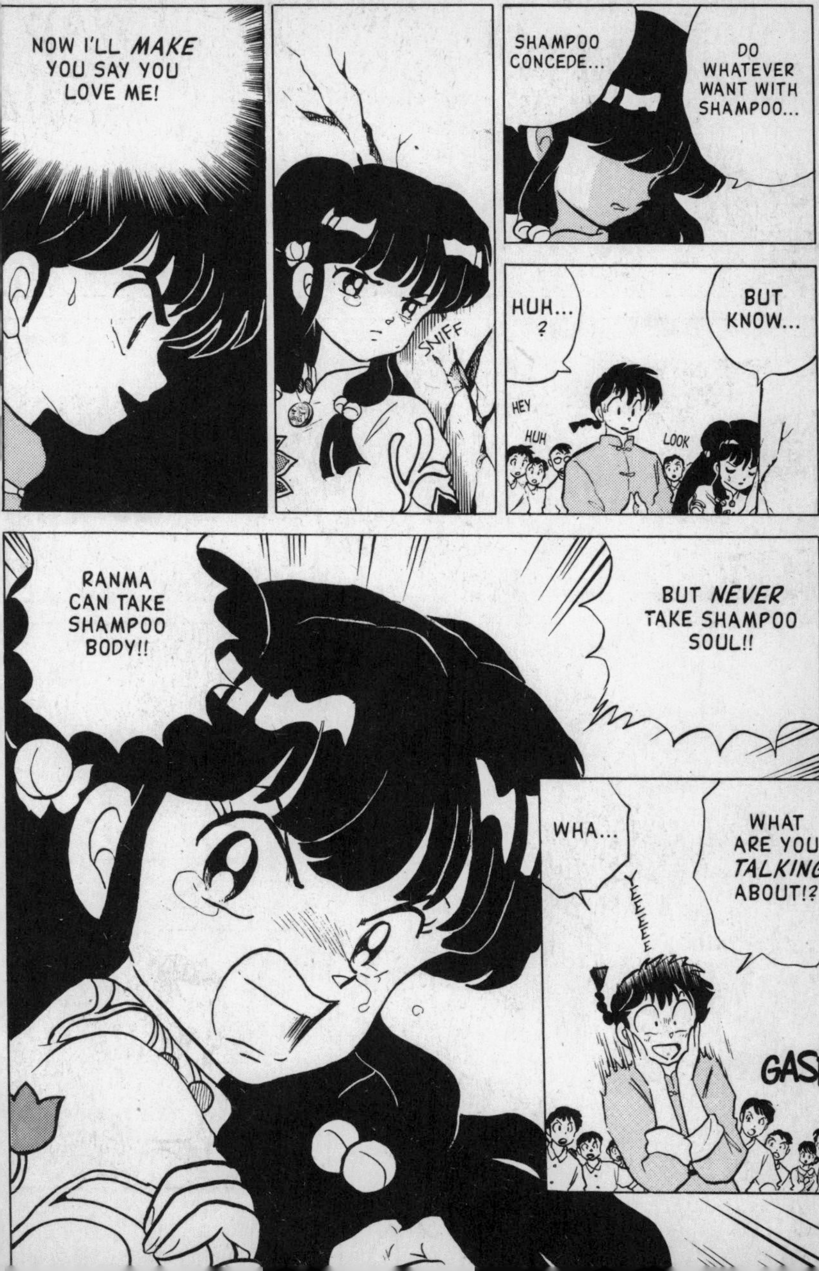
NOW I'LL MAKE YOU SAY YOU LOVE ME!
SNIFF
SHAMPOO CONCEDE...
DO WHATEVER WANT WITH SHAMPOO...
HUH... ?
BUT KNOW...
HEY
HUH
LOOK
RANMA CAN TAKE SHAMPOO BODY!!
BUT NEVER TAKE SHAMPOO SOUL!!
WHA...
WHAT ARE YOU TALKING ABOUT!?
YEEEEE
GASP

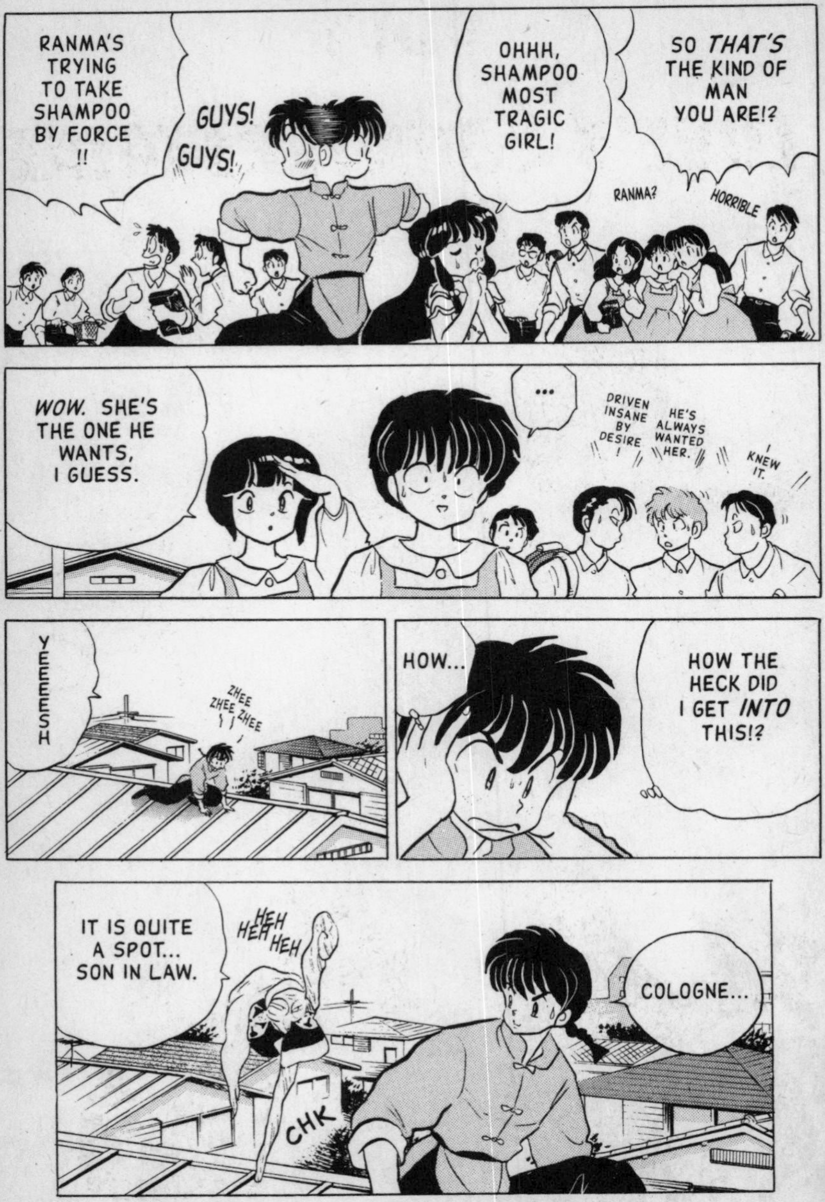
RANMA'S TRYING TO TAKE SHAMPOO BY FORCE !!
GUYS!
GUYS!
OHHH, SHAMPOO MOST TRAGIC GIRL!
SO THAT'S THE KIND OF MAN YOU ARE!?
RANMA?
HORRIBLE
WOW. SHE'S THE ONE HE WANTS, I GUESS.
...
DRIVEN INSANE BY DESIRE !
HE'S ALWAYS WANTED HER.
I KNEW IT.
YEEEESH
ZHEE ZHEE ZHEE
HOW...
HOW THE HECK DID I GET INTO THIS!?
IT IS QUITE A SPOT... SON IN LAW.
HEH HEH HEH
COLOGNE...
CHK

Part 9

LOVE'S COUNTERSTRIKE

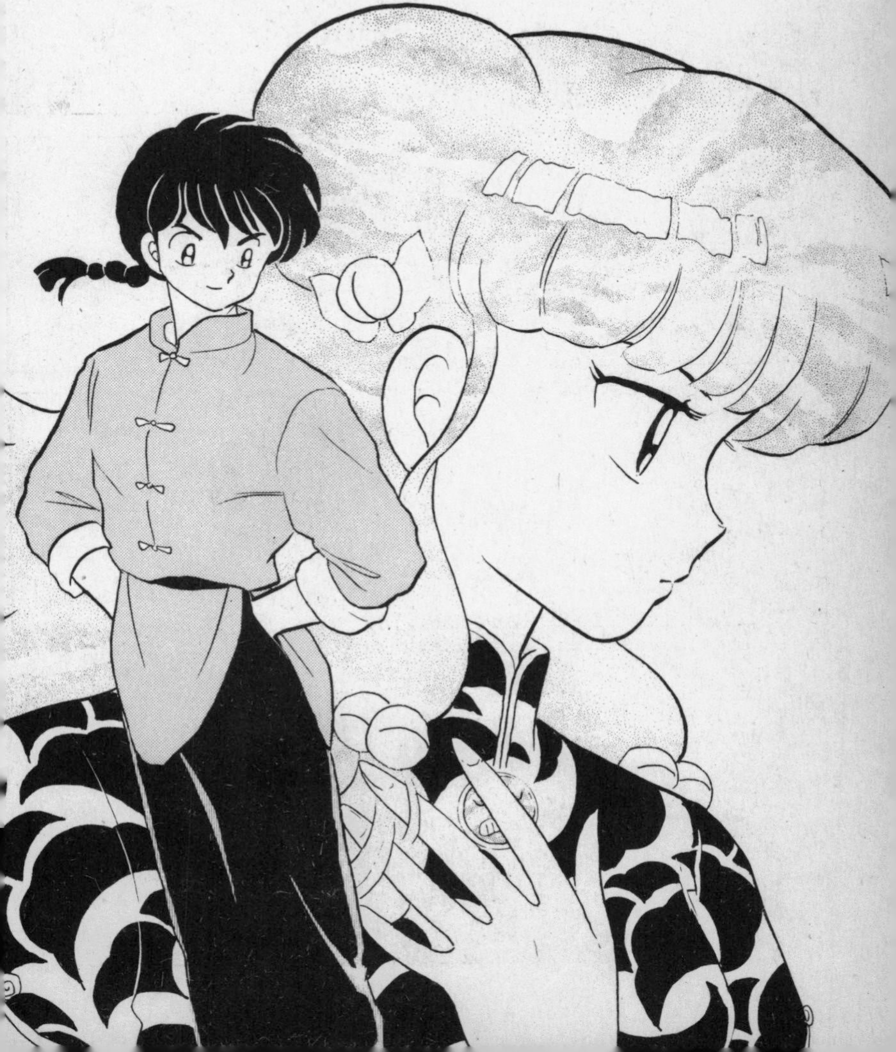

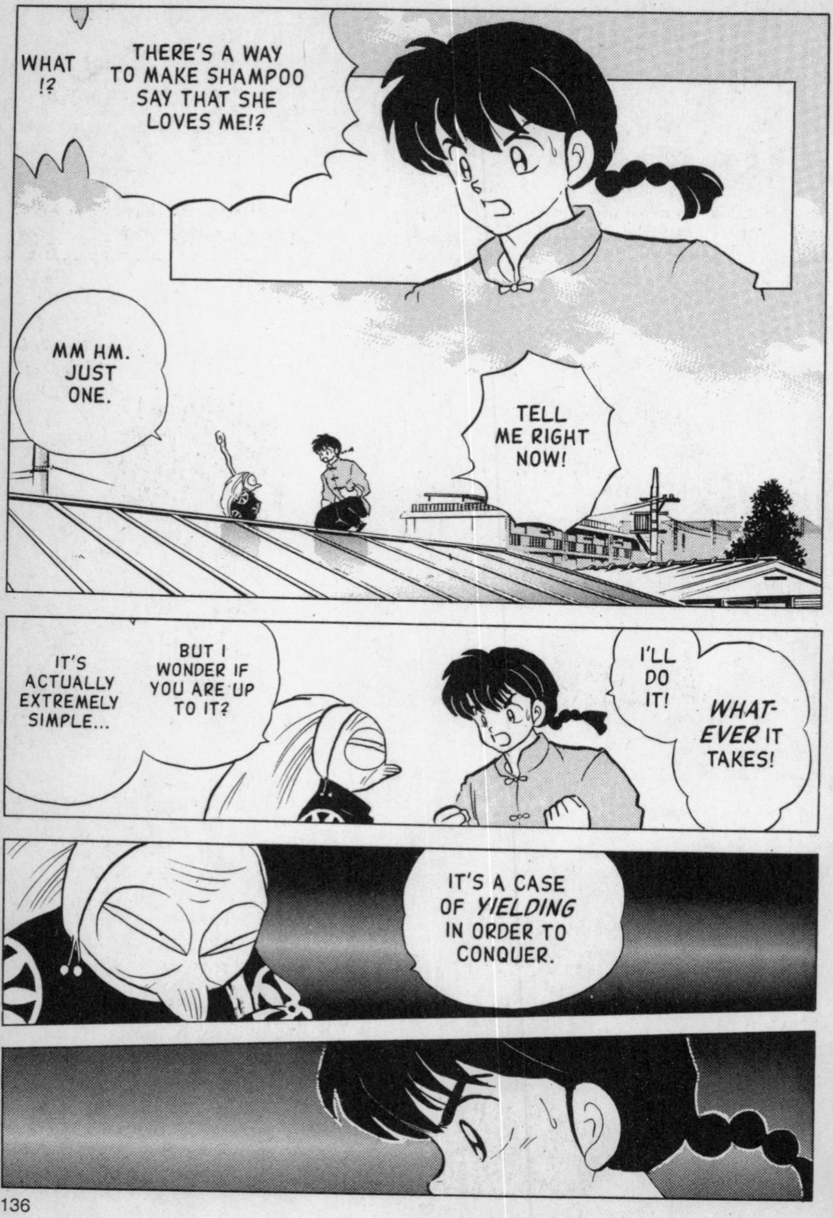
WHAT !?
THERE'S A WAY TO MAKE SHAMPOO SAY THAT SHE LOVES ME!?
MM HM. JUST ONE.
TELL ME RIGHT NOW!
IT'S ACTUALLY EXTREMELY SIMPLE...
BUT I WONDER IF YOU ARE UP TO IT?
I'LL DO IT!
WHAT-EVER IT TAKES!
IT'S A CASE OF *YIELDING* IN ORDER TO CONQUER.

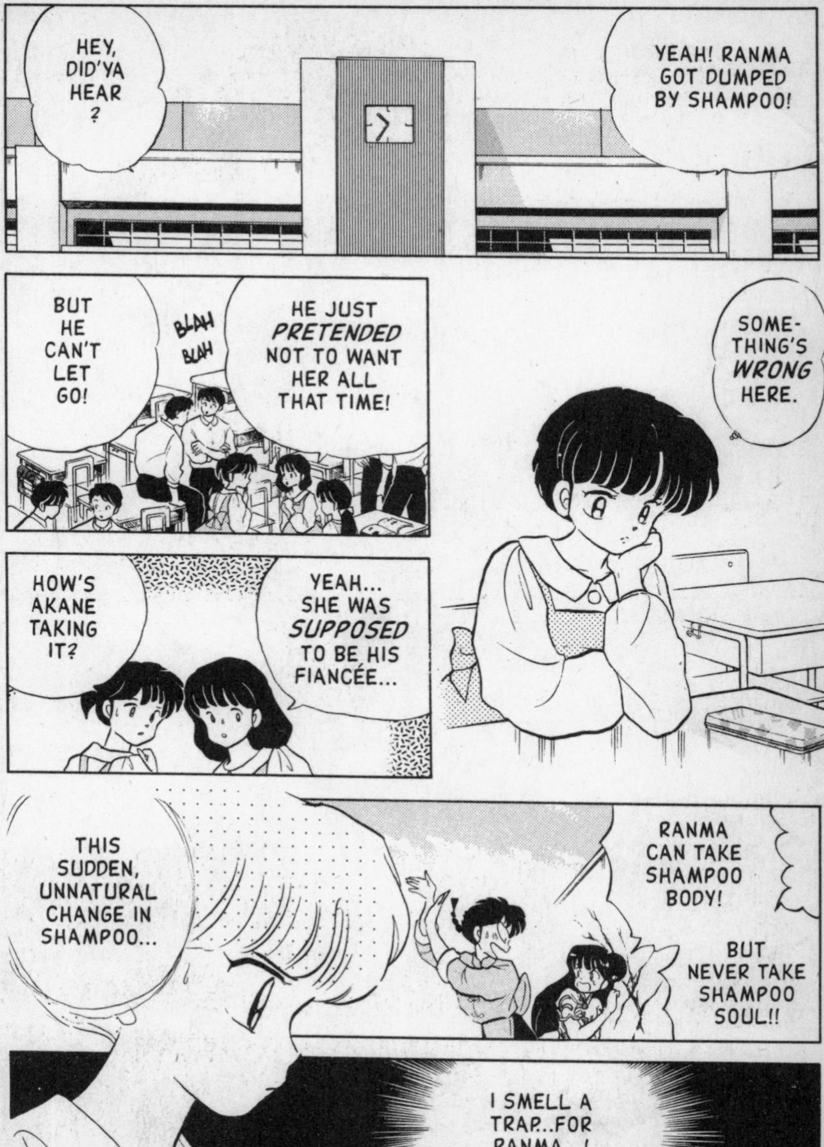
HEY, DID'YA HEAR?
YEAH! RANMA GOT DUMPED BY SHAMPOO!
BUT HE CAN'T LET GO!
BLAH BLAH
HE JUST *PRETENDED* NOT TO WANT HER ALL THAT TIME!
HOW'S AKANE TAKING IT?
YEAH... SHE WAS *SUPPOSED* TO BE HIS FIANCÉE...
SOME-THING'S *WRONG* HERE.
THIS SUDDEN, UNNATURAL CHANGE IN SHAMPOO...
RANMA CAN TAKE SHAMPOO BODY!
BUT NEVER TAKE SHAMPOO SOUL!!
I SMELL A TRAP...FOR RANMA...!

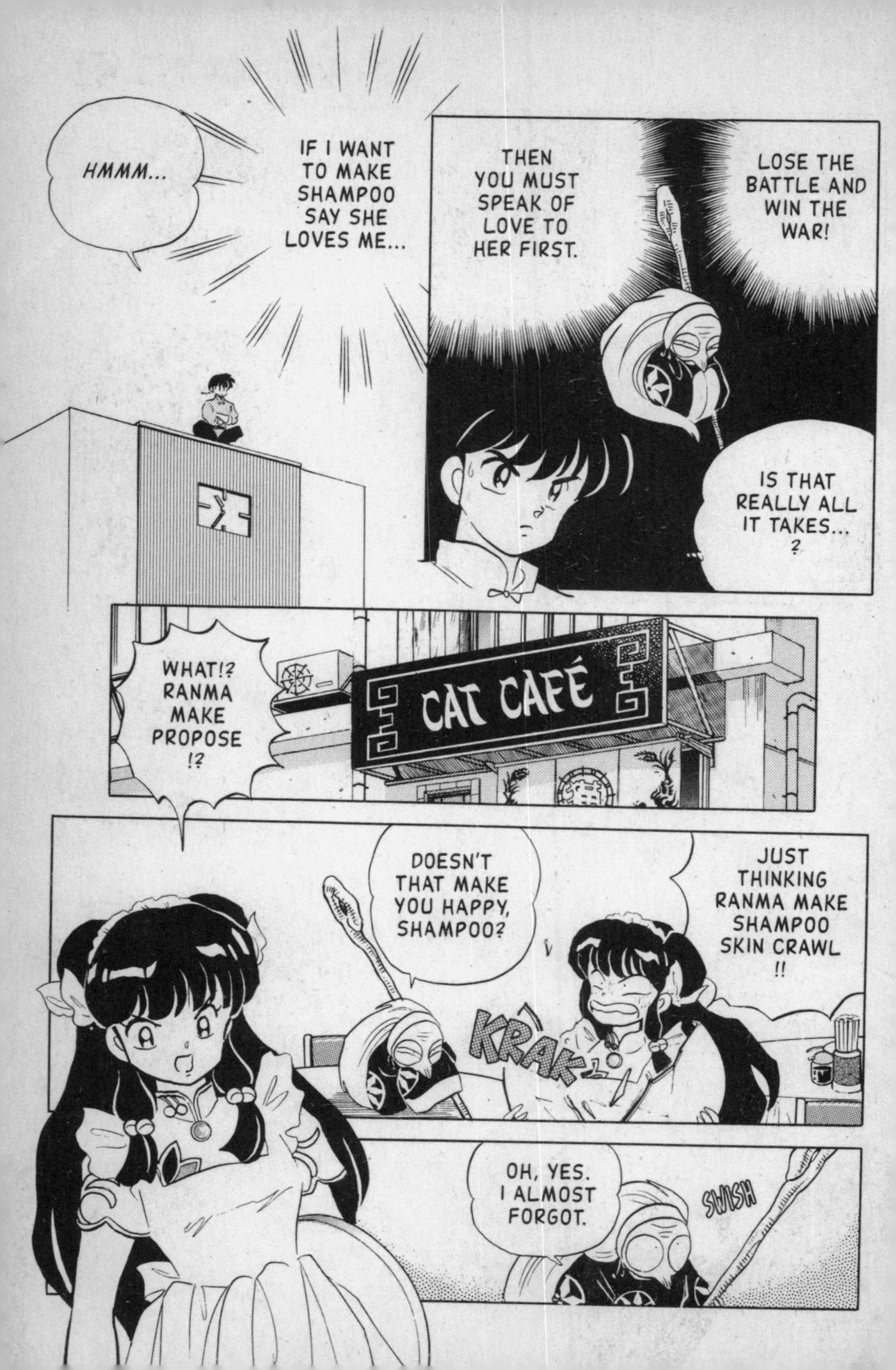
HMMM...
IF I WANT TO MAKE SHAMPOO SAY SHE LOVES ME...
THEN YOU MUST SPEAK OF LOVE TO HER FIRST.
LOSE THE BATTLE AND WIN THE WAR!
IS THAT REALLY ALL IT TAKES...?
WHAT!? RANMA MAKE PROPOSE!?
CAT CAFÉ
DOESN'T THAT MAKE YOU HAPPY, SHAMPOO?
JUST THINKING RANMA MAKE SHAMPOO SKIN CRAWL!!
KRAK
OH, YES. I ALMOST FORGOT.
SWISH

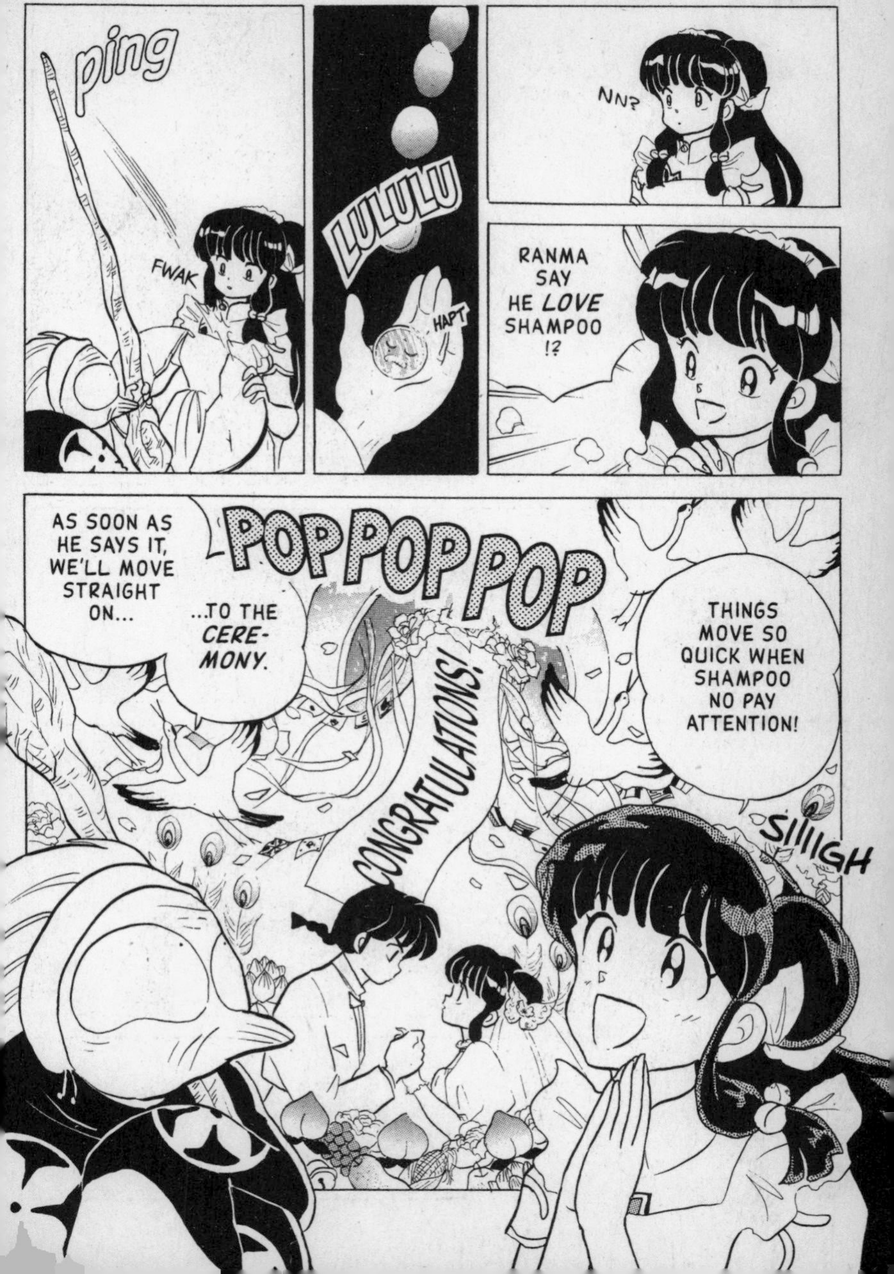
ping
FWAK
LULULU
HAPT
NN?
RANMA SAY HE *LOVE* SHAMPOO !?
AS SOON AS HE SAYS IT, WE'LL MOVE STRAIGHT ON...
...TO THE *CEREMONY.*
POP POP POP POP
CONGRATULATIONS!
THINGS MOVE SO QUICK WHEN SHAMPOO NO PAY ATTENTION!
SIIIIGH

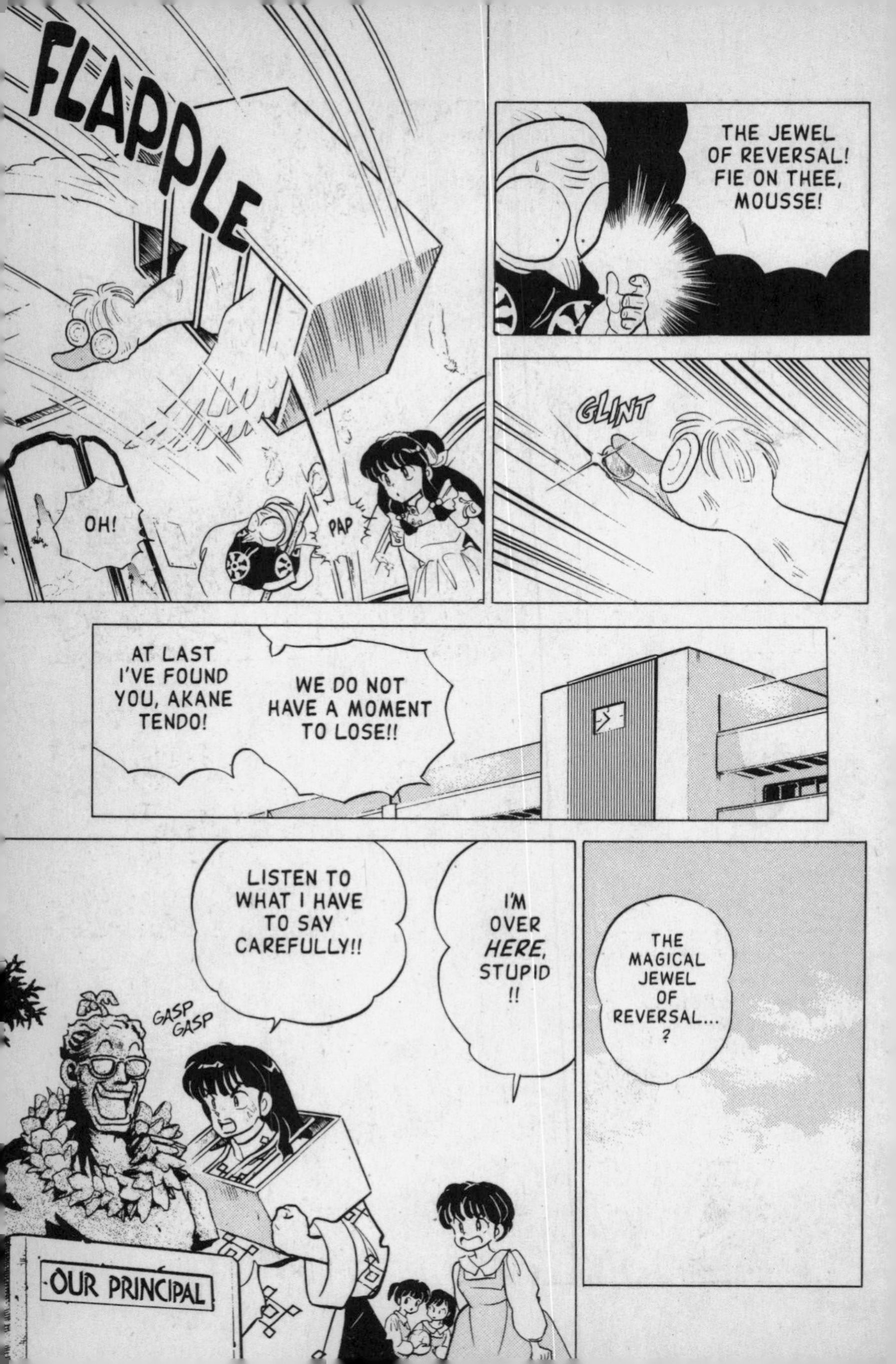
FLAPPLE
OH!
PAP
THE JEWEL OF REVERSAL! FIE ON THEE, MOUSSE!
GLINT
AT LAST I'VE FOUND YOU, AKANE TENDO!
WE DO NOT HAVE A MOMENT TO LOSE!!
LISTEN TO WHAT I HAVE TO SAY CAREFULLY!!
I'M OVER *HERE*, STUPID !!
GASP GASP
OUR PRINCIPAL
THE MAGICAL JEWEL OF REVERSAL... ?

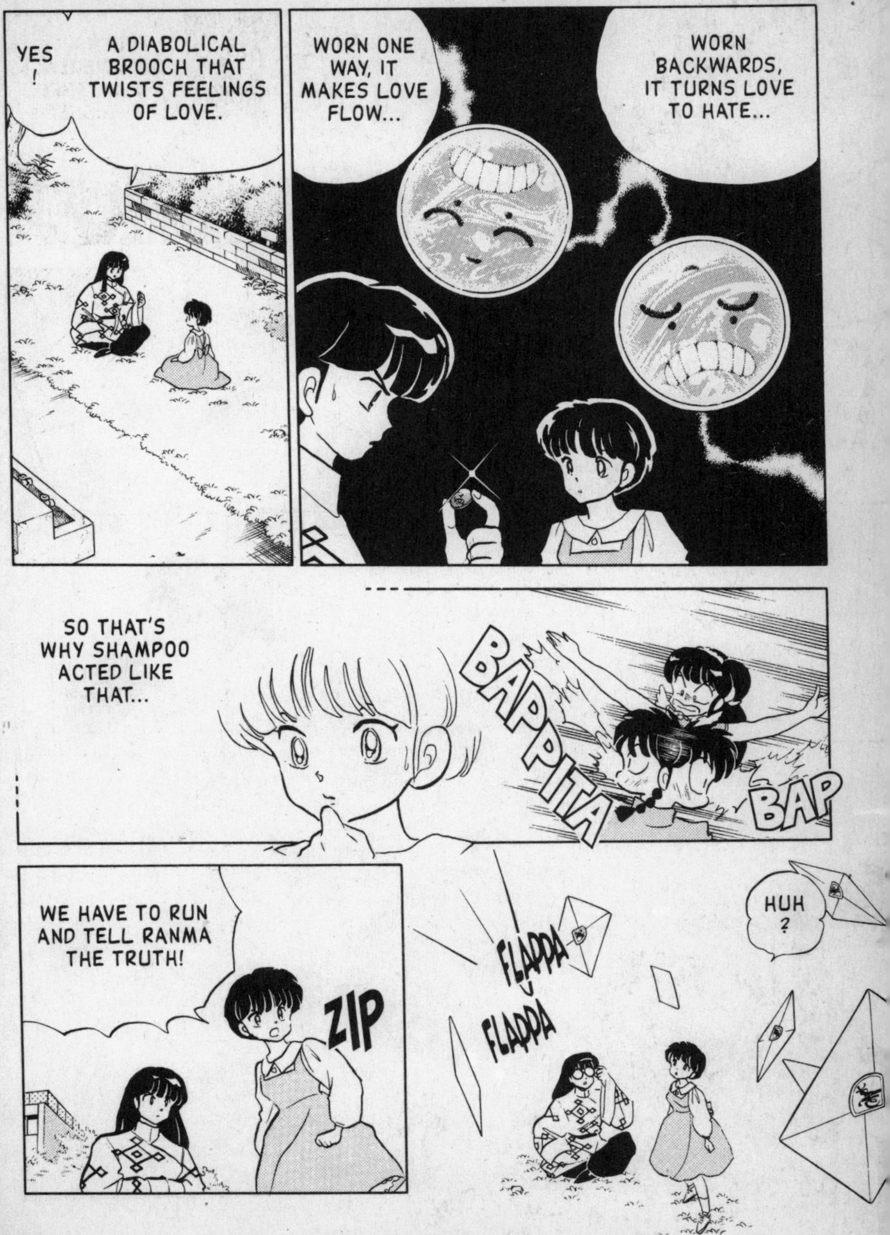
YES!
A DIABOLICAL BROOCH THAT TWISTS FEELINGS OF LOVE.
WORN ONE WAY, IT MAKES LOVE FLOW...
WORN BACKWARDS, IT TURNS LOVE TO HATE...
SO THAT'S WHY SHAMPOO ACTED LIKE THAT...
BAPPITA
BAP
WE HAVE TO RUN AND TELL RANMA THE TRUTH!
ZIP
FLAPPA
FLAPPA
HUH?

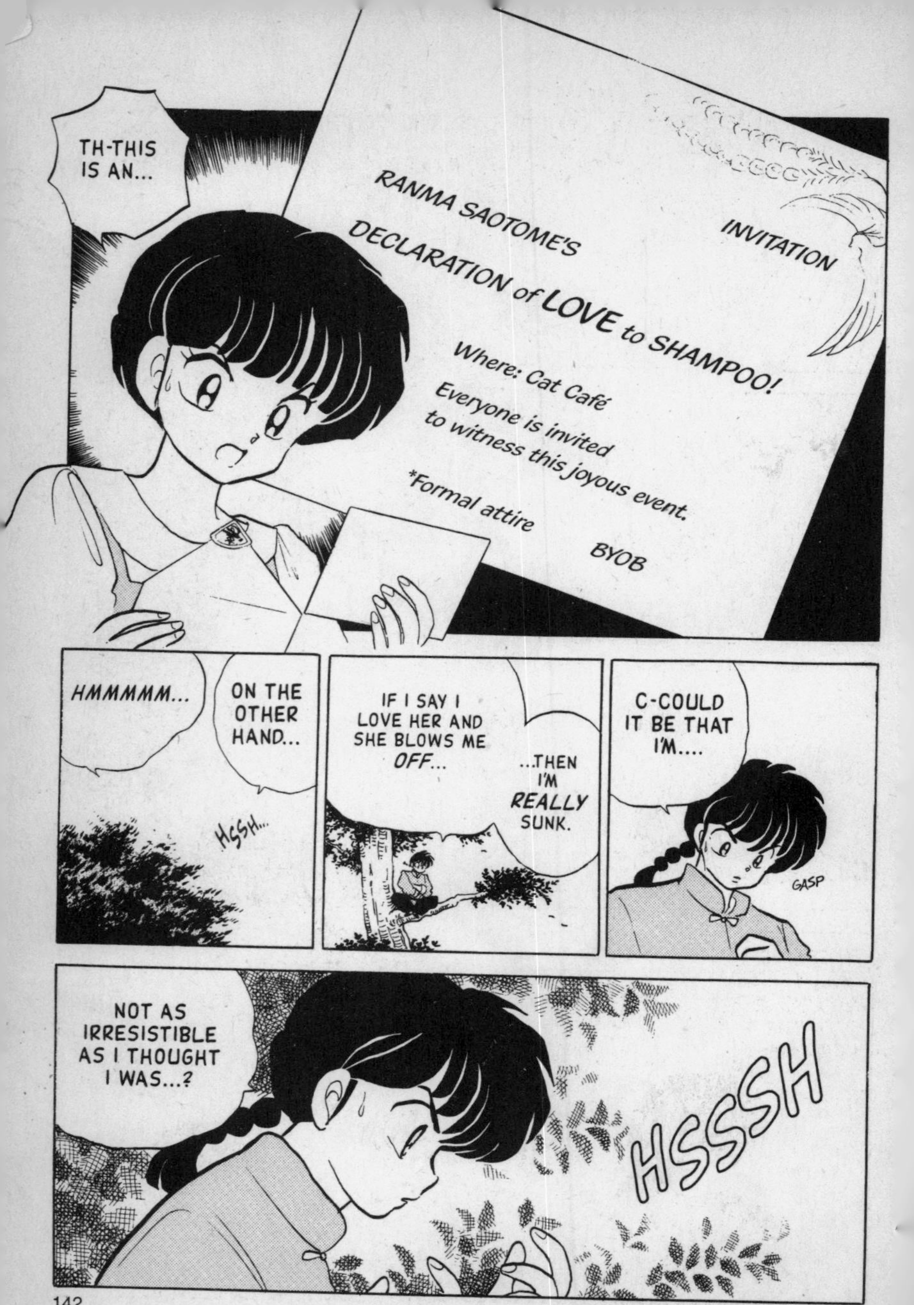

TH-THIS IS AN...
RANMA SAOTOME'S
INVITATION
DECLARATION of LOVE to SHAMPOO!
Where: Cat Café
Everyone is invited to witness this joyous event.
*Formal attire
BYOB
HMMMMM...
ON THE OTHER HAND...
HSSH...
IF I SAY I LOVE HER AND SHE BLOWS ME OFF...
...THEN I'M REALLY SUNK.
C-COULD IT BE THAT I'M....
GASP
NOT AS IRRESISTIBLE AS I THOUGHT I WAS...?
HSSSH

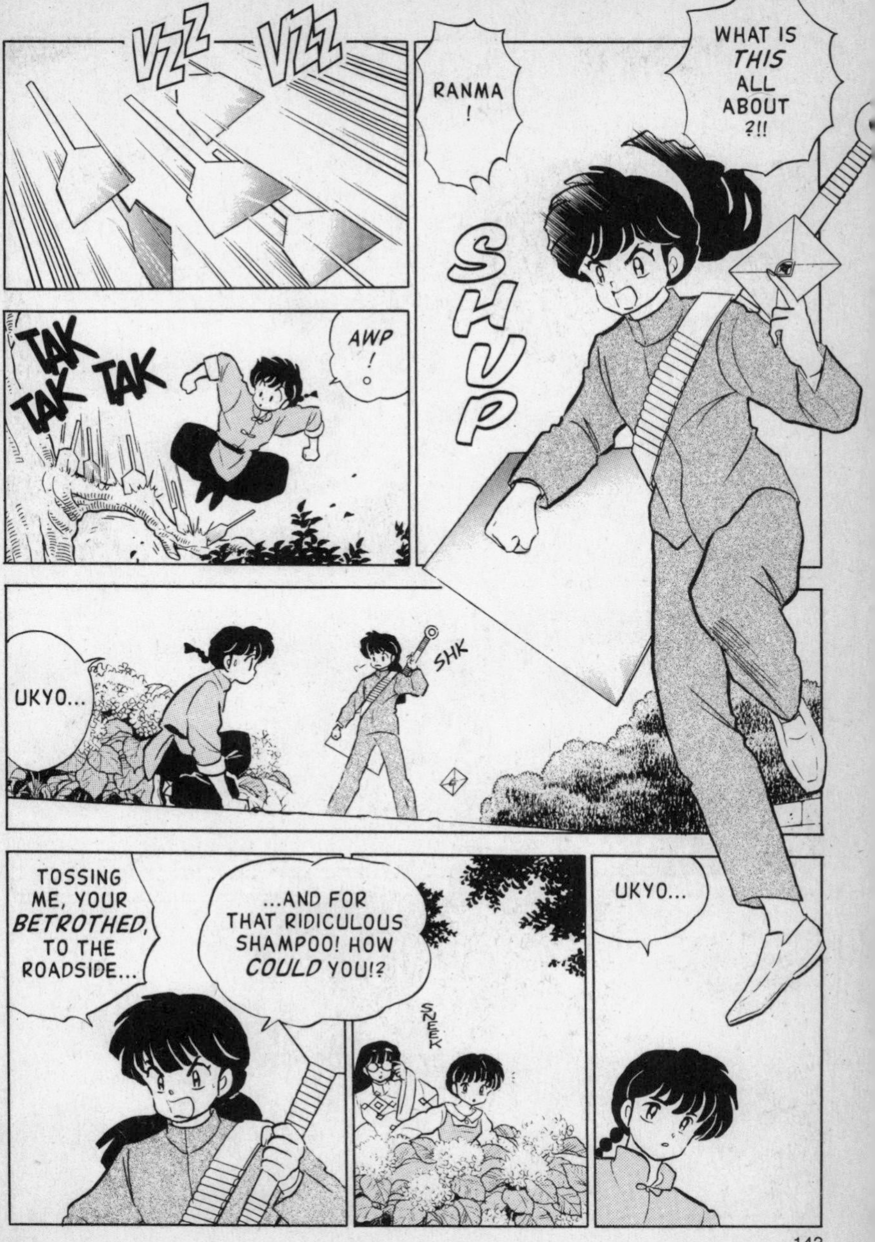
VZZ VZZ
TAK TAK TAK
AWP!
RANMA!
WHAT IS THIS ALL ABOUT?!!
SHUP
UKYO...
SHK
TOSSING ME, YOUR BETROTHED, TO THE ROADSIDE...
...AND FOR THAT RIDICULOUS SHAMPOO! HOW COULD YOU!?
SNEEK
UKYO...

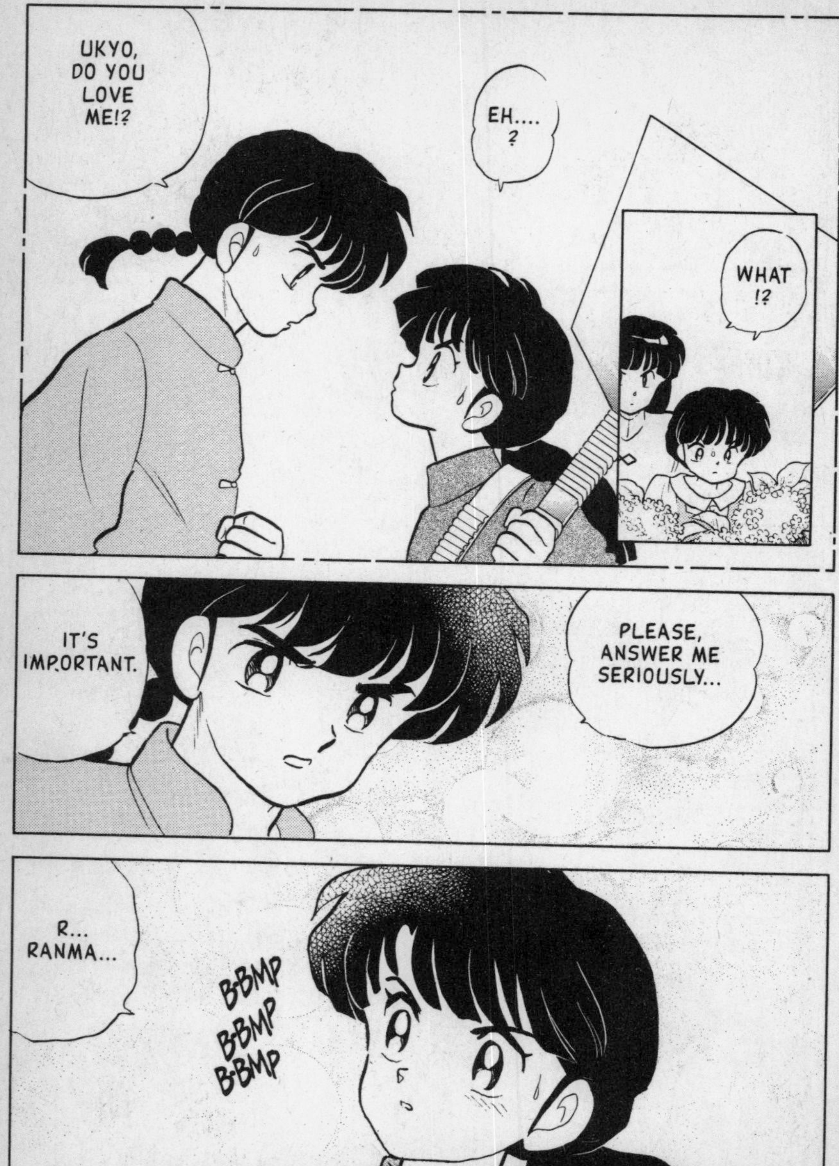
UKYO, DO YOU LOVE ME!?
EH.... ?
WHAT !?
IT'S IMPORTANT.
PLEASE, ANSWER ME SERIOUSLY...
R... RANMA...
B-BMP B-BMP B-BMP

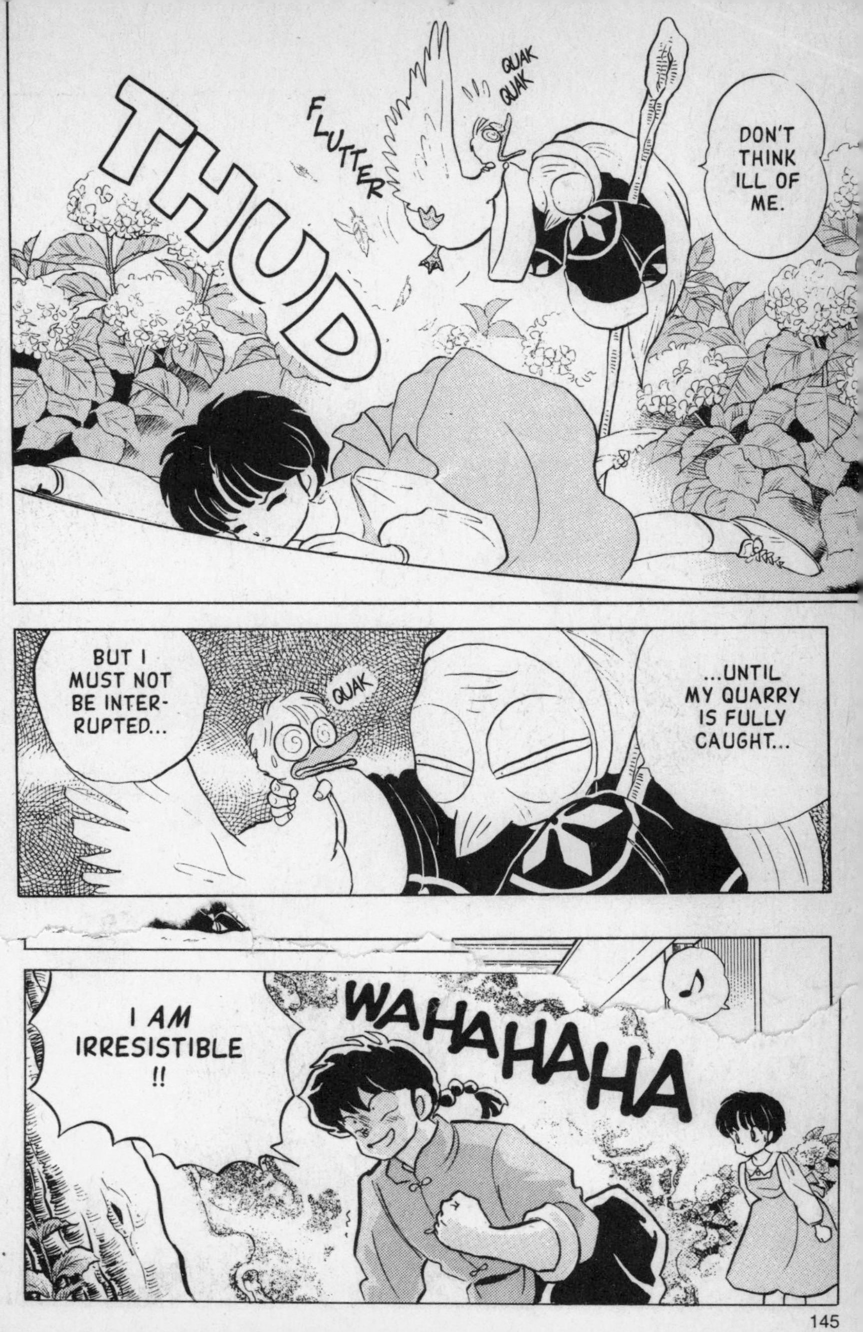
THUD
FLUTTER
QUAK QUAK
DON'T THINK ILL OF ME.
BUT I MUST NOT BE INTER-RUPTED...
QUAK
...UNTIL MY QUARRY IS FULLY CAUGHT...
I AM IRRESISTIBLE !!
WAHAHAHAHA
♪

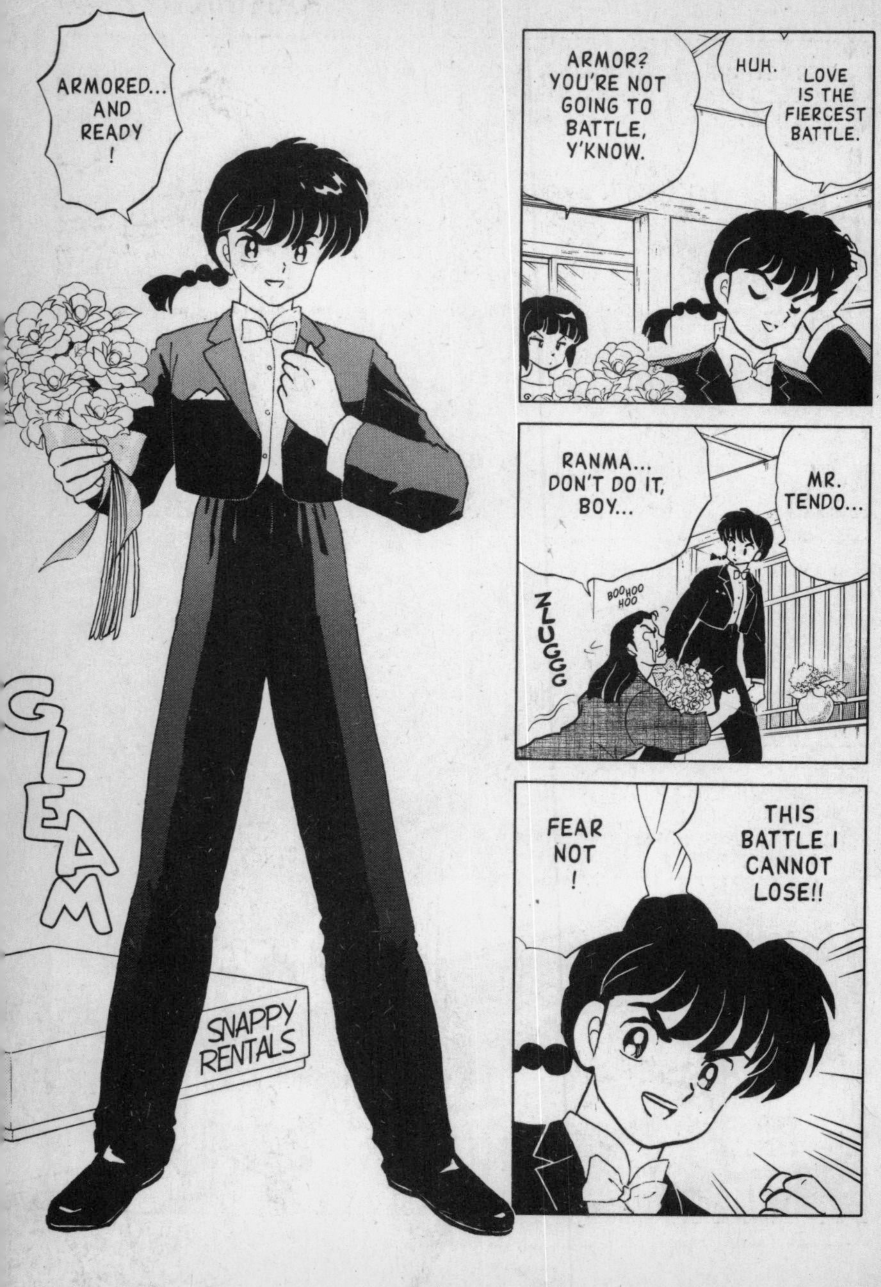
ARMORED... AND READY !
GLEAM
SNAPPY RENTALS
ARMOR? YOU'RE NOT GOING TO BATTLE, Y'KNOW.
HUH.
LOVE IS THE FIERCEST BATTLE.
RANMA... DON'T DO IT, BOY...
MR. TENDO...
ZLUGGG
BOO HOO HOO
FEAR NOT !
THIS BATTLE I CANNOT LOSE!!

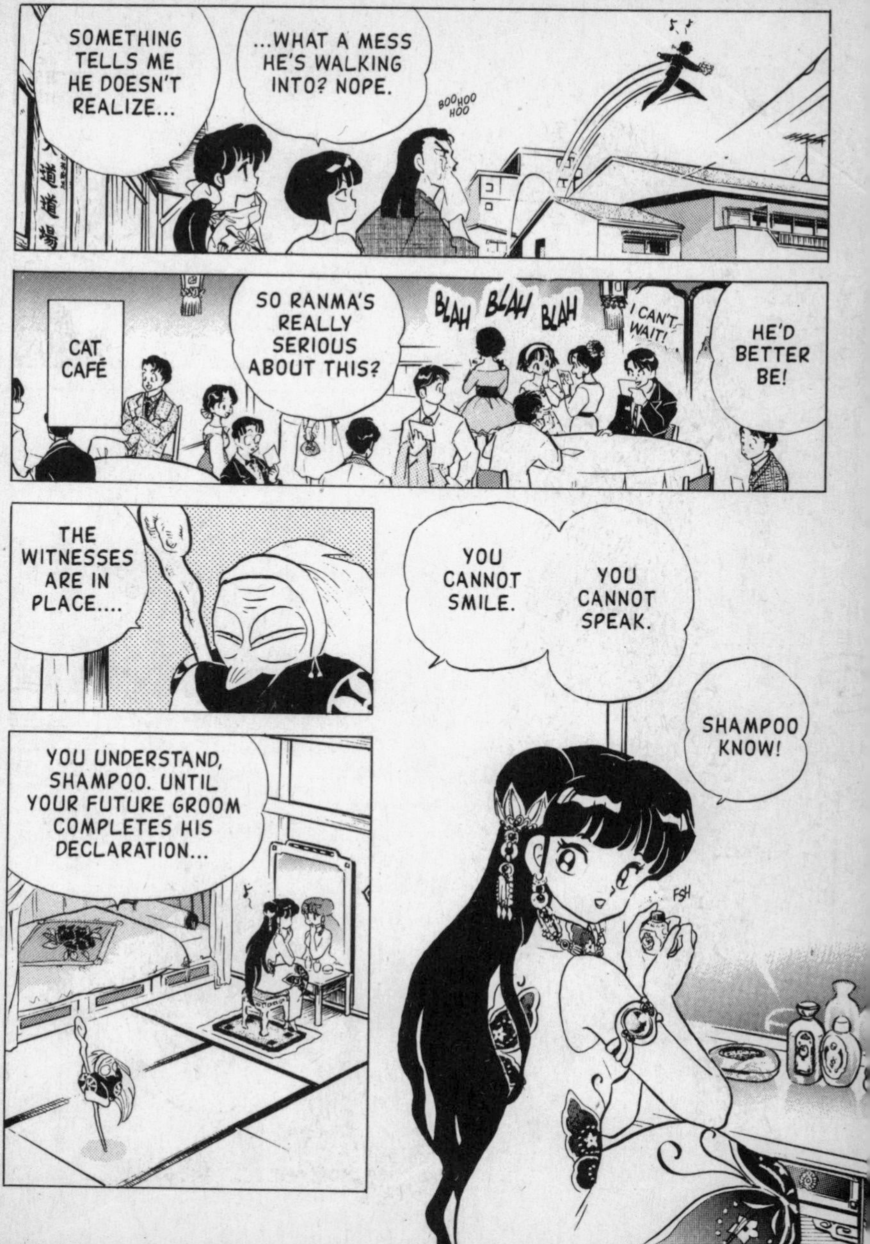
SOMETHING TELLS ME HE DOESN'T REALIZE...
...WHAT A MESS HE'S WALKING INTO? NOPE.
BOO HOO HOO
CAT CAFÉ
SO RANMA'S REALLY SERIOUS ABOUT THIS?
BLAH BLAH BLAH
I CAN'T WAIT!
HE'D BETTER BE!
THE WITNESSES ARE IN PLACE....
YOU UNDERSTAND, SHAMPOO. UNTIL YOUR FUTURE GROOM COMPLETES HIS DECLARATION...
YOU CANNOT SMILE.
YOU CANNOT SPEAK.
SHAMPOO KNOW!
FSH

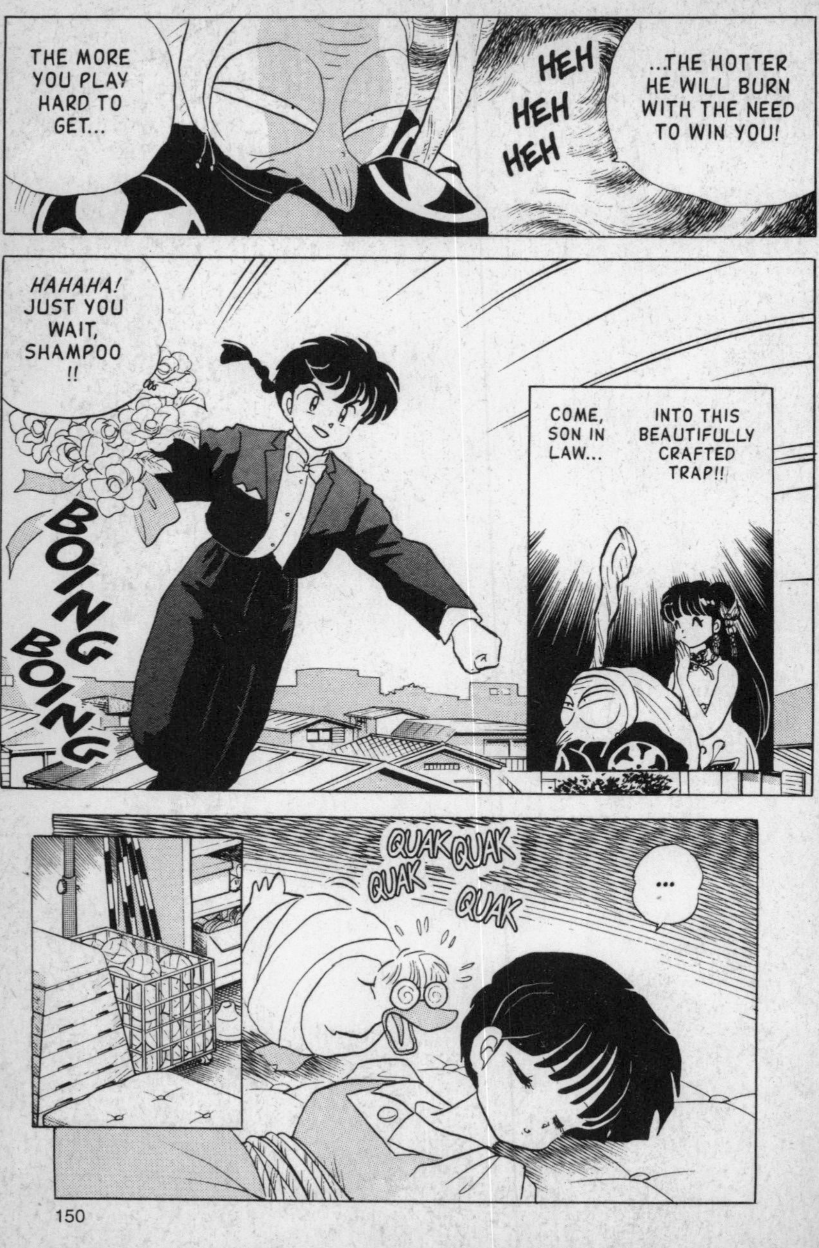

THE MORE YOU PLAY HARD TO GET...
HEH HEH HEH
...THE HOTTER HE WILL BURN WITH THE NEED TO WIN YOU!
HAHAHA! JUST YOU WAIT, SHAMPOO !!
BOING BOING
COME, SON IN LAW...
INTO THIS BEAUTIFULLY CRAFTED TRAP!!
QUAK QUAK QUAK QUAK
...

Part 10

WHO LOVES WHO?

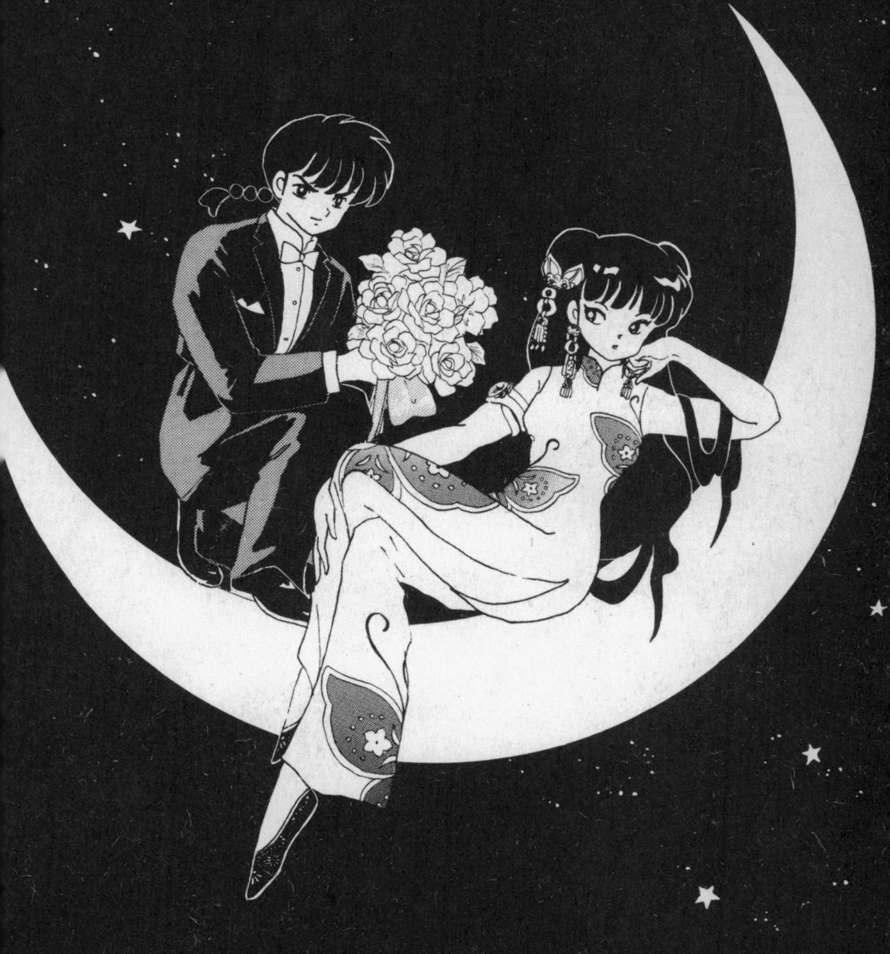

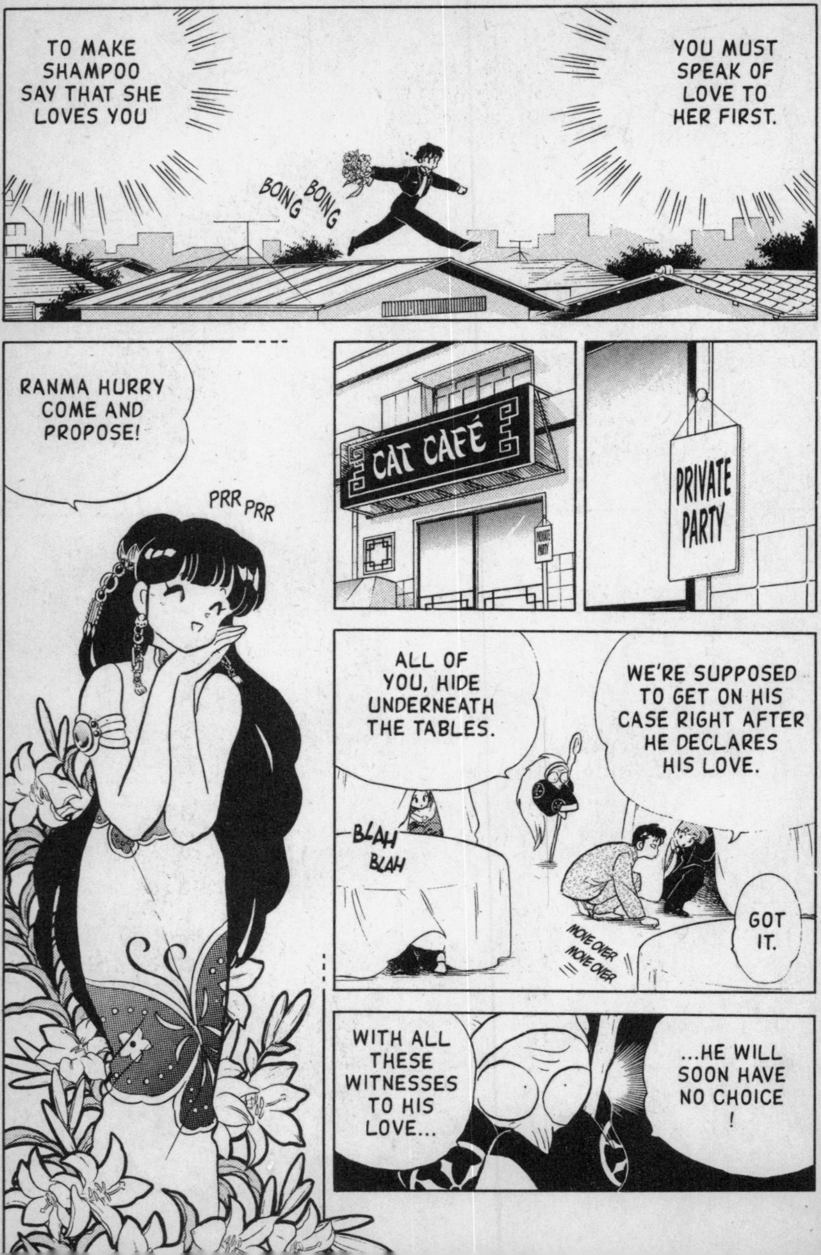

TO MAKE SHAMPOO SAY THAT SHE LOVES YOU
YOU MUST SPEAK OF LOVE TO HER FIRST.
BOING BOING
RANMA HURRY COME AND PROPOSE!
PRR PRR
CAT CAFÉ
PRIVATE PARTY
PRIVATE PARTY
ALL OF YOU, HIDE UNDERNEATH THE TABLES.
WE'RE SUPPOSED TO GET ON HIS CASE RIGHT AFTER HE DECLARES HIS LOVE.
BLAH BLAH
MOVE OVER MOVE OVER
GOT IT.
WITH ALL THESE WITNESSES TO HIS LOVE...
...HE WILL SOON HAVE NO CHOICE !

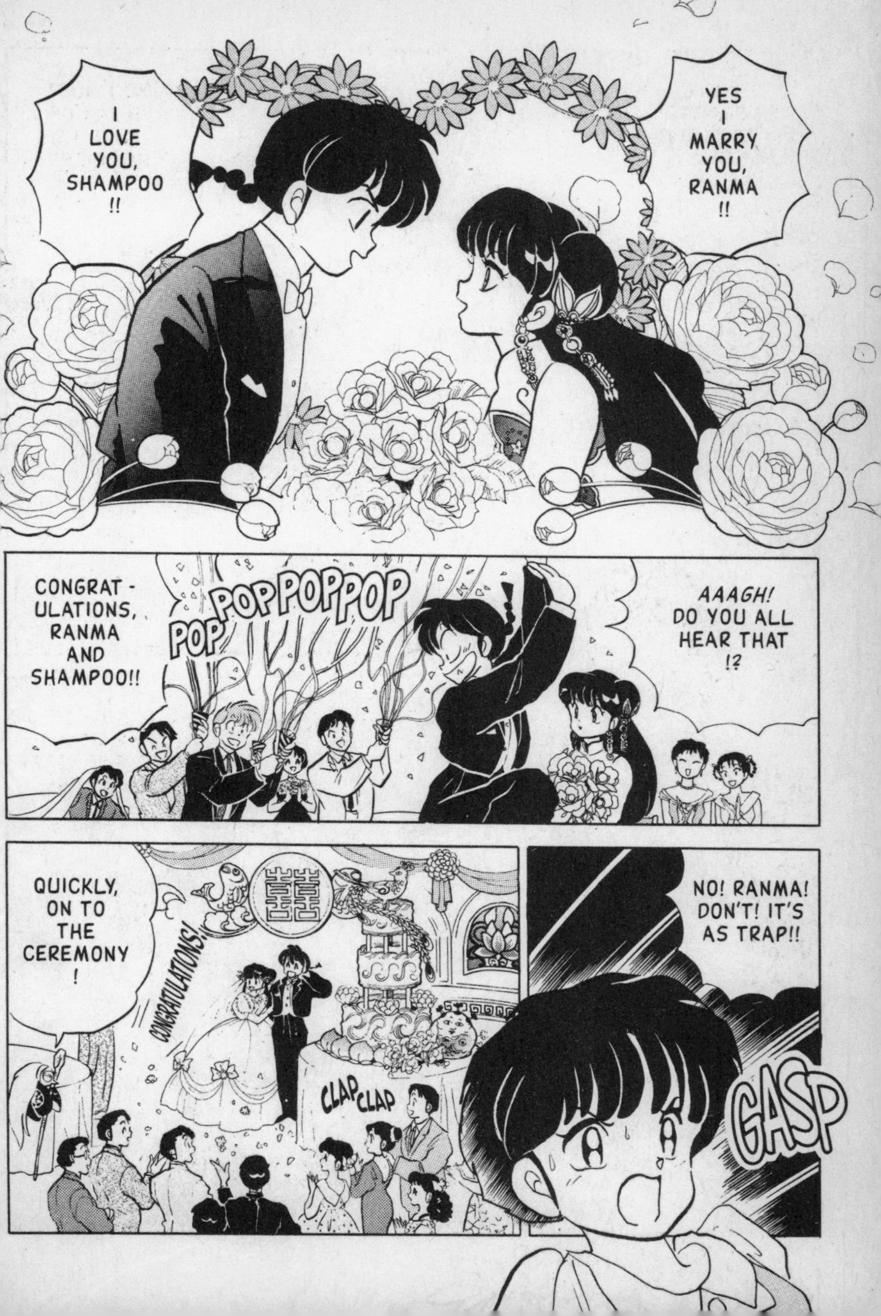
I LOVE YOU, SHAMPOO !!
YES I MARRY YOU, RANMA !!
CONGRAT - ULATIONS, RANMA AND SHAMPOO!!
POP POP POP POP
AAAGH! DO YOU ALL HEAR THAT !?
QUICKLY, ON TO THE CEREMONY !
CONGRATULATIONS!
CLAP CLAP
NO! RANMA! DON'T! IT'S AS TRAP!!
GASP

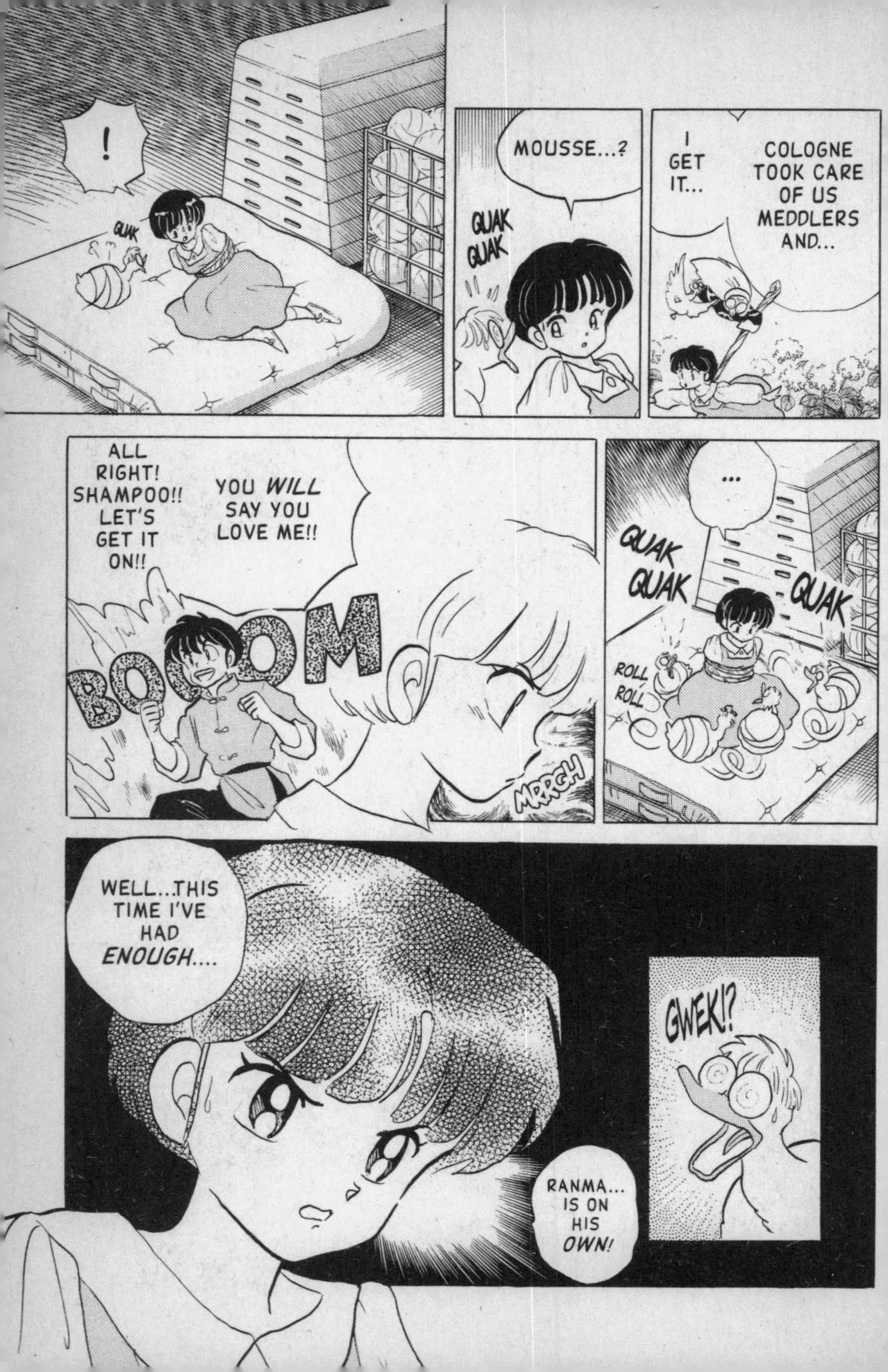
!
QUAK
MOUSSE...?
QUAK QUAK
I GET IT...
COLOGNE TOOK CARE OF US MEDDLERS AND...
ALL RIGHT! SHAMPOO!! LET'S GET IT ON!!
YOU WILL SAY YOU LOVE ME!!
BOOOM
MRRGH
...
QUAK QUAK
QUAK
ROLL ROLL
WELL...THIS TIME I'VE HAD ENOUGH....
RANMA... IS ON HIS OWN!
GWEK!?

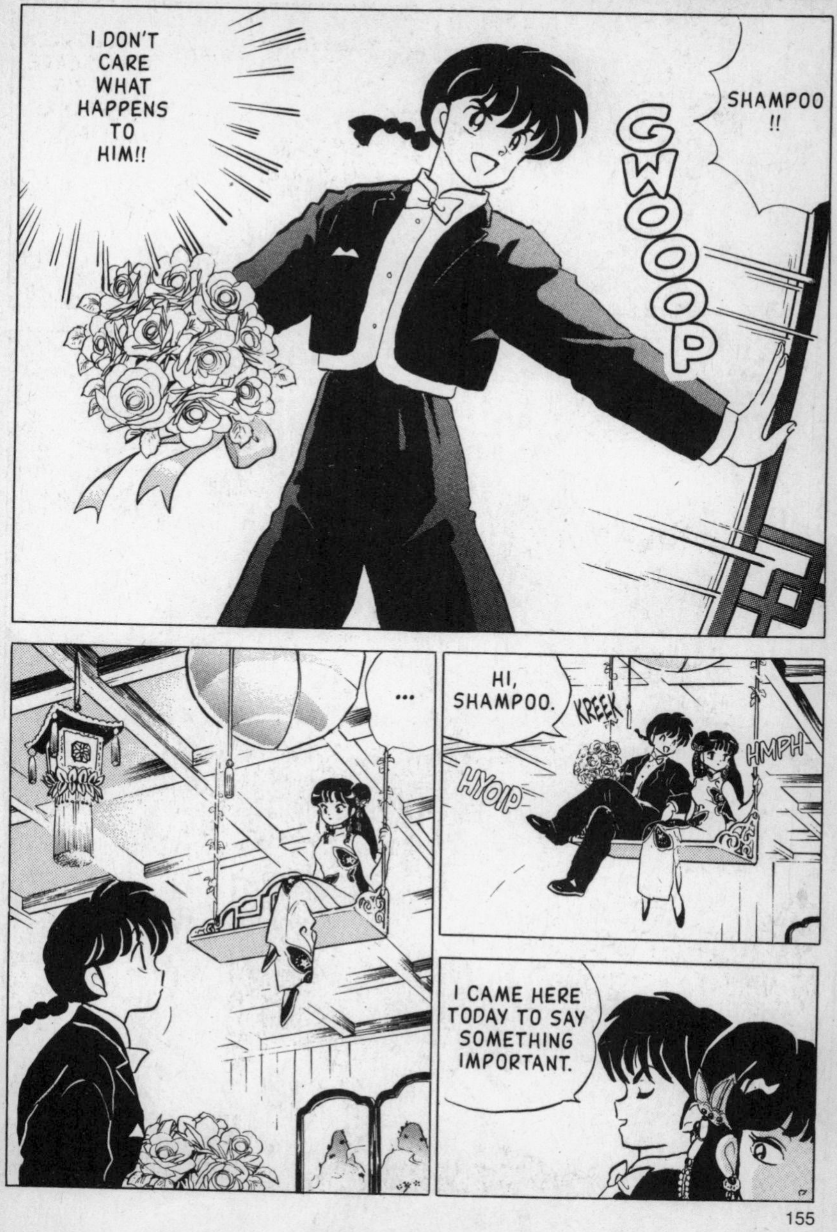
I DON'T CARE WHAT HAPPENS TO HIM!!
SHAMPOO !!
GWOOOP
...
HI, SHAMPOO.
KREEK
HMPH
HYOIP
I CAME HERE TODAY TO SAY SOMETHING IMPORTANT.

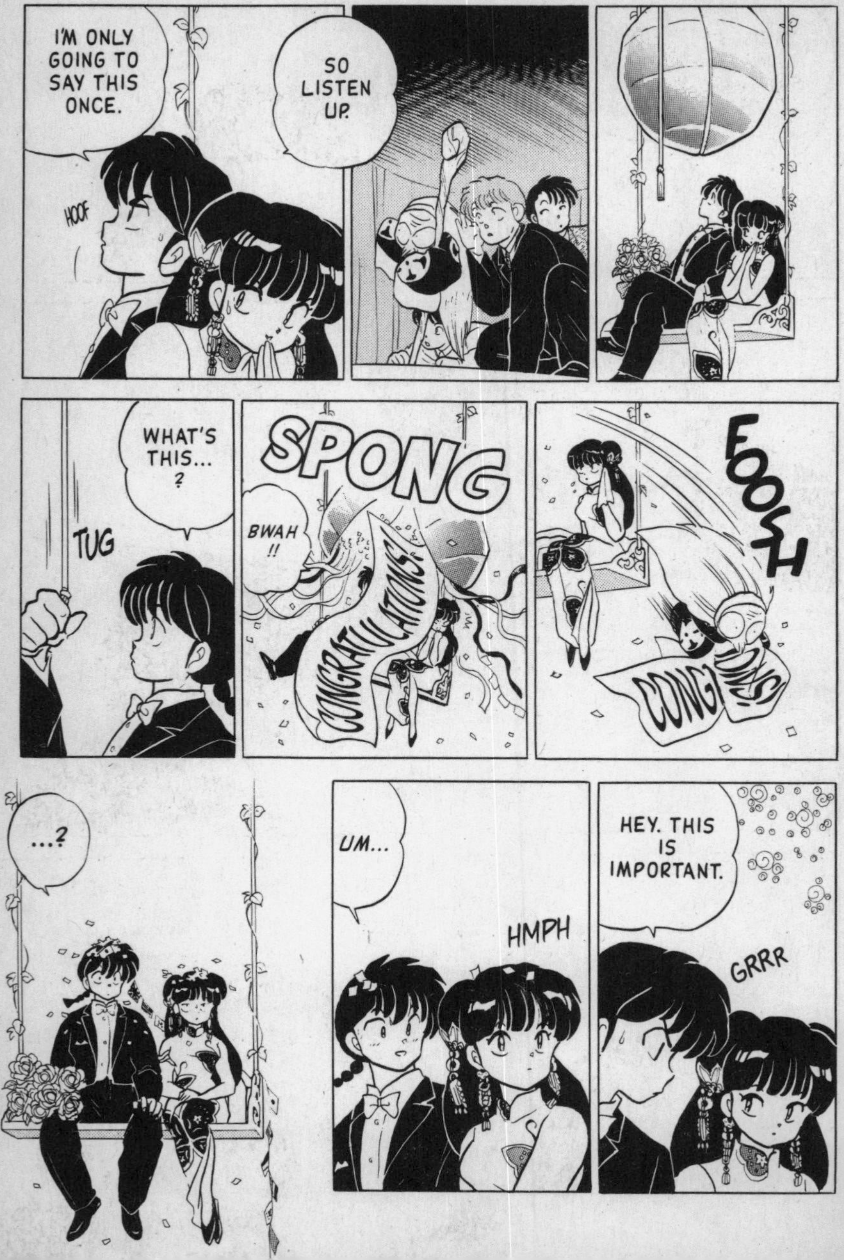
I'M ONLY GOING TO SAY THIS ONCE.
HOOF
SO LISTEN UP.
WHAT'S THIS... ?
TUG
SPONG
BWAH !!
CONGRATULATIONS!
FOOSH
...?
UM...
HMPH
HEY. THIS IS IMPORTANT.
GRRR

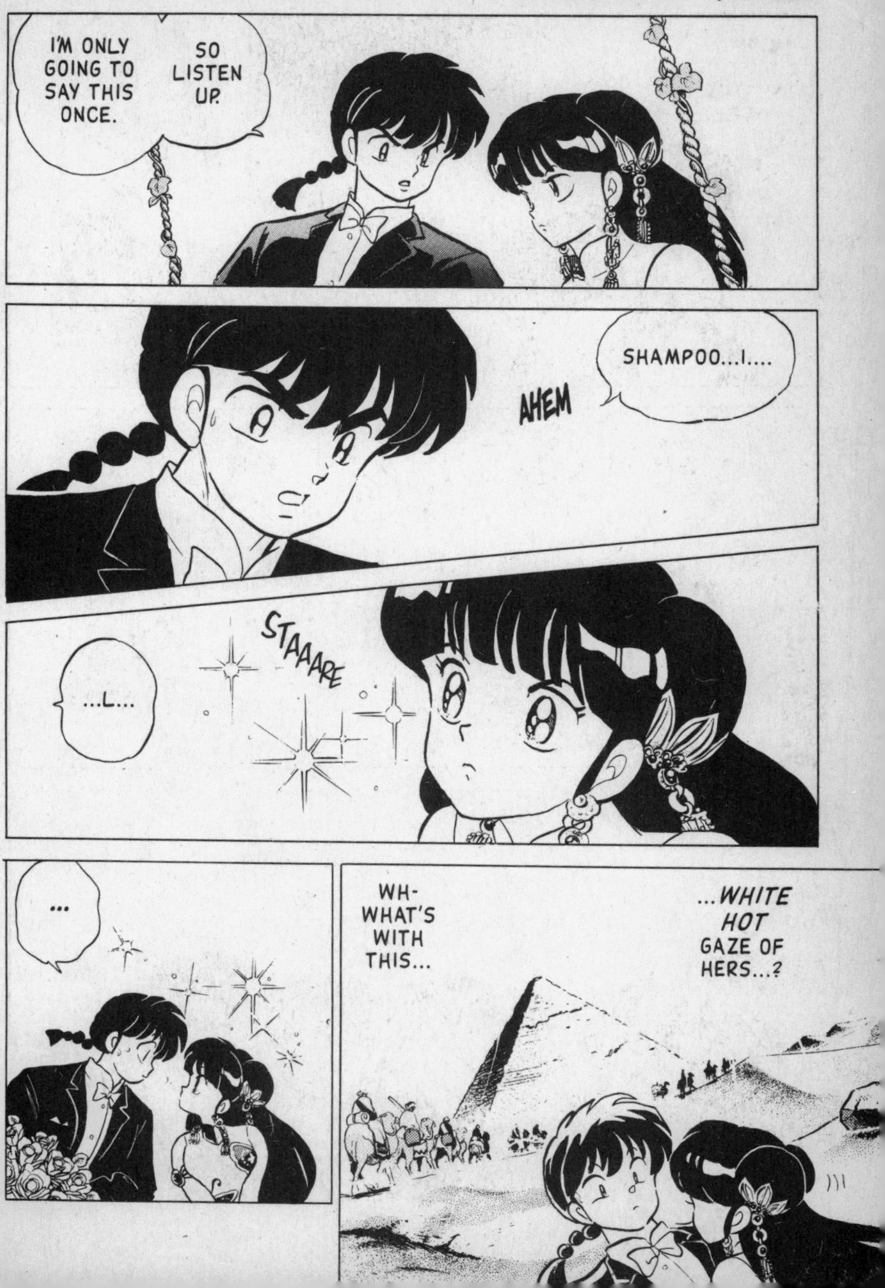
I'M ONLY GOING TO SAY THIS ONCE.
SO LISTEN UP.
AHEM
SHAMPOO...I....
...L...
STAAAARE
...
WH- WHAT'S WITH THIS...
...WHITE HOT GAZE OF HERS...?

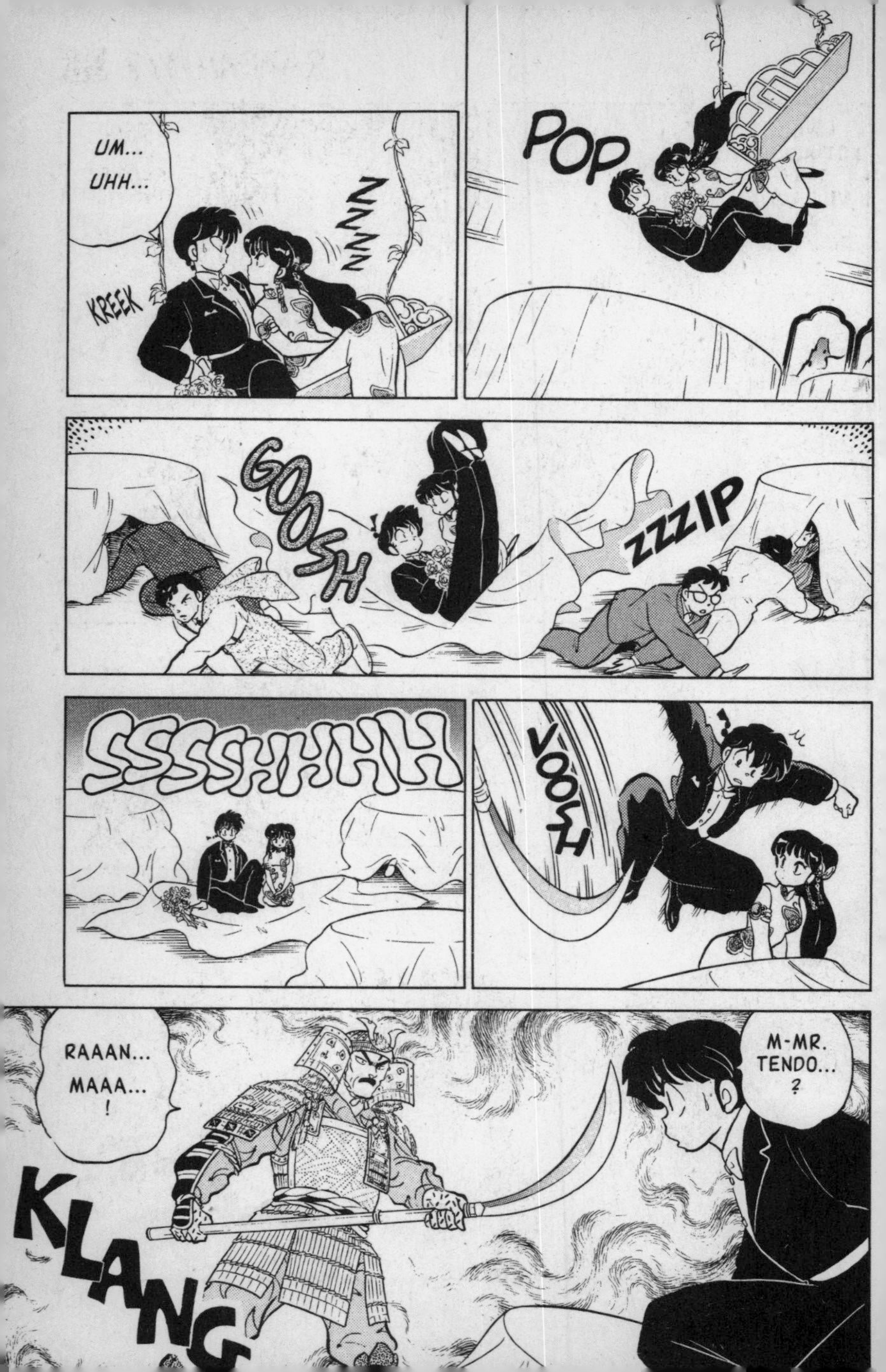
UM... UHH...
KREEK
ZZZZZ
POP
GOOSH
ZZZIP
SSSSHHHH
VOOSH
RAAAN... MAAA... !
KLANG
M-MR. TENDO... ?

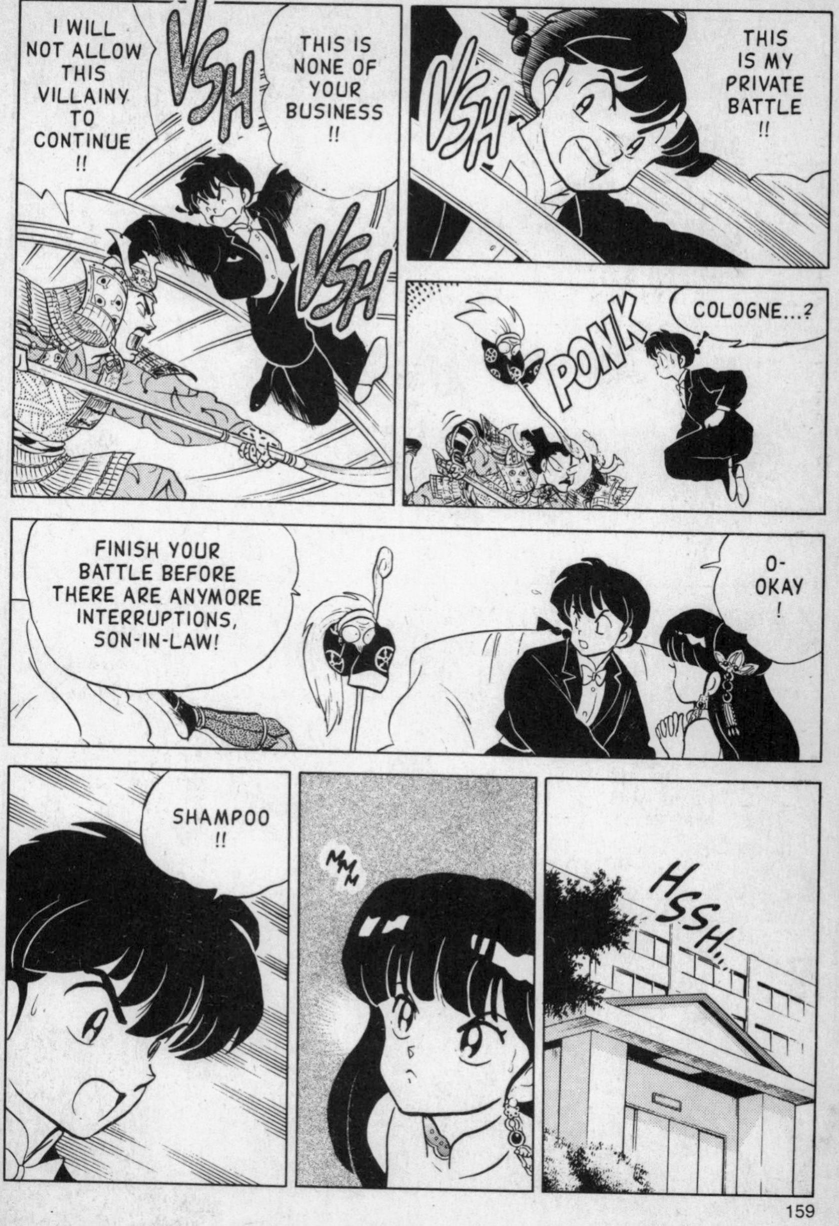
I WILL NOT ALLOW THIS VILLAINY TO CONTINUE !!
VSH
THIS IS NONE OF YOUR BUSINESS !!
VSH
VSH
THIS IS MY PRIVATE BATTLE !!
PONK
COLOGNE...?
FINISH YOUR BATTLE BEFORE THERE ARE ANYMORE INTERRUPTIONS, SON-IN-LAW!
O-OKAY !
SHAMPOO !!
MMM
HSSH...

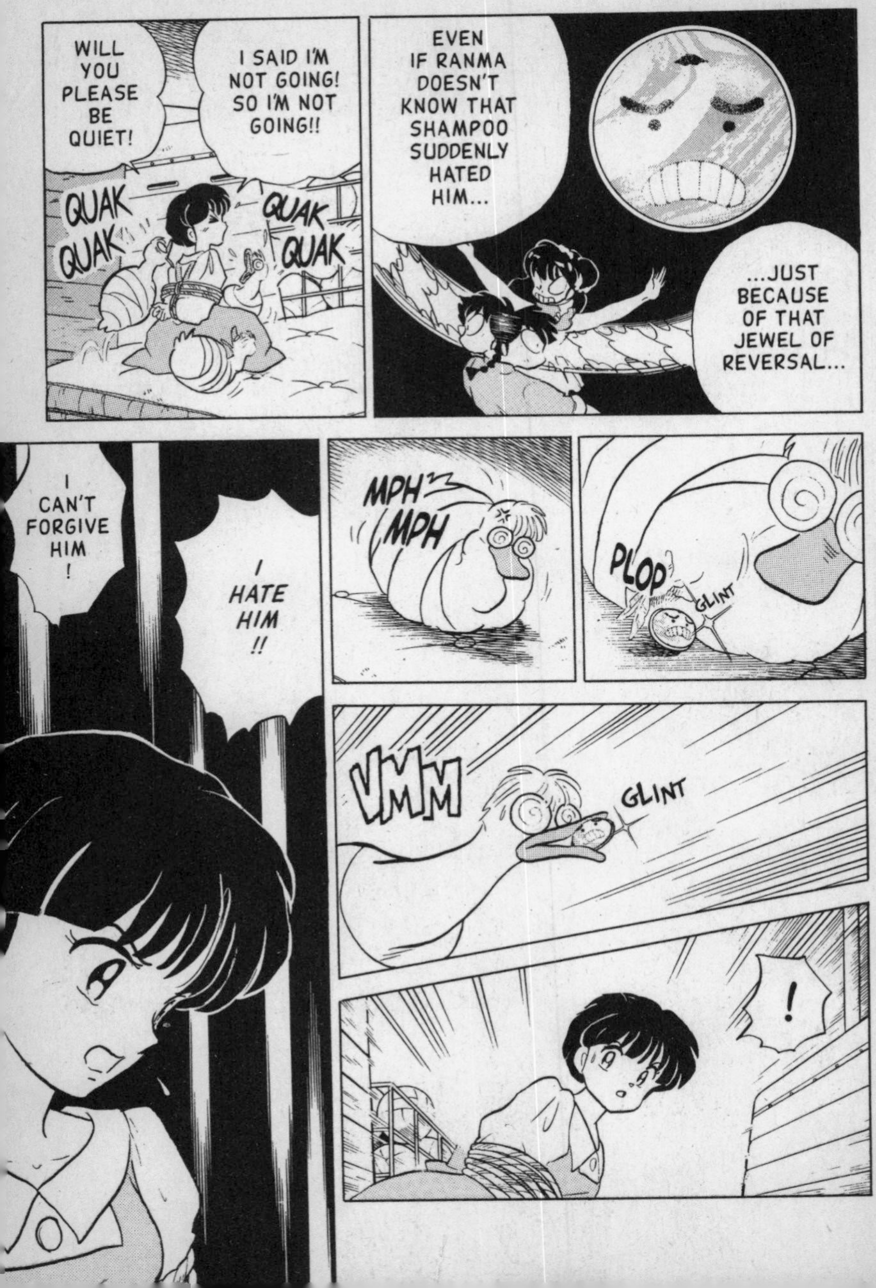
WILL YOU PLEASE BE QUIET!
I SAID I'M NOT GOING! SO I'M NOT GOING!!
QUAK QUAK
QUAK QUAK
EVEN IF RANMA DOESN'T KNOW THAT SHAMPOO SUDDENLY HATED HIM...
...JUST BECAUSE OF THAT JEWEL OF REVERSAL...
I CAN'T FORGIVE HIM !
I HATE HIM !!
MPH MPH
PLOP
GLINT
VMM
GLINT
!

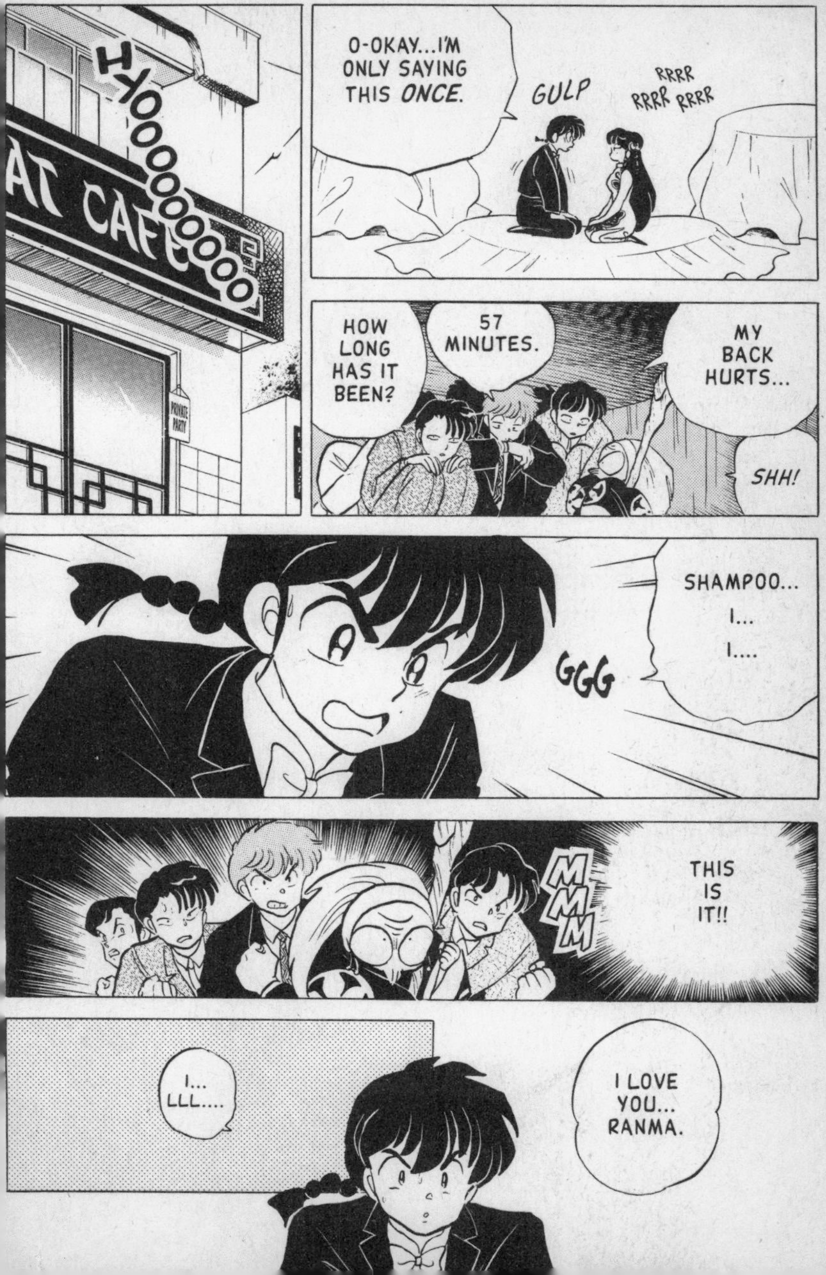
HYOOOOOOOOOOO
CAFE
PRIVATE PARTY
O-OKAY...I'M ONLY SAYING THIS ONCE.
GULP
RRRR RRRR RRRR
HOW LONG HAS IT BEEN?
57 MINUTES.
MY BACK HURTS...
SHH!
GGG
SHAMPOO... I... I....
MMMM
THIS IS IT!!
I... LLL....
I LOVE YOU... RANMA.

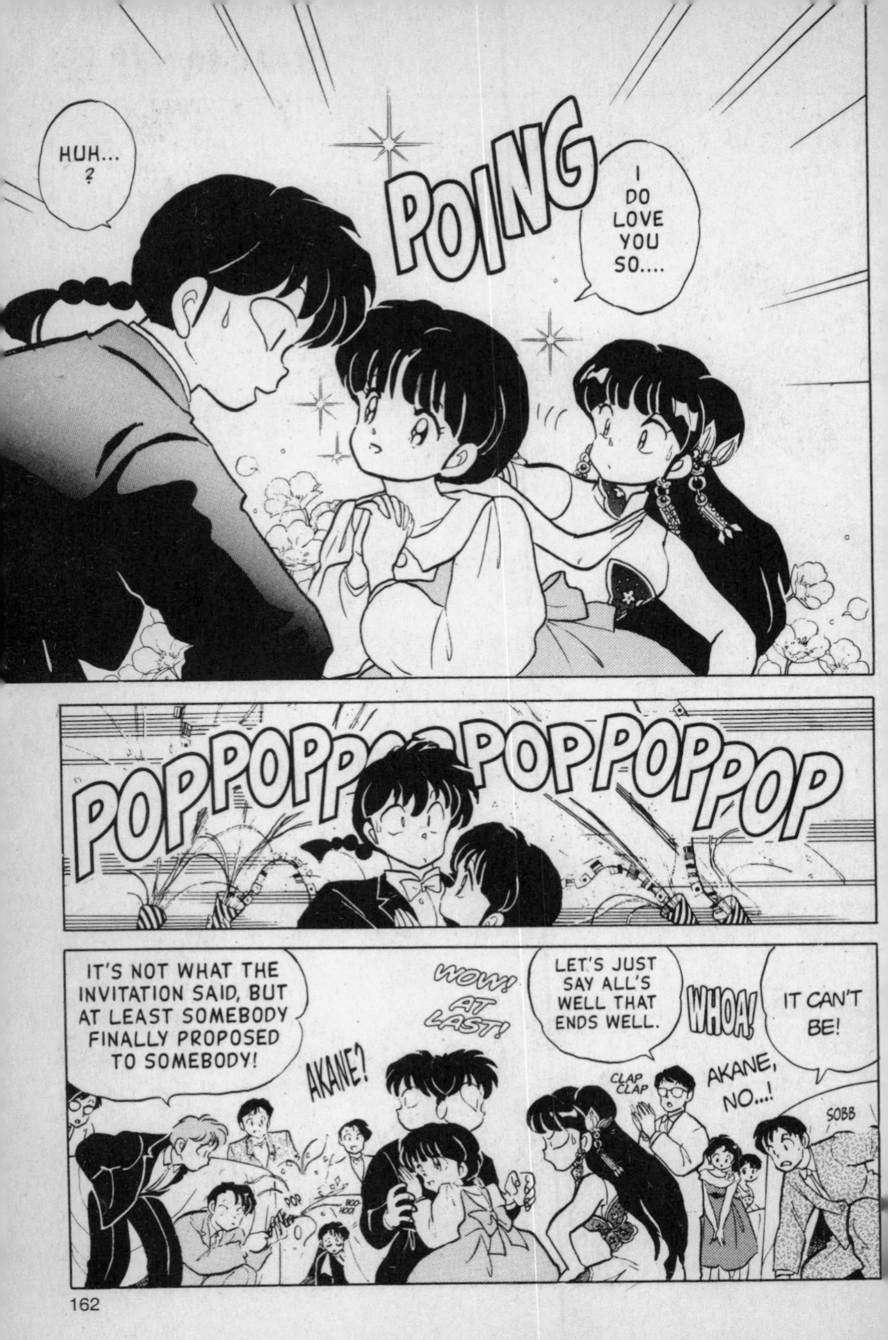
HUH... ?
POING
I DO LOVE YOU SO....
POPPOPPOPPOPPOPPOPPOP
IT'S NOT WHAT THE INVITATION SAID, BUT AT LEAST SOMEBODY FINALLY PROPOSED TO SOMEBODY!
WOW! AT LAST!
AKANE?
LET'S JUST SAY ALL'S WELL THAT ENDS WELL.
CLAP CLAP
WHOA!
AKANE, NO...!
IT CAN'T BE!
SOBB
POP
BOO-HOO!

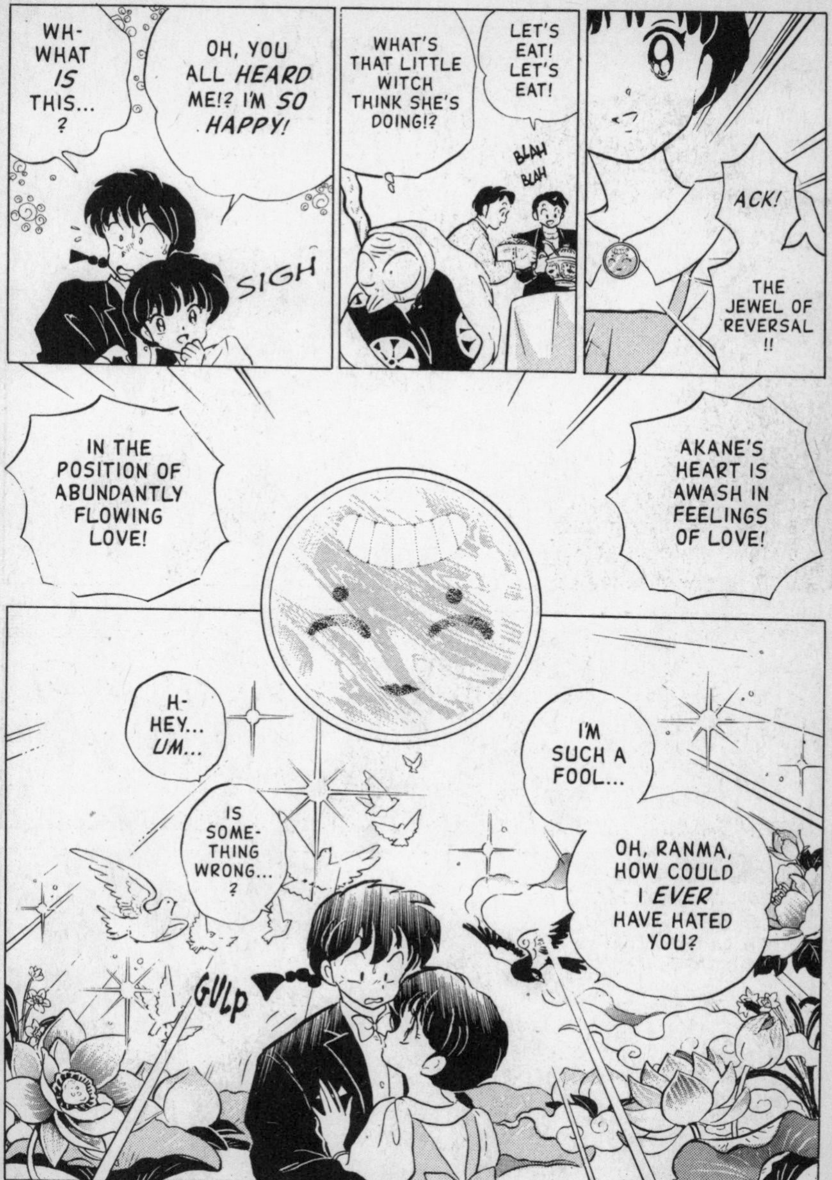
WH-
WHAT
IS
THIS...
?
OH, YOU
ALL *HEARD*
ME!? I'M *SO*
HAPPY!
SIGH
WHAT'S
THAT LITTLE
WITCH
THINK SHE'S
DOING!?
LET'S
EAT!
LET'S
EAT!
BLAH
BLAH
ACK!
THE
JEWEL OF
REVERSAL
!!
IN THE
POSITION OF
ABUNDANTLY
FLOWING
LOVE!
AKANE'S
HEART IS
AWASH IN
FEELINGS
OF LOVE!
H-
HEY...
UM...
IS
SOME-
THING
WRONG...
?
GULP
I'M
SUCH A
FOOL...
OH, RANMA,
HOW COULD
I *EVER*
HAVE HATED
YOU?

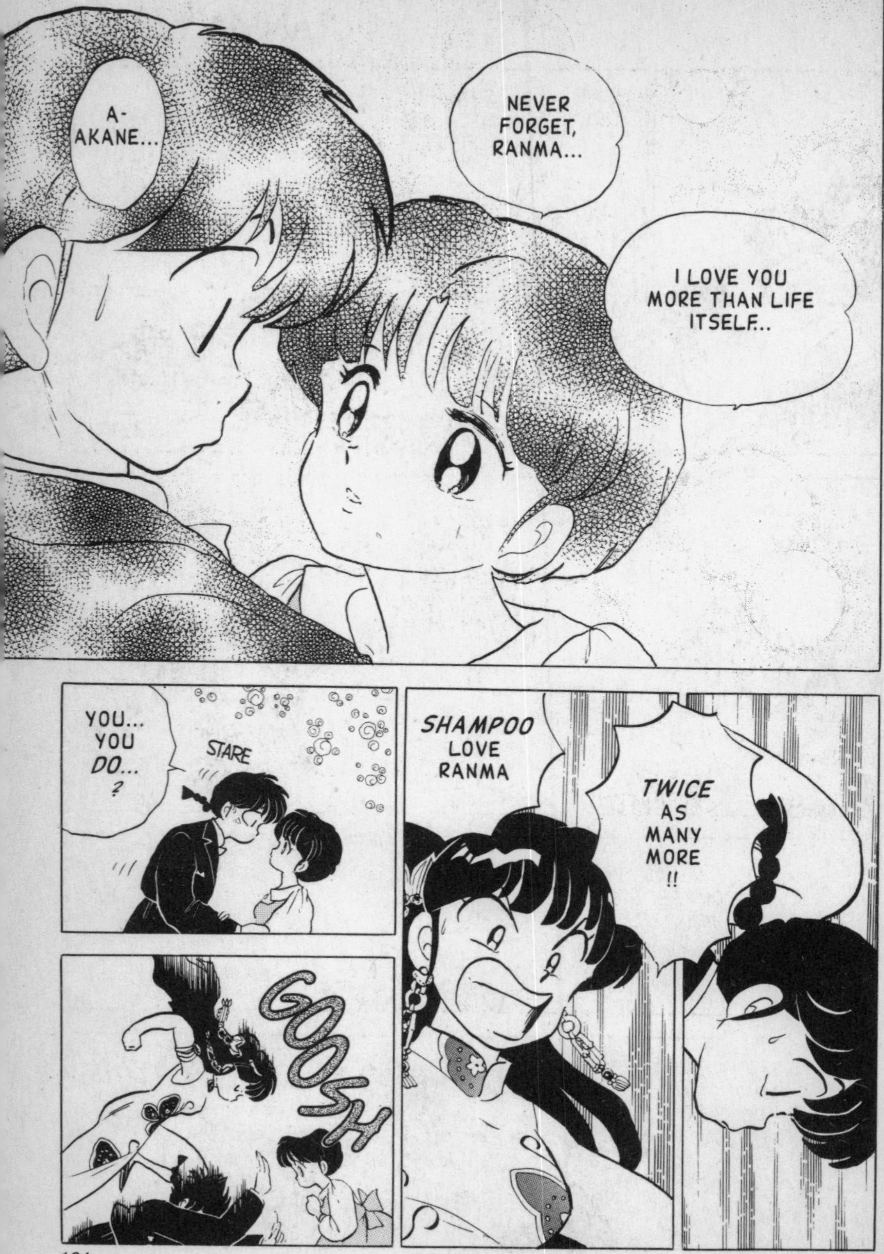
A- AKANE...
NEVER FORGET, RANMA...
I LOVE YOU MORE THAN LIFE ITSELF..
YOU... YOU *DO*... ?
STARE
GOOSH
SHAMPOO LOVE RANMA
TWICE AS MANY MORE !!

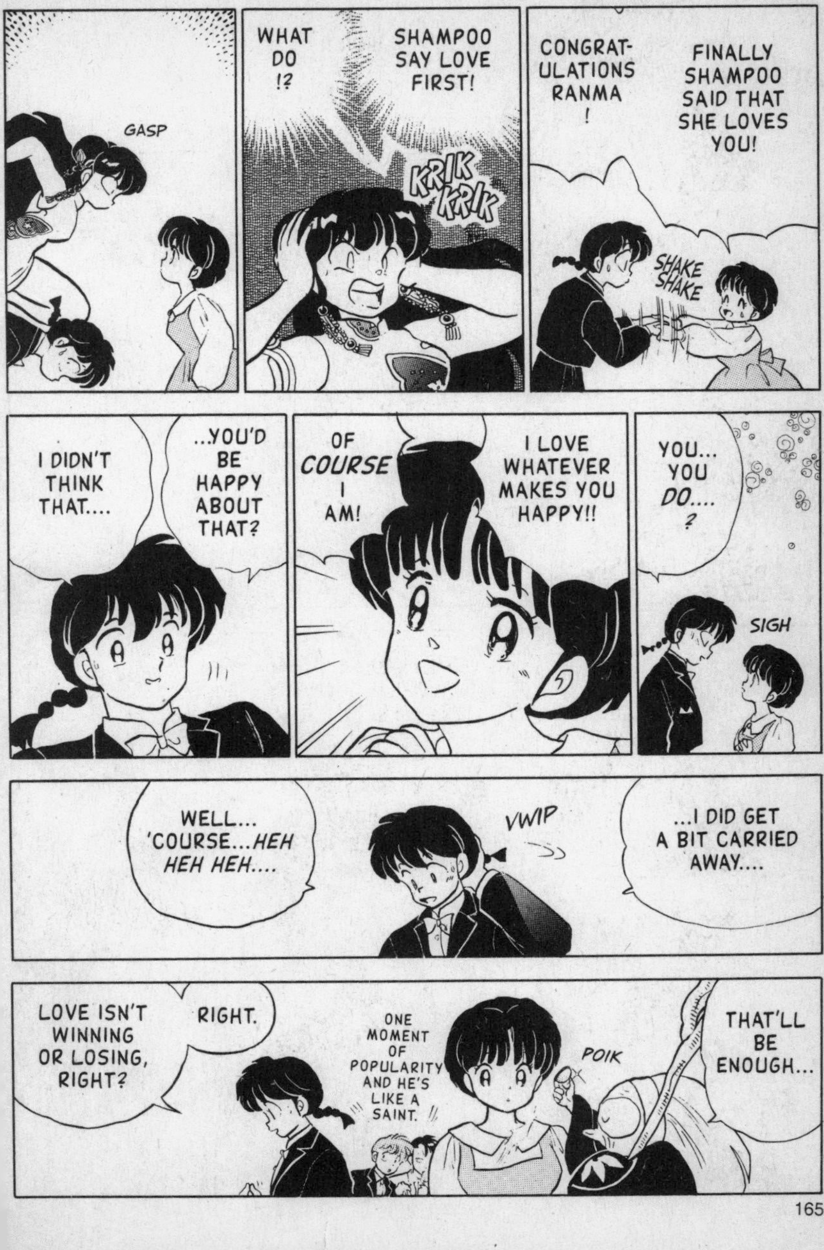
GASP
WHAT DO !?
SHAMPOO SAY LOVE FIRST!
KRIK KRIK
CONGRAT-ULATIONS RANMA !
FINALLY SHAMPOO SAID THAT SHE LOVES YOU!
SHAKE SHAKE
I DIDN'T THINK THAT....
...YOU'D BE HAPPY ABOUT THAT?
OF *COURSE* I AM!
I LOVE WHATEVER MAKES YOU HAPPY!!
YOU... YOU *DO*.... ?
SIGH
WELL... 'COURSE...*HEH HEH HEH*....
VWIP
...I DID GET A BIT CARRIED AWAY....
LOVE ISN'T WINNING OR LOSING, RIGHT?
RIGHT.
ONE MOMENT OF POPULARITY AND HE'S LIKE A SAINT.
POIK
THAT'LL BE ENOUGH...

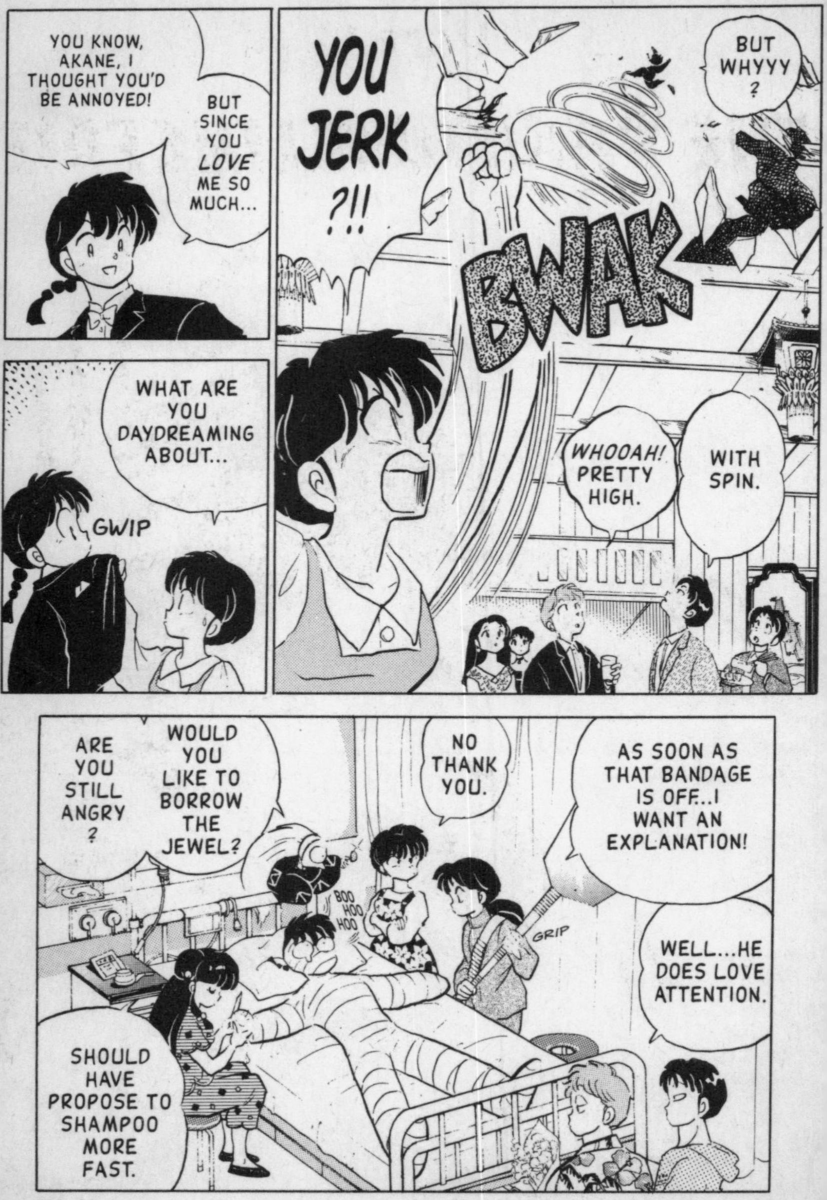
YOU KNOW, AKANE, I THOUGHT YOU'D BE ANNOYED!
BUT SINCE YOU *LOVE* ME SO MUCH...
WHAT ARE YOU DAYDREAMING ABOUT...
GWIP
YOU JERK ?!!
BUT WHYYY ?
BWAK
WHOOAH! PRETTY HIGH.
WITH SPIN.
ARE YOU STILL ANGRY ?
WOULD YOU LIKE TO BORROW THE JEWEL?
NO THANK YOU.
AS SOON AS THAT BANDAGE IS OFF...I WANT AN EXPLANATION!
BOO HOO HOO
GRIP
WELL...HE DOES LOVE ATTENTION.
SHOULD HAVE PROPOSE TO SHAMPOO MORE FAST.

Part 11

THE PHANTOM LINGERIE

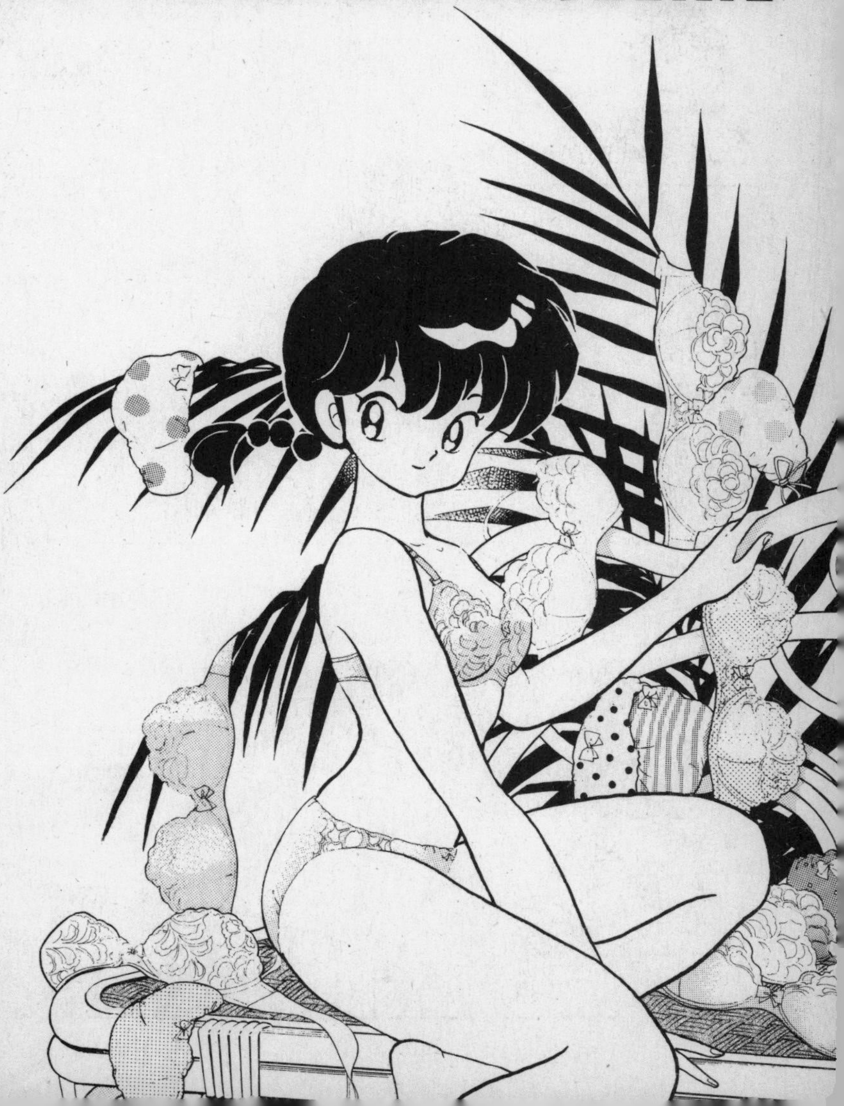

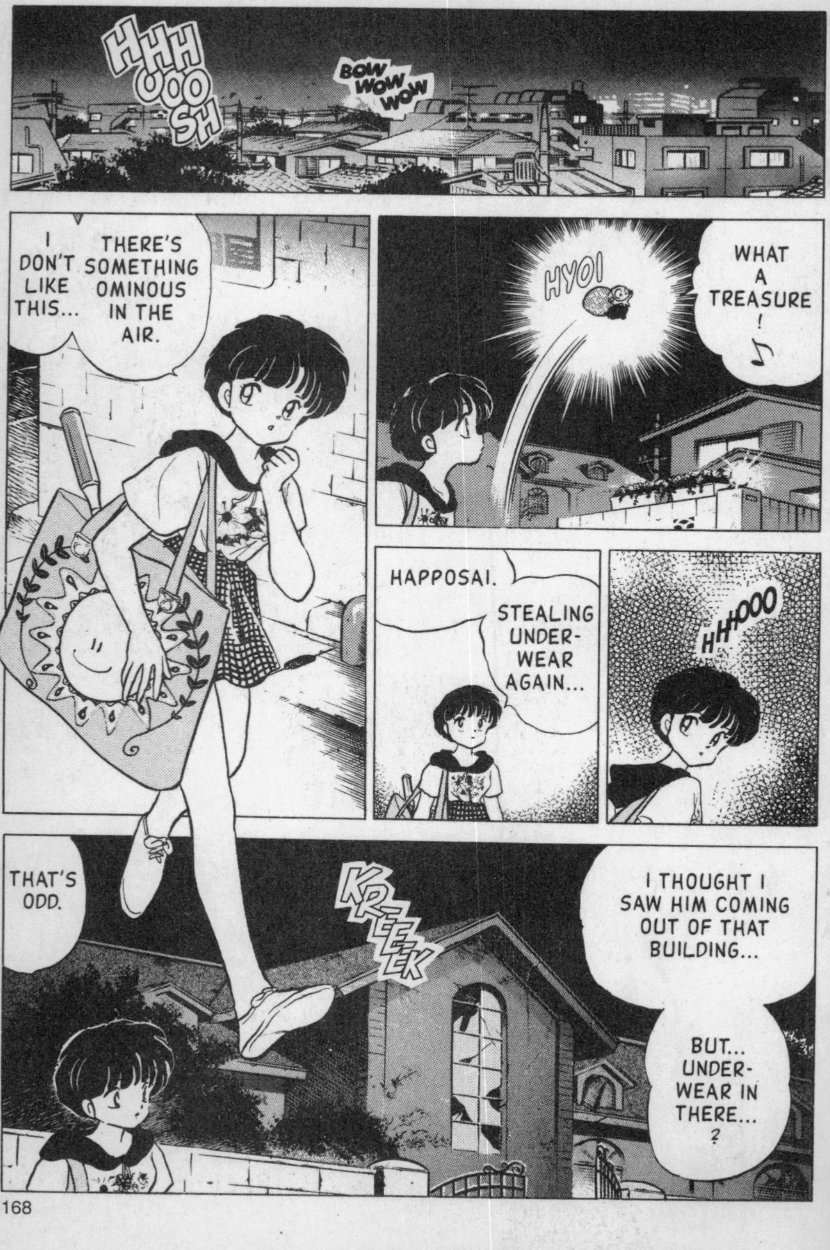
HHHOOOSH
BOW WOW WOW
I DON'T LIKE THIS...
THERE'S SOMETHING OMINOUS IN THE AIR.
HYOI
WHAT A TREASURE! ♪
HAPPOSAI.
STEALING UNDER-WEAR AGAIN...
HHHOOO
THAT'S ODD.
KREEEK
I THOUGHT I SAW HIM COMING OUT OF THAT BUILDING...
BUT... UNDER-WEAR IN THERE...?

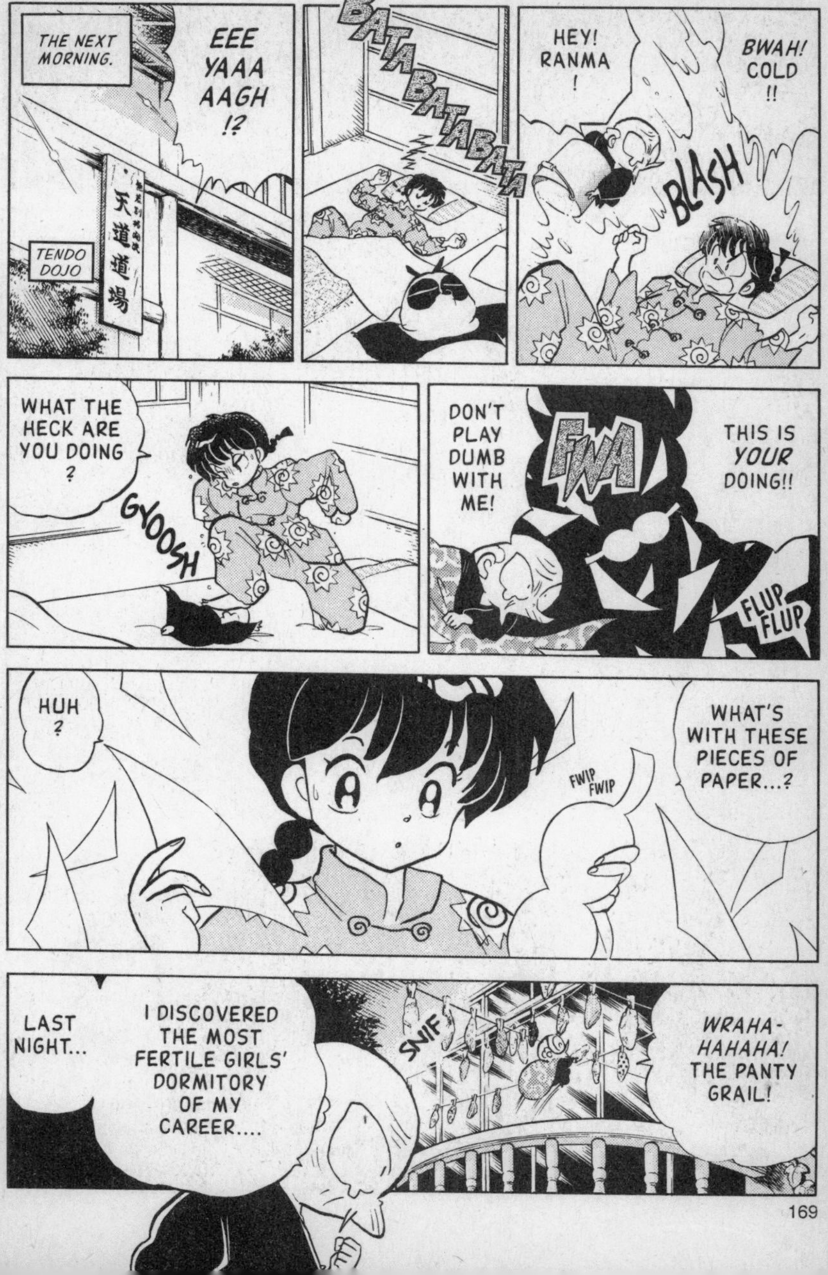
THE NEXT MORNING.
EEE YAAA AAGH !?
天道道場
TENDO DOJO
BATABATABATA
HEY! RANMA !
BWAH! COLD !!
BLASH
WHAT THE HECK ARE YOU DOING ?
GYOOSH
DON'T PLAY DUMB WITH ME!
FWA
THIS IS YOUR DOING!!
FLUP FLUP
HUH ?
FWIP FWIP
WHAT'S WITH THESE PIECES OF PAPER...?
LAST NIGHT...
I DISCOVERED THE MOST FERTILE GIRLS' DORMITORY OF MY CAREER....
SNIF
WRAHA-HAHAHA! THE PANTY GRAIL!

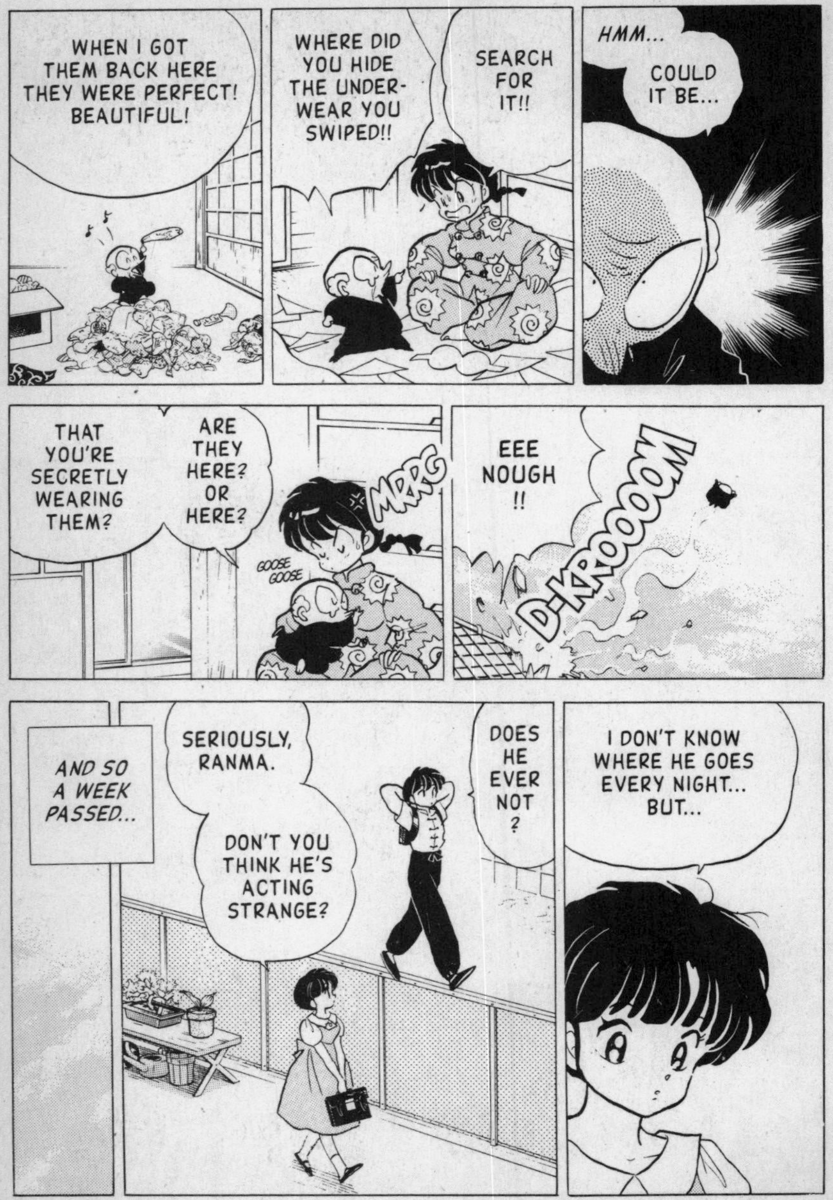
WHEN I GOT THEM BACK HERE THEY WERE PERFECT! BEAUTIFUL!
WHERE DID YOU HIDE THE UNDER-WEAR YOU SWIPED!!
SEARCH FOR IT!!
HMM...
COULD IT BE...
THAT YOU'RE SECRETLY WEARING THEM?
ARE THEY HERE? OR HERE?
MRRG
GOOSE GOOSE
EEE NOUGH !!
D-KROOOOM
AND SO A WEEK PASSED...
SERIOUSLY, RANMA.
DON'T YOU THINK HE'S ACTING STRANGE?
DOES HE EVER NOT ?
I DON'T KNOW WHERE HE GOES EVERY NIGHT... BUT...

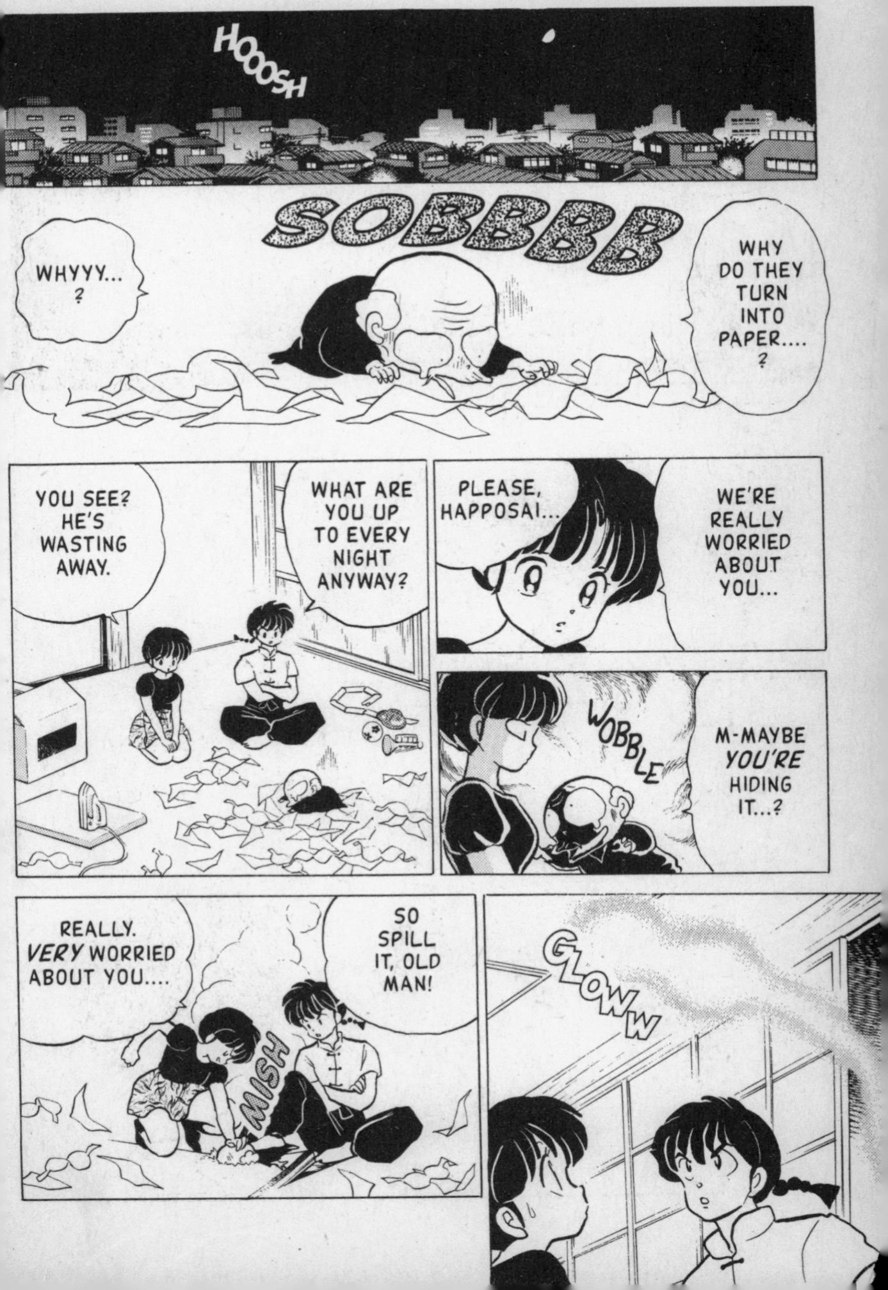
HOOOSH
WHYYY...?
SOBBBB
WHY DO THEY TURN INTO PAPER....?
YOU SEE? HE'S WASTING AWAY.
WHAT ARE YOU UP TO EVERY NIGHT ANYWAY?
PLEASE, HAPPOSAI...
WE'RE REALLY WORRIED ABOUT YOU...
WOBBLE
M-MAYBE *YOU'RE* HIDING IT...?
REALLY. *VERY* WORRIED ABOUT YOU....
SO SPILL IT, OLD MAN!
MISH
GLOWW

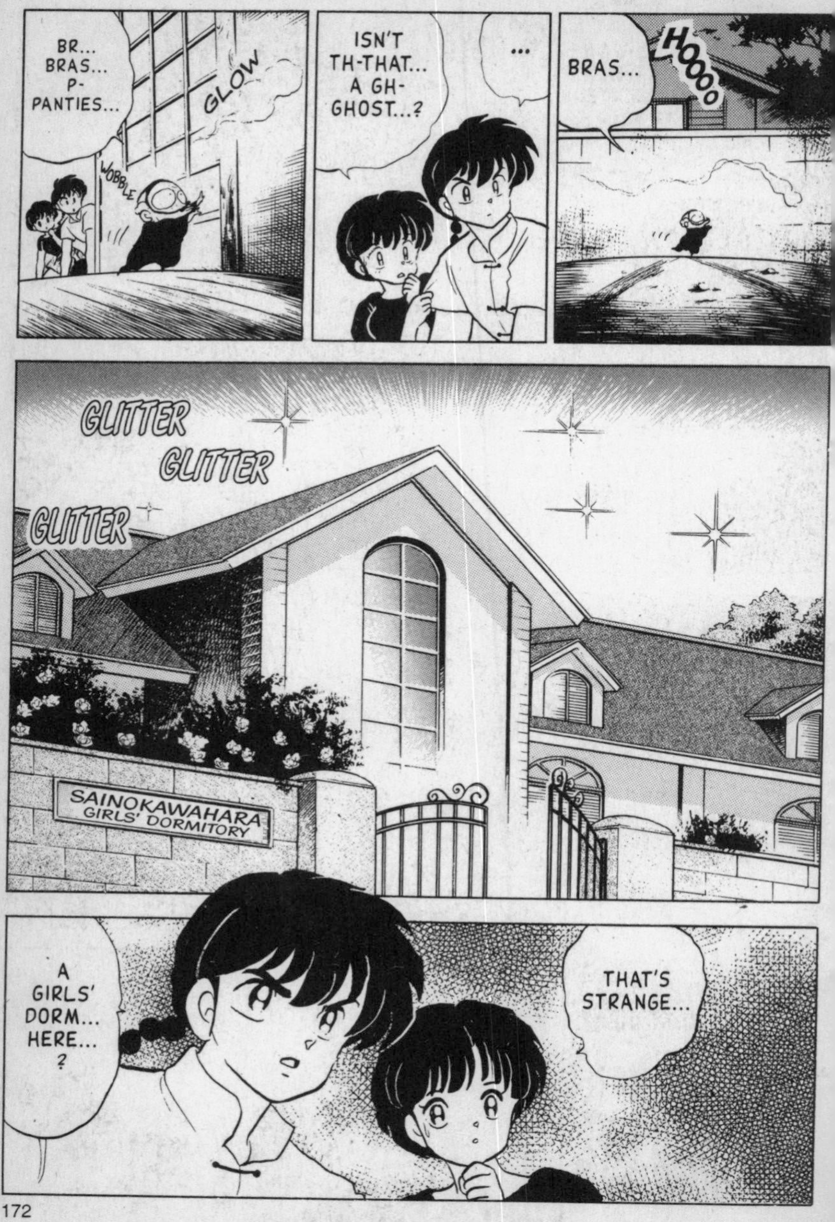
BR... BRAS... P-PANTIES...
GLOW
WOBBLE
ISN'T TH-THAT... A GH-GHOST...?
...
BRAS...
HOOOOO
GLITTER
GLITTER
GLITTER
SAINOKAWAHARA GIRLS' DORMITORY
A GIRLS' DORM... HERE...?
THAT'S STRANGE...

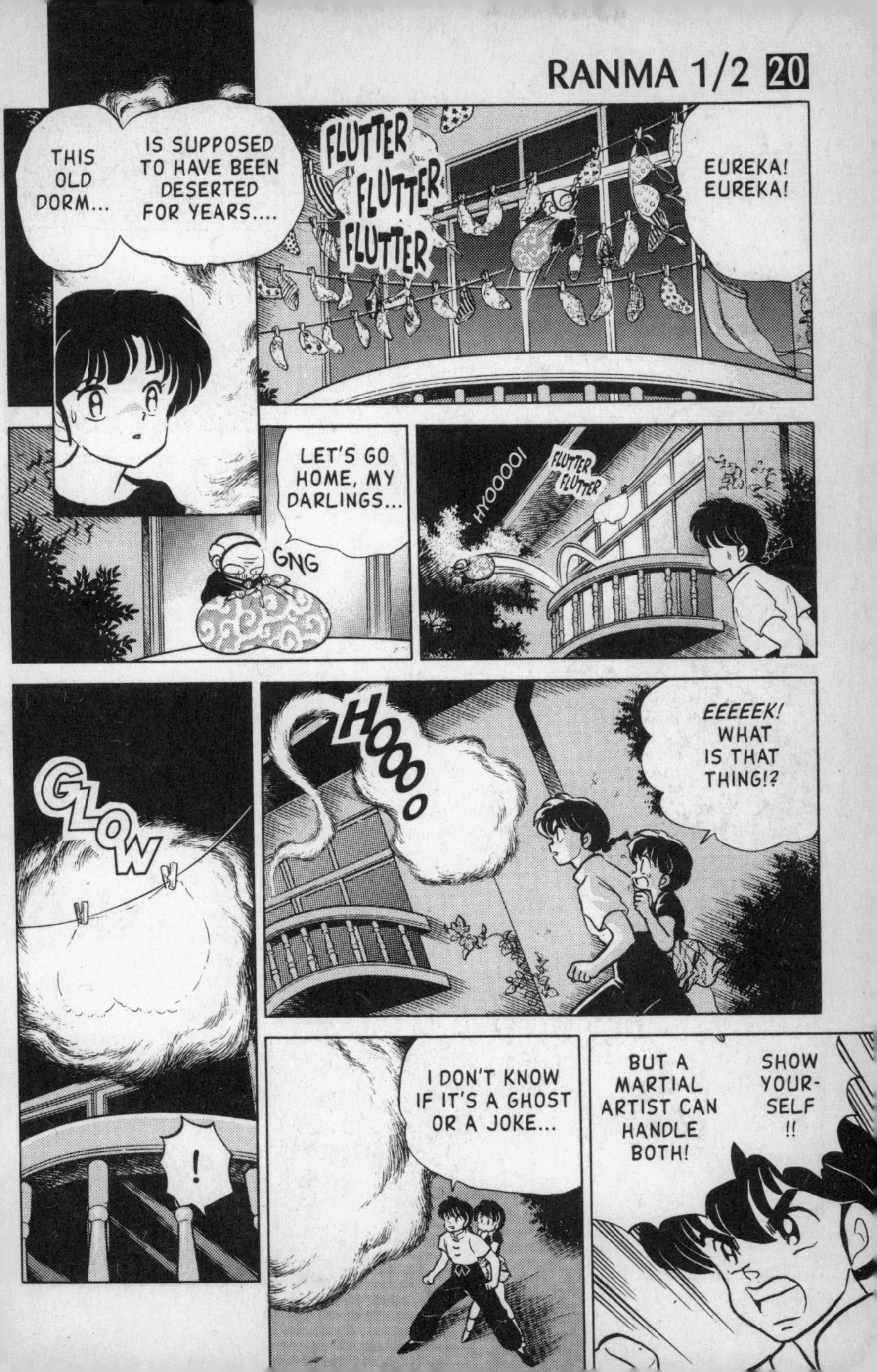
THIS OLD DORM...
IS SUPPOSED TO HAVE BEEN DESERTED FOR YEARS....
FLUTTER FLUTTER FLUTTER
EUREKA! EUREKA!
LET'S GO HOME, MY DARLINGS...
GNG
HYOOOO!
FLUTTER FLUTTER
GLOW
!
HOOOO
EEEEEK! WHAT IS THAT THING!?
I DON'T KNOW IF IT'S A GHOST OR A JOKE...
BUT A MARTIAL ARTIST CAN HANDLE BOTH!
SHOW YOUR-SELF !!

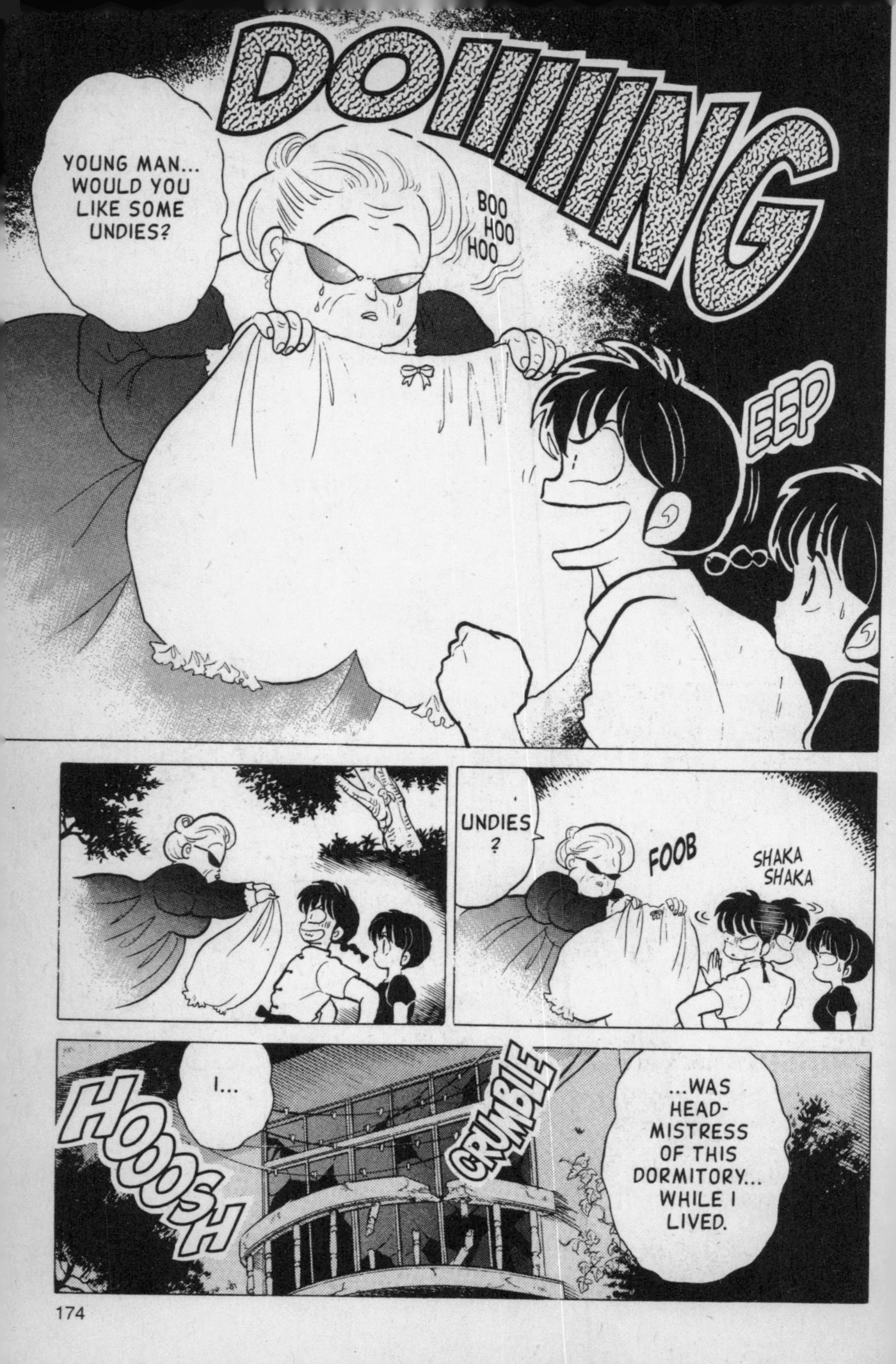
DOIIIING
YOUNG MAN... WOULD YOU LIKE SOME UNDIES?
BOO HOO HOO
EEP
UNDIES ?
FOOB
SHAKA SHAKA
HOOOSH
I...
CRUMBLE
...WAS HEAD-MISTRESS OF THIS DORMITORY... WHILE I LIVED.

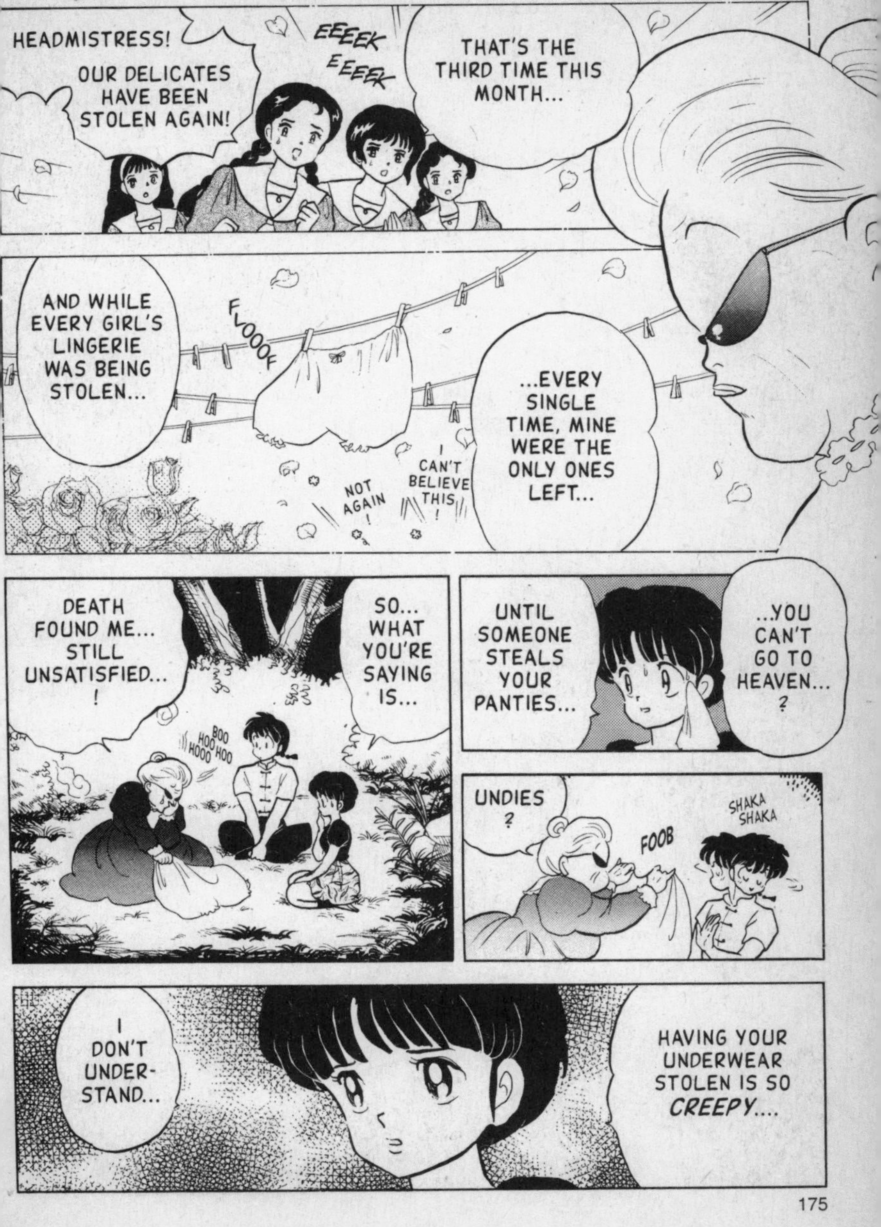
HEADMISTRESS!
OUR DELICATES HAVE BEEN STOLEN AGAIN!
EEEEK EEEEK
THAT'S THE THIRD TIME THIS MONTH...
AND WHILE EVERY GIRL'S LINGERIE WAS BEING STOLEN...
FVOOOF
I CAN'T BELIEVE THIS!
NOT AGAIN!
...EVERY SINGLE TIME, MINE WERE THE ONLY ONES LEFT...
DEATH FOUND ME... STILL UNSATISFIED...!
SO... WHAT YOU'RE SAYING IS...
BOO HOO HOO HOOO
UNTIL SOMEONE STEALS YOUR PANTIES...
...YOU CAN'T GO TO HEAVEN...?
UNDIES?
FOOB
SHAKA SHAKA
I DON'T UNDER-STAND...
HAVING YOUR UNDERWEAR STOLEN IS SO *CREEPY*....

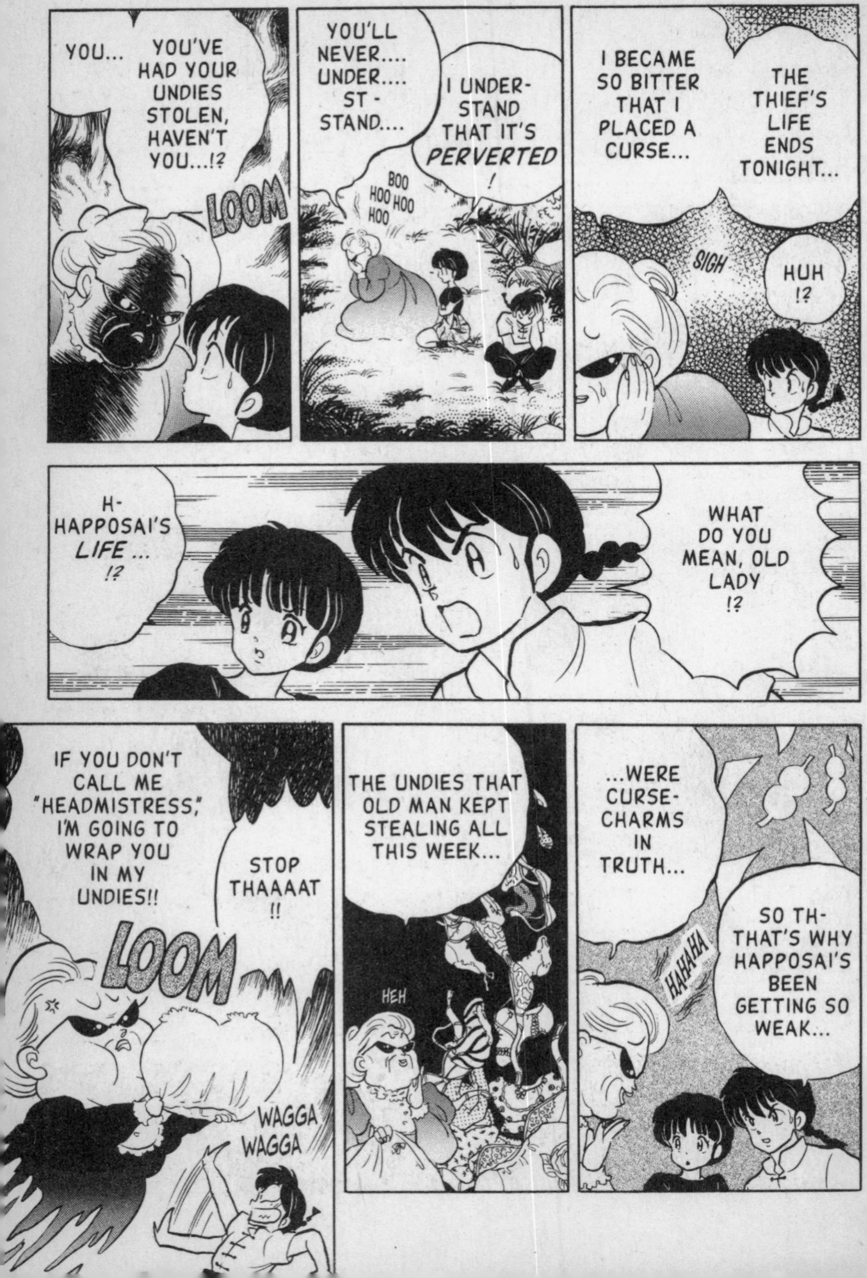

YOU... YOU'VE HAD YOUR UNDIES STOLEN, HAVEN'T YOU...!?
LOOM
YOU'LL NEVER.... UNDER.... ST - STAND....
I UNDER- STAND THAT IT'S PERVERTED !
BOO HOO HOO HOO
I BECAME SO BITTER THAT I PLACED A CURSE...
THE THIEF'S LIFE ENDS TONIGHT...
SIGH
HUH !?
H- HAPPOSAI'S LIFE ... !?
WHAT DO YOU MEAN, OLD LADY !?
IF YOU DON'T CALL ME "HEADMISTRESS," I'M GOING TO WRAP YOU IN MY UNDIES!!
STOP THAAAAT !!
LOOM
WAGGA WAGGA
THE UNDIES THAT OLD MAN KEPT STEALING ALL THIS WEEK...
HEH
...WERE CURSE- CHARMS IN TRUTH...
SO TH- THAT'S WHY HAPPOSAI'S BEEN GETTING SO WEAK...
HAHAHA

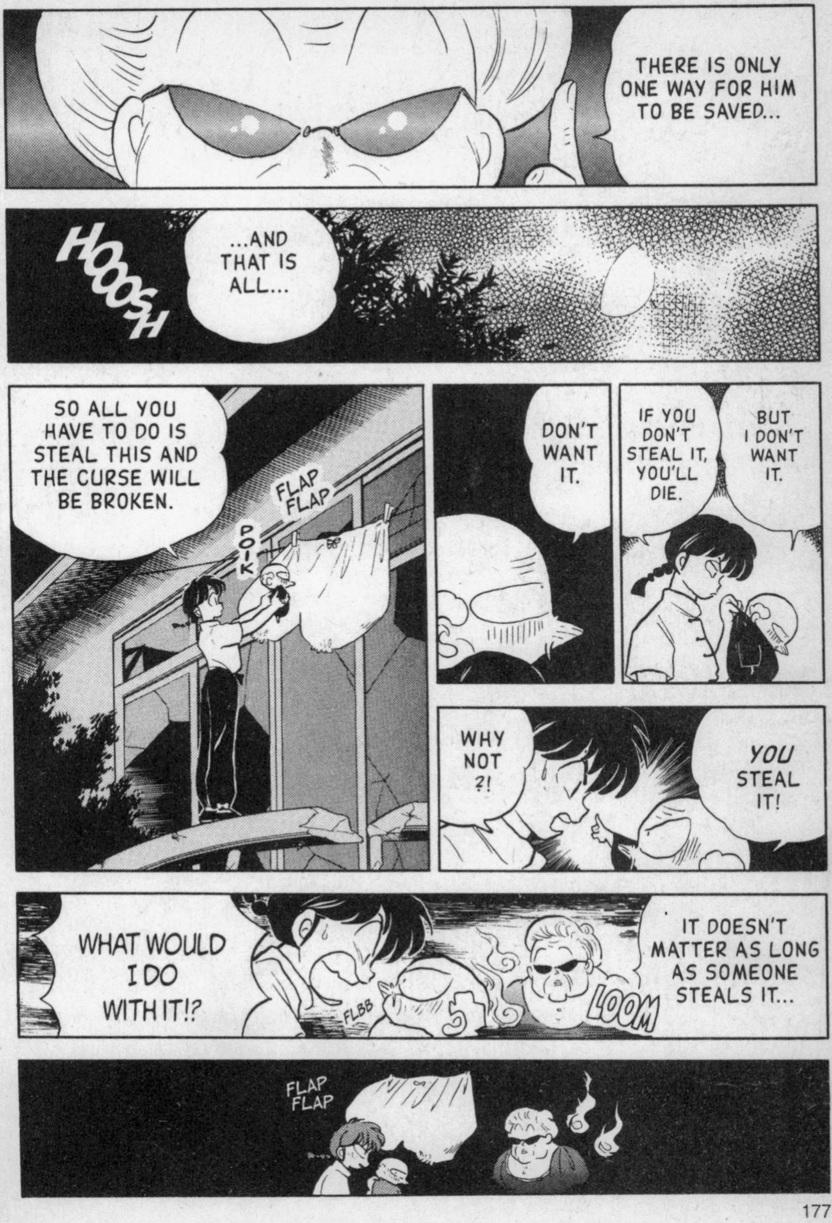
THERE IS ONLY ONE WAY FOR HIM TO BE SAVED...
HOOOSH
...AND THAT IS ALL...
SO ALL YOU HAVE TO DO IS STEAL THIS AND THE CURSE WILL BE BROKEN.
FLAP FLAP
POIK
DON'T WANT IT.
IF YOU DON'T STEAL IT, YOU'LL DIE.
BUT I DON'T WANT IT.
WHY NOT ?!
YOU STEAL IT!
WHAT WOULD I DO WITH IT!?
FLBB
LOOM
IT DOESN'T MATTER AS LONG AS SOMEONE STEALS IT...
FLAP FLAP

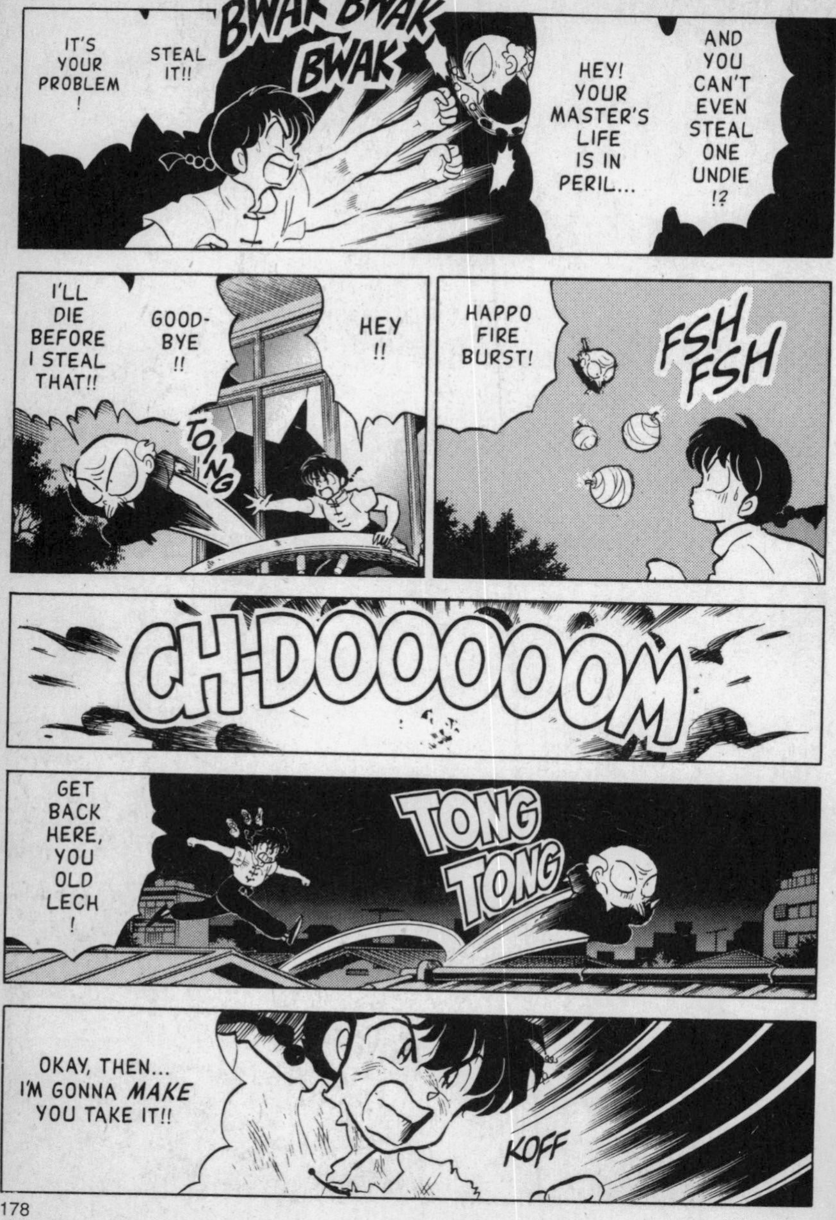
IT'S YOUR PROBLEM !
STEAL IT!!
BWAK BWAK BWAK
HEY! YOUR MASTER'S LIFE IS IN PERIL...
AND YOU CAN'T EVEN STEAL ONE UNDIE !?
I'LL DIE BEFORE I STEAL THAT!!
GOOD-BYE !!
HEY !!
TOING
HAPPO FIRE BURST!
FSH FSH
CH-DOOOOOM
GET BACK HERE, YOU OLD LECH !
TONG TONG
OKAY, THEN... I'M GONNA *MAKE* YOU TAKE IT!!
KOFF

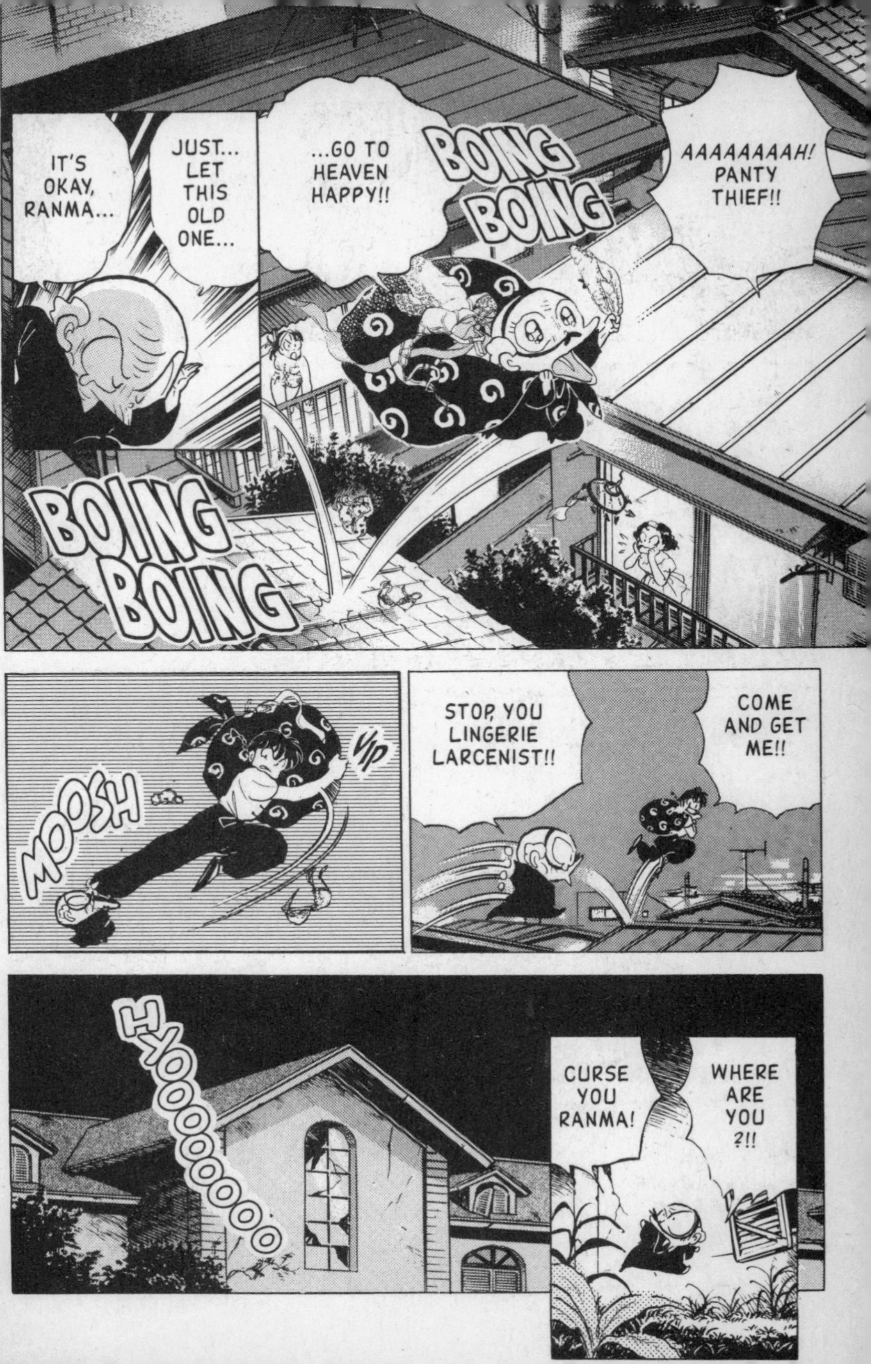
IT'S OKAY, RANMA...
JUST... LET THIS OLD ONE...
...GO TO HEAVEN HAPPY!!
BOING BOING
AAAAAAAAH! PANTY THIEF!!
BOING BOING
MOOSH
VIP
STOP, YOU LINGERIE LARCENIST!!
COME AND GET ME!!
HYOOOOOOO
CURSE YOU RANMA!
WHERE ARE YOU ?!!

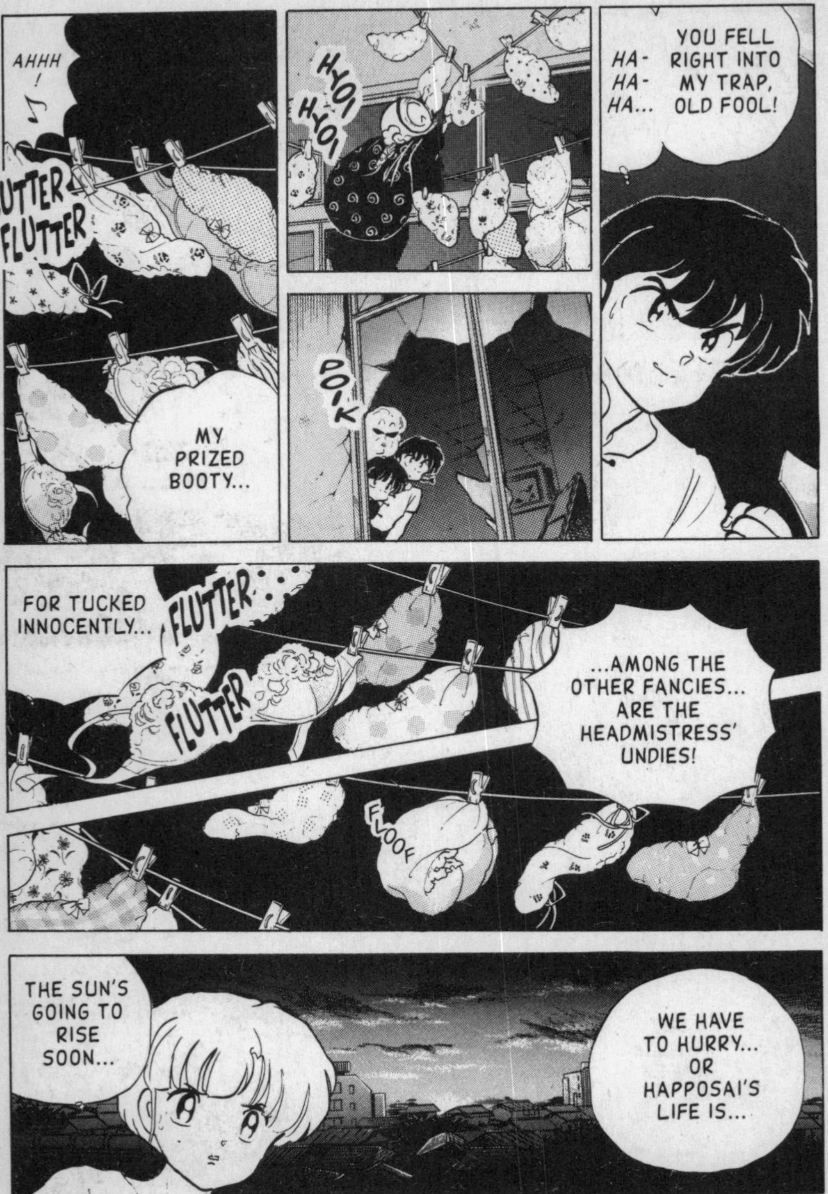
AHHH!
FLUTTER FLUTTER
MY PRIZED BOOTY...
HYOI HYOI
DOIK
HA-HA-HA...
YOU FELL RIGHT INTO MY TRAP, OLD FOOL!
FOR TUCKED INNOCENTLY...
FLUTTER
FLUTTER
...AMONG THE OTHER FANCIES... ARE THE HEADMISTRESS' UNDIES!
FLOOF
THE SUN'S GOING TO RISE SOON...
WE HAVE TO HURRY... OR HAPPOSAI'S LIFE IS...

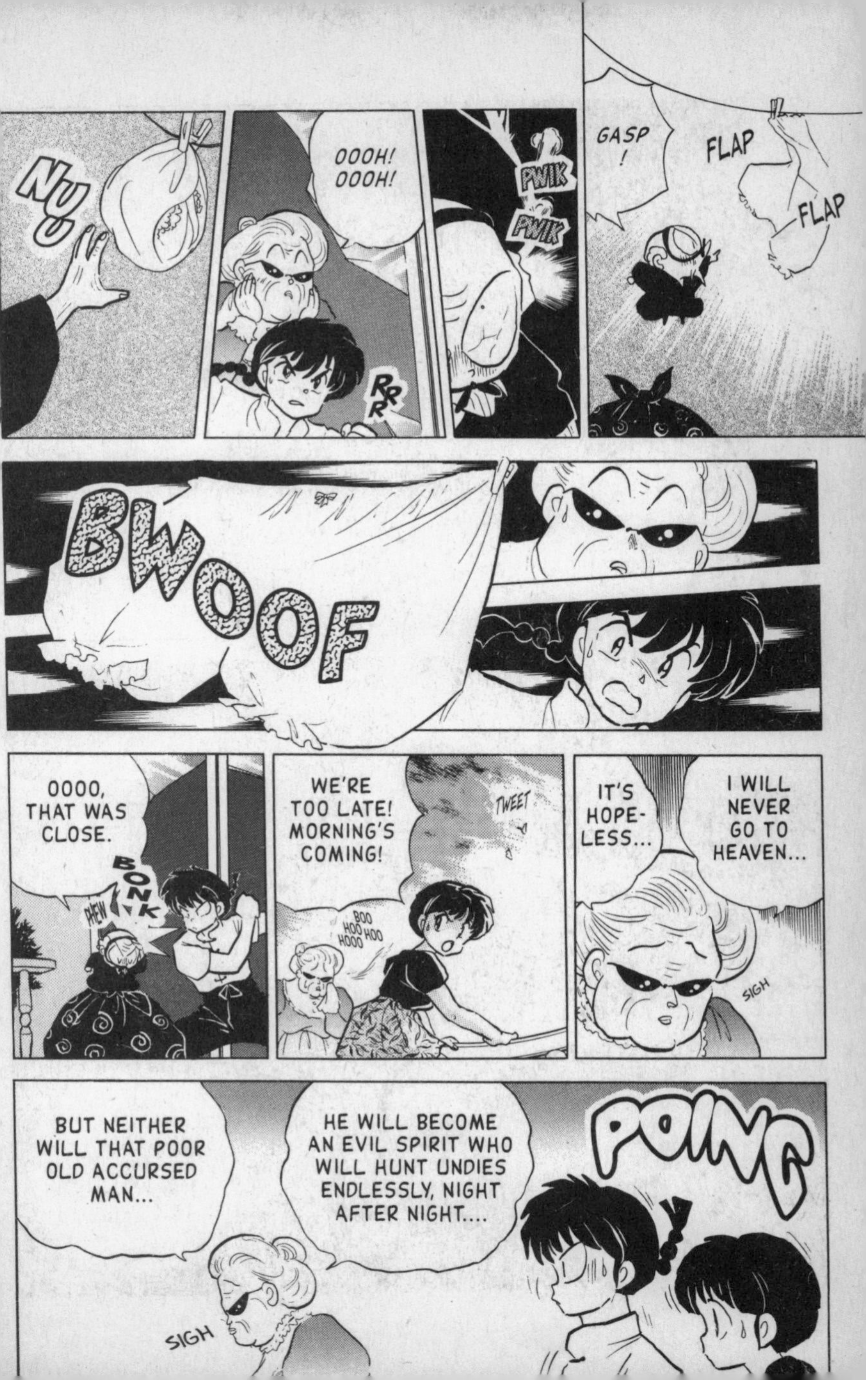
NU
OOOH! OOOH!
RRR
PWIK
PWIK
GASP!
FLAP
FLAP
BWOOF
OOOO, THAT WAS CLOSE.
BONK
PHEW
WE'RE TOO LATE! MORNING'S COMING!
TWEET
BOO HOO HOOO HOO
IT'S HOPE-LESS...
I WILL NEVER GO TO HEAVEN...
SIGH
BUT NEITHER WILL THAT POOR OLD ACCURSED MAN...
HE WILL BECOME AN EVIL SPIRIT WHO WILL HUNT UNDIES ENDLESSLY, NIGHT AFTER NIGHT....
POING
SIGH

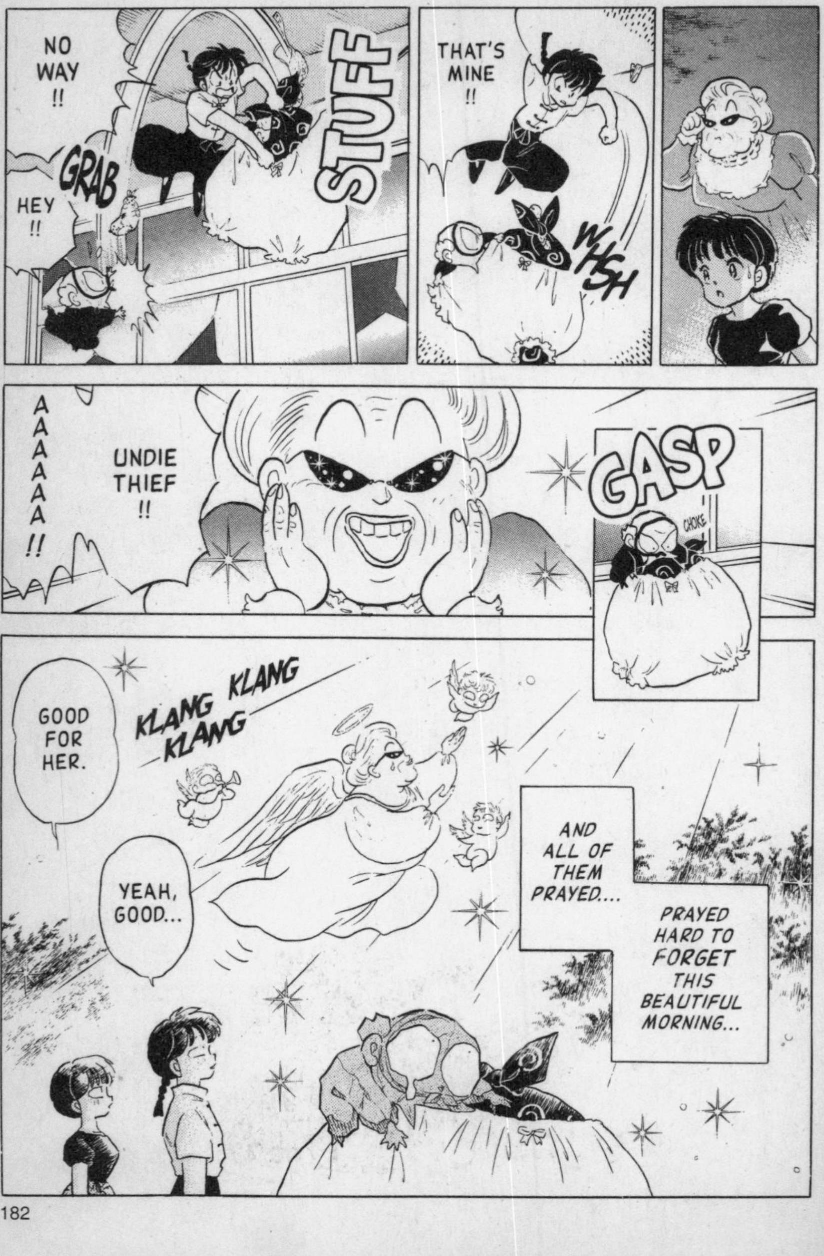
NO WAY !!
STUFF
GRAB
HEY !!
THAT'S MINE !!
WHSH
AAAAAAA!!
UNDIE THIEF !!
GASP
CHOKE
GOOD FOR HER.
KLANG KLANG KLANG
YEAH, GOOD...
AND ALL OF THEM PRAYED....
PRAYED HARD TO FORGET THIS BEAUTIFUL MORNING...

About Rumiko Takahashi

Born in 1957 in Niigata, Japan, Rumiko Takahashi attended women's college in Tokyo, where she began studying comics with Kazuo Koike, author of CRYING FREEMAN. She later became an assistant to horror-manga artist Kazuo Umezu (OROCHI). In 1978, she won a prize in Shogakukan's annual "New Comic Artist Contest," and in that same year her boy-meets-alien comedy series URUSEI YATSURA began appearing in the weekly manga magazine SHÔNEN SUNDAY. This phenomenally successful series ran for nine years and sold over 22 million copies. Takahashi's later RANMA 1/2 series enjoyed even greater popularity.

Takahashi is considered by many to be one of the world's most popular manga artists. With the publication of Volume 34 of her RANMA 1/2 series in Japan, Takahashi's total sales passed one hundred million copies of her compiled works.

Takahashi's serial titles include URUSEI YATSURA, RANMA 1/2, ONE-POUND GOSPEL, MAISON IKKOKU and INUYASHA. Additionally, Takahashi has drawn many short stories which have been published in America under the title "Rumic Theater," and several installments of a saga known as her "Mermaid" series. Most of Takahashi's major stories have also been animated and are widely available in translation worldwide. INUYASHA is her most recent serial story, first published in SHÔNEN SUNDAY in 1996.

**If you enjoyed this volume of Ranma 1/2,
then here is some more manga you might be interested in:**

Koko wa Greenwood © Yukie Nasu
1986/HAKUSENSHA, Inc.

HERE IS GREENWOOD

Perhaps written for a slightly older audience than
most of Rumiko Takahashi's work, Yukie Nasu's *Here is
Greenwood* is exactly like *Ranma 1/2*, except for the
martial arts (none), the wacky hijinks (almost none),
and the occasional depiction of the adult relationships
among its students. Okay, aside from the fact that they
both have male high school students in them, they
have nothing in common. But they're both cool!

HANA-YORI DANGO
© 1992 by YOKO KAMIO/SHUEISHA Inc.

BOYS OVER FLOWERS (HANA YORI DANGO)

Another tale of high school life
in Japan, *Boys Over Flowers*
(or "HanaDan" to most of its
fans) is not without its serious
side, but overall tends to fall
into the "rabu-kome" or
"love-comedy" genre.

CERES: CELESTIAL LEGEND
© 1997 Yuu Watase/Shogakukan, Inc.

CERES:CELESTIAL LEGEND

Aya Mikage is a trendy Tokyo teen with not
much else on her mind but fashion, karaoke, and
boys. But a terrible family secret involving an
ancient family "curse" is about to make things a
lot more difficult.

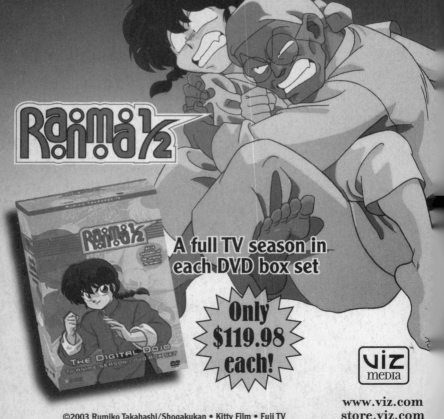

Half Human, Half

When Kagome discovers a well that transports her to feudal era Japan, she unwittingly frees a half-demon, Inuyasha, and shatters the sacred Jewel of Four Souls. Now they must work together to restore the jewel before it falls into the wrong hands...

INUYASHA

The manga that inspired a phenomenon!

FULL COLOR adaptation of the TV series!

Only $9.95!

Only $11.95!